Neo4j: The Definitive Guide

Hands-On Recipes for Production-Ready Graph Implementations

Luanne Misquitta and Christophe Willemsen

Foreword by Michael Hunger

Neo4j: The Definitive Guide
by Luanne Misquitta and Christophe Willemsen

Printed in the United States of America.

Published by O'Reilly Media, Inc., 141 Stony Circle, Suite 195, Santa Rosa, CA 95401

O'Reilly books may be purchased for educational, business, or sales promotional use. Online editions are also available for most titles (*http://oreilly.com*). For more information, contact our corporate/institutional sales department: 800-998-9938 or *corporate@oreilly.com*.

Acquisitions Editor: Aaron Black
Development Editor: Sarah Grey
Production Editor: Jonathon Owen
Copyeditor: nSight, Inc.
Proofreader: Helena Stirling
Indexer: nSight, Inc.
Cover Designer: Karen Montgomery
Cover Illustrator: José Marzan Jr.
Interior Designer: David Futato
Interior Illustrator: Kate Dullea

July 2025: First Edition

Revision History for the First Edition
2025-07-16: First Release

See *http://oreilly.com/catalog/errata.csp?isbn=9781098165659* for release details.

978-1-098-16565-9

[LSI]

Table of Contents

Foreword xi

Preface xv

1. How to Get Value from Graphs in Just Five Days 1
- Dissonance at ElectricHarmony 3
- Why Graph Databases? 4
- Graph Use Cases 6
  - Ultimate Beneficial Ownership Networks 6
  - Real-Time Recommendations 7
  - Law Enforcement 7
  - Cybercrime Networks 8
- Neo4j 9
  - Native Graph Databases 10
- Cypher 12
- The Song Recommendation System: A Proof of Concept 13
  - Day 1 14
  - Day 2 21
  - Day 3 32
  - Day 4 38
  - Day 5 42
- Summary 47

2. Importing (Much) More Data 49
- Database Transactions 50
  - The ~~Beat~~ Heap Box 52
  - Try It: Importing Data from Client Applications 57

Parallel Writes 64
Offline Import 73
Exploring Other Ingestion Tools 75
Summary 75

3. Revisiting Modeling Decisions.......... 77
It Depends 77
Principles of Modeling 82
Properties Versus Nodes 83
Properties That Decorate the Result 83
Key Takeaways 84
Traversing Across Commonalities 84
Key Takeaways 85
Modeling Concepts as Labels 85
Key Takeaways 87
Node Fanout 87
Key Takeaways 89
Supernodes 90
Key Takeaways 92
Relationship Granularity 92
Key Takeaways 95
Qualified Relationships 96
Bucketed Relationships 97
Key Takeaways 98
Bidirectional Relationships 98
Key Takeaways 104
Summary 104

4. Modeling and Refactoring Patterns.......... 105
Hyperedges: N-way Relationships 105
Key Takeaways 111
Time-Based Versioning 112
Key Takeaways 114
Representing Sequences 114
Key Takeaways 119
Refactoring Patterns 120
Refactoring to Change the Type of a Relationship 121
Refactoring to Create a Node from a Property 123
Refactoring to Create a Node from a Relationship 126
Key Takeaways 135
Summary 135

5. Query Analysis and Tuning.. 137
Query Execution 137
Pattern Anchors 138
Query Profiling 141
Row Cardinality 147
Matching Disconnected Patterns 148
Increasing Anchor Selectivity 151
Eliminating Redundant Filter Operations 153
Improving Anchor Selectivity in Queries with Predicates 156
Indexing Guidelines 161
Accessing Properties 162
Node Degrees 163
Don't Be Eager! 165
Sorting 168
I Want to Break Free (of the Planner) 172
Cypher Runtimes 176
Parameterizing Queries 178
Monitoring and Measuring Query Times 179
Summary 180

6. Securing Your Database.. 181
Spoofing 182
Authentication 182
Securing Access via the Neo4j browser 183
Best Practices 184
Tampering 184
Securing Communication Channels 184
Securing Data at Rest 185
Using Consistency Checks 185
Defending Against Cypher Injection Attacks 186
Implementing Role-Based Access Control 187
Using the Load CSV Command 193
Audit Logs 194
Constraints 194
Backups 194
Repudiation 195
Information Disclosure 196
Query Logs 196
Fine-Grained Access Control 196
Property Encryption 196

Denial of Service 197
Elevation of Privilege 198
Immutable Privileges 198
Least Privileges 199
Extensions 199
User and Privilege Reviews 199
File Permissions 200
Patches 200
Summary 200

7. Search. 201
What Is Search? 202
Text 202
Indexes 203
Searching for Data 204
Partial Searches 207
TEXT Indexes 208
Full-Text Indexes 211
Multitoken Searches 216
Phrase Searches 218
Wildcard Searches 219
Fuzzy Search 219
Additional Index and Query Considerations 220
Tokenization 220
Special Characters: Hashtags and Mentions 221
Identifiers, IP Addresses, and Other Nonword Terms 222
Stopwords: To Be or Not to Be 222
Performance with Graph Patterns 223
Summary 224

8. Advanced Graph Patterns. 225
Subqueries 225
CALL Subqueries 225
Post-Union Processing 229
Concurrent Transactions with CALL 230
Fine-Grained Relationship Types 230
Modeling Resolved Entities 238
Entity Groups 241
Fused Entities 242
Quantified Path Patterns: An Entity-Resolution Use Case 248
Security Modeling: Labels Versus Properties 252

Summary 256

9. **Backup and Restore** 257
The Write Path 257
Checkpoints 258
Transaction-Log Retention 260
How Aggressive Is Aggressive? 260
A Guided Example 261
Backups 267
Types of Backups 267
Restoring Backups 270
Cloud Backups 271
Remote Backups and VM Separation 272
Designing a Backup Strategy 272
Summary 274

10. **Clustering and Sharding** 277
Clustering for High Availability 277
Raft Protocol 278
Fault Tolerance 280
Secondaries 280
Deploying a Cluster 280
Cluster Degradation 283
Multidatabase Clusters 286
How Network Latency Affects Clustering 287
Scaling Reads with Secondaries 287
Using Secondary Servers for Backups 290
Causal Consistency 291
The Mythical 1+1 Cluster 292
Sharding and Federation 293
Summary 297

11. **Observability** 299
Harnessing the Power of Logs 300
Types of Logs in Neo4j 300
Configuring Neo4j Logs 301
Inspecting Logs 302
Taming the Query Log 307
Unveiling the Power of Metrics 313
Enabling Metrics 313
Server Load Metrics 315

Neo4j Load Metrics 315
Neo4j Workload Metrics 316
Bringing It All Together: Logs and Metrics with Grafana, Loki, and Prometheus 318
Setting Up the Observability Stack 318
Visualizing Metrics 319
Querying Logs 322
Other Tools 326
Summary 326

12. Practical Graph Data Science. 327
Introduction to the Graph Data Science Library 328
Algorithms 328
The Graph Catalog 328
AI-Driven Playlist Communities 329
Building a Co-Occurrence Graph 330
Using GDS 335
Real-World Applications of Community Detection 346
Playlist recommendations 346
User segmentation 347
Influencer discovery 348
Behavioral clusters 349
Content licensing strategy 350
Summary 351

13. The Future of Graphs with Generative AI. 353
Knowledge Graphs 354
Applications of Knowledge Graphs 357
Customer 360 357
Cybersecurity 357
Life Sciences 358
Retail 358
Criminal Investigations 358
GraphRAG 359
What About Vector Search? 361
Agentic AI Architectures 362
Knowledge Graph Creation 363
A Practical Example: Playlist Recommendations from Natural Language 364
Step 1: Communities from GDS 365
Step 2: Generate Summaries and Questions with an LLM 366
Step 3: Vectorize and Store in Neo4j 367

Step 4: The User Asks a Question 368
Step 5: Generate an answer 369
Step 6: Wrapping Up 370
Summary 371

Index. 373

Foreword

Graphs are everywhere you look: information is connected and doesn't exist in isolation. Especially now, in the age of smart agentic systems, having a reliable and performant full-stack database engine that is built from the ground up to deal with richly connected information is critical to grounding your LLM's language skills in trusted, contextual facts. Knowledge graphs are digital twins of your business that allow you to ask and answer more comprehensive questions and find the deeper insights hidden in your data. GraphRAG (*http://graphrag.com*) lets you use advanced retrieval augmented generation (RAG) patterns to make LLM output explainable and contextually grounded.

My own journey with graphs started in the 1990s, when I accidentally reinvented the Dijkstra pathfinding algorithm while building client-side tooling for a multiuser dungeon online text adventure. Later, in 2008, I met Emil Eifrem, one of the founders of Neo4j, at a geek-cruise conference on the Baltic Sea. I was intrigued to hear about Neo4j for the first time, as I was working in retail applications. I wanted to know more about the applications of graph models and queries in the complex hierarchies of data. I started building open source integrations for the Neo4j database (which was back then only a small Java library, hence the "4j" name) and joined the small Swedish startup in 2010 as employee number 10. I worked on all parts of the platform, contributing to everything from the kernel to Cypher (the world's best query language) to integration libraries for data import and application development (such as Spring Data Neo4j and GraphQL).

Fifteen years later, Neo4j is one of the Swedish "unicorns," serving thousands of large customers worldwide and offering a graph data platform that is well positioned to be a crucial part of the GenAI revolution. Coincidentally, that's the focus of my current role as VP of Product Innovation and Developer Experience.

If you're looking for a deep dive into Neo4j by two of the best experts on the technology, you don't have to look any further. The authors, my two amazing friends Luanne Misquitta and Christophe Willemsen, have been in the Neo4j graph space for a long time (almost as long as I have), working on open source projects as well as with a wide range of customer projects. They have been official Neo4j Ninjas for many years, answering thousands of questions, blogging, speaking, and training. We've shared in the Neo4j journey from both sides of the curtain: me contributing to building the database platform, and Luanne and Chris as customers, users, and contributors. Over the years I've worked with them a lot, in my capacity leading Developer Relations and Neo4j Labs and later Innovation and Developer Experience in Product Management, but also as a friend and mentor. I've always enjoyed their curiosity, smarts, and ability to take tough problems and break them down and execute on solving them in challenging production contexts.

Both are graph addicts who prove that graphs are everywhere: in human interactions (good and bad), scientific research, security and dependencies in IT infrastructure, supply chains in the global economy, digital humanities, and repositories of knowledge.

I encountered Luanne in 2010, when she was working in graph skills management and won our Heroku Neo4j challenge with a recipe recommendation application called Flavorwocky. Ever since then, Luanne has become an integral part of the Neo4j user community, writing articles, giving talks, and running training classes.

Chris started out working on open source graph projects while building software for the Belgian Navy. When we met, I was impressed by his inquisitive nature and always deep and critical feedback. His first open source project was Neoxygen Graphgen, which generated example graph models using the power of textual graph-pattern descriptions, not for querying, but for specifying data. Later, he created and maintained the neo4j-PHP driver for many years and worked on many integrations of Neo4j with different data technologies, including Camel, Kafka, Elasticsearch, and data lakes.

When Chris joined the Neo4j consultancy GraphAware as CTO and Luanne as VP of engineering, they could finally work on their passion technology full time. Not only do they work with demanding customers and projects every day, but they've also designed, built, and operated Hume, a comprehensive graph importation, exploration, and investigation platform with new and impressive features like complex graph analysis, virtual patterns, model mapping for massive data imports, and smart AI integrations. This book shares a lot of the tips and tricks that they've learned the hard way over the years.

This book will get you started on your graph journey, following the team at the fictional music company ElectricHarmony as they design, develop, tune, and productionize their graph-based recommendation engine. Besides explaining the practical applications of graph modeling, querying, and importing real-world data, they also show common stumbling blocks and how to address them properly. As we follow the team through their development cycles, we learn more about the power and possibilities of graphs and about the decisions that have to be made at each stage of development.

The book covers the recently released LTS version of Neo4j 5 as a robust foundation for your production deployment while also hinting at upcoming features and capabilities of the current development version. It also equips you for what's coming: larger sharded graphs, serverless graph computation, tight integrations with large data platforms, and a graph-based AI platform.

I hope you enjoy the book as much as I did and that you will become a graph addict too. You'll learn a lot here that you won't learn anywhere else.

Happy graphing!

— Michael Hunger
VP of Product Innovation, Neo4j
Author of DuckDB in Action *and*
GraphRAG: The Definitive Guide
Dresden, Germany, April 2025

Preface

Graph databases power mission-critical applications across thousands of enterprises, enabling everything from recommendation engines and fraud detection to supply-chain optimization and knowledge graphs. Neo4j, as a pioneer in this space and now a leading graph platform, plays a pivotal role in this evolution. Organizations are increasingly turning to graph-based solutions to extract deeper insights from their connected data. Yet the journey from concept to production remains challenging for many teams venturing into the world of graphs.

Whether you're looking to improve the performance of Cypher queries, model your graph to support diverse use cases, or comply with enterprise security requirements, this book is your companion on the road to production readiness. Within these pages, you'll find a curated collection of practical, concise lessons designed to help you solve real-world challenges with Neo4j. They're grounded in field-tested strategies from successful Neo4j deployments around the world.

Furthermore, with the explosion of generative AI driving even greater adoption of knowledge graphs, the need for practical implementation guidance has never been greater. From quick proof-of-concept implementations to full-scale production systems, we'll be your guides, keeping you on the path to success. Along the way, we'll explore common pitfalls, discuss the trade-offs behind different approaches, and help you build robust solutions that meet the demands of modern enterprise architectures.

After reading this book, you will have a clear understanding of what characteristics lend themselves to making native graph databases the best technology choice (as compared with multimodel databases) and graph modeling patterns' impact on a system's memory, CPU usage, performance, speed, and business SLAs. You will be able to make practical decisions in the proof-of-concept stage to maximize value, then revisit and revise those decisions when transitioning to production. You will also understand what it takes to run Neo4j in production at an enterprise scale, including how to configure your backups and logs and how to plan for running a cluster.

Why We Wrote This Book

The graph database space is relatively young. As some of the earliest practitioners on the scene, we've been involved with both organizations and individuals interested in using graphs, and particularly Neo4j, for decades. We've always been hands-on, training large and small teams, evaluating graph use cases, designing and reviewing graph architectures, conducting modeling sessions, and improving query performance. Starting as graph consultants, we went on to become key members of the team that conceptualized and built GraphAware's Hume, a connected data-analytics platform. The experience has been invaluable. Thanks to the very nature of graphs, every challenge is different, and there is always something new to learn. We felt it was time to share our experiences with everyone who wants to include Neo4j in their enterprise architecture and take it to production.

We believe that theoretical knowledge of graphs is best learned while implementing graph solutions in practical applications. Our observations about common mistakes and gotchas repeated across a wide range of organizations—despite plenty of documentation—drive our preferred method of sharing knowledge via trial and error. That's why, throughout this book, we guide you to try a seemingly natural way to approach a problem and then show you why it wasn't a good idea. This cements the concepts; you won't repeat these errors, and you'll understand the real reason behind the advice.

We wish you every success on your graph journey. More importantly, we wish you the thrill we both experience when we work with graphs.

Is This Book for You?

Let's start with who this book is not for, or not for yet: if you're new to graphs and Neo4j, we recommend that you come back to this book once you've completed beginner courses or have used graphs for a couple of use cases. GraphAcademy (*https://graphacademy.neo4j.com/*) is an excellent starting point.

The content of this book is targeted at intermediate to advanced graph database and Neo4j users. If you're a data engineer or experienced developer, you should already be able to ingest data into a graph and query it using Cypher. If you're a data scientist, you should have experimented with a couple of graph data science algorithms. For architects, principal engineers, and operations engineers, you should have some experience integrating a graph database into, perhaps, a nonproduction or proof-of-concept environment and have set up, administered, and monitored the database.

Essentially, if you're working with Neo4j today and you're already in production but have problems, or you're planning your path to production, this book is for you.

Navigating This Book

We recommend that you start with Chapter 1 to set the context for the rest of the book, especially the examples. Chapters 3 , 4, and 5 are closely related and best read together. The rest may be read in sequence, building on the foundations set in the early chapters, or visited as reference points.

Chapter 1, "How to Get Value from Graphs in Just Five Days," recaps why native graph databases matter and shows you how to build a proof of concept in a week. You'll touch a little of everything: modeling, ingesting data, and writing Cypher queries, including a simple but valuable recommendation query.

Chapter 2, "Importing (Much) More Data," moves beyond the proof-of-concept dataset and shows you how to ingest data at scale. It will help solidify your knowledge about database transactions, memory management, and parallel writes.

Chapter 3, "Revisiting Modeling Decisions," examines a couple of the modeling decisions taken in Chapter 1 and walks you through their pros and cons, as well as other factors to take into account when modeling a graph. Revisiting your graph model is a real-life process, and this chapter helps you to evolve out of your proof-of-concept model.

Chapter 4, "Modeling and Refactoring Patterns," catalogs different modeling patterns and in which situations they're best applied. You'll also learn techniques to refactor your model and graph.

Chapter 5, "Query Analysis and Tuning," is an in-depth treatment of how queries are planned, where the bottlenecks are, how to use the query profile, and how to massively improve the performance of your Cypher queries.

Chapter 6, "Securing Your Graph Database," exposes all the areas you should consider when it comes to securing your Neo4j database. From authentication and authorization to preventing tampering and elevation-of-privilege threats, this chapter is a comprehensive checklist to work through.

Chapter 7, "Search," shows you how to store and query textual data for relevant search results.

Chapter 8, "Advanced Graph Patterns," is a collection of patterns that you're bound to encounter as you get more experienced with Neo4j and start to see more advanced use cases. In this chapter, you'll find a treatment of subqueries, modeling resolved entities, quantified path patterns, and guidance for taking your security data modeling to the next level.

Chapter 9, "Backup and Restore," gives you nonnegotiable skills for operating Neo4j in production. Learn about types of backups, restoring them, and how to design your backup strategy.

Chapter 10, "Clustering and Sharding," prepares you and your growing graph for scale. You'll learn about clustering for high availability and the solution for sharding and federation: composite databases.

Chapter 11, "Observability," is all about robust strategies involving logs and monitoring to ensure that your graph is healthy and serving mission-critical use cases.

Chapter 12, "Practical Graph Data Science," introduces you to the graph data science library and how to use these algorithms to extract insights from your data.

Chapter 13, "The Future of Graphs with Generative AI," describes the symbiotic relationship between knowledge graphs and LLMs and why knowledge graphs are the present and future.

Conventions Used in This Book

The following typographical conventions are used in this book:

Italic
: Indicates new terms, URLs, email addresses, filenames, and file extensions.

`Constant width`
: Used for program listings, as well as within paragraphs to refer to program elements such as variable or function names, databases, data types, environment variables, statements, and keywords.

`Constant width bold`
: Shows commands or other text that should be typed literally by the user.

`Constant width italic`
: Shows text that should be replaced with user-supplied values or by values determined by context.

This element signifies a tip or suggestion.

This element signifies a general note.

This element indicates a warning or caution.

Using Code Examples

Supplemental material (code examples, exercises, etc.) is available for download at *https://github.com/neo4j-the-definitive-guide/book.*

If you have a technical question or a problem using the code examples, please send email to *support@oreilly.com*.

This book is here to help you get your job done. In general, if example code is offered with this book, you may use it in your programs and documentation. You do not need to contact us for permission unless you're reproducing a significant portion of the code. For example, writing a program that uses several chunks of code from this book does not require permission. Selling or distributing examples from O'Reilly books does require permission. Answering a question by citing this book and quoting example code does not require permission. Incorporating a significant amount of example code from this book into your product's documentation does require permission.

We appreciate, but generally do not require, attribution. An attribution usually includes the title, author, publisher, and ISBN. For example: "*Neo4j: The Definitive Guide* by Luanne Misquitta and Christophe Willemsen (O'Reilly). Copyright 2025 Luanne Misquitta and Christophe Willemsen, 978-1-098-16565-9."

If you feel your use of code examples falls outside fair use or the permission given above, feel free to contact us at *permissions@oreilly.com*.

O'Reilly Online Learning

For more than 40 years, *O'Reilly Media* has provided technology and business training, knowledge, and insight to help companies succeed.

Our unique network of experts and innovators share their knowledge and expertise through books, articles, and our online learning platform. O'Reilly's online learning platform gives you on-demand access to live training courses, in-depth learning paths, interactive coding environments, and a vast collection of text and video from O'Reilly and 200+ other publishers. For more information, visit *https://oreilly.com*.

How to Contact Us

Please address comments and questions concerning this book to the publisher:

O'Reilly Media, Inc.
141 Stony Circle, Suite 195
Santa Rosa, CA 95401
800-889-8969 (in the United States or Canada)
707-827-7019 (international or local)
707-829-0104 (fax)
support@oreilly.com
https://oreilly.com/about/contact.html

We have a web page for this book, where we list errata, examples, and any additional information. You can access this page at *https://oreil.ly/neo4j-definitive-guide*.

For news and information about our books and courses, visit *https://oreilly.com*.

Find us on LinkedIn: *https://linkedin.com/company/oreilly-media*.

Watch us on YouTube: *https://youtube.com/oreillymedia*.

Acknowledgments

We're grateful to you, Jim Webber, for introducing us to the lovely O'Reilly team, your support, and then your unforgiving technical review—your feedback pushed us to make this book a much better read. We promise not to use semicolons under pain of death.

To the crew at O'Reilly: Sarah Grey, for your patience, good humor, putting up with us as we wrote the book in no less than seven countries, and for never getting tired of Americanizing our writing; Aaron Black for believing in two first-time writers; Carol Keller for noticing subtle issues and your very thorough edit; Jonathon Owen and the publishing team.

In addition to Jim, we'd like to thank Michael Simons, Mats Bjerin, and Dennis Silva for the time you invested in reviewing our book and for sending us thoughtful and clear feedback.

The fact that we spent a decade of our lives at GraphAware also contributed heavily to our experience. The brilliant, graphy people of GraphAware, past and present, have pushed us to learn more and aim for the stars. Hume, a product we both love very much, was instrumental in keeping graphs our true passion over all these years.

Our graph of Neo4j friends has always been a community we've been proud to be part of—we've learned so much from you all. Being nodes in the Neo4j ecosystem has been enriching and fun.

Last but not least, we owe a huge thank you to our dear friend, Michael Hunger. Michael, we've known each other for ages, and your brilliance, enthusiasm, and open sharing of knowledge, support, and kindness have meant a lot to us. We're very thankful to you for not only your advice on book writing but for your very thorough technical reviews and constant stream of ideas. It is an honor to have our foreword written by you.

Luanne thanks her family especially Declan. Many weekend plans were sacrificed so that she could find the time to write.

Christophe wants to thank his partner and kids for their patience as he disappeared for countless "write time" sessions. And it is very fitting to end with the fact that he also thanks himself (*https://www.youtube.com/watch?v=wGRF3GQ4Wdk*).

CHAPTER 1

How to Get Value from Graphs in Just Five Days

All the world's a graph. The early 2010s saw modern enterprises adopting what was niche at the time—graphs—for use cases, such as online real-time recommendations or impact analysis. They chose graph databases over relational and other NoSQL databases because of their performance, scalability, and astonishing ability to traverse, in real time, relationships that connect data. The graph captured rich connections that mirrored the real world.

Fast forward 10 years, and the graph technology landscape has exploded. Beyond those initial use cases, graphs are the answer to a critical aspect of today's data: complexity.

The last two decades have been about data—data collection, analysis, prediction, and protection. Everything around us captures data. Some organizations exist solely to analyze data and provide insights. For others, the usage of data determines the success of the business.

Ever since Clive Humby (*https://oreil.ly/kcIc2*)[1] proclaimed that "data is the new oil" back in 2006, the imagination, creativity and technical innovation of various companies deriving value from data has seen no bounds. From the rise of NoSQL databases in the first decade of the 2000s to the mind-boggling pace of generative AI (GenAI) today, it is clear that we are not even close to being done with data. We live in the data age for sure, but more importantly, we live in the time of *connected* data—and value lies in the connections. As digital consumers, we now expect relevant, personalized experiences. The world is connected, data around the world is inherently connected,

1 Charles Arthur, ed., "Tech Giants May Be Huge, but Nothing Matches Big Data," *Guardian*, August 23, 2013.

and our digital footprints across devices and transactions leave rich stories to be uncovered.

Many large companies continue to silo their data across various enterprise systems, and even if in much better shape than a decade before, queries across these systems to unlock hidden value are still nonperformant.

Discovering and leveraging data from all corners of the organization has typically fallen to data engineers or scientists—but this takes analytics and data-driven decisions further and further away from those who need access to trustworthy data on a daily basis. How can we solve this?

Graphs democratize data. Graphs let us bring siloed data together into a model that is a digital twin of the organization, flexible enough to adapt to its evolving business needs. Relationships connect this data across disparate systems and serve as value multipliers. Suddenly, everyone can explore and work with business data directly. Analytics tools can connect to a single source of truth to provide the insights needed to validate hypotheses or back decisions, empowering those on the front lines of the business.

With the rise of GenAI, *knowledge graphs* are even more prominent: they capture explicit relationships, bringing institutional intelligence closer to the data. When paired with vector searches that reveal *implicit* relationships (those based on semantics), knowledge graphs ground responses from large language models (LLMs) in validated facts. GraphRAG (*https://oreil.ly/A4iwS*) is an approach that involves providing a richer and more relevant context to LLMs as compared to vector search. You'll read about these concepts in Chapter 13.

Graph technology is experiencing accelerated momentum. Gartner (*https://oreil.ly/74WmP*) predicts[2] that "by 2025, graph technologies will be used in 80% of data and analytics innovations, up from 10% in 2021, facilitating rapid decision making across the organization."

2 "Gartner Identifies Top 10 Data and Analytics Technology Trends for 2021," Gartner, March 16, 2021.

In this chapter, we guide you through a practical path to deliver graph value to your business in just one week. Neo4j lends itself well to an incremental style of development and delivery, a process modern enterprises favor over "big bang" approaches. A swift demonstration of value, followed by incremental iterations to show ongoing impact along the way, is one of the most successful routes to adopting a new technology.

Dissonance at ElectricHarmony

ElectricHarmony, an established music-streaming service, is exploring how it can use graph databases. As new music providers capture young people's attention, ElectricHarmony is struggling to stay competitive. In the last two quarters alone, they have lost a significant number of subscribers, who revealed that their listening experiences felt stale and uninspiring.

After a thorough analysis, ElectricHarmony concluded that it simply is not leveraging all the data it collects in various systems well enough to produce more relevant playlists. New data sources emerge rapidly, and the company can't keep up. Accompanying this is the expectation from the decision makers to implement ad hoc use cases to address immediate needs.

The engineering team at ElectricHarmony decides to experiment with Neo4j. They import a subset of data and learn the basics of Cypher very quickly, and soon they're writing queries that traverse effortlessly across artists, playlists, albums, and tracks. They can already see the benefits of connecting these key business entities in the graph. Instead of spending months trying to bring data together or find clever ways of querying across data in different sources in real time, they can spend their time working on critical business problems.

Stakeholders relate immediately to the team's line of thinking when they see it sketched on a whiteboard (as shown in Figure 1-1), and the excitement is palpable. New ideas start to pour in as the dots connect in everyone's minds.

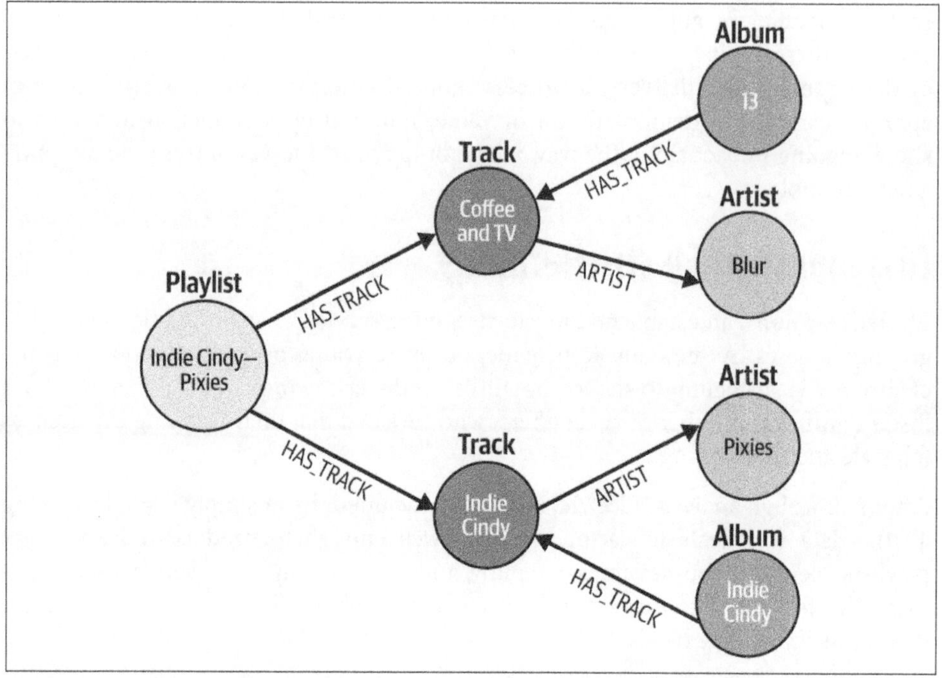

Figure 1-1. The whiteboard sketch from ElectricHarmony's discussion

The team theorizes that a connected data model is the answer to the problem of data silos and slow, expensive queries. Now they need to validate their theory with a short proof of concept—and *you're* joining the team to make it happen! In fact, throughout this book, you'll relate concepts and lessons learned to the music streaming domain and ElectricHarmony.

First, though, a detour to refresh your knowledge of graph databases and Neo4j.

Why Graph Databases?

Relational databases organize data in the form of tables. While applications may read data in this format, they frequently transform it into an object graph, which better aligns with how humans think about business domains. The mismatch occurs when the natural representation of the domain—entities with descriptive properties and relationships—have to be flattened to be stored in a relational database, then joined at query time to compose the real-world entity once again. This can lead to performance issues for the system and cognitive overhead for users to translate between both representations.

In database systems, an *impedance mismatch* is when the data's representation in the database differs from its representation in the application or the business domain.

The whiteboard sketch in Figure 1-1 demonstrates that graph models excel at solving this mismatch between the real world and the models (or schemas) that databases impose upon it. The beneficial side effect is that individuals, especially nonengineers, across all levels and functions in an organization now speak the same language. Graphs not only bring clarity to how data is used but also highlight gaps in data and misunderstandings about meaning or intent.

Figure 1-2 shows a relational representation of ElectricHarmony's data.

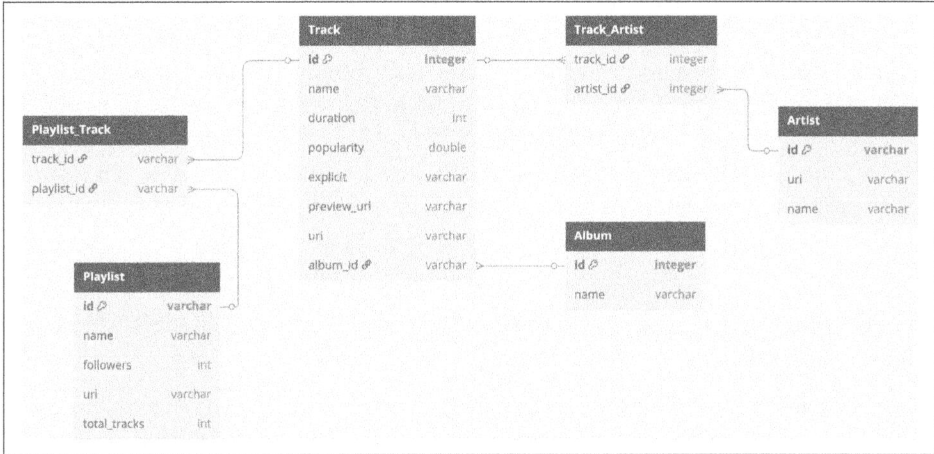

Figure 1-2. ElectricHarmony's relational database schema

Figure 1-3 is the graph model, equivalent to the business domain drawing on the whiteboard in Figure 1-1. Which one do you think is more intuitive?

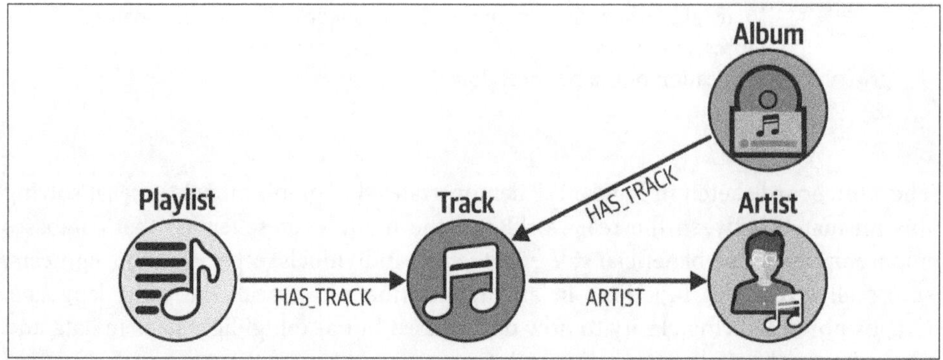

Figure 1-3. ElectricHarmony graph model representing the whiteboard sketch

Relational databases struggle with graph use cases because they rely heavily on join tables to represent relationships, which can lead to complex queries and performance bottlenecks, especially when dealing with highly interconnected data. The need to perform multiple joins at query time makes relational databases inefficient for traversing graphs. Additionally, their intricate database schemas are difficult for nontechnical stakeholders to understand, creating a significant gap between how the data is stored and how users conceptualize it, thus making the data less accessible and intuitive.

In our many years of consulting with clients, we've found that there's always an enjoyable aha moment where it suddenly all makes sense. Then that humble whiteboard begins to spark new use cases and ideas.

Graphs fit neatly into almost every domain, because the world is naturally connected. But the use cases that derive value from relationships are the ones that truly shine. The advantages of graphs increase with the size and complexity of the data, simply because graphs manage the inherent complexity for you and don't add more of their own in the form of normalization rules, many tables, index management, etc.

Graph Use Cases

To help you see the potential of graphs, let's look at four more ways they can solve real-world problems:

Ultimate Beneficial Ownership Networks

An *ultimate beneficial ownership* (UBO) is an individual or company that ultimately owns or controls another legal entity. It is a critical component of know your customer (KYC) processes; regulators require most financial institutions to verify the UBOs they do business with to prevent crimes such as money laundering or financing terrorism.

Imagine that Jane Doe owns 100% of Company A, which in turn owns 100% of Company B. Ultimately, Jane owns 100% of Company B through her ownership in Company A. In the real world, ownership structures can be far more complex. During our consulting work for several tax authorities, we've encountered real cases with 60 to 70 layers of ownership. Graphs are particularly well suited to traversing these deep and often circular networks efficiently, empowering anti-money-laundering analysts and tax investigators to uncover hidden beneficial ownership.

Real-Time Recommendations

Retailers, content providers, social networking platforms, and service providers all gain clear business advantages when they can provide their customers with recommendations in real time. Whether it is a product to purchase, a service that complements the product, or new social experiences and connections to discover, good recommendations are contingent on being able to quickly correlate data and incorporate new pieces of information (such as an action taken by a user).

Customers, the products they buy or are interested in, the services they subscribe to, their social circles, their preferences, and the content they consume are all highly interconnected. Recommender systems can use the power of the graph to traverse this interconnected data in order to perform content or collaborative filtering rapidly. The graph data science algorithms they use include *community detection* for customer segmentation, similarity algorithms to find similar items to recommend, and link prediction to train ML models to predict customer churn.

Law Enforcement

Network analysis is an indispensable tool in modern law enforcement—particularly link analysis, which helps reveal connections between people, places, and things. In this context, graphs offer a visual representation of relationships, where nodes represent individuals or entities and edges illustrate the connections between them. This type of analysis allows law enforcement agencies to uncover patterns in data, revealing connections between suspects, crime victims, and known criminals or gang members that may otherwise remain hidden.

For example, consider a large-scale investigation into organized crime, specifically drug trafficking. In such cases, criminal organizations often operate as complex networks, with different members performing specialized roles—such as money laundering, drug trafficking, or arms dealing. Traditional investigative methods might identify some key players, but network analysis can help map out the entire organization by connecting seemingly unrelated individuals through shared contacts, financial transactions, or common locations in order to build a complete picture of the criminal organization.

Investigators can analyze the data they collect from wiretaps, surveillance, and social media to identify the central figures in the network, as well as the lower-level members who serve as couriers or enforcers. By visualizing these relationships, investigators can see the hierarchy of the organization and identify the critical nodes—those individuals whose removal would cause the most disruption to the network's operations.

Furthermore, network analysis can help law enforcement predict future criminal activities by identifying emerging patterns or trends. For instance, if certain individuals or locations become increasingly central within a criminal network, this might indicate that they are becoming more involved in illicit activities, prompting further investigation.

Network analysis is also useful for solving individual crimes. For example, homicide investigators can create a network of all known associates of both the victim and any suspects, including friends, family, and coworkers. By examining the connections between these individuals, they may uncover a previously unknown relationship or motive that leads to the resolution of the case.

In short, network analysis allows law enforcement agencies to move beyond linear, list-based thinking and gain a more holistic view of criminal activities. By visualizing relationships between people, places, and things, agencies can not only solve crimes more effectively but also disrupt criminal networks before they can act.

Cybercrime Networks

The COVID-19 pandemic has made remote work today's "new normal," but this change also represents an immense opportunity for cyber attackers. In 2020 alone, the FBI reported (*https://oreil.ly/FDX3t*) a 300% increase in cybercrimes.

John Lambert, of Microsoft's Threat Intelligence Center, writes (*https://oreil.ly/uMhh8*)[3] that the "biggest problem with network defense is that defenders think in lists. Attackers think in graphs. As long as this is true, attackers win." His point is that defenders traditionally rely on lists, such as logs and alerts from software tools, while attackers are more opportunistic in thinking of their target network. After gaining access to one node, they build an *attack graph*—a representation of all the possible paths of attack against a cybersecurity network—to gain access to the most valuable systems. Defenders can enhance their security by building a *digital twin* of their infrastructure: a digital representation of a physical object, person, or process, contextualized in a digital version of its environment. Digital twins (*https://oreil.ly/BADL1*)[4] can help an organization simulate real situations and their outcomes

3 John Lambert, "Defender's Mindset," Medium, November 21, 2021.

4 "What Is Digital-Twin Technology?," McKinsey & Company, August 26, 2024.

and identify their most valuable assets, the impact on downstream components, and suspicious patterns. Ultimately, this helps the organization make better decisions.

These use cases are just the beginning; later in the book, we'll delve deeper into the use of knowledge graphs in GenAI workflows.

First, however, you might be wondering: since there are several graph databases to choose from, why would you use Neo4j?

Neo4j

Neo4j is one of the most mature and frequently deployed (*https://oreil.ly/XrVoJ*) graph solutions,[5] having created the graph database category in the early 2010s. Neo4j is available today in a variety of offerings: as an open source Community edition, a commercial Enterprise edition, and a service on all major cloud platforms. Its flexible graph modeling, however, is not the sole reason to adopt another database. Neo4j has many beneficial qualities that may drive this decision:

- It is highly performant when querying complex data.
- It uses a powerful query language, Cypher, that expresses traversals intuitively.
- It is highly scalable.
- It is operationally sound, with atomicity, consistency, isolation, durability (ACID) transactions, cluster support, and runtime failover.

Neo4j is a labeled property graph. *Property graph models* are very popular for graph databases. They consist of nodes and relationships, each of which can contain zero or more properties that describe their characteristics (you can think of *properties* as key-value pairs). Figure 1-4 depicts a property graph model.

---

5 For more differences between a graph database and a relational database management system (RDBMS), see this infographic from Neo4j (*https://oreil.ly/qOuqL*).

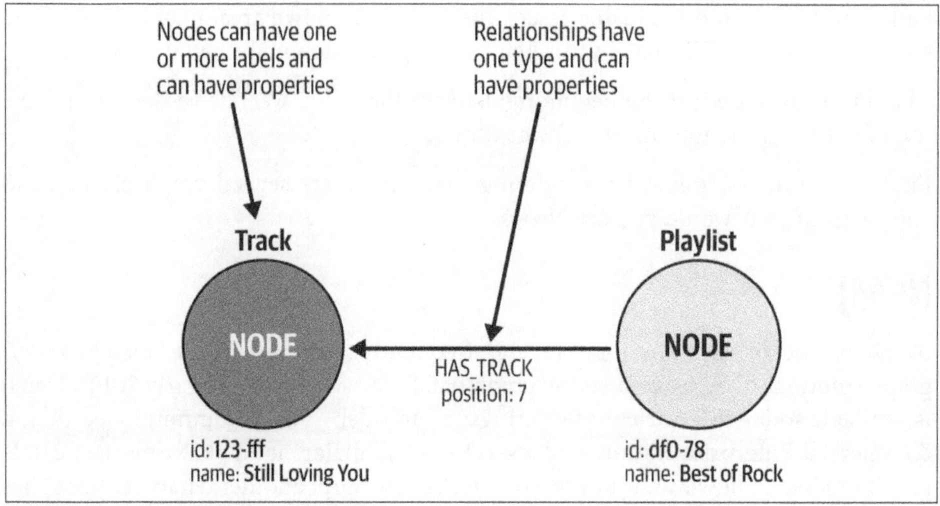

Figure 1-4. Property graph model

Nodes represent *entities,* such as people, vehicles, locations, songs, suppliers, orders, and so forth. *Relationships* represent the connections between entities. Relationships are the "first-class citizens" of graphs. Relationships have a *type* and *direction*: examples are `DRIVES`, `PERFORMS`, `SUPPLIES`, and `LIVES_AT`.

Labeled property graphs let you assign zero or more *labels* (denoting tags or categories) to nodes. A label categorizes the *type* of the node. For example, a node might have just the label `Person`, or it might have `Person`, `Customer`, `Location`, and other labels. Keep in mind that there is no semantic structure or relationship imposed between labels.

Native Graph Databases

Neo4j is also a *native* graph database. Native graph databases are architected specifically for graphs. This enables them to perform graph queries faster and more efficiently because they are designed to store and process data as a graph. This is a major difference between Neo4j and other multimodel databases built over other types of database structures, such as key-value or relational. Such databases may support some graph operations, but not as a primary use case.

When we say that relationships matter, we mean that it is important to be able to traverse those relationships or connections in a performant manner—quickly and with efficient resource usage. How these connections are represented—whether they are *materialized* (their structure is physically represented in the storage) or joined at query time—is crucial. In general, you will favor materializing the relationships for better performance.

Neo4j stores graph data efficiently using *index-free adjacency*, meaning that each node is linked to its connected nodes through relationships that maintain direct references. This allows fast traversal between related nodes without needing to search through a global index. Under the hood, relationships are stored separately and include references to the start and end nodes, as well as pointers that make it efficient to navigate through what's called a *relationship chain*. In practice, this means Neo4j can access connected data quickly, as illustrated in Figure 1-5.

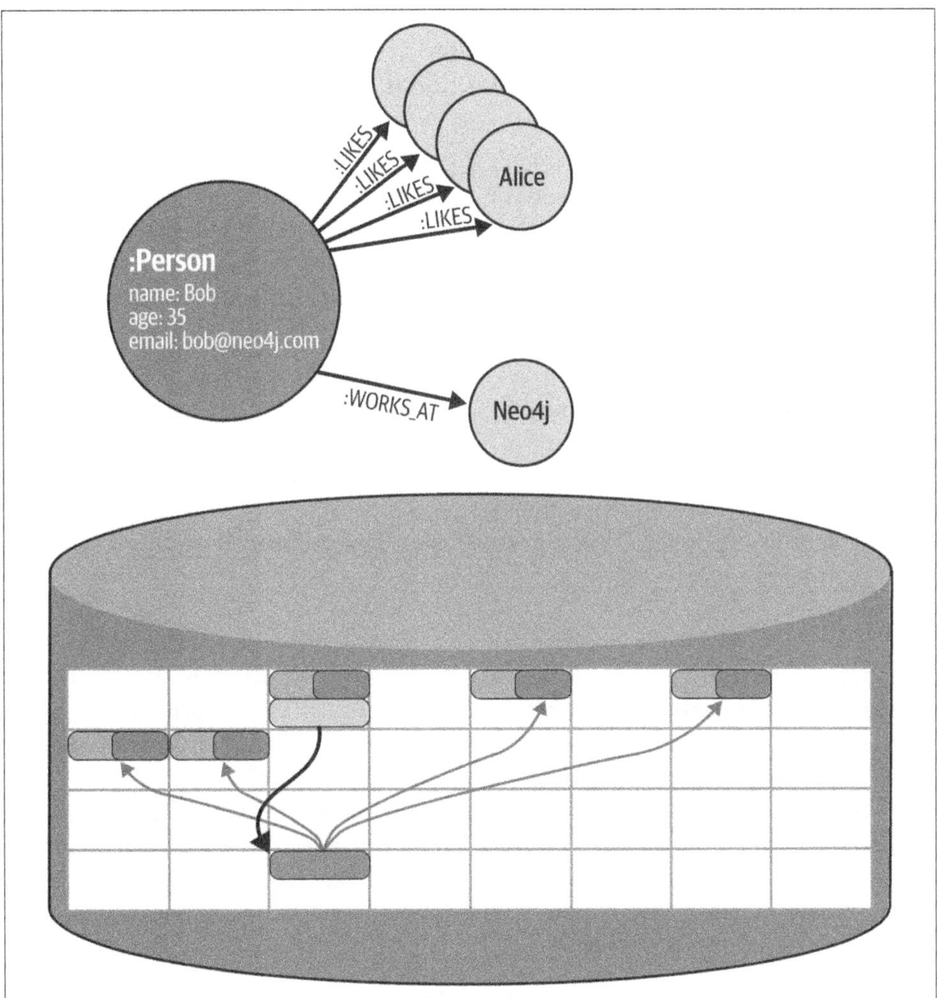

Figure 1-5. In Neo4j's block-storage engine, a node's relationships are a linked list with pointers to other nodes.

Nonnative graph stores, by contrast, suffer the cost of *joins* to find related entities, which are typically achieved by performing repeated index lookups to determine the next connection. While this is only of trivial importance at a couple of hops (a hop is the navigation across a relationship to land at the connected node), querying gets exponentially slower and more expensive as the depth of the connections and the size and complexity of the data increase.

Native graph databases allow graph algorithms that rely on pathfinding to shine when working with network-based cases. Some examples:

- How are people connected to each other in a social network? Are they immediate contacts, or are they two (friend-of-friends) or three or even more levels apart? What's the shortest path that connects them? Facebook and LinkedIn are definitely modern examples of such.
- What will the impact on the electrical grid be if a particular power plant has an outage? How should the network be reconfigured to minimize outage time for a particular area? In case of an outage at a power plant or along transmission lines, a graph algorithm can help efficiently reroute power through alternative paths, minimizing disruption and restoring power quickly. It identifies the shortest or most reliable routes in the network to redistribute the load effectively.
- What is the fastest route from Clapham South station to King's Cross in London? Here, a graph models the transport network as nodes (stations) and edges (connections). A graph algorithm calculates the optimal path by considering factors like distance, transit time, and potential delays. By analyzing real-time data, the algorithm identifies the most efficient route, adjusting dynamically for disruptions to provide the best possible option for the user.

Cypher

The query language that Neo4j uses is called Cypher. Created by Neo4j in 2011, it was so intuitive and popular that in 2017 it resulted in an open source implementation called openCypher (*https://opencypher.org*), which many graph databases use. Today, Graph Query Language (*https://gqlstandards.org*) (GQL), derived from Cypher, is only the second database query language after Structured Query Language (SQL) to be standardized by the International Organization for Standardization (ISO) and International Electrotechnical Commission (IEC). Neo4j's Cypher supports the majority of mandatory GQL features and at the time of writing this book, support for optional GQL features is increasing.

Cypher is a *declarative* query language; it focuses on describing *what* the user wants to create or find in the database rather than *how* to do so.

Cypher is also a visual query language that is based on ASCII art. It uses parentheses "`()`" to describe nodes and lines "`--`" with arrows "<>" for directions to describe relationships.

Figure 1-6 expresses a pattern that reads like this: "A playlist has a track." The two entities in rounded parentheses are *nodes*. The nodes are represented by identifiers `p` and `t` and have labels `Playlist` and `Track`, respectively. The relationship type, `HAS_TRACK`, is in square brackets. Finally, the dashes are an arrow that tells you that the playlist is connected to a track via an outgoing relationship.

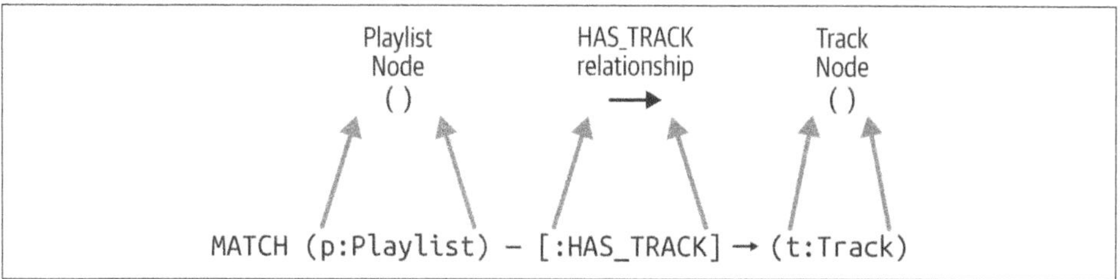

Figure 1-6. Cypher's ASCII art. Nodes are represented by parentheses and relationships by lines and arrows.

Cypher is very powerful and would probably require an entire book in itself. We'll explain the queries throughout the book, but for a complete overview of Cypher and its capabilities, visit the Cypher manual section (*https://oreil.ly/2VFT2*) of the Neo4j documentation.

Now that the benefits of Neo4j are clear, we return to ElectricHarmony, where you and the team will demonstrate that recommendations powered by Neo4j will help solve the company's current problem.

The Song Recommendation System: A Proof of Concept

We assume that you have previous experience with Cypher and labeled property graphs like Neo4j. If you've loaded data into Neo4j in any way, written Cypher queries, or built an application with Neo4j as the backing database, then you're at the right level to proceed reading this book. If you're a beginner, fear not: Neo4j is a very friendly database, and it's easy to get started. We recommend that you learn the fundamentals of graph databases, modeling, and Cypher and then return. GraphAcademy (*https://graphacademy.neo4j.com*) is an excellent resource that offers free, hands-on Neo4j training.

Through our decade-long Neo4j consulting experience, we've found that we consistently advise on commonly repeated patterns and gotchas. Our approach in this book is to demonstrate how you might instinctively do the same, and then explain why there are better solutions. We find that this method helps good practices stick better.

ElectricHarmony's analytics show that a listener often skips over the recommended songs when the listener's playlist comes to an end. Research from the company's sociomusicology group shows that users prefer to listen to music that others with similar musical tastes like. The surprise effect is also important, as discovering new artists or tracks increases users' engagement time. Serendipity in recommender systems is a much-written-about subject. Recommendations that produce something unexpected broaden users' experience and, if crafted well, result in delight and novel discoveries. The group's hypothesis is that listeners will respond positively to recommendations based on these principles, so they ask the development team to quickly deploy a proof of concept that they can test with real users.

Recommender systems are an entire discipline in themselves and can be very complex. This book is not meant to teach you how to build recommendation engines. We use simple examples for clarity and to showcase the benefits of using graph databases for analytical workloads. Recommendations produced by traditional systems are often a closed box—difficult to reason about and less explainable. This magnifies the gap between highly specialized engineers and stakeholders who are unclear about how and why recommendations are produced. Graphs, on the other hand, help with traceability, as you will see in the following sections.

The development team members agree that they'll consider the evaluation successful if it can do all of the following:

- Detect similar playlists based on how many tracks they share.
- Compute a track recommendation based on similar playlists; find similar playlists that share the same last track. The more similar the playlist, the better the recommendation.
- Discard recommendations for tracks that are too popular.
- Compute recommendations in less than 200ms.

Day 1

Today is day one. Over the next five days, you and the team will get value out of the graph database by building the proof of concept. We encourage you to participate in this very realistic exercise by following along and reflecting on your accomplishments at the end of each section (day).

Installing Neo4j

A companion GitHub repository (*https://oreil.ly/SVnwo*) is available to help you follow along with the examples and code in this book. Follow the instructions in the README file in the repository in order to get all the necessary software installed and to get up and running locally. The examples in this book use the most recently released LTS version of Neo4j, currently 5.26.

If you prefer a fully managed option, Neo4j Aura (*https://oreil.ly/bqKp6*) offers Neo4j as a service in the cloud, removing the need to install or operate database infrastructure yourself. Aura is available in several tiers, Aura Free, Professional, and Enterprise, so you can choose what fits your needs.

For those working with large-scale graph analytics, Neo4j launched serverless Graph Analytics (*https://oreil.ly/9e7q1*) in May 2025. This new option allows you to run graph data science (GDS) workloads on demand without provisioning a database—ideal for elastic, analysis-driven use cases. Other Neo4j deployment options are listed in the Neo4j Deployment Center (*https://oreil.ly/mL3jz*).

Ingesting your first datasets

To demonstrate the song-recommendation use case, you can draw from two of ElectricHarmony's data sources. The first contains track, artist, and album information. The second contains playlists, including their IDs, playlist names, and references to tracks and their positions in the playlist.

In this case, the most practical way to import a limited set of this data into Neo4j is by exporting a sample of the source databases into CSV format.

The CSV files are in the *docker/import* directory in the GitHub repository, while the Cypher queries for this chapter are in the *chapter01/cypher* directory and referenced as a comment with the filename.

If not already done, start up Neo4j with the following command:

```
cd book/docker
docker-compose up -d
```

Once Neo4j is running, go to *http://localhost:7474/* and log in with the following credentials:

> Username: **`neo4j`**
> Password: **`password`**

The Neo4j browser will show (as seen in Figure 1-7) that you are connected to the default database named `neo4j`.

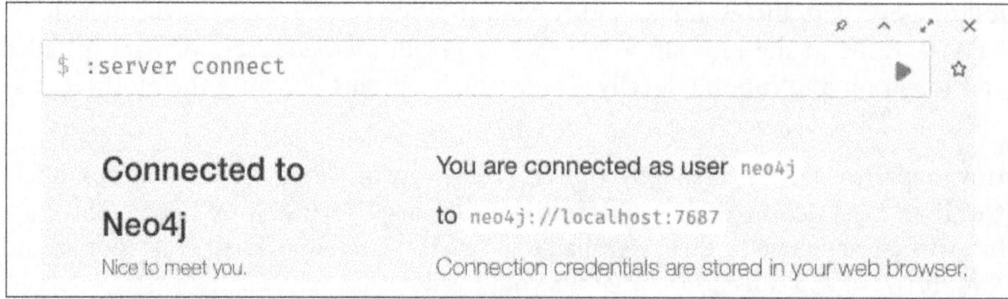

Figure 1-7. Successful authentication in the Neo4j browser

The sample datasets are mounted on the Neo4j docker container and are available as *sample_tracks.csv* and *sample_playlists.csv* in the */import* directory, which is the only folder accessible by Neo4j by default.

Before you create any data, create a new database. You'll build upon this database in this chapter and use it again in Chapters 3 and 4:

```
//000-create-database.cypher
CREATE DATABASE chapter01 WAIT;
```

Then, switch to that database with `:use chapter01`.

Previewing the data

The `LOAD CSV` clause is suitable for ingesting data at the proof-of-concept stage. It's easy to use and gets your data into the graph quickly. We'll cover other methods in the next chapter. To get accustomed to the shape of the data, run the following in the Neo4j browser (see Figure 1-8):

```
//001-preview-data.cypher
LOAD CSV WITH HEADERS FROM "file:///sample_tracks.csv" AS row
RETURN row
LIMIT 5;
```

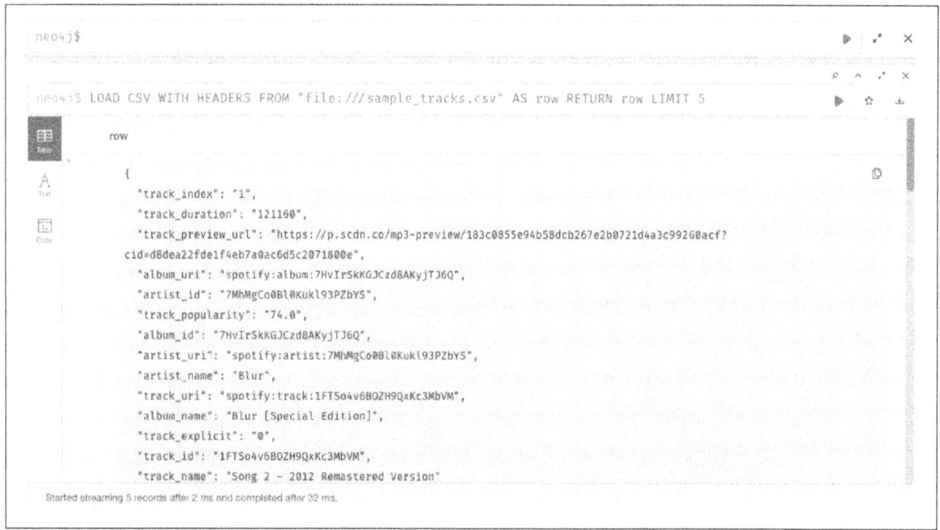

Figure 1-8. `LOAD CSV` preview of five rows of the sample tracks file

If the CSV has a header line, the `WITH HEADERS` option allows you to refer to each field by its column name. This is because each row in the file is represented as a map, such as in Figure 1-9, as opposed to an array of strings for a file without headers. It's good practice to add a header to your CSV files—it makes the data easier to understand and handle.

You can do the same for the playlist sample file:

```
//001-preview-data.cypher

LOAD CSV WITH HEADERS FROM "file:///sample_playlists.csv" AS row

RETURN row

LIMIT 5;
```

Figure 1-9 shows the preview you should see.

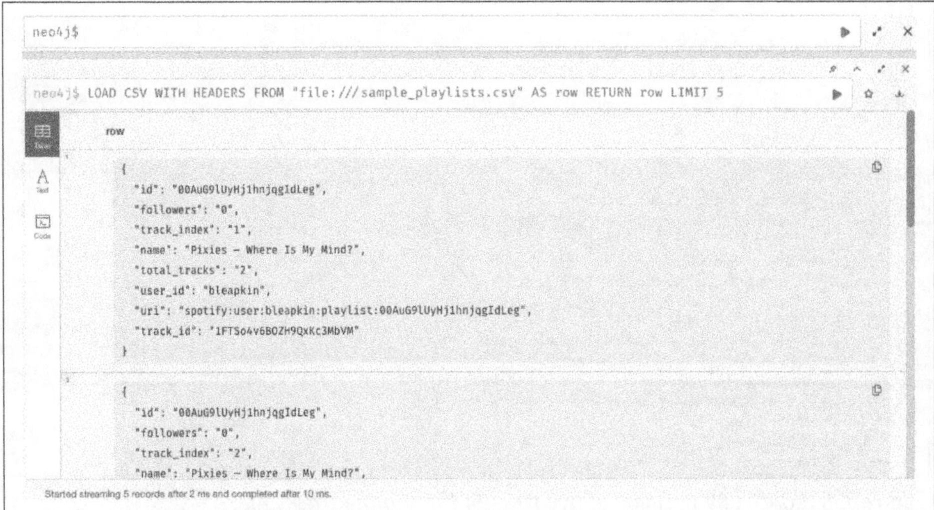

Figure 1-9. `LOAD CSV` *preview for the playlists dataset*

Our experience shows that many graph users like the ease of previewing their CSV files in the Neo4j browser; however, other options exist, such as csvkit (*https://oreil.ly/j2pP2*), xsv (*https://oreil.ly/C8yNW*), and similar.

Designing your graph model

Before you can ingest data into the graph, you and the team have to decide on the first version of your graph model.

You can think of a graph model as akin to a schema in other types of database systems. A *graph model* (sometimes referred to as a data model) represents the conceptual structure of the graph and should be a metamodel of your business domain. It contains:

- Nodes and their labels
- How they are related to each other
- The types of those relationships
- The properties of both nodes and relationships with their data types
- Optional constraints

Graph modeling is driven by use cases. A use case elaborates the goal that you're trying to achieve and the concepts involved to reach it. This makes it very different from creating a schema for a relational database, for example, where you would generally follow normalization rules without having to know anything about the types of queries users will be executing. This will work to our advantage as the system evolves.

Initially, the best tool for graph modeling is a whiteboard. You and the team grab some coffee and assemble in front of one, ready to get started.

First, it's important to clarify the specific use case. The goal is to provide a recommendation when a playlist ends. This recommendation is based on how similar other playlists are to the one just played, specifically by analyzing the number of tracks they share. The last track of the finished playlist plays a key role in this process: the more similar playlists that share this final track, the stronger the recommendation will be. There are many more ways to determine the next track to be played, but for simplicity, the last track is used.

You get started by drawing the key entities, which will represent nodes in your graph (see Figure 1-10). A handy tip is to start by picking out the nouns from the use case—more often than not, they're entities that have some conceptual identity. In this use case, the nouns are *user*, *playlist*, and *track*, and they also serve as appropriate labels. Similarly, relationships are usually the verbs or actions in your use case. A user owns playlists, and playlists have tracks, so you draw those relationships using arrows, indicating the direction of the relationship.

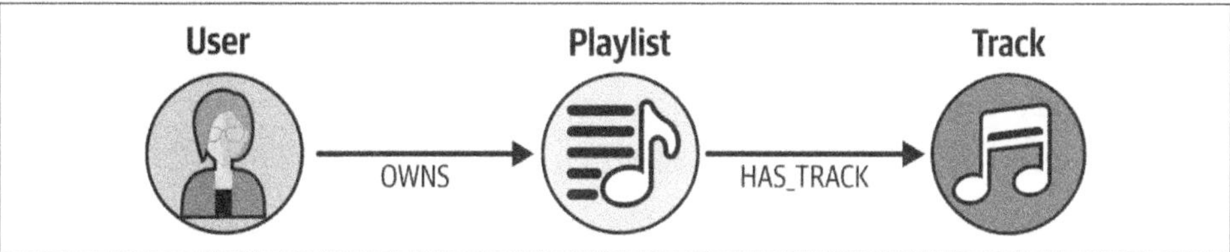

Figure 1-10. The graph model with key entities

The datasets contain information about the artist and album as well, but you don't strictly need that information in order to fulfill the use case. So what should you do with it?

There are two ways to go here. One approach is to simply not ingest that data now and bring it into the graph later, when you need it. The second is to model it in a straightforward way, keeping in mind that the model can change as the use case gets clearer. You decide as a group to add both labels to the graph model; they're fairly obvious and will make validating and reasoning about the recommendation results easier. Now your whiteboard looks like Figure 1-11.

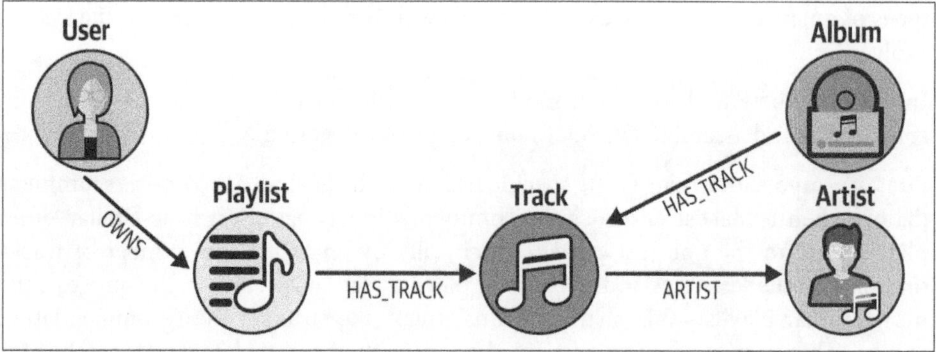

Figure 1-11. The extended graph model

Walking the graph

Now you take a step back and look at the graph model. You can "walk the graph" on the whiteboard. This exercise might feel strange to you if you've never done it before, but trust us: with time, it will come naturally!

Here's how to walk this graph:

- Start all the way on the left. Point at the `User` and state the first relationship: "a `User` owns a `Playlist`."
- Follow the arrow to point at the `Playlist`, narrating what you see on the board.
- Hop over to the tracks, saying, "a playlist has tracks."
- Now follow the `HAS_TRACK` and `Artist` relationships: "the artist of a track is…" and land on the artist node.
- Do the same with the `Album`: "an album has tracks"—and arrive back at the `Track` node.
- "A track is part of other playlists"—back to the `Playlist`.
- And "a playlist is owned by another user." You've reached the start again.

You've discovered the next track to play—and you've articulated the business domain *and* the graph model with the same language.

Now that you have the idea of the graph model, you're ready to start ingesting data tomorrow! You'll see that the schema will develop along the way.

Key takeaways

The barrier to getting started with Neo4j is extremely low, and the Neo4j ecosystem is geared toward developer friendliness and ease of use. Designing your first graph model is very intuitive—what the team draws on the whiteboard will turn out to be your initial graph model.

Day 2

The team is eager to see data in the graph!

Creating nodes and relationships

You've wisely decided to do a dry run of the ingestion with a single row of data (`LIMIT 1` in the following query) so that you can inspect the graph and see if the model makes sense before going any further.

This query will create the `Track`, `Album`, and `Artist` nodes as well as the relationships between them. While the file contains many properties that will be useful later, the only important ones now are `id`, `name`, and `uri`. Here's the statement to import that first row of data:

```
//002-one-track.cypher
LOAD CSV WITH HEADERS FROM "file:///sample_tracks.csv" AS row
WITH row LIMIT 1

CREATE (track:Track {id: row.track_id}) ❶
SET track.uri = row.track_uri,
track.name = row.track_name ❷

CREATE (album:Album {id: row.album_id}) ❸
SET album.uri = row.album_uri,
album.name = row.album_name ❹

CREATE (artist:Artist {id: row.artist_id}) ❺
SET artist.uri = row.artist_uri,
artist.name = row.artist_name ❻

CREATE (album)-[:HAS_TRACK]->(track) ❼
CREATE (track)-[:ARTIST]->(artist); ❽
```

❶ Creates a Track node with its id property

❷ Sets the uri and name properties on the track node

❸ Creates the Album node and sets its id

❹ Sets the uri and name properties on the album node

❺ Creates the Artist node and sets its id

❻ Sets the uri and name on the Artist node

❼ Creates the HAS_TRACK relationship from the album to the track

❽ Creates the ARTIST relationship from the track to the artist

Now you retrieve the data you just created:

```
MATCH path=(artist:Artist)<-[:ARTIST]-(t:Track)<-[:HAS_TRACK]-(album:Album)
RETURN path;
```

Your results look like the ones in Figure 1-12.

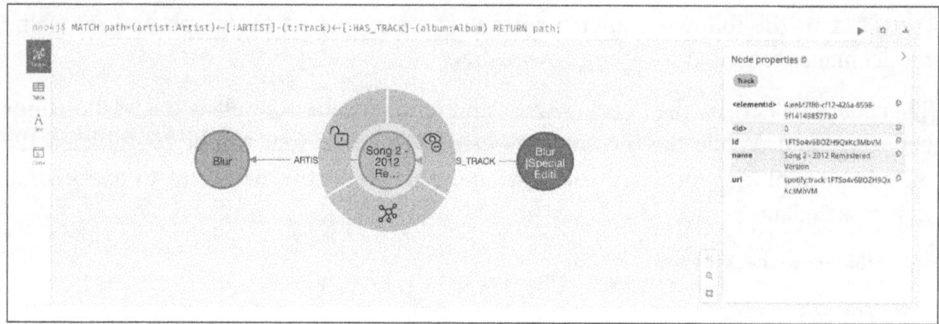

Figure 1-12. Result of a Cypher pathfinding query matching artists, tracks, and albums

Do the same for the playlists sample file. As with the previous file, you're only interested in properties that represent the IDs and the tracks' positions in a playlist:

```
//003-one-playlist.cypher
LOAD CSV WITH HEADERS FROM "file:///sample_playlists.csv" AS row
WITH row LIMIT 1

CREATE (playlist:Playlist {id: row.id})
SET playlist.name = row.name

CREATE (user:User {id: row.user_id})

CREATE (track:Track {id: row.track_id})

CREATE (user)-[:OWNS]->(playlist)
CREATE (playlist)-[:HAS_TRACK {position: row.playlist_track_index}]->(track);
```

Match the playlist that was just created and view the results in the Neo4j browser (see Figure 1-13) to see if this subgraph makes sense:

```
MATCH path=(user:User)-[:OWNS]->(p:Playlist)-[:HAS_TRACK]->(t:Track)
RETURN path;
```

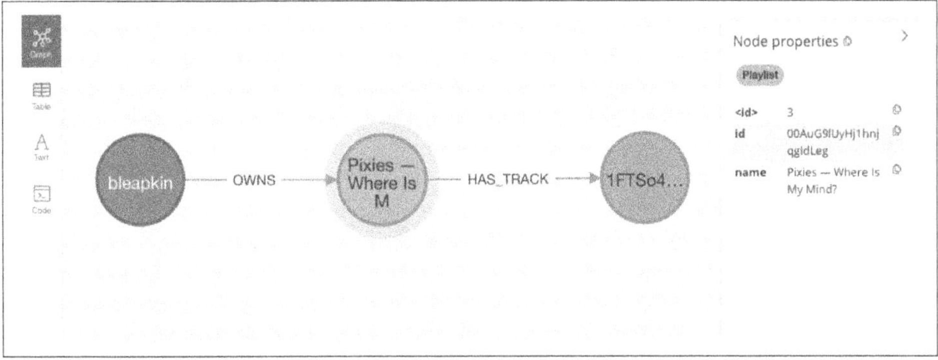

Figure 1-13. Cypher query result showing a user named "bleapkin" who owns a playlist with one track

Querying across datasets

Now the team checks what their "single source of truth" looks like after having ingested a row from each dataset. You start to write a Cypher query to find patterns that represent playlists that have tracks and their artists or albums. This query traverses from the `Playlist` node to the `Artist` and `Album` nodes:

```
MATCH path=(p:Playlist)-[:HAS_TRACK]->(track:Track)<--(albumOrArtist)
RETURN path;
```

The label of the `albumOrArtist` node in the pattern is not specified. The same applies to the relationship between the `track` and the `albumOrArtist` node—it isn't specified between the dashes connecting them, resulting in just a double dash. This allows you to match any node or relationship that can exist at that place in the pattern in a concise and friendly form.

Alas, no results are returned, which tells you that something went wrong during the data ingestion. Run the following query to have an overview of the whole graph (see Figure 1-14):

```
MATCH (n)
OPTIONAL MATCH (n)-[r]->(o)
RETURN *
```

Since there is a very small amount of data in the graph, this query is suitable: it matches everything and you can visualize the results. In real graphs with millions or billions of nodes and relationships, you wouldn't be able to return the whole graph to your screen.

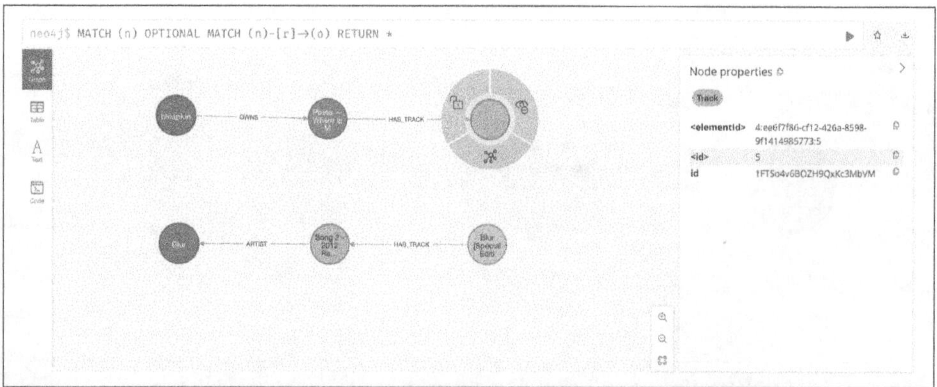

Figure 1-14. Cypher query result showing all the graph data in the database

Indeed, it doesn't look quite right. The first pattern represents a row from the playlists file:

```
(:User)-[:OWNS]->(:Playlist)-[:HAS_TRACK]->(:Track)
```

The second pattern represents a row from the tracks file:

```
(:Album)-[:HAS_TRACK]->(:Track)-[:ARTIST]->(:Artist)
```

The track in both patterns is the same track and should be the same node. To correct this, you use the `MERGE` clause rather than the `CREATE` clause you used in the CSV loading scripts.

Merging (safely) to avoid duplicates. In the queries above, you used `CREATE`, which simply created a node or relationship as instructed. But it's important to remember that every track in the CSV has a unique track ID. If this track exists in the graph already, you do not want to create it again.

`MERGE` is a combination of `MATCH` and `CREATE`. It will try to find the pattern you're looking for in the graph in its entirety, and if it does, nothing is created. Only if the pattern cannot be matched will the whole pattern be created.

As you're looking to avoid duplicate track nodes, `MERGE` needs a key that it can use effectively to `MATCH` a track first. In this case, the ID of the track, album, or artist is unique and can be reliably used to determine if the node exists in the graph. You'll also want to create a unique constraint for this property to ensure that duplicates are not created when ingesting data into the graph in parallel. For your current use case, which is the ease of loading data into Neo4j and preventing duplicates, you use the unique identifiers available in the dataset.

MERGE explained

Working with MERGE needs some care, and we advise that you keep it simple. Always remember that MERGE will attempt to match the *entire* pattern. When it cannot, it will create the *entire* pattern. Here are a couple of examples:

```
MERGE (n:Artist {name:"Wham!", origin:"UK"})
```

A single node is a pattern too. If you expected this MERGE statement to match a node in your graph and therefore not create another one, your graph would have to already have:

- A node labeled `Artist` (other labels may exist and do not matter)
- A property "name" with value "Wham!" and a property "origin" with value "UK" (other properties may exist and do not matter)

If the artist node in your graph contained the property "name" with the value "Wham!" but no "origin" property the pattern does not match, and a new node with label `Artist` and the two properties would be created. Now you'd have two artist nodes for Wham! (assuming a unique constraint did not fail).

The same applies to patterns that contain relationships. Suppose you want to create the pattern between a track and an artist:

```
MERGE (t:Track {name:"Last Christmas"})-[:ARTIST]->(a:Artist {name:"Wham!"})
```

You now you have the artist, Wham!, in the graph, so this MERGE will create the track node for "Last Christmas" and the ARTIST relationship to Wham!, right?

Wrong. The entire pattern could not be matched since the track wasn't in the graph, so MERGE went ahead and created the entire pattern. You have two Wham!'s now.

Keep it simple. Merge individual nodes on their key and leave off other properties, and then use those identifiers to merge in the relationships, like this:

```
MERGE (t:Track {name:"Last Christmas"})
MERGE (a:Artist {name:"Wham!"})
MERGE (t)-[:ARTIST]->(a)
```

You can find more examples in an article (*https://oreil.ly/XYjOe*) we wrote a long time ago.

Before re-ingesting the data with the updated query using MERGE, remove what the previous LOAD CSV created.

Use the following query to delete all nodes and relationships from the graph:

```
MATCH (n)
DETACH DELETE n
```

DETACH DELETE ensures that all relationships of the node are deleted. Using the single DELETE clause would fail on nodes that contain at least one relationship, as orphan relationships (relationships not connected to existing nodes) are forbidden in a graph.

Do not attempt the previous query on a large graph. How to perform operations affecting large graphs is covered in Chapter 2.

Now, recreate the data using the MERGE clause instead of CREATE. Start with the sample tracks file first:

```
//004-merge-one-track.cypher
LOAD CSV WITH HEADERS FROM "file:///sample_tracks.csv" AS row
WITH row LIMIT 1

MERGE (track:Track {id: row.track_id})
SET track.uri = row.track_uri,
track.name = row.track_name

MERGE (album:Album {id: row.album_id})
SET album.uri = row.album_uri,
album.name = row.album_name

MERGE (artist:Artist {id: row.artist_id})
SET artist.uri = row.artist_uri,
artist.name = row.artist_name

MERGE (album)-[:HAS_TRACK]->(track)
MERGE (track)-[:ARTIST]->(artist);
```

Do the same with the sample playlists:

```
//005-merge-one-playlist.cypher
LOAD CSV WITH HEADERS FROM "file:///sample_playlists.csv" AS row
WITH row LIMIT 1

MERGE (playlist:Playlist {id: row.id})
SET playlist.name = row.name

MERGE (user:User {id: row.user_id})

MERGE (track:Track {id: row.track_id})

MERGE (user)-[:OWNS]->(playlist)
MERGE (playlist)-[:HAS_TRACK {position: row.track_index}]->(track);
```

This time, since the Track was created in the graph with the previous ingest of the track's CSV, the MERGE (track:Track {id: row.track_id}) found the track by its

ID during its MATCH phase and hence did not create anything. It is this node, identified by track, that will be connected to the playlist node via the HAS_TRACK relationship.

Now verify that you can navigate between a playlist and album or artist nodes via the same track node:

```
MATCH path=(user)-[:OWNS]->(p:Playlist)
-[:HAS_TRACK]->(track:Track)--(albumOrArtist)
RETURN path;
```

This picture, as represented by Figure 1-15, looks much better! It clearly represents a connected set of data—a track that is on an album and is part of a playlist, along with the artist, just like you intended with your model in Figure 1-11.

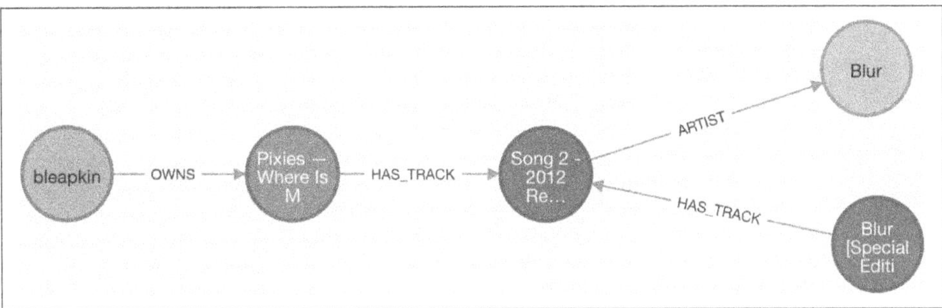

Figure 1-15. Cypher query result showing all the graph data after using the MERGE clause

You can now ingest the remaining of the sample data by removing the one-row limit. Start with the sample tracks. The only thing that has changed in this query is that the LIMIT 1 has been removed:

```
//006-merge-all-sample-tracks.cypher
LOAD CSV WITH HEADERS FROM "file:///sample_tracks.csv" AS row

MERGE (track:Track {id: row.track_id})
SET track.uri = row.track_uri,
track.name = row.track_name

MERGE (album:Album {id: row.album_id})
SET album.uri = row.album_uri,
album.name = row.album_name

MERGE (artist:Artist {id: row.artist_id})
SET artist.uri = row.artist_uri,
artist.name = row.artist_name

MERGE (album)-[:HAS_TRACK]->(track)
MERGE (track)-[:ARTIST]->(artist);
```

Repeat for the playlists' file, removing the `LIMIT` clause:

```
//007-merge-all-sample-playlists.cypher
LOAD CSV WITH HEADERS FROM "file:///sample_playlists.csv" AS row

MERGE (playlist:Playlist {id: row.id})
SET playlist.name = row.name

MERGE (user:User {id: row.user_id})

MERGE (track:Track {id: row.track_id})

MERGE (user)-[:OWNS]->(playlist)
MERGE (playlist)-[:HAS_TRACK {position: row.track_index}]->(track);
```

Now, you can run the following query to have a high-level overview of the connected graph (see Figure 1-16):

```
MATCH (n) OPTIONAL MATCH (n)-[r]->(o) RETURN *
```

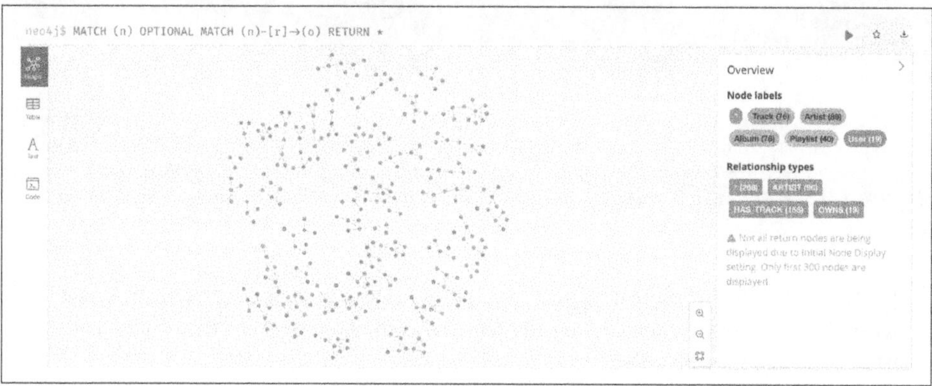

Figure 1-16. Visualizing the graph data in the database. You can see this picture in color and full resolution in the book's GitHub repo (https://oreil.ly/mkzXh).

Beautiful, isn't it?

Exploration and refactoring. Just as a business undergoes constant change and optimizations, so does a graph. As you work with graph databases, it's common to find yourself understanding the shape of the graph as it evolves and refactoring it to accommodate new use cases or improve performance. Often, exploring the graph also reveals connections that were not apparent earlier and can also uncover new use cases.

Before jumping into the new recommendation query, you and the team now run some basic queries for insights into the limited data you've ingested into the graph.

How many playlists does the graph contain? The first query is simple and tells you how many playlists are in the graph:

```
MATCH (n:Playlist)
RETURN count(n) AS playlistCount;
```

The output is:

playlistCount
40

Forty isn't much, but perhaps enough to prove the concept. However, you need more information to determine how connected the data is.

Are any tracks present in more than one playlist? The proof-of-concept recommendation query is based on playlists that share tracks. The following query matches all tracks that are in more than one playlist:

```
MATCH (t:Track)<-[:HAS_TRACK]-(p:Playlist)
WITH t AS track, count(p) AS playlistCount
WHERE playlistCount > 1
RETURN track.name as trackName, playlistCount;
```

The output is:

trackName	playlistCount
Where Is My Mind?	2

There's just one track that appears on two playlists. It's getting clear that the amount of data you've ingested so far isn't going to be enough.

Who are the five artists most featured in playlists? Check for the five artists who are featured the most in playlists and count how many playlists they're part of:

```
MATCH (a:Artist)<-[:ARTIST]-(track)<-[:HAS_TRACK]-(p:Playlist)
RETURN a.name AS artistName, count(distinct p) AS playlistCount
ORDER BY playlistCount DESC
LIMIT 5;
```

The output is:

artistName	playlistCount
Pixies	3
Tristesse Contemporaine	1
Mos Def	1
DJ Shadow	1
Blur	1

Using `count(distinct p)` ensures that playlists are counted only once. This could be the case when artists have multiple tracks on a playlist.

Which artist has the most tracks in the last position of a playlist? The recommendation query for the proof of concept is based on the last track of the playlist. As a reminder, the last track is simple logic for demonstration purposes. To find which artists are commonly in this place, you need to know how many tracks are in the playlist, then use that number to match a track at the last position. A `COUNT` subquery in the `WHERE` clause does the trick:

```
MATCH (a:Artist)<-[:ARTIST]-(t:Track)<-[r:HAS_TRACK]-(p:Playlist)
WHERE r.position = COUNT { (p)-[:HAS_TRACK]->() }
RETURN a.name AS artist, count(*) AS numberOfTracks
ORDER BY numberOfTracks DESC
LIMIT 1;
```

The output is:

```
(No changes, no records)
```

This is puzzling. It's quite impossible to have playlists without a track in the last position. Perhaps something went wrong with the data ingestion? You check five such tracks to see if their position is set in playlists with the following query:

```
MATCH (a:Artist)<-[:ARTIST]-(t:Track)<-[r:HAS_TRACK]-(p:Playlist)
RETURN a.name AS artist, t.name as track, r.position as position
LIMIT 5;
```

That's it! Look at the results in the table for `position` column, then check the `WHERE` clause of the query:

```
WHERE r.position = 1
```

The `1` in the `WHERE` clause is expressed as a number, not a string, but the table results clearly show that the position is a string. You realize that you used the `LOAD CSV` command to ingest data, and the nature of CSV files is that every single cell is typed as a string.

You could modify your query to use a string condition for the value `1`, but it wouldn't be very elegant compared to storing the data with the correct type. Fortunately, one of Neo4j's great benefits is that it's easy to refactor data you've already stored in the graph—whether that means changing the data values, its types, or the graph model itself. Figure 1-17 illustrates results in table view.

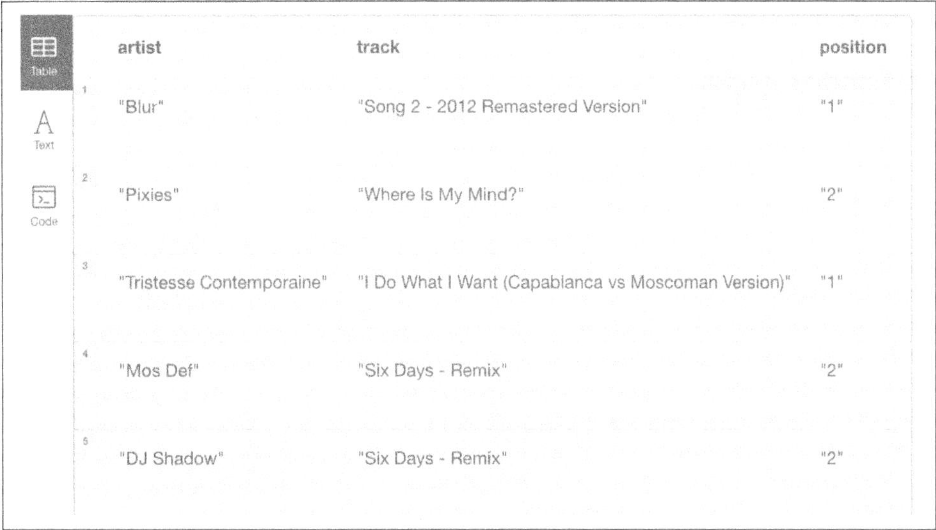

	artist	track	position
1	"Blur"	"Song 2 - 2012 Remastered Version"	"1"
2	"Pixies"	"Where Is My Mind?"	"2"
3	"Tristesse Contemporaine"	"I Do What I Want (Capablanca vs Moscoman Version)"	"1"
4	"Mos Def"	"Six Days - Remix"	"2"
5	"DJ Shadow"	"Six Days - Remix"	"2"

Figure 1-17. Cypher query result for track position in playlists. When your query doesn't return graph data (nodes, relationships, paths) but scalar values, the Neo4j browser switches to table-result view.

Neo4j is a schema-free database. The word *schemaless* is also common, but we prefer *schema-free*. No dataset is schemaless. A schema exists, logically, even if it's undocumented. Neo4j gives you total control and dictates nothing, which enables you to get any sort of data into your graph very quickly, without regard for types or structures. You can then modify or refactor them, gently molding them into shape as you proceed.

Schema-free databases also give you the flexibility to impose a schema when required, in the form of constraints on your graph. This is usually done to ensure data quality and adhere to a documented or communicated graph model.

You change the type of the values stored on the `position` property of the `HAS_TRACK` relationships to be an integer:

```
MATCH (p:Playlist)-[r:HAS_TRACK]->()
SET r.position = toInteger(r.position);
```

Results are now returned for your initial query:

```
MATCH (a:Artist)<-[:ARTIST]-(t:Track)<-[r:HAS_TRACK]-(p:Playlist)
WHERE r.position = COUNT { (p)-[:HAS_TRACK]->() }
RETURN a.name AS artist, count(*) AS numberOfTracks
ORDER BY numberOfTracks DESC
LIMIT 1;
```

The output is:

artist	numberOfTracks
Pixies	2

No artist other than the Pixies has tracks in the last position of a playlist. With such sparse data, it's a bit of a problem to fulfill the use case. Very often, we see teams struggle to realize their use case or answer queries satisfactorily, simply because the data required might belong to other systems that they have no access to, or the data really isn't captured in the first place. Graphs help expose this problem and the business benefits by correcting this to enable newer use cases. However, ElectricHarmony does have more data and you've detected this early enough, so you're going to ingest some more tomorrow and see if that solves the problem.

Key takeaways

There are many ways to get data into the graph. In a production system, you might use a connector or driver to connect to another data source and transfer data, but one of the easiest ways to get started is a simple CSV dump of limited data, which you can import into Neo4j with `LOAD CSV`. Neo4j browser is an excellent companion to help you get your hands on the graph, ingest data, query it, and visualize the results.

The schema-free nature of Neo4j removes another barrier by not imposing any rigid structure in the early stages, making it easy to refactor, extend the model, and change data types or properties.

Day 3

Thanks to your discovery the day before, you're going to ingest a larger dataset using the previous `LOAD CSV`. Simply change the filenames in queries 006 and 007 to *file:///medium/sample_tracks_medium.csv* and *file:///medium/sample_playlists_medium.csv*. And you wait.

Fifteen minutes later, you're still waiting? Does ingesting a fairly small amount of data (approximately 10,000 rows) really take so long? Well, no. Most teams stumble upon this problem early in the process. The solution to faster ingesting is easy: it's called indexing.

Wait a minute. We said earlier that Neo4j offers index-free adjacency. So why is the solution indexes? The difference lies in how and why you access the data.

In the database world, indexes usually make identity lookups faster. They offer an efficient way to find a particular entity by the value of some identifier, typically a key.

When you write a Cypher query, the starting point for the traversal—a pattern specified in the `MATCH` clause—consists of nodes or relationships, which should be accessed as quickly as possible by the query engine to stay performant. Consider this query:

```
MATCH (t:Track {id: 501})<-[:HAS_TRACK]-(p:Playlist)
RETURN p.name;
```

It gets expensive to scan through *all* the nodes or relationships to find the track with ID 501. Indexes help you get to the starting point of the traversal quickly—in this case, the track with ID 501. From this point on, you can traverse the graph at lightning speed without indexes, by following pointers. This is the index-free adjacency that Neo4j provides.

Indexes for boosting data ingestion speed

The bottleneck in your query is the `MERGE`. You learned earlier that `MERGE` can be a `MATCH` or `CREATE`. Without indexes, if you ask Neo4j to `MATCH` (i.e., find the `Track` node with a particular ID, say `1FTSo4`), it will iterate over all nodes with the `Track` label and, for each of those nodes, filter the ones that have the value `1FTSo4` for the `id` property. If the graph has a hundred tracks, this would result in 200 operations (100 for extracting each node with the `Track` label and 100 for filtering on the property). If there are 100,000 tracks in the graph, this would result in 200,000 operations. And that's just for one type of node: the `Track`.

The query you are running, however, creates more than one type of node. Apart from the `Track`, it also creates `Album` and `Artist` nodes, and the number of operations increases drastically as the dataset grows.

When you want to ensure fast ingestion of large datasets, you can add a constraint on all labels for their respective `id` property. Constraints are backed by indexes, so they provide the same performance benefits while also ensuring data integrity:

```
//008-index-creation.cypher
// The NODE KEY constraint ensures the id property is present AND unique
CREATE CONSTRAINT playlist_id FOR (n:Playlist) REQUIRE n.id IS NODE KEY;
CREATE CONSTRAINT user_id FOR (n:User) REQUIRE n.id IS NODE KEY;
CREATE CONSTRAINT track_id FOR (n:Track) REQUIRE n.id IS NODE KEY;
CREATE CONSTRAINT album_id FOR (n:Album) REQUIRE n.id IS NODE KEY;
CREATE CONSTRAINT artist_id FOR (n:Artist) REQUIRE n.id IS NODE KEY;
```

With these constraints—and subsequently, indexes—in place, every `MATCH` will have only one operation, the index lookup, providing a better `O(log(n))` complexity.

Try running the `LOAD CSV` queries 006 and 007 with the medium-sized csv again. They should complete now in seconds!

Minimum data quality

Just before lunch, your team runs into exactly the same situation you'd puzzled over just the day before: the query *which artist has the most tracks in the last position of a playlist?* For a moment or two you all wonder why you don't see the results you expect, and then you facepalm as you realize that the track position in the playlist is *again* a string.

This is the double-edged sword of Neo4j's schema-free design. While it enables quick wins, its lack of schema enforcement allows data-quality issues to slip in. You will want to prevent situations where you suddenly don't have any results because of a type mismatch between how the data is stored and how you refer to it in your queries.

Refactoring the graph, just like you did yesterday, is always possible. But refactoring operations take longer to execute as the dataset grows because they typically work over all data of a specific type or types. To maximize your effort on solving business problems and minimize the time spent on these issues caused by data quality, you want to ensure this never happens again. Let's see how you can do that.

First, try to add a property-type constraint on the `position` property on the `HAS_TRACK` relationship between the `Playlist` and `Track` nodes so that it accepts only values of type `integer`:

```
//009-constraint-creation.cypher
CREATE CONSTRAINT has_track_position_integer
FOR ()-[r:HAS_TRACK]-()
REQUIRE r.position IS TYPED INTEGER;
```

A property-type constraint will ensure that a property has the required type for all nodes with a specific label or all relationships of a specific type. Any query that violates this constraint will fail. Property-type constraints are useful because you can have two properties with the same name on two different nodes with the same label, but each of these properties have values that have different data types!

Since you ingested some of the sample dataset as strings yesterday, you find that you cannot create the constraint. A `ConstraintCreationFailed` error is produced because some of the existing data in the graph is in violation. At this prototypical stage, it's easier to just drop the data and reingest it.

To drop the data, use the following query:

```
MATCH (n)
DETACH DELETE n
```

Then move the type transformation (from string to integer) using the `toInteger` function to the data-ingestion level like so, in the `LOAD CSV` statements that follow:

```
MERGE (p)-[:HAS_TRACK {position: toInteger(row.track_index)}]->(t)
```

Now you're ready to ingest the larger dataset. Start with a larger tracks file, *sample_tracks_medium.csv*:

```
//010-merge-tracks-medium.cypher
LOAD CSV WITH HEADERS FROM "file:///medium/sample_tracks_medium.csv" AS row

MERGE (track:Track {id: row.track_id})
SET track.uri = row.track_uri, track.name = row.track_name

MERGE (album:Album {id: row.album_id})
SET album.uri = row.album_uri, album.name = row.album_name

MERGE (artist:Artist {id: row.artist_id})
SET artist.uri = row.artist_uri, artist.name = row.artist_name

MERGE (album)-[:HAS_TRACK]->(track)
MERGE (track)-[:ARTIST]->(artist);
```

Repeat for the playlists—*sample_playlists_medium.csv*:

```
//011-merge-playlists-cast-integer-medium.cypher
LOAD CSV WITH HEADERS FROM "file:///medium/sample_playlists_medium.csv" AS row

MERGE (playlist:Playlist {id: row.id})
SET playlist.name = row.name

MERGE (user:User {id: row.user_id})

MERGE (track:Track {id: row.track_id})

MERGE (user)-[:OWNS]->(playlist)
MERGE (playlist)-[:HAS_TRACK {position: toInteger(row.track_index)}]->(track)
```

Now that you have a higher volume of data ingested in about 2 seconds, and you've ensured that the right constraints are in place, guaranteeing data type quality, you're ready to start constructing the recommendation query.

Finding similarities

The very nature of a graph is its *expressive model*: it stores data in a form that represents the real world.

When you look at the model in Figure 1-18, it's easy to see that two playlists have some similarity if they share a connection to the same track. For ElectricHarmony's purposes, they decide that the similarity between two playlists is greater when they contain tracks at exactly the same position.

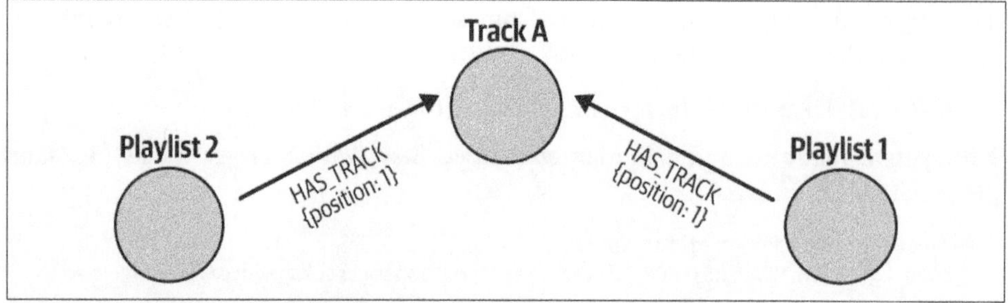

Figure 1-18. Playlists are similar when they share tracks.

You explore the similarities between these playlists and decide to look for playlists that have a track in common at the same position:

```
MATCH path=(n:Playlist)-[r1:HAS_TRACK]->(track)<-[r2:HAS_TRACK]-(other:Playlist)
WHERE r1.position = r2.position
RETURN path
LIMIT 10;
```

In this query, the whole pattern that connects two playlists via a shared track is assigned to `path`—this is a set of nodes connected by relationships and can be either returned, as in this case, or further operated on later in the query. This query produces the graph in Figure 1-19.

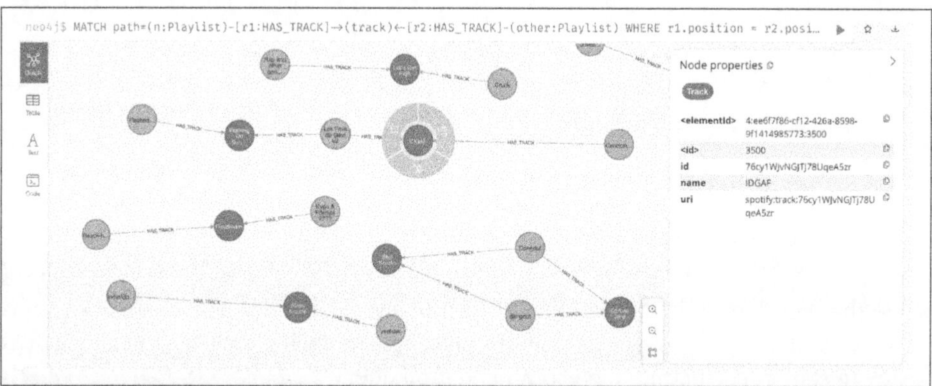

Figure 1-19. Playlist similarity: you can easily identify which playlists share two tracks.

To find similar playlists with at least five tracks in common, count the number of tracks with the same position and those without:

```
//012-find-similar-playlists.cypher
// find playlists sharing tracks
MATCH path=(p:Playlist)-[r1:HAS_TRACK]->(track)<-[r2:HAS_TRACK]-(other:Playlist)
WITH
    p AS playlistLeft,
    other AS playlistRight,
```

```
    collect( ❶
        {
            track: track,
            positionLeft: r1.position,
            positionRight: r2.position
        }
    ) AS commonTracks

WHERE size(commonTracks) > 5 ❷
RETURN
    playlistLeft.name,
    playlistRight.name,
    size([track in commonTracks
        WHERE
            track.positionLeft = track.positionRight])
        AS tracksWithSamePosition,
    size([track in commonTracks
        WHERE NOT
            track.positionLeft = track.positionRight])
        AS tracksAtDifferentPosition
ORDER BY tracksWithSamePosition DESC;
LIMIT 100;
```

❶ Collect the track and left, right positions

❷ Omit if they don't share at least 5 tracks

This returns the query results in Figure 1-20. As you can see, playlists can be similar to themselves. You didn't add a condition to the query to prevent this, but you could do so by simply adding `AND p <> other` in the `WHERE` clause.

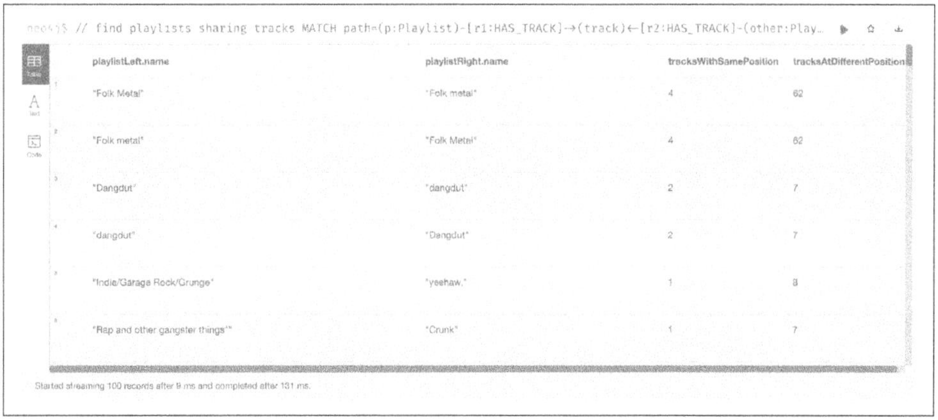

neo4j$ // find playlists sharing tracks MATCH path=(p:Playlist)-[r1:HAS_TRACK]→(track)←[r2:HAS_TRACK]-(other:Play...

playlistLeft.name	playlistRight.name	tracksWithSamePosition	tracksAtDifferentPosition
"Folk Metal"	"Folk metal"	4	62
"Folk metal"	"Folk Metal"	4	62
"Dangdut"	"dangdut"	2	7
"dangdut"	"Dangdut"	2	7
"Indie/Garage Rock/Grunge"	"yeehaw."	1	8
"Rap and other gangster things""	"Crunk"	1	7

Started streaming 100 records after 9 ms and completed after 131 ms.

Figure 1-20. Playlists with a minimum of 5 tracks in common

Key takeaways

A schema-free database allows you to get data into the graph quickly. Since you can add a schema incrementally, such as a data type constraint, you can also find and fix data-quality issues early.

Day 4

Now that ElectricHarmony has a query to find similar playlists, you need to think about how and when to compute their similarity.

Materializing similarities

You don't need to compute similar playlists for every single user request at this stage. Instead, you will want to materialize the fact that two playlists are similar by explicitly creating a `SIMILAR` relationship between two similar playlists, along with a similarity score. By explicitly storing these relationships, the graph becomes even easier and more efficient to traverse, especially when dealing with large datasets or frequent queries.

Yesterday, you wrote a query to find similar playlists. Now you use the same query, but add a `MERGE` as shown below to create a `SIMILAR` relationship between playlists that have at least 5 tracks in common. Your statement will also record the number of tracks in the same or different positions as properties on the `SIMILAR` relationship:

```
//013-merge-similarities.cypher
// find playlists sharing tracks
MATCH path=(p:Playlist)-[r1:HAS_TRACK]->(track)<-[r2:HAS_TRACK]-(other:Playlist)
WITH
    p AS playlistLeft,
    other AS playlistRight,
    collect( ❶
        {
            track: track,
            positionLeft: r1.position,
            positionRight: r2.position
        }
    ) AS commonTracks

WHERE size(commonTracks) > 5 ❷
WITH
    playlistLeft,
    playlistRight,
    size([track in commonTracks
        WHERE
            track.positionLeft = track.positionRight])
    AS tracksWithSamePosition,
    size([track in commonTracks
        WHERE NOT
            track.positionLeft = track.positionRight])
```

```
        AS tracksAtDifferentPosition
    MERGE (playlistLeft)-[r:SIMILAR]->(playlistRight)
    SET
        r.samePosition = tracksWithSamePosition,
        r.notSamePosition = tracksAtDifferentPosition;
```

1. Collect the track and left, right positions

2. Omit if they don't share at least 5 tracks

This created 308 `SIMILAR` relationships; you can verify it by running the query:

```
MATCH path=(p1:Playlist)-[:SIMILAR]->(p2:Playlist)
RETURN count(path)
```

The graph you now have is the final version for this chapter. You will use this graph database again in Chapter 3.

You can now inspect the similar playlists quite easily:

```
MATCH path=(playlist1)-[:SIMILAR]-(playlist2)
RETURN path
LIMIT 100
```

This produces the graph in Figure 1-21.

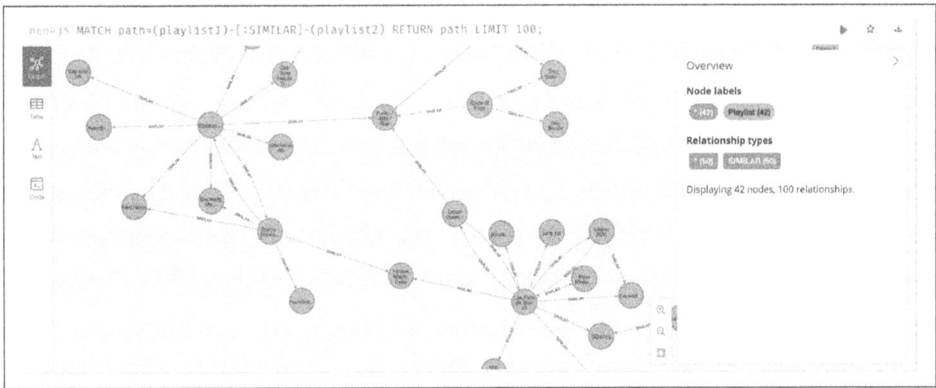

Figure 1-21. Similar playlists

The duplication of the `SIMILAR` relationships between two playlists is a common graph-modeling gotcha. We cover best practices for handling this in Chapter 3.

Implicit relationships

Look at the updated graph model with the new `SIMILAR` relationship between playlists (see Figure 1-22). It doesn't take your team long to realize that you can consider two users to be potentially similar if they own similar playlists or identify groups of users having similar tastes!

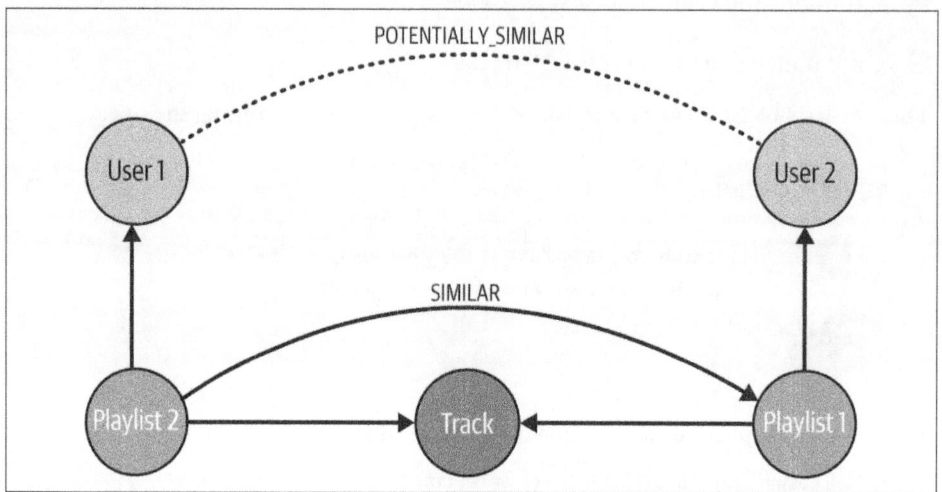

Figure 1-22. The dotted line between two users represents an implicit relationship between them based on other explicit relationships in the graph.

But since the potential number of similar playlists between two users is low, there is probably no need to materialize this fact as an explicit relationship, since traversing between users via their shared playlists will be very fast. These implicit relationships are revealed by other data connections and provide another dimension of insights.

You're now ready to write the final recommendation query.

Recommending a track when the playlist ends

To recommend tracks, you will need to first express how you would like to query the data from the graph, then translate that to Cypher.

While the last song of a user's playlist is playing, you want your query to perform the following steps in order:

1. Calculate the 10 most popular tracks by the number of playlists in which they appear.
2. Find the last track of the playlist currently being played.
3. Get the previous tracks from the playlist (since you do not want to recommend tracks that are already in this playlist).

4. Find other playlists that have the same last track and are similar to the given playlist.
5. Find other tracks on those playlists that are not in the given playlist.
6. Exclude the 10 most popular tracks because you want listeners to discover new music as much as possible.
7. Score the remaining tracks by the number of times they appear, so that tracks that appear more frequently in similar playlists rank higher.

This is the query you will write:

```
// Find the 10 most popular tracks
WITH COLLECT {
    MATCH (popularTrack:Track)-[:HAS_TRACK]-(:Playlist)
    WITH popularTrack, count(*) as playlistCount
    ORDER BY playlistCount DESC
    LIMIT 10
    RETURN popularTrack
} AS popularTracks

MATCH (p:Playlist) WHERE p.name = "all that jazz" ❶


WITH p, popularTracks,
COLLECT {
    MATCH (p)-[r:HAS_TRACK]->(t)
    WITH t, r
    ORDER BY r.position DESC
    RETURN t
} AS playlistTracks ❷

WITH
    p AS playlist,
    popularTracks,
    head(playlistTracks) AS lastTrack,
    tail(playlistTracks) AS previousTracks

MATCH (lastTrack)<-[:HAS_TRACK]-(otherPlaylist)-[:SIMILAR]-(playlist)
WHERE otherPlaylist <> playlist ❸

MATCH (otherPlaylist)-[:HAS_TRACK]->(recommendation)
WHERE NOT recommendation IN previousTracks
AND NOT recommendation IN popularTracks ❹

RETURN
recommendation.id as recommendedTrackId,
recommendation.name AS recommendedTrack,
otherPlaylist.name AS fromPlaylist,
count(*) AS score ❺
ORDER BY score DESC
LIMIT 10;
```

❶ For a given Playlist

❷ Collect the tracks in reverse position

❸ Find other playlists that have the same the last track

❹ Find other tracks which are not in the given playlist

❺ Score them by how frequently they appear

The first set of results are shown in Table 1-1.

Table 1-1. Scoring track recommendations

recommendedTrackId	recommendedTrack	fromPlaylist	score
"7N2UmTJG5Uv6zQvjf4eIjd"	"Now See How You Are - Remastered"	"smooth jazz"	2
"1Z9XpsIg7YlzDTGbLQyXMK"	"Stompin' at the Savoy"	"smooth jazz"	2
"4T0ohWvlVJenmxPUVeuaue"	"The Folks Who Live On The Hill"	"smooth jazz"	2
"0pmO0O5FCPYri3rVycwl00"	"I May Be Wrong"	"smooth jazz"	2
"5NliRTDw7ktmLDtUH2Dvqr"	"Intermezzo"	"smooth jazz"	2

Note that you may see different recommendations due to the high number of matches with score 2. The recommendation is computed in a couple of milliseconds, proving that traversing relationships in the graph is really efficient.

Key takeaways

As insights are discovered in the graph—in this case, similar playlists—you can materialize them by creating new nodes and/or relationships. This enriched graph serves as a foundation upon which more complex queries can be performed. The recommendation query builds on the concept of similar playlists and shows how real-time recommendations can be generated quickly and easily.

Day 5

Your work is producing some recommendations on a limited dataset—brilliant! You can expect even richer results once all data is ingested. But how do you know if the recommendations are any good? Is this feature ready to roll out to a small set of users?

The nice thing about a graph is that it makes recommendation results explainable—no closed box involved. It's easy to trace why a particular song is recommended. Not only does this help you test the query, but it also means you can elicit and account for negative feedback from users, to build a pattern of which songs the system should *not* recommend to that user.

Say a user routinely skips over recommended tracks. If you query these tracks to see what they have in common, you might find that they're performed by the same artist or belong to the same genre. That information will feed back into the recommendation query to avoid repeating the same mistake and make more relevant recommendations.

As a test, you decide to take the results of yesterday's recommendation query and see if they make sense.

The playlist titled "all that jazz" is over. The next song to be played could be any of the five listed in Table 1-1. Take the first one: "Now See How You Are - Remastered," with track ID `7N2UmTJG5Uv6zQvjf4eIjd`.

The first thing to observe is that this track is on a playlist called "smooth jazz." That's a good start—it sounds logical.

What was the last track on "all that jazz"? You can reuse a part of the recommendation query to find it:

```
// For a given Playlist
MATCH (p:Playlist) WHERE p.name = "all that jazz"

// Find the last track
MATCH (p)-[r:HAS_TRACK]->(t)
WHERE r.position = COUNT {(p)-[:HAS_TRACK]->()}
RETURN t;
```

You double-click the `Track` node to expand its connections (see Figure 1-23) and see that the last track, "Journey into Melody - 2007 Digital Remaster/Rudy Van Gelder Edition" by Stanley Turrentine, is actually on both playlists.

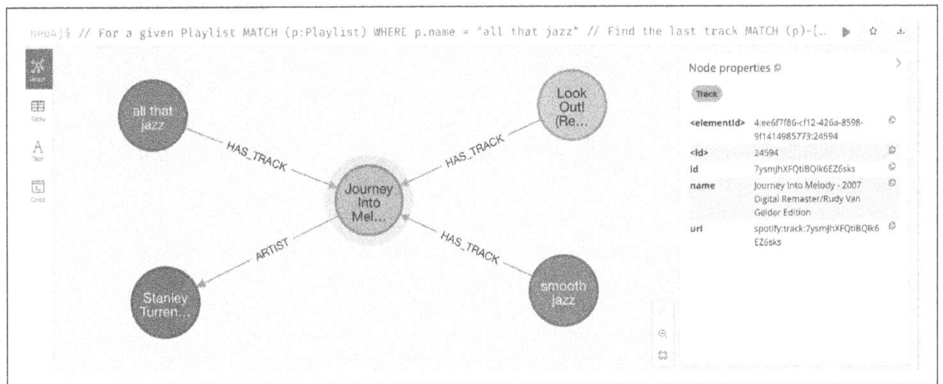

Figure 1-23. The query returns the Track node; double-clicking the node expands its relationships.

If smooth jazz is your genre of music, you probably don't need much more explanation to know that the recommended track sounds like a good bet. If it isn't, though, then seeing how both tracks are connected is a quick way to feel your way around the graph and explore why this particular track is being recommended.

Using the track IDs of each track, you set out to find all connections between them, to a depth of 5. Why 5? There isn't any magic formula for this. Consider tracks that are connected because they share an artist or an album or a playlist—the two tracks are separated by 3 hops. A path of length 4 separates two tracks that might be connected in this fashion: `(Track1)--(Artist)--(Track)--(Album)--(Track2)`. A 6-hop path such as `(Track1)--(Album)--(Track)--(Playlist)--(Track)--(Album)--(Track2)` is a bit too long for our recommendation—the tracks are too far apart. So, we go with the middle ground of 5. We could have tried the `shortestPath` first, like this:

```
//015-shortest-1.cypher
MATCH (t1:Track {id: "7ysmJhXFQtiBQlk6EZ6sks"})
MATCH (t2:Track {id:"7N2UmTJG5Uv6zQvjf4eIjd"})
MATCH path = SHORTEST 5 (t1)-[r:HAS_TRACK]-+(t2);
RETURN path
```

`SHORTEST` is a function that returns the path between two nodes with the fewest relationships connecting them (see Figure 1-24). You can define and constrain the path pattern by, for example, specifying relationship types. In this case, you're interested in any kind of relationship, but don't want to find paths longer than 5 hops away, so you set an upper bound of 5.

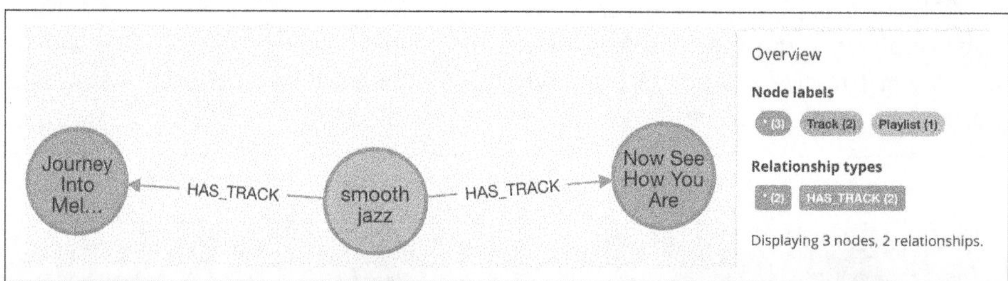

Figure 1-24. The query returns the Track node; double-clicking the node expands its relationships.

You don't want deep traversals to bring in so much of the graph that it adds more noise than value. The depth of 5 is just right in this case:

```
//016-shortest-2.cypher
MATCH (t1:Track {id: "7ysmJhXFQtiBQlk6EZ6sks"})
MATCH (t2:Track {id:"7N2UmTJG5Uv6zQvjf4eIjd"})
MATCH p = ((t1)-[*..5]-(t2))
RETURN p
```

On the far left and right of the graph in Figure 1-25, you see the two tracks, along with their artists and the common paths between them, via the playlists they're on.

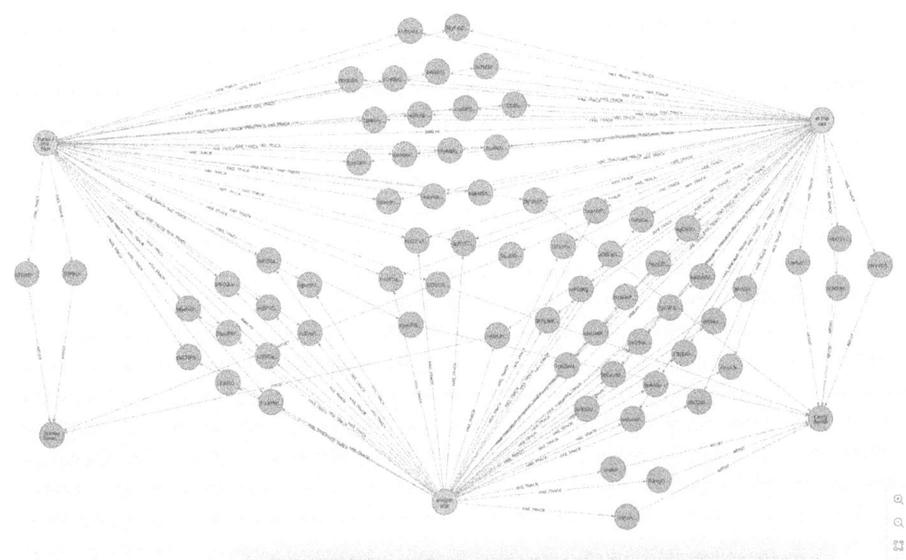

Figure 1-25. Paths between tracks up to a depth of 5 (https://oreil.ly/1P-0E)

The query returns *Midnight Blue*, an album recorded in 1963 by Kenny Burrell that features Stanley Turrentine on tenor saxophone. Sounds like a good recommendation. You and the team have achieved what you set out to do this week and with time to spare. Congratulations!

There's one thing left to do this week: it's time to sum up the results of your work for ElectricHarmony's stakeholders.

The proof is in the pudding, so your team starts off by asking one of the stakeholders to pull up one of her playlists. You run the recommendation query for that playlist and tell everyone which song will be played next. The recommendation gets it right. Instead of a Top 40 track with no real relevance to her tastes or a totally random track, it's a song she likes.

The executives are impressed! They all agree that this simple recommendation is already improving their experience.

Next, you present the current version of the graph model (see Figure 1-26).

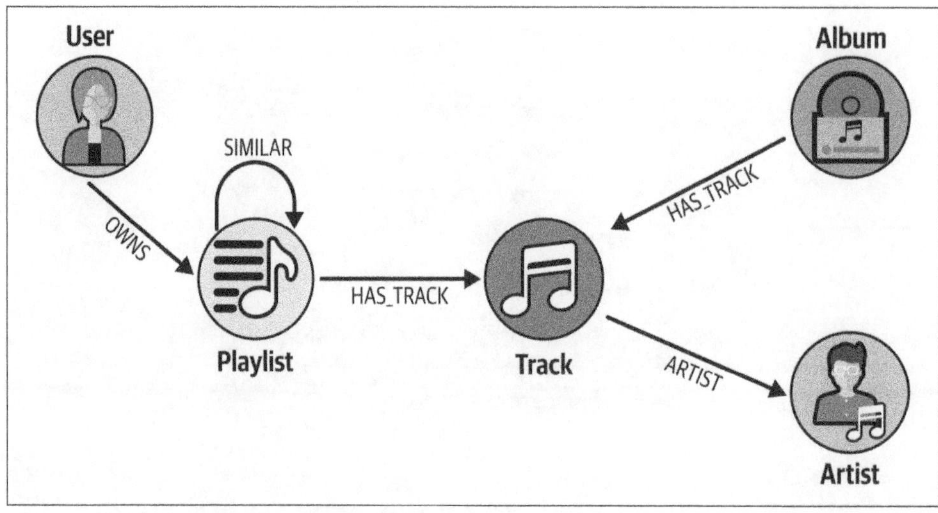

Figure 1-26. Latest version of the graph model

This graph has been populated with limited data from two data sources that exist in different systems at ElectricHarmony. You explain that you created the `SIMILAR` relationship by matching playlists that share a number of tracks at the same position. This makes explicit the knowledge that was already in the data but was obscured. The executives are surprised at how easy it is for them to understand the graph model even though they're not very technical and that it represents their worldview of the domain.

You elaborate that the clear relationships in the graph enabled the team to build a simple recommendation query that could traverse from the last track played in a playlist to a similar playlist, exclude any tracks in common, and pick the next track to be played to the user, with a relatively high chance of success and an execution time of milliseconds.

Another stakeholder points out that he sees a way for the company to leverage the implicit relationship your team has discovered: that users can be considered similar if they own similar playlists, forming "peer groups" of users with shared preferences. These peer groups can be useful for clustering and segmenting users, allowing the company to develop new features like "users to follow" or "suggested playlists" based on these groups.

The executives ask your team to do some A/B testing with a subset of users in the following weeks to gather feedback about whether this feature improves their listening experience. Feedback is also an interesting aspect to capture in the graph. For example, you might experiment with extending the graph model to include a

`LISTENED` relationship between a user and track. You can go a step further to capture more advanced metrics like a feedback score: did they listen to the whole track, or half of it, or did they skip it after the first few seconds? The executives also ask you to test ways to extend the system to use the artists and albums present in the graph, working from users' favorite artists or revealing rare albums.

Summary

It's time to celebrate: you and the team have got yourselves a graph database that opens up many exciting opportunities!

While you made mistakes along the way, you learned from them, and now you all have a better understanding of the value that graphs provide. Using the graph database allows you to focus on validating business ideas in a short time.

As you continue to refine your evaluation and build additional use cases, you will need to adjust your interaction patterns to ensure optimal performance as you scale up your usage of Neo4j. This will help you maintain efficiency and handle increased data volumes effectively.

In the rest of this book, we'll take you beyond the proof of concept and build on use cases in the music domain. While they are fictitious, they closely mirror real-world paths to production and address typical issues you're likely to encounter on your own journey. The next chapters are designed to help you circumvent those issues by providing you with best practices, built upon our years of experience developing and deploying Neo4j for all sizes and kinds of applications. Chapter 5 explores query profiling and tuning, while understanding the write path of transactions is covered in Chapter 9. In the next chapter, we'll look at how to efficiently ingest a much bigger dataset.

CHAPTER 2

Importing (Much) More Data

You and your team at ElectricHarmony are now faced with the challenge of importing a massive amount of data—which will better represent your total user base—to provide recommendations for users.

You try the method you used for ingesting data in Chapter 1, but it proves to be slow as you increase the size of the tracks' dataset from a hundred thousand to a million rows. This often leads to the dreaded "spinning wheel of death," making you wonder if your database choice is effective at scale.

Your concerns are valid. You need to answer key questions from your team and stakeholders, such as:

- Can the system ingest data as fast as the business produces it?
- Can the system serve recommendations in near real time and keep up with the data produced by other systems?
- In case of a disaster, how long would recovery take?

This chapter shows you how to ingest the large datasets necessary to answer these questions.

Your journey begins with an easy-to-understand introduction to database management system internals, including transactions and memory management. Next, you'll learn how to optimize the `LOAD CSV` commands you used in Chapter 1. You'll then move on to more production-like scenarios, importing data using automated programs in your preferred programming language. You will also experiment with different locking strategies to understand when and how parallel data import is feasible without negative impact and conclude with offline data-import strategies.

Database Transactions

Transactions ensure data integrity by grouping a set of operations into a single unit that either succeeds entirely or fails entirely. Database constraints, such as uniqueness and type constraints, enforce rules to maintain consistency and accuracy. Transactions ensure that all operations adhere to these constraints, but many checks (such as uniqueness) are often deferred until the end of the transaction (at commit time). This allows flexibility during updates such as temporarily violating a constraint while transitioning data from one state to another. If any operation violates a constraint, the entire transaction will fail and rollback, ensuring no partial changes are applied and preventing data inconsistencies.

As you saw in Chapter 1, you already have some experience with database constraints. For instance, you created one to ensure that the `position` property of the HAS_TRACK relationship is an integer:

```
CREATE CONSTRAINT has_track_position_integer
FOR ()-[r:HAS_TRACK]-()
REQUIRE r.position IS TYPED INTEGER
```

What happens if you try to write some data that doesn't adhere to the defined constraint, like the following Cypher query?

```
CREATE (n:Playlist)-[:HAS_TRACK {position: 'some string'}]->(track);
```

This won't work; instead, the error message shown in Figure 2-1 is displayed. In database terminology, your transaction has been aborted due to a constraint violation.

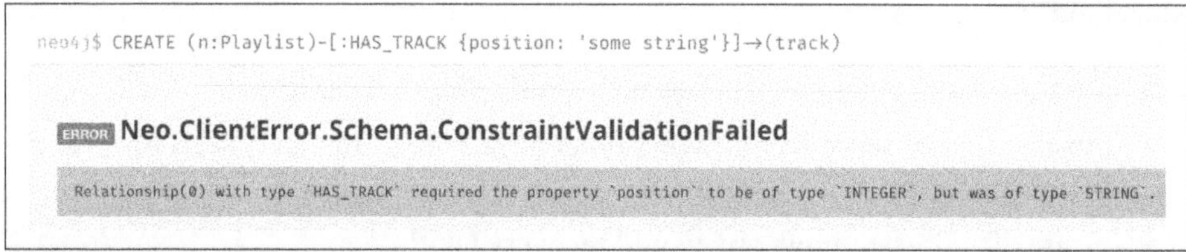

Figure 2-1. The error message produced by attempting to execute a query that does not comply with the database constraints

But wait, you didn't even use the word *transaction*—in fact, you haven't seen that word anywhere so far! The Neo4j browser *implicitly* uses transactions and most of the Neo4j drivers offer methods where you don't necessarily need to worry about managing transactions yourself. Just know that everything in Neo4j is transactional.

So, what is really happening under the hood? This sequence of steps is executed:

1. The Neo4j server opens a transaction.
2. It executes changes (like creating data) on the database.
3. It commits the transaction (changes are applied) or rejects it (changes are discarded).

The sequence of steps respects the characteristics necessary for transactions in database systems, both relational and nonrelational, to achieve safety. Those properties are commonly named the ACID properties; the initials stand for:

Atomicity
: This property treats all the operations to be executed as one single unit. You wouldn't want half-constructed objects in your database: it's all or nothing.

Consistency
: This ensures that transactions move the database from one valid state to another, maintaining the integrity of the data.

Isolation
: Transactions are executed independently of each other; even if multiple transactions are executing simultaneously, their intermediate state is not visible to each other. This is how Neo4j operates, as its isolation level is `READ COMMITTED` by default.

Durability
: Once a transaction has been committed successfully, it is permanently recorded, even in the event of a power failure or crash.

Transactions ultimately write data to the transaction log on disk, as shown in Figure 2-2, for durability. For the purpose of this chapter, you only need to know that the speed (the number of input/output operations per second, or IOPS) of your disks matters: the faster the better. Chapter 9 will cover the write path in detail, including transaction logs.

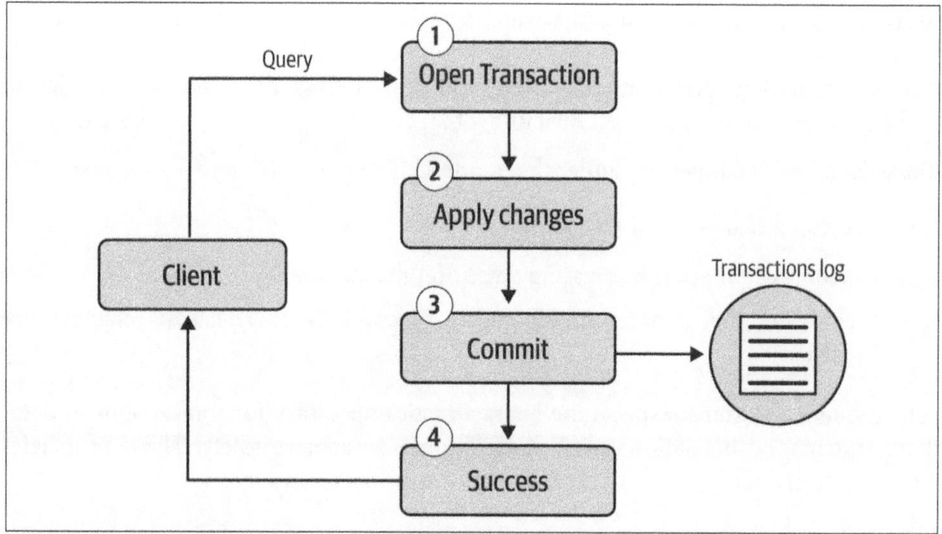

Figure 2-2. Flow of a successful transaction

At its core, a transaction ensures that additions or removals of data are performed safely and consistently. However, this approach has its limits, a topic we will explore in the following section.

The ~~Beat~~ Heap Box

Neo4j is developed in Java and runs on the Java virtual machine (JVM), which introduces you to a crucial feature known as the heap. The *heap* is a dedicated memory area for Java objects and stores all working data that Java applications need to maintain. Whenever Neo4j generates new entities, such as nodes, their transactional state can be stored either on-heap or off-heap. However, the process of generating the transaction log requires creating transaction log commands on the heap.

The heap is managed by the JVM, which automatically allocates space for new objects and reclaims space from objects that are no longer in use. This reclamation process is referred to as *garbage collection*, and it allows for effective memory reuse. Figure 2-3 illustrates a finite space reserved for the heap, with allocated objects claiming space inside it.

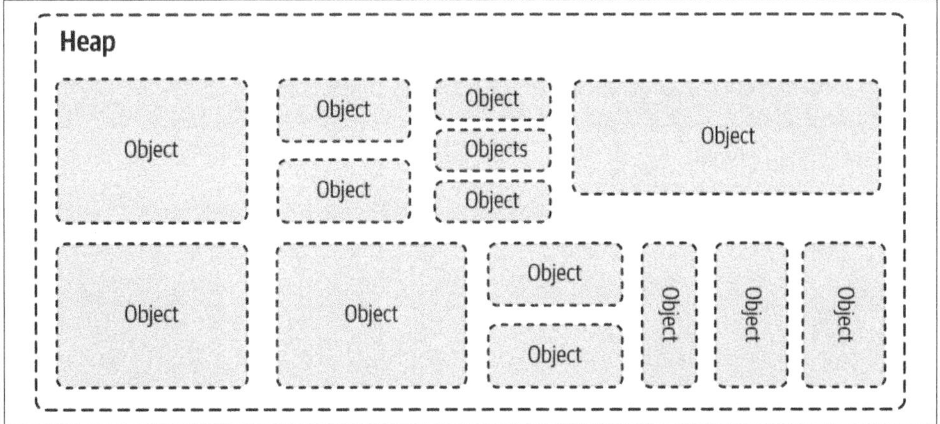

Figure 2-3. The heap, with objects taking up space in it

The heap serves a critical role beyond just writing data to the database; during read transactions, it also temporarily holds information within this memory space, such as query execution plans, states of transactions, intermediate query state, and query outcomes.

Like a physical box, the heap's capacity is finite. Recall that the heap is a segment of memory: its size is thus inherently constrained by the total amount of memory available on your machine or on the servers hosting Neo4j. Real-world applications built on Neo4j often execute multiple transactions simultaneously. All these transactions compete for memory space in the heap.

When you import data using the `LOAD CSV` command (as you did in Chapter 1), each creation of a node, property, or relationship consumes space on the heap (as shown in Figure 2-4). Consequently, the heap's size limits the number of CSV rows you can import in a single transaction without exhausting the heap.

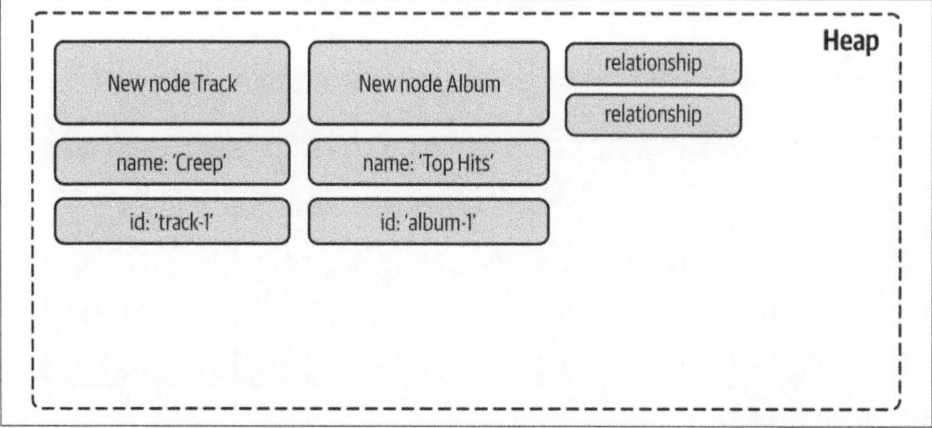

Figure 2-4. Objects created by the `LOAD CSV` clause using space on the heap

If you attempted to import a CSV file containing 1 million rows, it might exceed the configured heap's maximum memory, and your transaction would fail. Depending on how you import your data, there are several ways to address this issue. While `LOAD CSV` offers a convenient option, this chapter will also explore strategies for importing data directly from your applications using your preferred programming language.

The setting in the Neo4j server to configure the maximum heap memory allocation is called `server.memory.heap.max_size`. In the example Docker Compose, the heap is limited to 512 megabytes (MB). A reference to configuration settings can be found in the operations manual (*https://oreil.ly/-r5TJ*).

The CALL IN TRANSACTIONS operation

Cypher enables you to specify how many rows you wish to commit in a single transaction. If you have a CSV file containing 100,000 rows and you set a threshold of 10,000 rows per commit, this will result in 10 separate transactions, each of which will process 10,000 rows, as illustrated in Figure 2-5.

Splitting an operation into multiple transactions only makes sense if that operation does not require full atomicity. Each transaction commits independently, meaning that partial updates may occur if one of them fails. Bulk imports and large-scale data transformations are typical use cases where full atomicity is not essential.

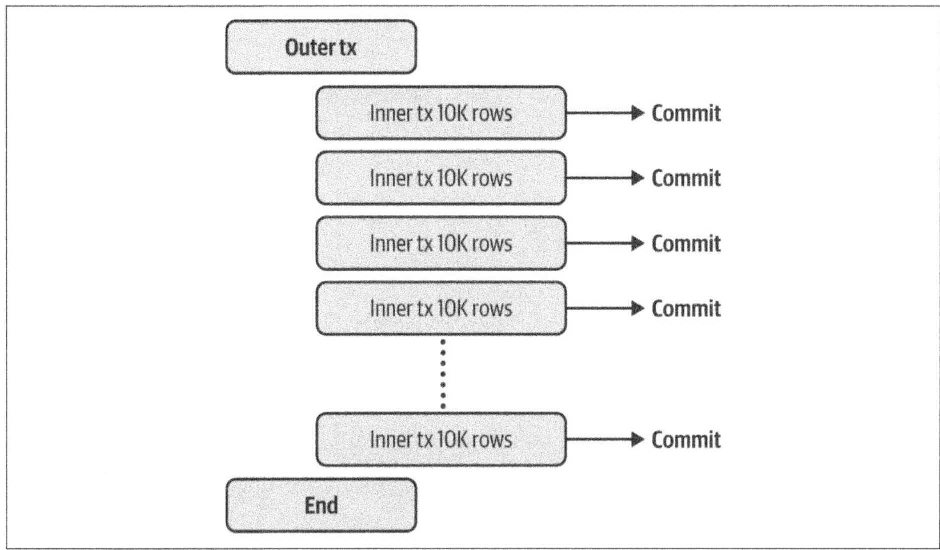

Figure 2-5. Incremental commits per 10,000 CSV rows

To commit rows incrementally, in transactions, you will need to wrap your statement in a subquery and add the `IN TRANSACTIONS` modifier after it:

```
LOAD CSV WITH HEADERS FROM "file:///mydata.csv" AS row
CALL(row) {
  MERGE ...
  MERGE ...
} IN TRANSACTIONS OF 10_000 ROWS;
// The underscore _ in 10_000 helps with readability and the
// value 10000 will effectively be used
```

If you do not specify the number of rows per inner transaction, the default value of 1,000 rows will be used.

Are you ready to get hands-on with this technique? You will now explicitly *reduce* the amount of heap memory available to Neo4j to 128MB, create a new test database, and import the same sample file you used in Chapter 1.

In the example Docker Compose in the GitHub repository for this book, uncomment the following line by removing the # character:

```
NEO4J_server_memory_heap_max__size: "128M"
```

Now restart the Neo4j container by running the `docker compose up -d` in your terminal. Go to the Neo4j browser and run the following commands that will create a new database named `testload`; switch to it and create a constraint for tracks only:

```
//001-create-database.cypher
CREATE DATABASE testload WAIT
```

```
:use testload
CREATE CONSTRAINT FOR (n:Track) REQUIRE n.id IS NODE KEY;
```

Switch to the new database with `:use testload`. Then create the constraint:

```
//002-create-constraint.cypher
CREATE CONSTRAINT FOR (n:Track) REQUIRE n.id IS NODE KEY;
```

Now import the same CSV file of sample tracks you used at the end of Chapter 1. This time, you'll load only the tracks:

```
//003-load-tracks.cypher
LOAD CSV WITH HEADERS FROM "file:///medium/sample_tracks_medium.csv" AS row
MERGE (track:Track {id: row.track_id})
SET track.uri = row.track_uri,
track.name = row.track_name;
```

After a couple of seconds, you should see an error message like the one in Figure 2-6, explaining that you tried to execute a transaction that consumes more memory than the maximum allocated to Neo4j.

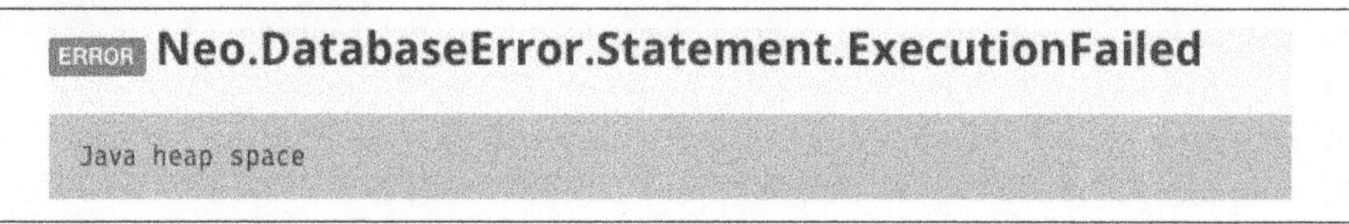

Figure 2-6. The error message received when going over the memory limit in a transaction, also called an `OutOfMemory` error

The CSV file is just about 100,000 rows. Commit after every 10,000 rows to release the memory it occupies after each iteration:

```
//004-call-in-transactions.cypher
:auto // necessary if you run this query in the Neo4j browser
LOAD CSV WITH HEADERS FROM "file:///medium/sample_tracks_medium.csv" AS row
CALL(row) {
    MERGE (track:Track {id: row.track_id})
    SET track.uri = row.track_uri,
    track.name = row.track_name
} IN TRANSACTIONS OF 10_000 ROWS;
```

`:auto` is a Neo4j browser-only command that instructs the browser to send the Cypher query in an auto-commit transaction. In general, using auto-committing transactions is not recommended because they do not support automatic retries on failure. However, certain queries, such as `CALL { ... } IN TRANSACTIONS`, must be executed this way to function properly in the Neo4j browser.

Congratulations—you've imported your data into a Neo4j database using a drastically reduced amount of memory.

`CALL IN TRANSACTIONS` is not specific to `LOAD CSV`. You can use it in other large-scale update operations, like deleting relationships of very dense nodes in smaller increments to ensure controlled and steady memory usage.

`LOAD CSV` in the browser is not what you would use in production to automate your imports.

The next section details how to perform the same operation from a client application in Python.

Try It: Importing Data from Client Applications

In this section, you will learn how to efficiently import data from client applications.

Cypher query parameters

Cypher's query parameters allow you to query or modify data using the same query string while varying the input values. This enables Neo4j to reuse cached execution plans, which optimizes performance by avoiding repeated parsing and planning. Query parameters are especially useful for application developers, who can run many queries with different inputs efficiently. Chapter 4 provides deeper insights into Neo4j's query-analysis process, and Chapter 6 shows how query parameters help guard against malicious injection attacks.

Named placeholders for parameters are prefixed with the $ (dollar) sign:

```
CREATE (track:Track {id: $id})
RETURN track
```

You can try to create a Track in the `testload` database by declaring some parameters and their values before executing the query:

```
:params {id: 'test-track', name: 'Thunderstruck'};
CREATE (track:Track {id: $id}) SET track.name = $name RETURN track;
```

Neo4j Drivers

A *driver* is a software component that enables communication between a program and a database. In the context of Neo4j, drivers facilitate interactions with the Neo4j database, allowing developers to query and manipulate data using various programming languages such as Java, Python, and JavaScript. These drivers provide an interface for applications to connect to and interact with Neo4j databases. When you run the previous code, from the perspective of a Neo4j driver, you're passing parameters as a dictionary along with the query.

Note: The Neo4j manual (*https://oreil.ly/BVJmo*) contains guides to drivers for various languages. GraphAcademy also features courses (*https://graphacademy.neo4j.com/categories/development*) on how to build applications with Neo4j drivers.

Here is an example of using parameters with the Neo4j driver for Python:

```
001-cypher-parameters.py
from neo4j import GraphDatabase
from neo4j import Result

URI = 'bolt://localhost:7687'
AUTH = ('neo4j', 'password')

query = '''
    CREATE (track:Track {id: $id})
    SET track.name = $name
    RETURN track
    '''

def create_track(driver, parameters):
    record = driver.execute_query(
        query,
        parameters,
        database_='testload',
        result_transformer_=Result.single
        )
    return record['track']['name']

with GraphDatabase.driver(URI, auth=AUTH) as driver:
    t1 = create_track(driver, {'id': 'track-01', 'name': 'Sin City'})
    t2 = create_track(driver, {'id': 'track-02', 'name': 'Creep'})
```

Note: The GitHub repository contains all instructions for running the code examples.

You've now seen how Cypher parameters work and are ready to move on to the next section.

Processing batches of data with UNWIND

The `UNWIND` clause in Cypher is used to break down a list (a collection of values) into individual rows. This allows each item in the list to be processed separately, making it a powerful tool for handling data in batches:

```
UNWIND [1, 2, 3] AS x
RETURN x

//Result
1
```

Combining Cypher parameters with the UNWIND clause is the secret sauce for efficiently importing data with Cypher. UNWIND is not limited to simple lists; it can also turn lists of dictionaries (called *maps* in Neo4j) into rows:

```
UNWIND [
{id: 'track-7', name: 'Start me up'},
{id: 'track-8', name: 'I feel good'}
] AS trackInfo
CREATE (track:Track {
  id: trackInfo.id,
  name: trackInfo.name
})
RETURN track
```

A Cypher parameter can be a list of maps (or dictionaries), commonly used when importing data into Neo4j from a client application. This section explores how to work with such parameters effectively.

First, you need to collect some objects to create a temporary list on the client side. Then you'll execute a query using UNWIND and pass the temporary list to the query as a Cypher parameter. The following code illustrates these concepts all together.

Python:

```
#002-cypher-unwind-parameters.py
query = '''
    UNWIND $trackInfos AS trackInfo
    CREATE (track:Track {id: trackInfo.id})
    SET track.name = trackInfo.name
    RETURN track
    '''

def create_tracks(driver, tracks):
    records, _, _ = driver.execute_query(
        query,
        trackInfos=tracks,
        database_='testload'
        )
    for record in records:
        print(record['track']['name'])

with GraphDatabase.driver(URI, auth=AUTH) as driver:
  # collect a certain amount of tracks
    all_tracks = []
    all_tracks.append({'id': 'track-01', 'name': 'Sin City'})
    all_tracks.append({'id': 'track-02', 'name': 'Creep'})
```

```
    # execute the query with the tracks collection
    create_tracks(driver, all_tracks)
```

In order to get out of proof-of-concept mode and work with real volumes of data, you will now import the standard `tracks` CSV file using Python. Each line will be converted into a dictionary that you can add to a collection and pass as Cypher a parameter.

First, you'll batch all lines into a single collection. Then you'll try to reproduce the `OutOfMemoryError` you received when you attempted to import the whole file at once with `LOAD CSV`:

```
#003-read-csv-1.py
import csv
from neo4j import GraphDatabase

URI = 'bolt://localhost:7687'
AUTH = ('neo4j', 'password')

all_rows = []

with open('./files/sample_tracks_medium.csv', 'r') as file:
    reader = csv.DictReader(file)
    # accumulate all rows of the file
    # into the all_rows variable
    for row in reader:
        all_rows.append(row)

query = '''
    UNWIND $trackInfos AS trackInfo
    CREATE (track:Track {id: trackInfo.id})
    SET track.name = trackInfo.name
    '''

with GraphDatabase.driver(URI, auth=AUTH) as driver:
    records, _, _ = driver.execute_query(
        query,
        trackInfos=all_rows,
        database_='testload'
    )
```

Running this script should produce the expected error: `java.lang.OutOfMemoryError: Java heap space`.

Batch sizing

Creating a single batch that contains all the rows of the CSV file is as problematic as trying to import the whole file with `LOAD CSV`. The solution is to periodically commit *smaller* batch sizes as you iterate over the entire dataset to import it.

This code demonstrates the application of the batch sizing outlined earlier, following the logic illustrated in Figure 2-7:

```
#004-import-sized-batch.py
import csv
from neo4j import GraphDatabase

URI = 'bolt://localhost:7687'
AUTH = ('neo4j', 'password')
driver = GraphDatabase.driver(URI, auth=AUTH)

query = '''
    UNWIND $trackInfos AS trackInfo
    CREATE (track:Track {id: trackInfo.id})
    SET track.name = trackInfo.name
    '''

BATCH_SIZE = 10_000
current_batch = []

def commit_batch(current_batch):
    records, _, _ = driver.execute_query(
        query,
        trackInfos=current_batch,
        database_='testload'
    )
    # reset current_batch to empty list
    current_batch.clear()

def process_row(row, current_batch):
    current_batch.append(row)
    if len(current_batch) >= BATCH_SIZE:
        commit_batch(current_batch)

with open('./files/sample_tracks_medium.csv', 'r') as file:
    reader = csv.DictReader(file)
    for row in reader:
        process_row(row, current_batch)
    else:
        commit_batch(current_batch)
```

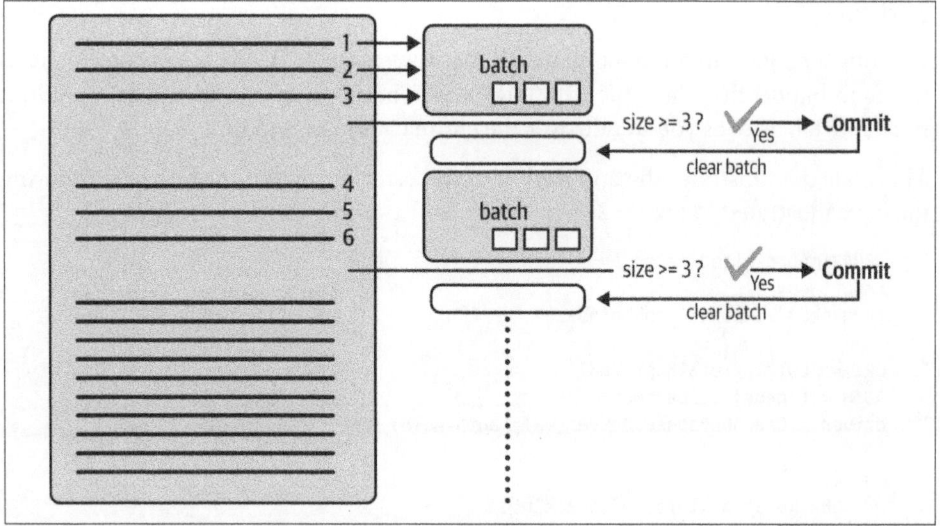

Figure 2-7. Batching statements programming flow

The Python code is a typical example of what you'll be writing day in and day out for importing data into Neo4j. As you work with it, you'll also need to keep an eye on how the program's transactions perform against Neo4j. If the batch size is too low, it will limit how fast you can write to Neo4j. On the flip side, if it's too high, it could saturate heap memory usage, causing issues for other transactions that are running.

If you're working with CSV files, you might wonder: why not just use `LOAD CSV` directly? It's a valid question. `LOAD CSV` is great for many use cases, especially quick imports and simple pipelines. However, in real-world applications, data rarely arrives in such a clean, straightforward format. More often than not, you'll be handling dynamic input, conditional logic, error handling, and monitoring, all of which are far easier to manage in a general-purpose programming language. Understanding how batching and transactions work at this level is essential, even if `LOAD CSV` is sometimes the right tool for the job.

UNWIND Idiosyncrasies

The `UNWIND` clause has a peculiarity that perplexes developers to this day, often leaving them frustrated until the aha moment. But not you, because you're reading this section now!

As we've mentioned, the `UNWIND` clause turns a list into rows. However, if the list is empty, no rows are produced, and the rest of the query is not executed. The following

Cypher query will not return any result, because the second UNWIND didn't produce any rows:

```
UNWIND [1,2,3] AS i
UNWIND [] AS x
RETURN i, x
```

As your datasets become more varied, chances are high that you will use data structures more complex than simple CSV rows—such as JSON objects.

Let's say the following JSON object represents the structure of a User object in your data.

```
{
    "id": "user-789",
    "podcasts": [],
    "playlists": [
        "playlist-12",
        "playlist-14"
    ]
}
```

You would naturally construct your Cypher queries following the order of your data structure:

```
MERGE (u:User {id: $id})
WITH u
UNWIND $podcasts AS podcast
  MERGE (p:Podcast {id: podcast})
  MERGE (u)-[:SUBSCRIBED_TO]->(p)
WITH u
UNWIND $playlists AS playlist
  MERGE (pl:Playlist {id: playlist})
  MERGE (u)-[:HAS_PLAYLIST]->(pl)
```

Executing the query, with the JSON object above passed as a Cypher parameter, will create the user, but not any of that user's relationships to playlists, because the UNWIND on $podcasts does not produce any rows. To solve the problem, wrap the portion of the query that creates playlists into a dedicated subquery:

```
MERGE (u:User {id: $id})
WITH u
CALL(u) {
    UNWIND $podcasts AS podcast
    MERGE (p:Podcast {id: podcast})
    MERGE (u)-[:SUBSCRIBED_TO]->(p)
    RETURN count(*) AS podcasts
}
CALL(u) {
    UNWIND $playlists AS playlist
    MERGE (pl:Playlist {id: playlist})
    MERGE (u)-[:HAS_PLAYLIST]->(pl)
    RETURN count(*) AS playlists
```

```
}
RETURN podcasts, playlists
```

Note: The `RETURN count(*)` in each subquery is used to control cardinality. In Cypher, *cardinality* refers to the number of rows being processed at any given stage of a query. Managing cardinality is essential when working with subqueries, as the results of one part of the query can inadvertently multiply rows in subsequent operations. This can lead to unexpected results, particularly when creating or merging nodes and relationships.

You can experiment with the behavior of the two queries by simulating their parameters in the Neo4j browser:

```
:params {id: "user-789", podcasts: [],
  playlists: ["playlist-12", "playlist-14"]}
```

Using Cypher parameters and proper batch sizing is the key to speedy, successful large data imports (as well as developer happiness).

Parallel Writes

To speed up data imports, developers sometimes run multiple Neo4j queries in parallel. While this sounds straightforward, it involves complex considerations. This section will give you the essentials for implementing parallel queries effectively and address potential challenges to keep your project moving smoothly. It's a practical guide, designed to enhance your skills and ensure a successful, efficient parallel data importation process.

Competing for memory

If two transactions are attempting to use the heap concurrently, the heap will need to be large enough to accommodate two transactions at the same time. In the situation depicted in Figure 2-8, if a third transaction attempts to write the same amount of data as the two transactions already running, your Neo4j server will reach its heap memory capacity and reject your transaction. Or worse, it will shut down.

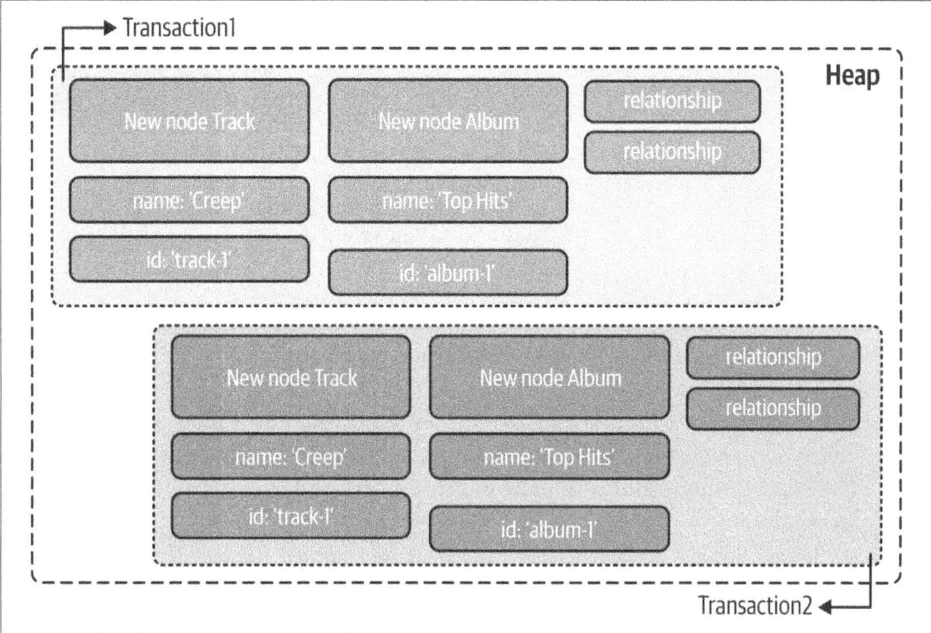

Figure 2-8. Units of work from multiple transactions occupying space on the heap

Make sure your heap is configured with enough memory to sustain the concurrent transaction workloads that you can reasonably foresee. Don't forget that read transactions use memory, too.

To limit memory usage for transactions, you need to configure two key settings. The `db.memory.transaction.max` setting defines the maximum memory a single transaction can use, while the `db.memory.transaction.total.max` setting limits the total memory usage for all transactions within a database. You can also estimate the amount of memory a particular Cypher query would consume by profiling it, which is explained in Chapter 5.

Locking mechanisms

When write operations occur, Neo4j acquires locks to preserve data consistency. If you try to modify the same record from two different transactions, one of the transactions will have to wait for the other one to complete before being able to commit.

Figure 2-9 illustrates this concept by representing transaction 1 deleting a node, while transaction 2 tries to update a property of the same node.

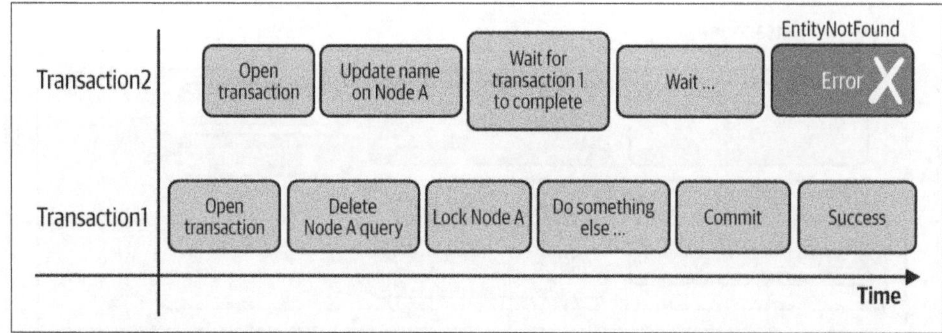

Figure 2-9. Timeline of concurrent transactions attempting to modify the same node

To deepen your understanding of this mechanism, this section focuses on hands-on experimentation. These exercises are designed to provide practical insights that are rarely explored, giving you a unique opportunity to gain a comprehensive grasp of these concepts.

First, create a new database:

```
//005-create-database-locking.cypher
CREATE DATABASE locking WAIT
```

Then switch to it with `:use locking`.

Next, look at the following Cypher query. The `apoc.util.sleep` procedure allows you to pause the transaction for the specified amount of time (in milliseconds) before processing any further. This easy trick will prove useful in future testing scenarios!

Running this query will make your Neo4j browser show a spinning wheel for 60 seconds as it waits for the transaction to commit:

```
//006-merge-wait-spinning.cypher
MERGE (n:Track {id: 1})
WITH n
// the transaction will be paused for 60 seconds
CALL apoc.util.sleep(60000)
// the transaction now continues
SET n.name = 'Creep'
RETURN n
```

Neo4j procedures are prebuilt or user-defined functions written in Java that extend the capabilities of Cypher queries. They enable advanced operations, such as data processing, custom algorithms, or integrations, directly within the database. A popular library, Awesome Procedures on Cypher (APOC), provides a rich collection of procedures and functions, offering solutions for tasks like data import/export, graph algorithms, and schema management. Procedures are invoked using the `CALL` keyword in Cypher, enhancing Neo4j's flexibility and power. APOC is already enabled in the Docker Compose from the GitHub repository.

Simultaneous updates to nodes and relationships

Inevitably, you'll encounter scenarios where you need to update the graph from different parts of your code, increasing the likelihood of simultaneous attempts to modify identical nodes or relationships. This section aims to show you how locking mechanisms affect your attempts and provides strategies to minimize such occurrences.

For this experiment, you will simulate two concurrent transactions with two Neo4j browser tabs opened, using the transaction pause trick in one of them.

In your first browser tab, create a node that both transactions will try to modify at the same time:

```
//007-create-node-1.cypher
CREATE (t:Track {id: 1})
```

Now, in the first Neo4j browser tab, issue the following Cypher query:

```
//008-tab-1-1.cypher
MATCH (t:Track {id: 1})
SET t.name = 'Creep'
WITH t
CALL apoc.util.sleep(60000)
RETURN t
```

Issue the following query in the second tab:

```
//009-tab-1-2.cypher
MATCH (t:Track {id: 1})
SET t.name = 'Creep from transaction 2'
RETURN t
```

You will observe that despite not using the *apoc.util.sleep* procedure, the query in the second tab also shows a spinning wheel icon for about 60 seconds. This indicates that its transaction is waiting for the other one to complete, as shown in Figure 2-10. Observe, too, that the final name value for the track is the value set by the second transaction.

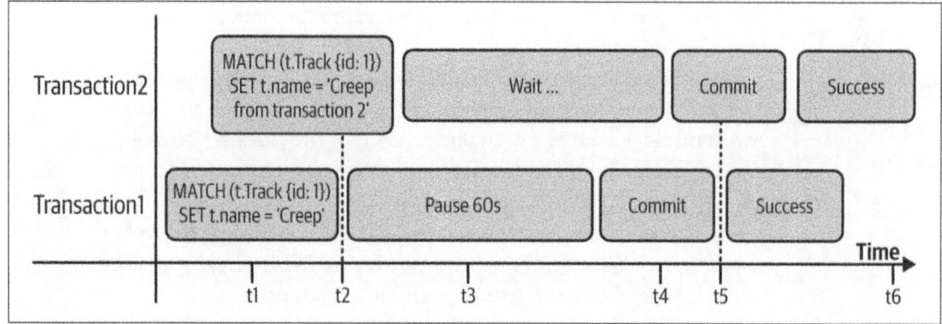

Figure 2-10. One transaction is waiting for another one to complete before proceeding.

You can inspect the state of transactions with the `SHOW TRANSACTIONS` command. Run the following code in your Neo4j browser while both previous queries are idle:

```
//010-transactions-info.cypher
SHOW TRANSACTIONS YIELD *
RETURN transactionId, status, currentQueryId, currentQuery,
resourceInformation.lockMode AS lockMode,
resourceInformation.resourceType AS lockOnResource
```

In the result, seen in Figure 2-11, the status of the second transaction is blocked by the first transaction.

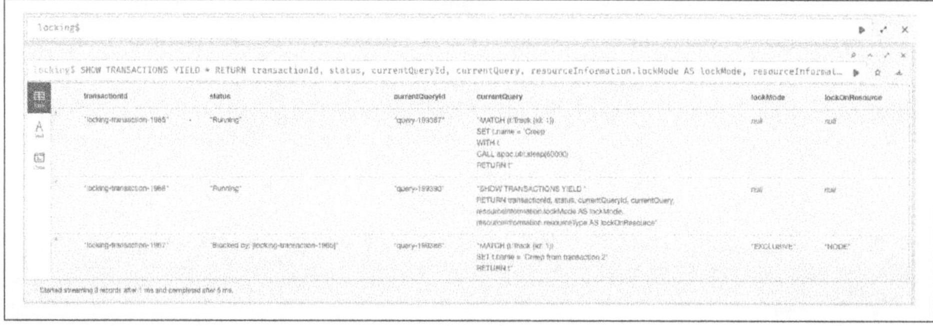

Figure 2-11. One transaction is blocked by another transaction and is waiting before proceeding.

To minimize locking conflicts during concurrent import pipelines, it's essential to structure the import process in a way that reduces contention. One effective approach involves dividing the import tasks among concurrent threads so that each thread handles distinct portions of the data. For example, threads can process nodes with specific labels or those whose identifiers fall within designated alphanumeric ranges, ensuring that no two threads attempt to modify the same nodes simultaneously.

Locking conflicts can arise when multiple transactions try to access the same nodes or relationships concurrently, leading to congestion. While Cypher load statements like LOAD CSV can handle a significant amount of data efficiently, improper batching or overlapping node processing can cause contention, especially in large-scale imports (see Figure 2-12). Structuring imports to avoid such overlaps helps alleviate these issues.

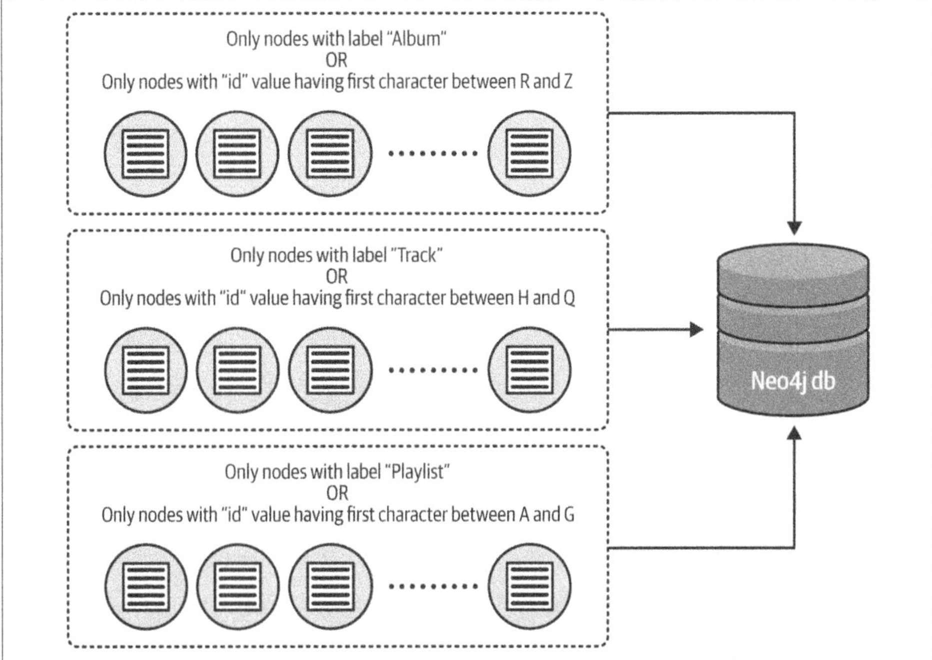

Figure 2-12. Sticky load balancing of statements in transaction pools

Creating nodes and relationships concurrently

When you're bootstrapping a fresh database with minimal existing data, you'll often find yourself juggling two datasets: one for creating nodes and another solely for various types of relationships that's packed with node identifiers (generally a primary key property such as `id`).

You'll be tempted to load those two datasets simultaneously, but here's the twist: as you begin writing relationships to your database, you aren't certain whether the corresponding nodes have already been created from the other dataset. This might push you toward a tempting but tricky solution: using `MERGE` on node identifiers backed by a unique or node key constraint (here comes locking again!).

To simulate this scenario, you'll use two browser tabs. In one, you will `MERGE` a node on its identifier; in the second tab, you will `MERGE` two nodes, again on their identifiers, and attempt to create a relationship between them:

```
//011-tab-2-1.cypher
// browser tab 1
MERGE (t:Track {id: '123'})
WITH t
CALL apoc.util.sleep(60000)
RETURN t

//012-tab-2-2.cypher
// browser tab 2
MERGE (t1:Track {id: '123'})
MERGE (t2:Track {id: '234'})
MERGE (t1)-[:SIMILAR_TO]->(t2)
```

You cannot believe your eyes: the second query returns immediately, successfully creating both the nodes and the relationships in no time, while the first query is still paused. Did the authors of this book get it wrong? No, this little surprise is intentional. Identifier uniqueness guarantees are enforced with the usage of *uniqueness constraints*. These are enforced using locks to prevent concurrent transactions violating the constraint.

Try it out. Remove all the test data and add a uniqueness constraint for the nodes with label `Track`:

```
//013-unique-constraint.cypher
MATCH (n) DETACH DELETE n;
CREATE CONSTRAINT track_uk FOR (t:Track) REQUIRE t.id IS UNIQUE;
```

After you repeat the previous locking experiment queries, the second transaction is effectively waiting for the first one to complete, ensuring that only one node with a label `Track` and the ID `123` can exist in the database.

Adding relationships concurrently

Starting with Neo4j version 5.23 and the introduction of the new store format, called `block` (*https://oreil.ly/0f43v*), it is now possible to create relationships between two nodes even when other transactions hold a write lock on one of the nodes. This behavior can be demonstrated using the following queries:

```
//014-tab-3-1.cypher
// In browser tab 1
MATCH (t1:Track {id: 1})
SET t1.popularity = 0.9
WITH t1
CALL apoc.util.sleep(60000)

//015-tab-3-2.cypher
// In browser tab 2
MATCH (t1:Track {id: 1})
MATCH (t2:Track {id: 2})
CREATE (t1)-[r:SIMILAR]->(t2)
```

You'll observe that the relationship-creation query executes and returns instantaneously.

Transactions also acquire locks on relationships when modifying or deleting them. Figure 2-13 shows what happens when two simultaneous transactions attempt to delete the same relationship—the second transaction waits for the first to complete because of the lock on the relationship and then fails.

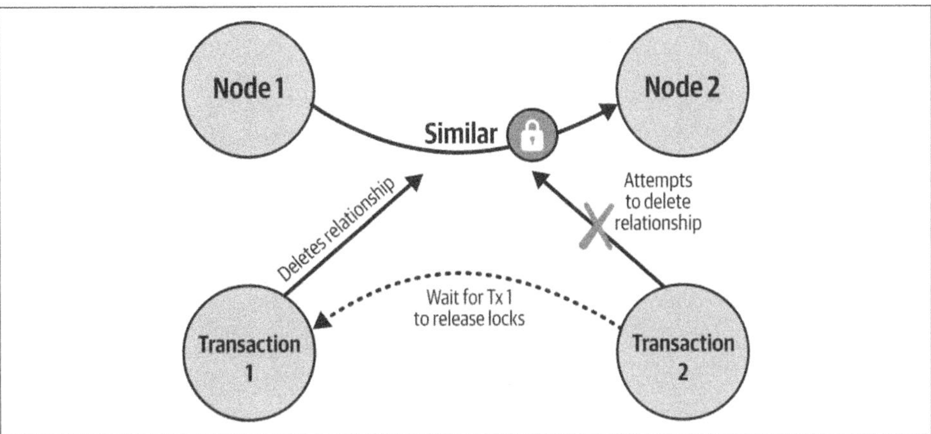

Figure 2-13. Locks when two transactions attempt to delete the same relationship

Finally, you might encounter a situation where locks on nodes can still be taken. This situation becomes very apparent when you're materializing similarity relationships between nodes (as depicted in Figure 2-14, based on the graph model presented in Chapter 1).

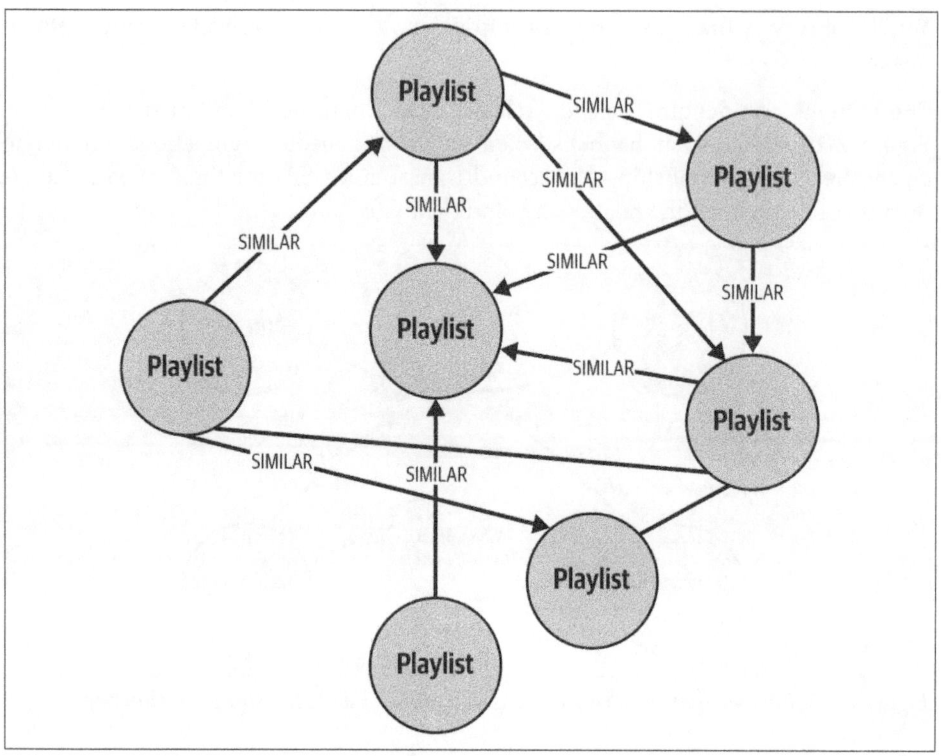

Figure 2-14. A typical graph model representing a similarity network between playlists.

Because the similarities between playlists will change over time, you might have to delete many old similarity relationships and insert newly computed ones.

Nodes keep track of the first relationship for each group (relationship type), as shown in Figure 2-15.

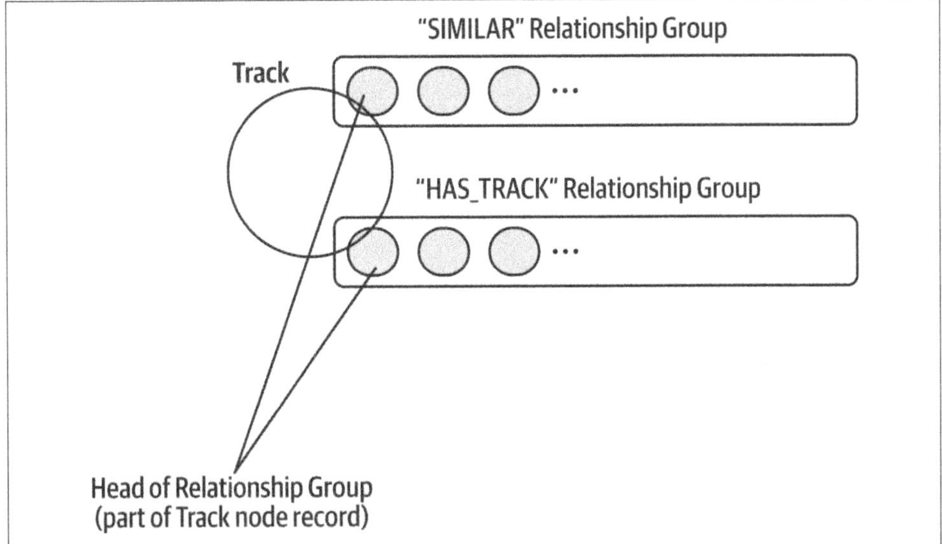

Figure 2-15. Representation of the head of a relationship group, with relationships grouped by type and direction

When two concurrent transactions are competing to replace the head of a node's relationship group, the first transaction takes a lock on that node as well.

Locking mechanisms are crucial to ensuring your database's consistency in all circumstances. To ensure a safe, successful, and smooth writing experience with Neo4j, you'll need to understand the nuances of these locks and incorporate this knowledge into how you design your import pipelines.

Offline Import

Neo4j has specialized tooling for fast offline import of an initial dataset called the *admin import* feature that lets you load data from CSV files directly into the database's storage layer, circumventing the transactional layer and the locking mechanisms. This approach maximizes your machine's resource utilization by engaging all available CPU cores and I/O.

Most relational database systems offer the capability to export data into CSV format. As long as the transformation from relational tables to a graph model is straightforward and minimal, this method is particularly advantageous for initially importing data.

Most of your effort will go toward generating the necessary CSV files. You'll need one or more files for each node type, along with corresponding relationship CSV files that include columns for the start and end node IDs, as illustrated in Figure 2-16.

Track.csv

track_id:ID	name	length	...
123-fff	Creep	173	...
...	...	...	...

Playlist.csv

playlist_id:ID	name	total_tracks	...
456-ddd	Rock Compilation	47	...
...	...	...	...

Playlist_track.csv

:START_ID(Playlist)	:END_ID(Track)	Track_index	...
456-ddd	123-fff	47	...
...	...	...	...

Figure 2-16. Typical CSV file structure suitable for use with the `neo4j-admin` import tool

You can download the complete dataset in CSV format from this book's accompanying GitHub repository and test the import process. The performance metrics provided below are based on importing the dataset using a 12-core MacBook Pro with the following command:

```
./bin/neo4j-admin database import full
--nodes=:Track=import/full/track.csv
--nodes=:Playlist=import/full/playlist.csv
--relationships=:HAS_TRACK=import/full/track_playlist1.csv
--skip-duplicate-nodes
--multiline-fields=true tracksdb

IMPORT DONE in 1m 23s 708ms.
Imported:
  14336944 nodes
  125451006 relationships
  358453696 properties
Peak memory usage: 1.674GiB
```

The admin import tool offers a wide range of configuration possibilities: you can import incremental data, supply headers through separate files, manage duplicates,[1] specify the number of cores to utilize, and handle multiline values, among other things. Neo4j has developed comprehensive guides (*https://oreil.ly/-jLjy*) to assist you in using this tool, tailored to the characteristics of the CSV files you are able to produce.

The neo4j-admin import tool is designed for clean datasets. In this context, "clean" means your CSV files must not contain duplicate node IDs and should avoid relationships that point to nonexistent nodes. The tool performs strict validation and will fail the import if duplicate node IDs are detected. It also checks for relationships that reference undefined nodes, and if the proportion of such missing references exceeds a certain threshold, the import will be aborted. This is a high-performance, create-only process, so it's essential to preprocess and verify your data carefully before using it.

Exploring Other Ingestion Tools

While this chapter focused on foundational techniques for getting data into Neo4j, the ecosystem offers a wide range of other tools designed to support more advanced or continuous ingestion workflows. Depending on your architecture, you might benefit from Neo4j's Change Data Capture (CDC) feature for streaming updates from transactional systems or from Kafka Connect plugins that integrate Neo4j into event-driven data pipelines. If you're working in a Java-based environment or integrating with BI tools, neo4j-jdbc can help you treat Neo4j like a traditional data source. These tools are particularly useful in production environments that require real-time updates, synchronization with external systems, or tighter integration with enterprise data platforms. We encourage you to explore these options as your needs evolve or as your software stack demands.

Summary

You now have the tools to import data efficiently, no matter the stage of your project. By leveraging the `CALL IN TRANSACTIONS` clause of the `LOAD CSV` statement, you can efficiently import and experiment with large volumes of data. Batching data imports provides a seamless solution when connecting to Neo4j from your own applications. However, while lightning-speed offline imports are possible with Neo4j admin import, they may not be ideal for extensive data transformations between original formats and graph models.

1 The tool is optimized for clean datasets, so we recommend that you eliminate duplicates from your CSV files before using it.

CHAPTER 3
Revisiting Modeling Decisions

Graph modeling is an intuitive process that requires a clear understanding of the use cases in your business. It's different from relational schema design, and the flexibility and lack of fixed rules can be bewildering at first, but as you get used to the process, you'll find that it is a rewarding exercise.

You'll use the graph you created in Chapter 1 to try some of the queries that follow.

It Depends

Let's say you've been given a dataset that contains tracks, albums, artists, and their genres, and you want to design a schema for a relational database management system (RDBMS). You'd probably apply the familiar set of normalization rules (*https://oreil.ly/syey6*)[1] and end up with a similar structural model—table and column names might vary—as in Figure 3-1.

1 Wikipedia. "Database normalization." Last modified April 23, 2025.

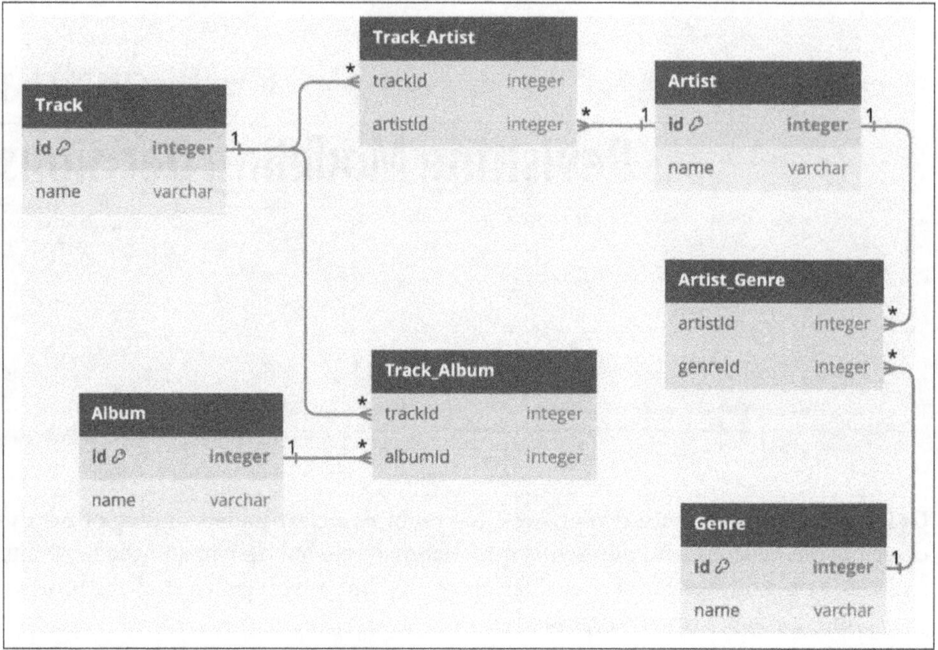

Figure 3-1. Schema for an RDBMS

How do you model this as a graph? Your answer, as a seasoned graph modeler, should be, "It depends!" Really? Yes, really. Figures 3-2 to 3-4 show three graph models, all of which are valid.

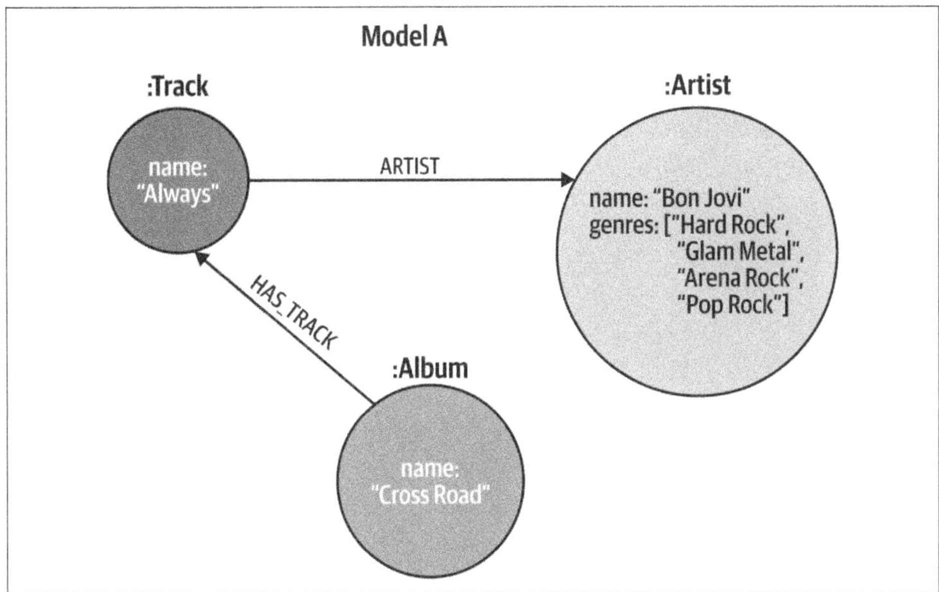

Figure 3-2. Model A models genres as a property of the artist.

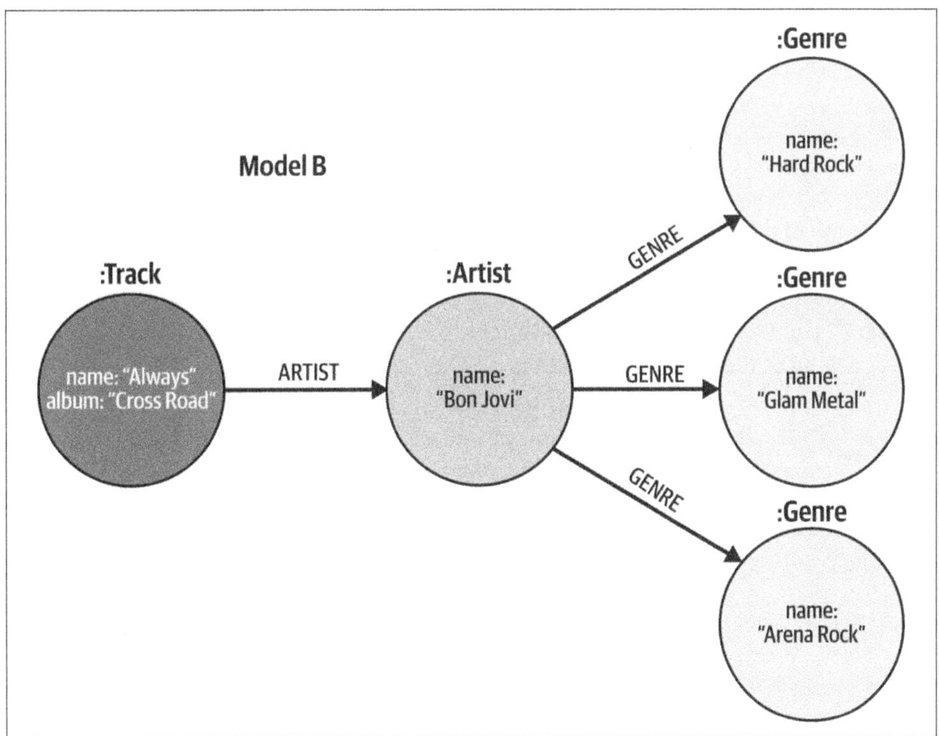

Figure 3-3. Genres are nodes and the album is a property in Model B.

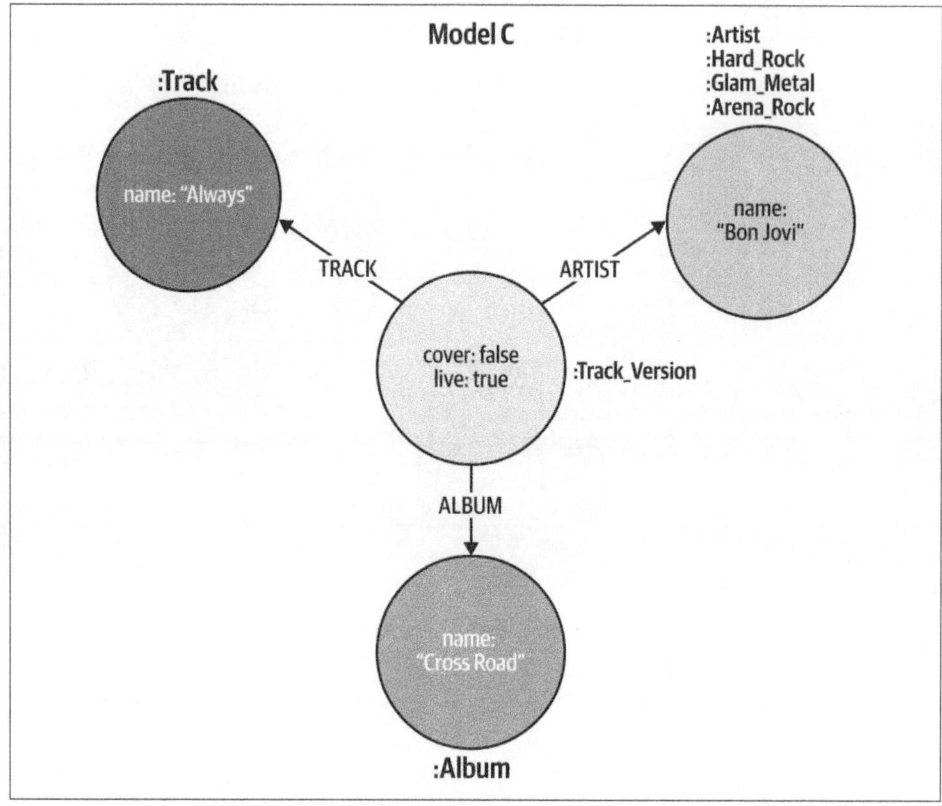

Figure 3-4. Model C with a `TRACK_VERSION` node and genres as labels

Add more entities to the dataset, and the number of possible models grows. No model is incorrect; their suitability depends on the use case. That's why the next thing you say, as a seasoned graph modeler is, "What questions do you want the graph to answer?" The use case determines which model is optimal to answer the question(s) you're asking of the graph and perform efficient queries.

We strongly advise you, as with everything else, to keep it simple. Model just enough, but no more—and don't optimize prematurely.

You can always refactor your graph model; this is not considered to be an antipattern. A graph model should constantly evolve as the business changes. You may find yourself refactoring primarily when the following events occur:

- New kinds of data
- New use cases
- The volume of data increases sharply
- The business domain evolves or changes

If all the models in Figures 3-2 to 3-4 are valid, which one should you pick? Which is the "right" one? It depends on your use case! Right now, your primary use cases are to:

- Find tracks on an album with the track artist.
- Find all tracks by an artist and the albums they're on.
- Whenever the artist is listed, also list artist genres.

Model A in Figure 3-2 will work. The album, artist, and track are modeled as nodes. It doesn't use the genres as part of any query criteria; they are simply a returned property and are modeled as such. Modeling the genre as a node or as labels, as in Models B and C, would be overkill.

Let's stay with the same data, but try two different use cases:

- Find all artists in one or more genres and return their tracks, along with their albums.
- Find artists that share genres.

Model B shown in Figure 3-4 is suitable for these tasks. Since the genres are modeled as nodes, queries can start from them or traverse through them. The album isn't of note, so it can start as a property of the track till it gains importance.

Model C would not suit the query to "find artists that share genres," since Neo4j traverses the graph along the relationships between nodes, and labels are used to filter. Finding shared genres across artists would not use the power of Neo4j's traversals and instead would have to compare labels across individual artist nodes. However, it is more specific and covers these use cases:

- Find all the artists that have covered a track, and the albums they're on.
- Categorize artists by genre.
- Given a genre, find tracks in that genre, and then find artists that have performed the same track.

As you can see, knowing the use case and the questions they need to answer is the only way to arrive at an appropriate graph model. You might also use the three models to visualize how use cases evolve and how the graph model evolves with them—if perhaps you start off with the first set but then grow to the third, the graph model would need to be refactored.

There are many factors to consider when deciding whether to model your data as nodes, properties, or labels. First, though, it is vital to understand the principles behind these factors.

Principles of Modeling

The characteristics of a well-tuned graph model are:

Human intuitiveness
: The appeal of a graph database is the intuitiveness of its model. It should directly represent the business and be whiteboard-friendly and clear to stakeholders.

Query simplicity
: Cypher was designed to be an expressive query language. Query simplicity derives directly from the model, so an unnecessarily complex graph model results in unnecessarily complex queries, which in turn leads to increased cognitive load for the engineers maintaining or tuning these queries.

Query performance
: A well-designed graph model, backed by reasoned choices of indexes and constraints, aids query performance (which we cover in Chapter 5). For now, think of *query performance* as how much work the graph engine must do to access, traverse, and fetch data to answer your use case questions. In this chapter, we will frequently refer to how accessible a graph element (a node, relationship, property, or label) is and how much processing the query engine must do to execute the query.

Read/write trade-off
: In Chapter 2, you learned approaches to ingesting high volumes of data. *Reading* data at scale is the other side of the coin. Your goal is to understand your application's read and write requirements and then tweak your graph model to achieve an optimal balance between the two.

We'll adopt a problem-solution approach in the following sections to help you to recognize modeling patterns in your own graphs and apply good practices.

Properties Versus Nodes

Examine figures 3-2 and 3-3 again. Notice how Model A represents the album *Cross Road* as a node, and Model B represents it as a property of the track. Which one is better? By now, you know that it depends on a couple of things.

Properties That Decorate the Result

First, consider the use case: when fetching tracks, the query should return the album as well. The album is a *decorating* property: it enriches the result but is not itself used in the query, neither to navigate the graph nor as a predicate. This case is quite easily fulfilled by Model B.

If you add cardinality to the picture, what is the cardinality of the association between a track and an album? If it is one-to-one, Model B is still quite suitable. You can look up the node by the track or album name and return the node and both properties easily. Modeling the album as a separate node, however, has no value and results in an extra traversal to fetch the album every time a track needs to be returned.

Cardinality in the context of databases describes the numerical relationship between entities on either side of a relationship. A one-to-many cardinality between label A and label B indicates that one node with label A is related to many nodes with label B.

What if the album had a couple more properties, such as a release date and a link to the cover art? It is still okay to add these properties to the track node, as seen in Figure 3-5.

Figure 3-5. A representation of a nested object within a node

What if you're dealing with one-to-many cardinality? One track can be on multiple albums. This is not yet a dealbreaker, in the absence of other use cases. Figure 3-6 shows how you can still store the album name as a property on the track node; only now, the data type of this property is a list.

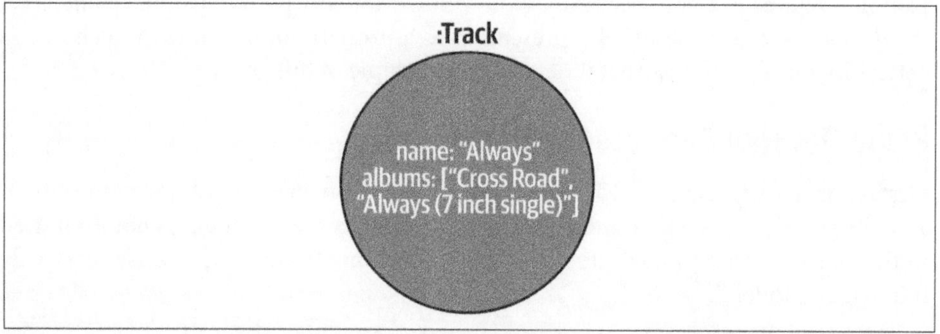

Figure 3-6. The `albums` property is now a list of strings.

This does not work if you need a richer representation of an album. Adding release dates and a link to cover art would require storing the album as a nested object (an object embedded in an object), which Neo4j does not currently support. Hacks to get around this include transforming the object to a JSON string, but then engineers must do extra work on the client side to reconstruct the object from its string representation. In addition, you'll suffer the drawback of being unable to sort on a list property or enforce uniqueness constraints. In this case, you are better off representing the album as a node, as in Model A, since it is an entity in its own right.

Key Takeaways

Simple pieces of data that serve as decorators and are not of use while querying should not be stored in the graph. If they must for various reasons, such as that the graph is the only database or that it is infeasible to separate them into another database, then they can be modeled as properties on a node. The downside of this approach is that the information in these properties is duplicated across the graph. This redundancy also implies updates in multiple places instead of one.

Traversing Across Commonalities

A frequent use case for graphs is to find entities that share something in common. For example, which tracks share the same album as a given track? If the album were a property of the track, the query would look like this:

```
MATCH (t:Track {id:1})
MATCH (otherTrack:Track)
WHERE otherTrack.album = t.album
RETURN otherTrack
```

This is not a performant query, because it will gather and inspect all tracks and discard any that do not contain the same album as track 1. It also has to be written differently if the album property is a list—instead of a simple comparison. The query would have to check that the intersection of both lists is not empty, making it even more unintuitive. Furthermore, list properties are not indexed, preventing quick access to the value. In use cases such as this, the album ceases to be a decorator: it is a first-class entity and should be represented as a node, as in Model A.

The query then changes to:

```
MATCH (t:Track {id:1})<-[:HAS_TRACK]-(a:Album)-[:HAS_TRACK]->(otherTrack:Track)
RETURN otherTrack
```

A query navigating through the `HAS_TRACK` relationships is very performant and only gathers tracks it needs to return. Tracks that belong to other albums are not traversed, unlike the previous query.

Key Takeaways

When you find yourself referring to some data as an entity or an important concept in the business domain, and the data is a shared concept between other entities, then traversing through nodes and relationships is more intuitive and performant. Model the entity as a node.

Modeling Concepts as Labels

An artist's genre is represented in three different ways in Figures 3-2 to Figure 3-4 —as a list property, as nodes, and as labels. Genre is an example of a categorical variable, as are characteristics like the artist's country of origin, status, or gender. A *categorical variable* is a variable that can have a limited and finite number of possible values. These types of data are the ones that raise the most questions when you're modeling a graph because they can be modeled in many different ways.

Model A expresses genres as properties. Just like you saw in the previous section, where it is not performant to find tracks that belong to the same album, modeling the genre as a property also makes it difficult to find artists that share genres.

Model B represents genres as nodes: this is great for representing one-to-many cardinality, as well as traversing to other entities such as artists, tracks, or albums based on shared (common) genres.

Model C uses labels for genres. This is an interesting modeling approach that is typically considered for categorical variables with a small number of values, where the values assigned to the node have a low *change velocity* (that is, they are not frequently updated on nodes) and when their primary purpose is categorization.

Using labels is inappropriate when your queries involve traversing through the category. For example, this query, "Find tracks from artists who share genres with the artists in my favorites playlist," is unwieldy to write—and wouldn't perform well either. The labels of a node can be queried using the `labels(node)` function; it returns a list of strings, and finding shared genres once again would result in a predicate that finds the intersection of lists—not very graphy.

Labels are primarily used to group nodes into sets. Labels are backed by indexes that are implicitly created by the database, so matching the starting set of nodes in a query using labels is efficient. We'll show you more about how labels aid query performance in Chapter 5; for now, it is sufficient to know that to make your query both performant and readable, you should start it by finding nodes in specific genres, as in the following query:

```
MATCH (a:Artist&HardRock&ArenaRock)
```

There are related factors to consider with this type of modeling. Labels are implicitly Boolean: they are either present or absent. No other meaning, conditions, or states are involved. Labels on a node also imply an overlap of categories. The meaning of labels should be clear, semantically.

In the `MATCH` from the previous query, the use of genres is clear, but that's not always the case. This query uses labels indiscriminately:

```
MATCH (:Artist&Songwriter&Producer&Grammy&HardRock&PowerUpTour)
```

Does the absence of the `Grammy` label indicate that the artist has never won a Grammy Award or that there is no information about it? Was the `Grammy` for the `Producer` category or the `SongWriter` category or was it for a song or the album? Is the `PowerUpTour` in the `HardRock` genre or is the artist in this genre?

Apart from unclear semantics, there is another downside to having too many labels. Neo4j preallocates a certain amount of storage for labels—if you go above that limit, Neo4j has to allocate extra space and do more work to keep database statistics up to date, which can affect performance. You could go up to 30 or 40 labels on a node without slowing things down, but there's rarely any justification for using more than 20 labels on a node (one justification is using labels to model security roles—a topic that we will cover in Chapter 8).

Finally, if the change velocity of a categorical variable is high, the cost of Neo4j acquiring a lock on the node for every change can be significant. As you learned in Chapter 2, you should take locking into account when doing parallel writes or heavy updates on the graph.

Key Takeaways

Labels are great for performance, as you'll see in the next chapter, especially when used as a lookup. When using labels, make sure that they:

- Are Boolean
- Stay semantically clear (a good example: a set of a few categorical values that clearly represent some property of an entity, such as status)
- Have low change velocity
- Are primarily used for looking up collections of nodes of the same type or role

Avoid these:

- Treating labels as you would a relationship, such as to connect nodes
- Overloading nodes with labels

Node Fanout

Node fanout refers to the number of related entities that a node has.

Let's look at two examples. The node in Figure 3-7 has no fanout and compresses all information into properties.

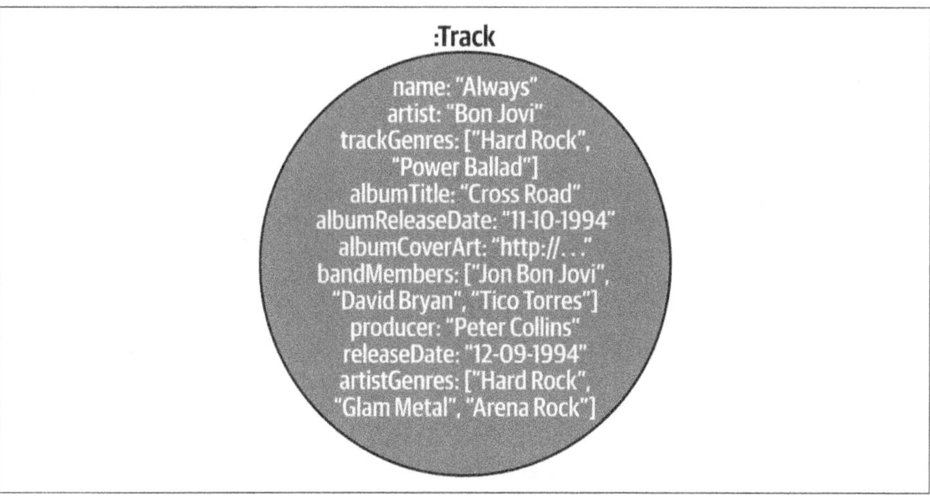

Figure 3-7. A node with no fanout. All the information about a track is stored on the track node itself.

The other extreme is the model in Figure 3-8.

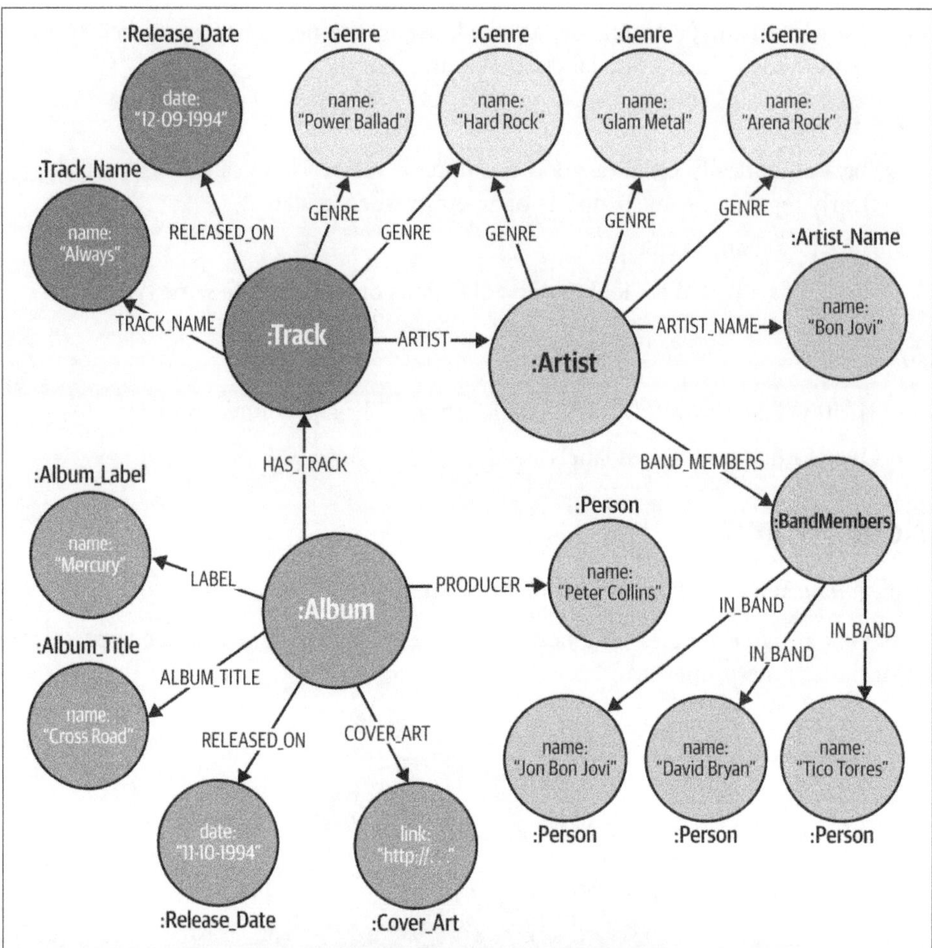

Figure 3-8. This model represents maximum fanout, where every property has been modeled as a node. This is similar to a Resource Description Format (https://www.w3.org/TR/rdf12-concepts/) (RDF) model.

Neither of these models is viable. They suffer from traversal problems such as:

- No relationships to take advantage of when traversing in Figure 3-7
- High number of traversals when gathering fine-grained properties to return in Figure 3-8
- Duplicated values

- Extra inspection work done by the database due to gathering too many nodes up front, then discarding them when they fail the inspection criteria

By contrast, the model in Figure 3-9 strikes the right balance.

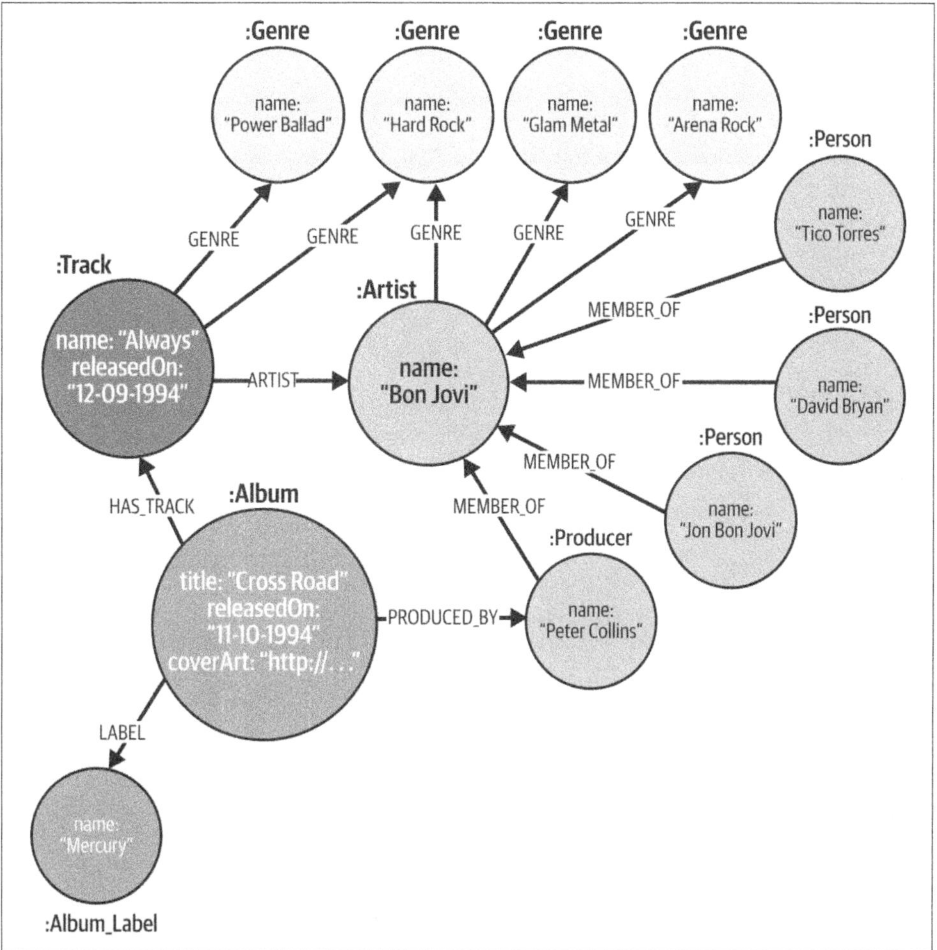

Figure 3-9. Balanced fanout on nodes

Key Takeaways

Aim to control node fanout by:

- Identifying navigation points such as entities that are shared or traversed through and turning them into nodes
- Reducing repetition of values so that updates are localized to a single place

- Reducing the number of nodes to be traversed when gathering properties that decorate the output
- Reducing the number of nodes to be inspected and discarded when checking property conditions

Supernodes

As your graph grows, you may encounter a categorical variable that you modeled as a node becoming a *supernode*: a node that has an extremely high number of relationships, disproportionately higher than for other nodes of the same type. There is no exact answer to "How high is high?" It could be thousands, tens of thousands, or millions of relationships. Supernodes are easy to spot when you visualize your graph: they're the ones causing the "hairball" effect (see Figure 3-10).

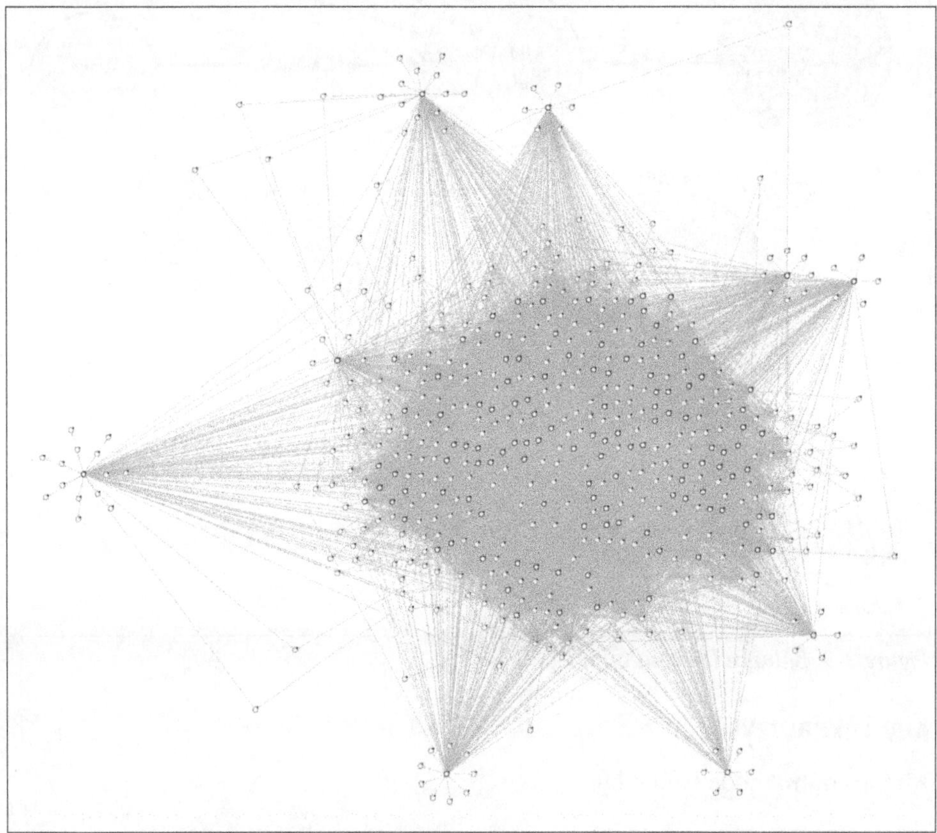

Figure 3-10. A typical hairball visualization

You can predict some supernodes and avoid them. An example would be modeling gender as a node. If ElectricHarmony's user base numbers in the tens of millions, each Gender node will have tens of millions of relationships to users, as the team verified by pulling these statistics from their RDBMS sources.

Some nodes start off innocently but grow into supernodes over time. Imagine a case where users can follow artists. In the beginning, the FOLLOWS relationships are fairly well distributed.

Then, some event occurs that propels a particular artist to fame. Suddenly, this artist starts to collect millions of fans, and their node crosses some threshold to become a supernode. Not only does this create issues with graph visualizations and skew recommendations in favor of this supernode artist, it also adversely impacts the performance of queries that traverse through this artist node. Think of it as a variation of the node fanout problem: Every time the query engine hits the artist node, the number of paths it can traverse explodes along the FOLLOWS relationship.

Imagine that ElectricHarmony decides to query the graph to suggest other listeners that a user might want to connect with at the after-party of a concert they're attending, based on whether these listeners follow the same artists as the user:

```
MATCH
(u:User {id:500})-[:FOLLOWS]->(:Artist)
<-[f:FOLLOWS]-(other)-[:ATTENDS]->(c:Concert)
<-[:ATTENDS]-(u)
RETURN other
```

Does the user with ID 500 follow the famous supernode artist? Probably, but it would be unfortunate if the number of FOLLOWS relationships identified by f in the query could reach the millions, and Neo4j would need to traverse each of those paths further to find concerts in common.

Paths *ending* at the supernode are not a problem—just those that traverse *through* it.

There are some techniques to get around the supernode problem, depending on your domain and use cases. Some of them involve query hints, which will be covered in Chapter 5. Others involve excluding the supernode from path traversals. This is highly dependent on your use case, but it would be a possible solution for ElectricHarmony: they'd have too many listeners at their concert after-party just because of the supernode artist. ElectricHarmony can monitor the graph at frequent intervals to detect supernodes and, when found, add a special Supernode label to the Artist node. Then they can exclude any supernode artists by modifying the query like this:

```
MATCH
(u:User {id:500})-[:FOLLOWS]->(:Artist&!Supernode)
```

```
<-[f:FOLLOWS]-(other)-[:ATTENDS]->(c:Concert)
<-[:ATTENDS]-(u)
RETURN other
```

You might also prefer to remove supernodes from the graph altogether (or not even ingest them) if they offer no value in graph analysis. You can also consider sharding the supernode into buckets based on some key, such as time or geography, and then use bucketed relationships to connect them. Bucketed relationships are explained later in this chapter. Sometimes the node can be represented as a property instead, like gender.

You don't always have to get rid of supernodes. In fact, some use cases revolve around identifying these dense nodes, and therefore they cannot be modeled in any other way.

Key Takeaways

Weigh the costs and benefits of supernodes in your graph. If they are undesirable, consider detecting and skipping them prior to ingesting the data. Otherwise, if they turn out to add tremendous navigational overhead, you might try ways to exclude them from traversals. This can be done quite efficiently with degree counts; you'll learn about this in Chapter 8. However, supernodes might be an important aspect of your domain and aid you in finding, for example, clusters with graph data science algorithms, which you'll read about in Chapter 12.

Relationship Granularity

How generic or specific should your relationship types be? Recall the model employed in Chapter 1 (Figure 1-3), which we've reproduced in Figure 3-11. The `HAS_TRACK` relationship connects a `Track` to both a `Playlist` and an `Album`.

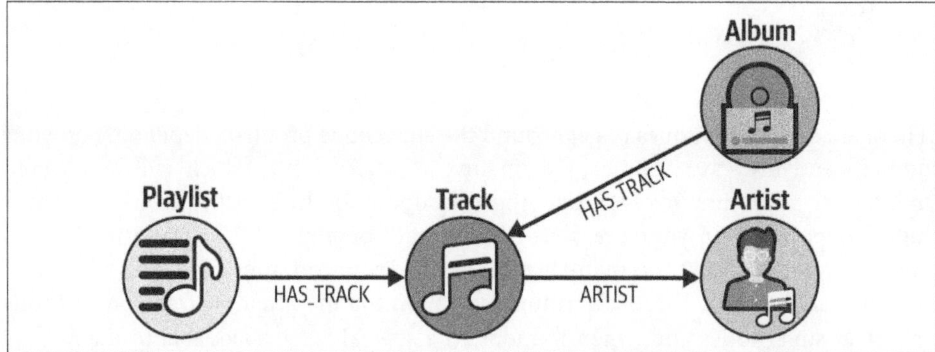

Figure 3-11. This graph model uses the HAS_TRACK relationship between tracks and playlists or albums.

Figure 3-11 depicts a generic relationship. If the major use case for ElectricHarmony is to start from either a playlist or an album, navigate to their tracks, and then continue as in the next query, this works quite well. Here is that query:

```
//001-generic-relationship-1.cypher
MATCH (n {id:"0eLgWXRdFvQWb5Ch6Hm33Z"})-[:HAS_TRACK]->(t:Track)
-[:ARTIST]->(a:Artist) //this n matches an album
```

It also works for use cases that start from a track and want to traverse to all entities that contain this track in the future, such as playlists, albums, or anything else:

```
//002-generic-relationship-2.cypher
MATCH (t:Track {id: "0kish3Tobj6Wq0we74343q"})<-[:HAS_TRACK]-(n)
RETURN n.name, labels(n)
```

This particular track was on one album and one playlist, as shown in Table 3-1.

Table 3-1. Results of the query to find all entities that contain track `t`

n.name	labels(n)
"Road Trip Punta Fuego"	["Playlist"]
"Cross Road"	["Album"]

Consider the following query:

```
//003-generic-relationship-3.cypher
MATCH (t:Track {id:"15vzANxN8G9wWfwAJLLMCg"})<-[:HAS_TRACK]-(a:Album)
RETURN t,a
```

If the primary use cases consist of finding albums on which a certain track appears, this query can turn out to be inefficient—depending on how dense the track's playlist relationships are (see Figure 3-12):

- The query starts by anchoring itself on the `Track` node with the given ID.
- The query traverses every `HAS_TRACK` relationship.
- The nodes on the other end are filtered based on whether they contain the `Album` label or not.

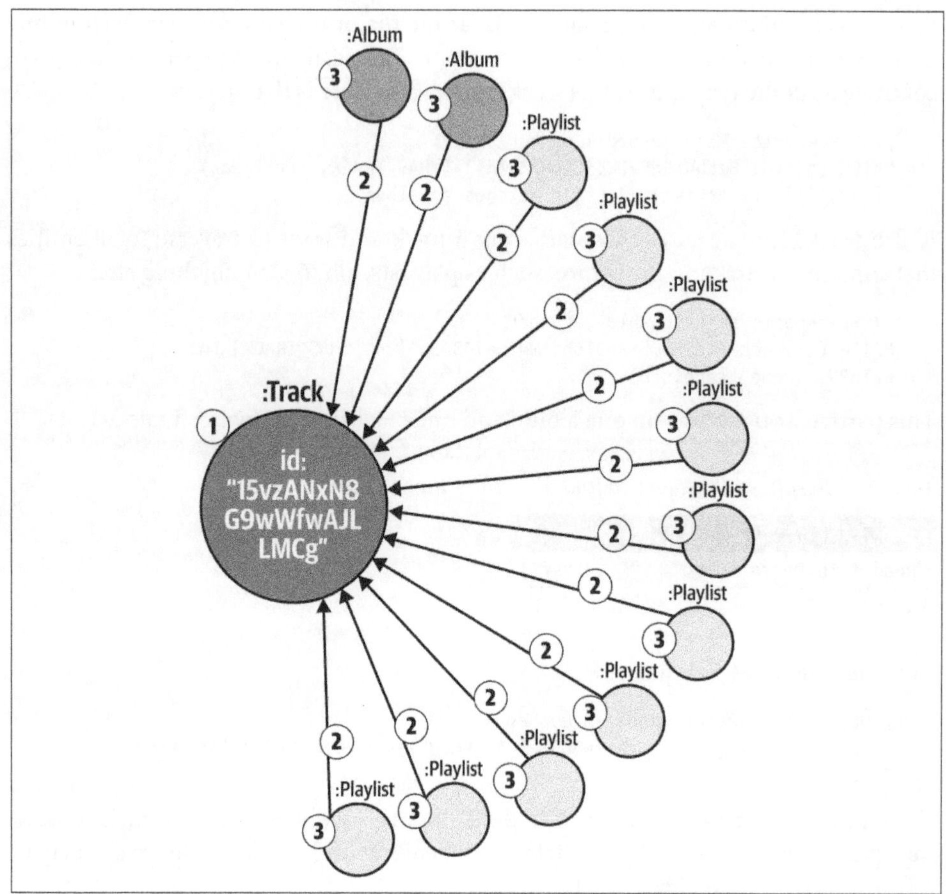

Figure 3-12. Steps taken by the Cypher execution engine to find albums of a track

This results in extra work to filter and discard the HAS_TRACK relationships to playlists. In this case, you'd refactor your graph model to find a more specific relationship type (see Figure 3-13).

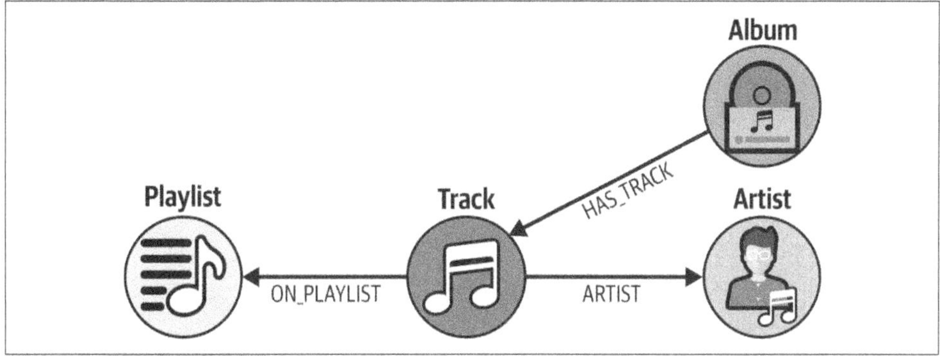

Figure 3-13. A specific relationship, `ON_PLAYLIST`, replaces the generic `HAS_TRACK` between a playlist and a track.

In cases where both traversal patterns are important, you may consider maintaining both relationship types, as in Figure 3-14. This way, generic and specific traversals remain optimal: you'd use either the `HAS_TRACK` relationship type *or* the `ON_PLAYLIST` relationship type in your queries.

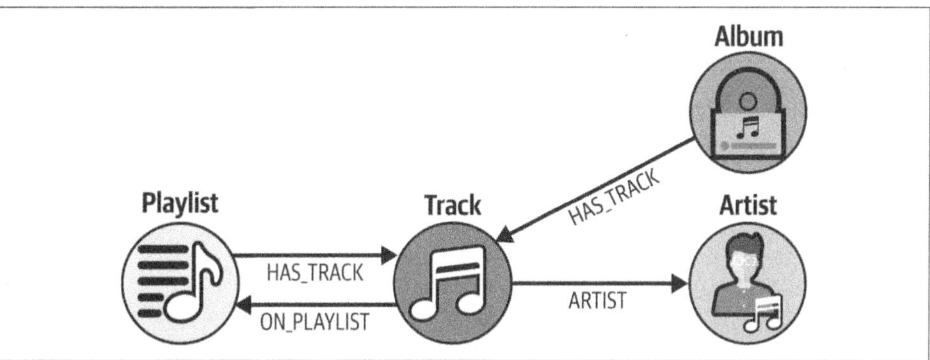

Figure 3-14. The best of both worlds: maintaining specific and generic relationships between playlists and tracks

Note that the redundancy in relationship types now means that track nodes are twice as dense, so you will incur a maintenance cost. Every time a relationship between a track and a playlist is created, updated, or deleted, the operations must be applied to two relationships instead of one.

Key Takeaways

Prefer the specific relationship as much as possible. In cases where you want to use a single relationship type to connect nodes with different labels, consider the performance hit.

Qualified Relationships

Sometimes you need to quantify the strength or weight of a relationship. You can do that in two ways: with the relationship type or with a property on the relationship.

Consider how listeners feel about a song. Figure 3-15 shows how this is modeled with a relationship type.

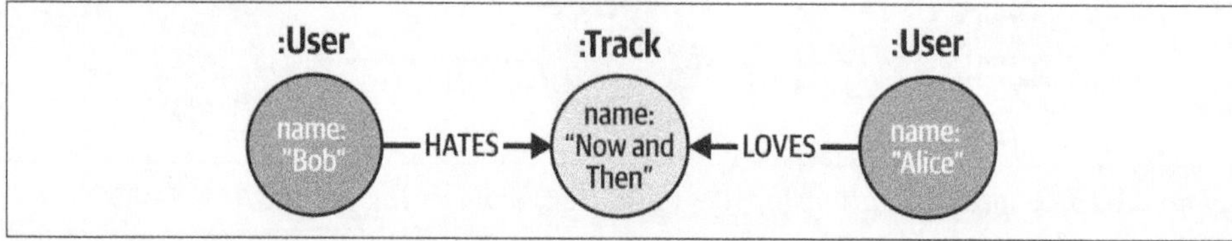

Figure 3-15. Modeling a listener's love or hate relationship with a song

The relationship types, `LOVES` or `HATES`, are explicit and simple.

You can also use a generic relationship type, as depicted in Figure 3-16. Here, a property called `level` indicates the strength of this relationship, with level 0 equivalent to "hate" and 5 meaning "love." This model supports different grades: for example, a 4 might be a "like."

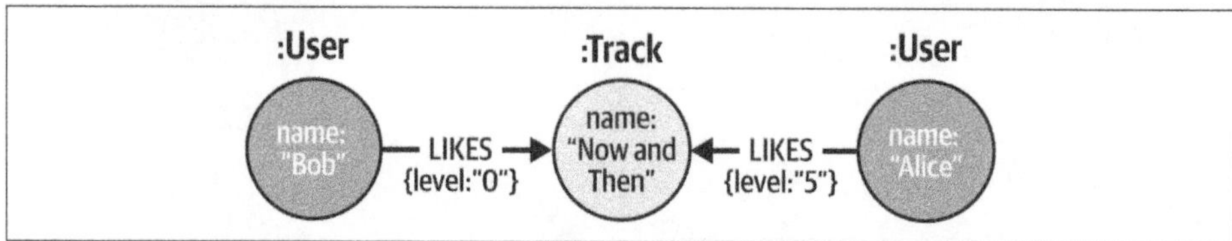

Figure 3-16. Using a quantified relationship instead of specific types

There is no single best model—your use case will help you pick the more suitable one.

If ElectricHarmony believes that its recommendations benefit from knowing whether a user loves or hates a track, then the specific relationships are perfect. When querying for tracks that a user loves, the graph traverses only the `LOVES` relationships. The `HATES` relationships don't incur any extra traversals.

What if ElectricHarmony decides to introduce a new feature by which users can rate how much they like tracks on a scale from 0 to 5? They would need to refactor the model to use a property on the relationship. All existing queries that use the `LOVES` or `HATES` relationship would also need to be refactored to use the new `LIKES` relationship type and its `level` property. As with everything, it is not worth designing this prematurely. With a property, every time the query needs to find tracks that this user hates, it will gather every `LIKES` relationship between the user and the track to inspect the `level` property and discard any that do not have value 0—wasting a lot of work.

However, if ElectricHarmony supports track ratings from the get-go, then using a generic relationship type with a property would be the right way to start, even if it only supports two values at first, 0 and 5. When ElectricHarmony is ready to introduce the equivalent of a "likes" or "OK," it won't need to refactor any existing queries. Only the value of the property will be updated or queried accordingly. Also, the property is useful to compare how different two users are when it comes to their taste for a song, or to average and calculate some score for a track. As in the previous discussion, if both cases are important, it's worth considering using both the property and the relationship, which acts as a shortcut, with maintenance as the trade-off.

Bucketed Relationships

Here is another use case that blends the previous concepts: when relationship granularity is neither coarse nor specific, the relationships are all quantified in some way, and their volume in the graph is very high.

Let's say ElectricHarmony extends its graph model with a `PLAYED` relationship. Every time a user listens to a song, a `counter` property on the `PLAYED` relationship is incremented. ElectricHarmony frequently runs demographics-based targeted campaigns, and they want to find all users aged 20 to 30 who've listened to a particular song 100 to 250 times. Executing this query execution involves:

- Traversing the coarse-grained `PLAYED` relationship between all users in this age group and the track
- Inspecting the `counter` property on all these relationships
- Retaining only the relationships with a `counter` value between 100 and 250 and discarding the rest

A specific relationship type isn't practical here, either, due to the continuous nature of the `counter` property. Neither is an alternative model where you create a `PLAYED` relationship between the user and a song every time the song is played. This would be too fine-grained and wasteful when calculating aggregate statistics.

To constrain the number of relationships traversed to the ones that you're interested in, you can create specific relationship types per bucket: for example, `PLAYED_0_99`, `PLAYED_100_250`, etc. Then, when you query for the users who listened to a song between 100 and 250 times, the query can use the `PLAYED_100_250` relationship type. Other such buckets could categorize by date ranges, scores, or weights. Only consider this approach when you can't further improve performance of the `PLAYED` relationship with a counter, since it does increase maintenance costs.

Key Takeaways

Are your queries making Neo4j do extra work to gather and discard results because a relationship type is too broadly defined? Options to improve this include using specific relationships, quantified relationships, and—if really necessary—bucketed relationships.

Bidirectional Relationships

Every relationship in Neo4j must have a *type, a direction* (outgoing or incoming), a *start node*, and an *end node*. Together, these characteristics give semantic meaning to the relationship that connects two nodes.

Even though relationships must be stored with a direction, they can be traversed or queried in either direction with no performance penalty (unlike some nonnative graph databases (*https://oreil.ly/pSrIc*)). Modeling symmetric relationships in Neo4j is an antipattern; there is no reason to do so. A *symmetric relationship* is one that is true in either direction—it means the same thing, no matter which way it is traversed.

In Chapter 1, you created a `SIMILAR` relationship between similar playlists (see Figure 3-17). This is a good example of a symmetric relationship. No matter which way the traversal goes between the two playlists, playlist A is similar to playlist B and playlist B is similar to playlist A.

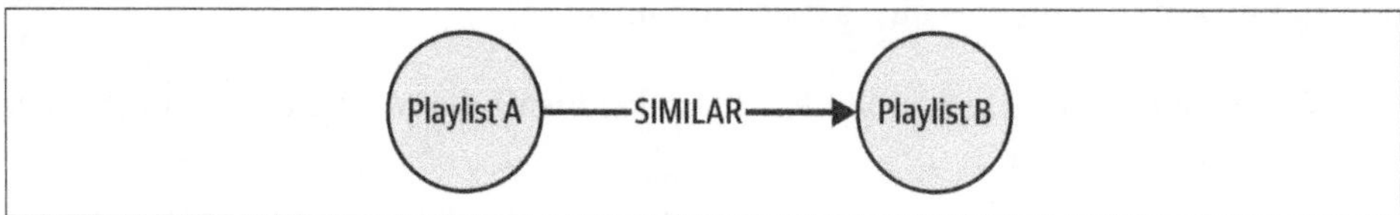

Figure 3-17. Representing a symmetric relationship

Storing the relationship in both directions, as in Figure 3-18, is redundant and causes two significant problems.

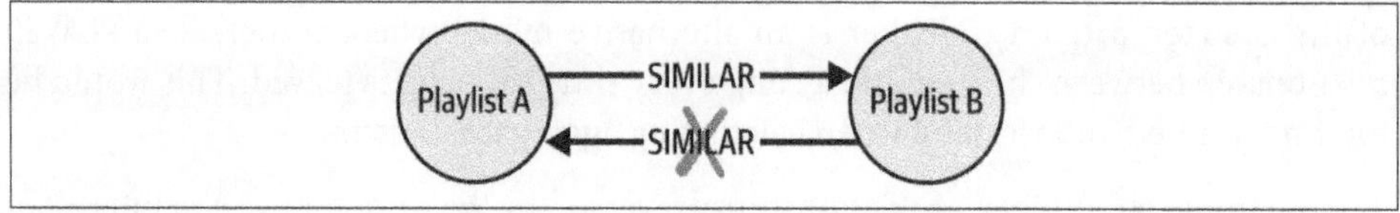

Figure 3-18. Do not store symmetric relationships in both directions.

First, it duplicates data, doubling the amount of data that must be stored. The second is that traversal will occur in both directions—one traversal across each relationship—when matching with an undirected pattern. For example:

```
MATCH (a:Playlist)-[:SIMILAR]-(b:Playlist)
RETURN a,b
```

In Chapter 1 (see Figure 1-20), you created bidirectional relationships, resulting in an extra traversal for each pair of playlists. Here's an example of this double traversal:

```
//005-double-traversal.cypher
MATCH path=(track1:Track {id:"0BB9eUBBaaX6GALSYNcEp7"})-
[*3]-(track2:Track {id:"2KmEgiY8fQs0G6WNxtzQKr"})
RETURN path
```

This query finds paths of length 3 between two tracks. Using the graph built in Chapter 1, this query matches 10 paths because it traverses the `SIMILAR` relationship twice in connected playlists. The bidirectional relationships stand out in the graph results in Figure 3-19.

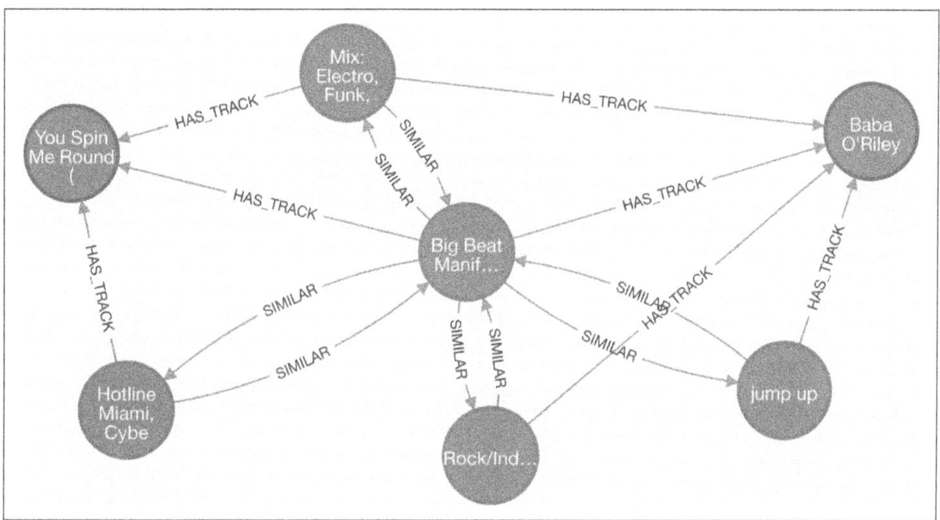

Figure 3-19. `SIMILAR` relationships were previously stored in both directions.

Switch to the table view to see the number of paths (records) returned. Figure 3-20 shows that 10 were matched: twice the number of playlists.

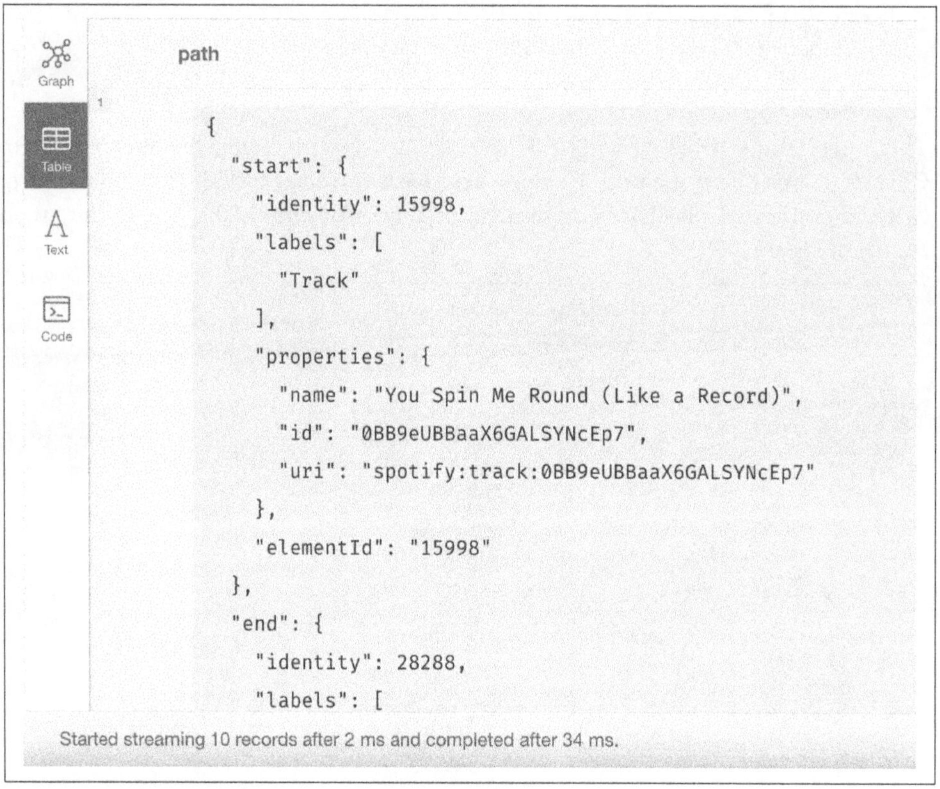

Graph
Table
Text
Code

path


```
{
  "start": {
    "identity": 15998,
    "labels": [
      "Track"
    ],
    "properties": {
      "name": "You Spin Me Round (Like a Record)",
      "id": "0BB9eUBBaaX6GALSYNcEp7",
      "uri": "spotify:track:0BB9eUBBaaX6GALSYNcEp7"
    },
    "elementId": "15998"
  },
  "end": {
    "identity": 28288,
    "labels": [
```


Started streaming 10 records after 2 ms and completed after 34 ms.

Figure 3-20. Five playlists were expected to match, but 10 records were returned due to the traversal in either direction across the `SIMILAR` relationships.

You will now apply the good modeling practice you've just learned and refactor your graph to keep just one `SIMILAR` relationship between playlists. The graph is pretty small, so you will first drop all `SIMILAR` relationships and then re-create them.

To drop all `SIMILAR` relationships, run:

```
//006-drop-similar.cypher
MATCH ()-[r:SIMILAR]-()
DELETE r
```

Then re-create them, using the query from "Materializing similarities" in Chapter 1 but with one modification: you'll remove the direction from the `MERGE` of the `SIMILAR` relationship:

```
//007-single-similar-rel.cypher
MATCH path=(p:Playlist)-[r1:HAS_TRACK]->(track)<-[r2:HAS_TRACK]-(other:Playlist)
WITH p AS playlistLeft, other AS playlistRight,
     collect({track: track,
              positionLeft: r1.position,
              positionRight: r2.position}) AS commonTracks
WHERE size(commonTracks) > 5
WITH playlistLeft, playlistRight,
     size([track in commonTracks WHERE
           track.positionLeft = track.positionRight])
           AS tracksWithSamePosition,
     size([track in commonTracks WHERE NOT
           track.positionLeft = track.positionRight])
           AS tracksAtDifferentPosition
MERGE (playlistLeft)-[r:SIMILAR]-(playlistRight)
SET r.samePosition = tracksWithSamePosition,
r.notSamePosition = tracksAtDifferentPosition
```

This doesn't mean that there is no direction now. In fact, Neo4j simply does not allow us to create relationships that look like the ones in Figure 3-21.

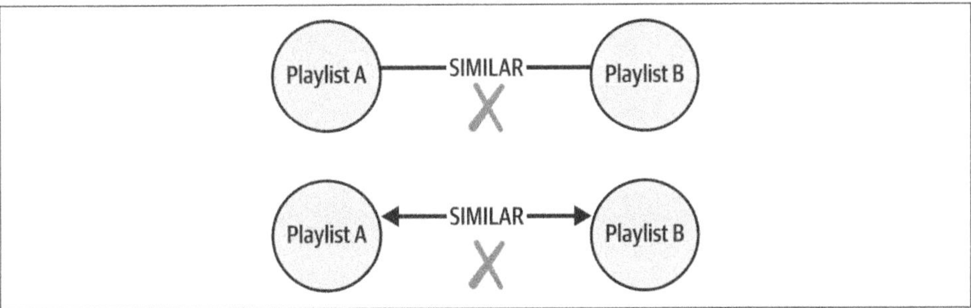

Figure 3-21. Every relationship in Neo4j is stored with a direction. The two patterns above are disallowed.

`MERGE` is `MATCH` or `CREATE`. Since `MATCH (playlistLeft)-[r:SIMILAR]-(playlistRight)` will find a `SIMILAR` relationship between two playlists if it exists in either direction, it will not create a new one. This results in one and only one `SIMILAR` relationship connecting two playlists. If nothing is matched, then the relationship is created in the outgoing direction from the left node to the right, since the direction is not explicitly mentioned.

Now run the pathfinding (*005-double-traversal.cypher*) query again. Apart from the cleaner visual (see Figure 3-22), it has matched half the number of paths we expected.

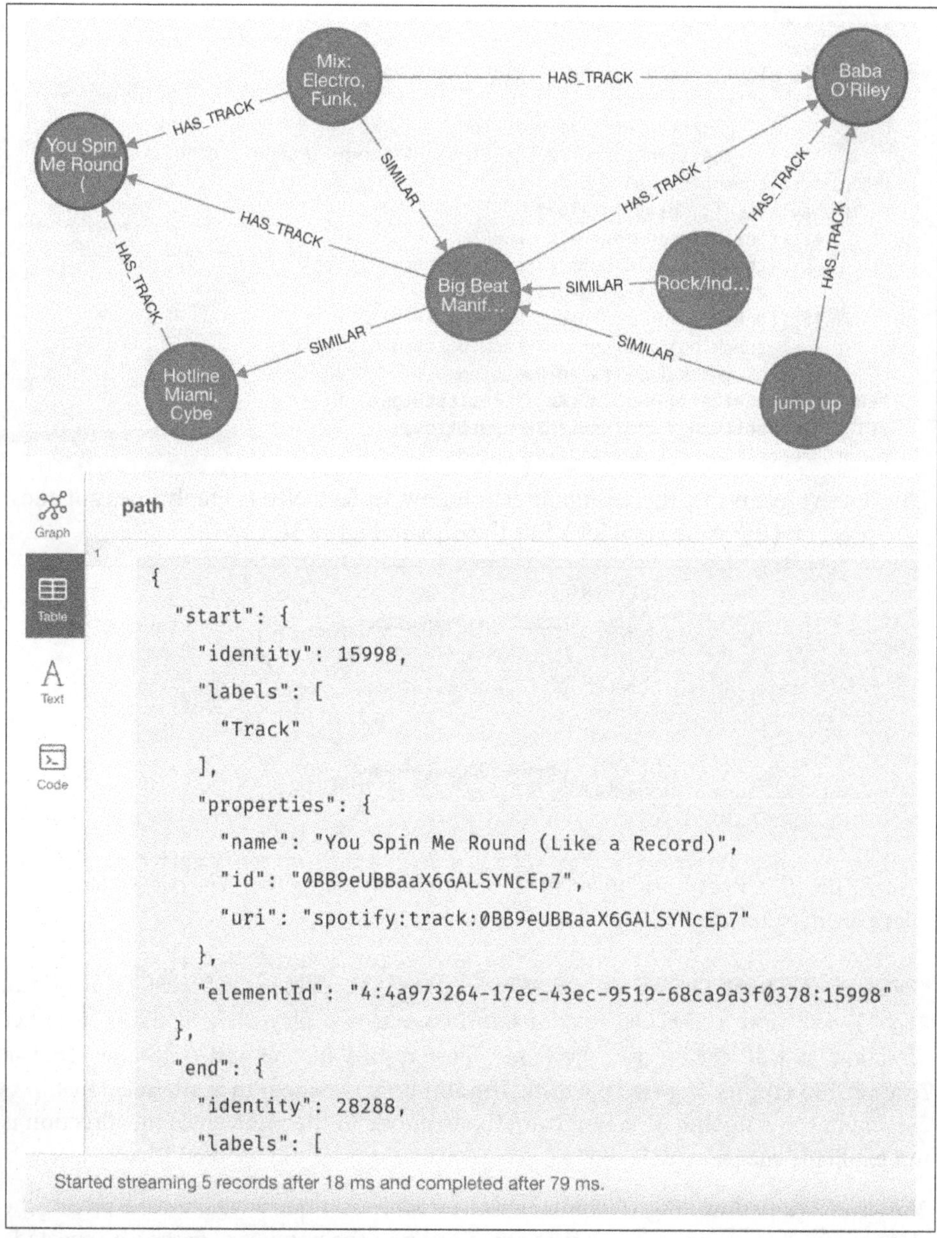

Figure 3-22. A single `SIMILAR` relationship results in half as many records as compared to the initial query.

Other examples of symmetric relationship types are `SPOUSE`, `PARTNER`, `SIBLING`, and `LIVES_WITH`. The `HAS_TRACK` relationship in Figure 3-23, outgoing from `Album` to `Track`, embodies the semantics that an album has a track.

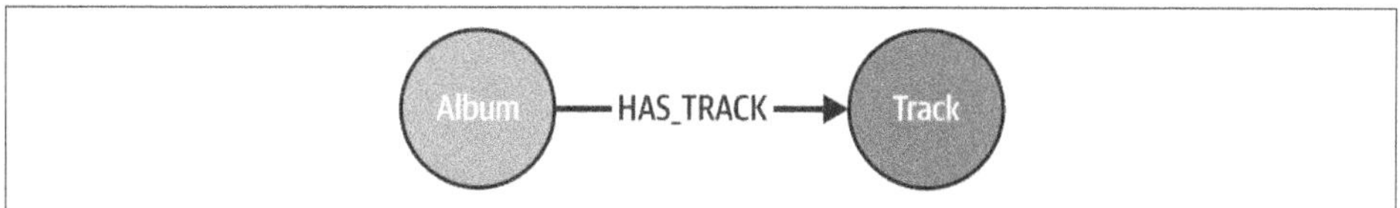

Figure 3-23. The relationship between an album and a track

`HAS_TRACK` implies that the track is on the album. Traversing from the track to the album requires reversing direction and produces identical results. Adding a relationship in the opposite direction with `ON_ALBUM`, to make it "bidirectional," such as in Figure 3-24, is redundant and not recommended.

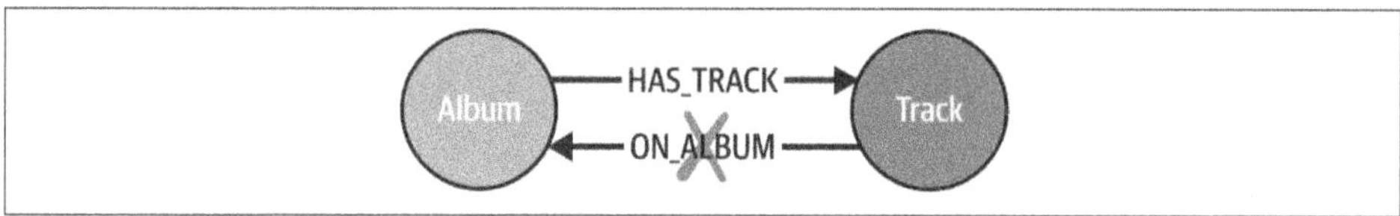

Figure 3-24. Do not add redundant relationships to navigate in the opposite direction.

When choosing names for relationships, choose the one that is most commonly used in your business domain. If you are modeling family relations and you always speak of "parents" ("A is the parent of B"), then use `PARENT`. But, if the more frequent usage is "child" ("B is the child of A") then use `CHILD`. It helps greatly when reading queries—you won't have to reverse the concept in your head. It also makes it much easier for business stakeholders to understand the model. Of course, now that you've read this section, you will *not* model it like in Figure 3-25.

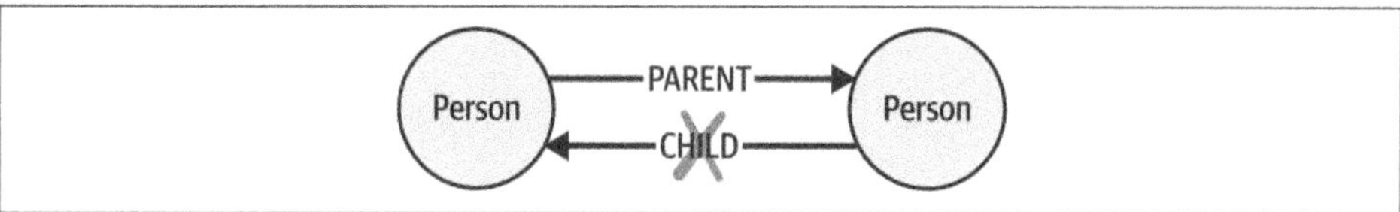

Figure 3-25. Choose the relationship type that better matches your domain and omit the reverse concept.

Conversely, a relationship like `FOLLOWS` (think of a person following another person on X/Twitter) is not symmetric, so creating two relationships—one in either direction—is the right thing to do.

Key Takeaways

Maintain a single relationship for a symmetric or bidirectional concept. The relationship type should be named so that it is coherent with your domain.

Summary

In this chapter, you've learned the principles of graph modeling and how your use cases will determine the most appropriate solution. As with most things, there are trade-offs between various models, and you're now equipped to spot them and pick the optimal model for your use case. The next chapter continues with modeling and highlights common patterns, as well as how to refactor your graph.

CHAPTER 4

Modeling and Refactoring Patterns

Now that you've mastered the principles of graph modeling, you're ready to explore some other modeling patterns. You'll learn to recognize when to apply these patterns and weigh their pros and cons. Sooner or later you'll also need to refactor your graph as your use cases and model evolve, so the second half of this chapter takes you through refactoring patterns with a hands-on approach.

Hyperedges: N-way Relationships

There's a new trend—everybody appears to be interested in covers of songs. ElectricHarmony wants to jump onto the bandwagon by introducing a new feature that helps listeners find covers of their favorite tracks easily. This feature should also help them discover if some of their favorite tracks are indeed covers—and, if so, who the original artist is. You find yourself at the whiteboard with the team once again to model this use case.

The most obvious way to start is like in Figure 4-1: by specifying whether the artist's recording of the track is a cover or not on the `ARTIST` relationship to the `Track`.

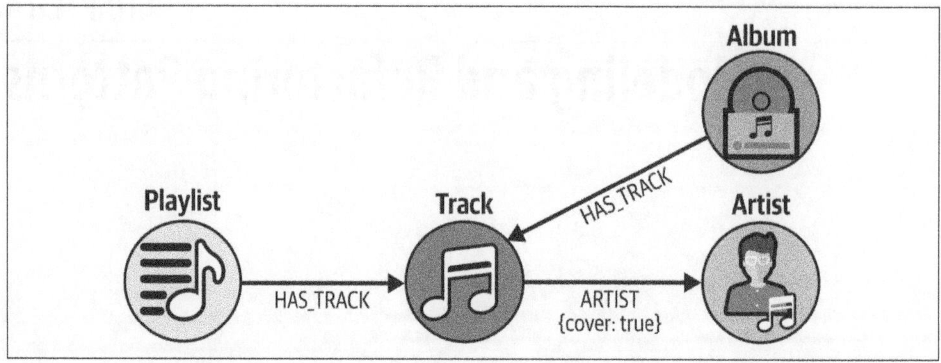

Figure 4-1. Quantifying the `ARTIST` relationship to indicate whether the track is a cover or not

Good modeling practice involves revisiting existing use cases to see if your refactoring has impacted them (perhaps adversely). You immediately think back to a key use case—fetching the track artist. So far, ElectricHarmony has leaned toward always showing a track's original artist, and you don't want that to change. However, now that this information is contained in a property on the relationship, Neo4j is doing extra work to traverse all the `ARTIST` relationships from a `TRACK`, examine the `cover` property value, and discard the majority. While that isn't a major problem (because it is rare for tracks to have an extremely high number of artists), your team doesn't feel like this is the right solution.

Instead, based on what you've learned in the previous chapter about relationship granularity, you decide to introduce a new relationship type: COVERED_BY (see Figure 4-2).

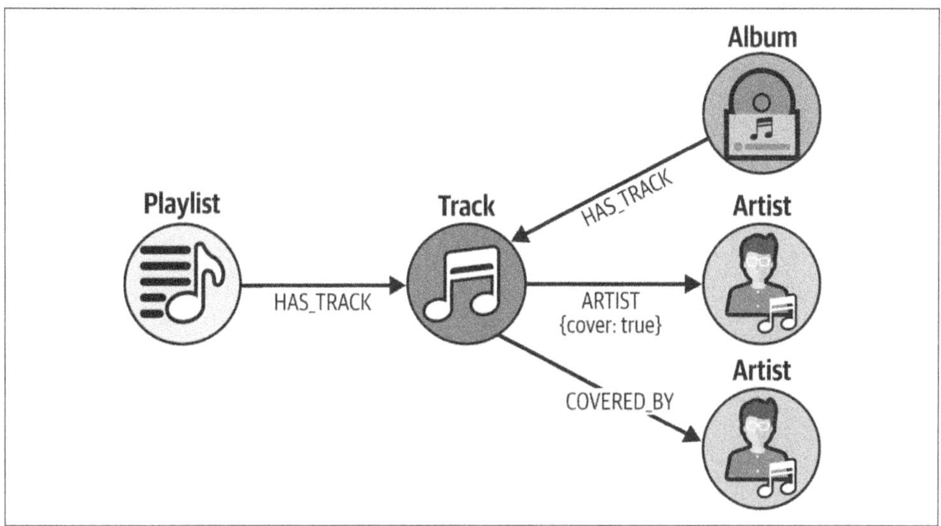

Figure 4-2. COVERED_BY is a new relationship type introduced to represent the fact that an artist has covered a track.

This leaves the key use case undisturbed. When Neo4j needs to fetch covers—or conversely, find all tracks that a particular artist has covered, it traverses the COVERED_BY relationship.

What about finding any artist who has performed any version of the track? Simply include both relationship types in the pattern and Neo4j will traverse them both:

```
MATCH (t:Track {id:"4J4gApJKSC0himDViFotdy"})-[:ARTIST|COVERED_BY]-(a:Artist)
RETURN a
```

Draw some examples on the whiteboard (like in Figure 4-3) to validate that this approach works.

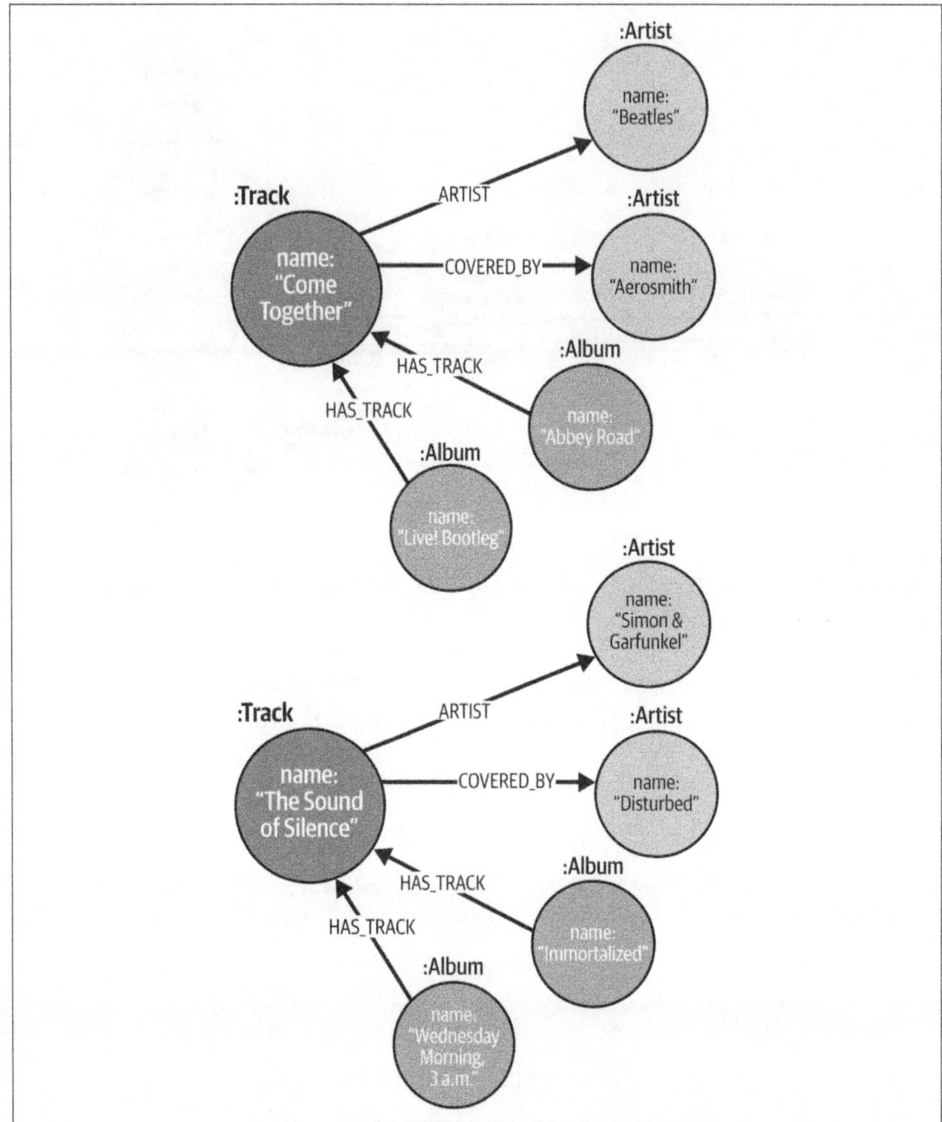

Figure 4-3. Representing some data using the new model to validate use cases

It does work: it's easy to find both the original artist and other artists who've covered these tracks. But does it really work? Are you now asking your team whether it was Simon & Garfunkel or Disturbed who recorded the album *Immortalized*? What happened?

The model has now lost information: it is no longer possible to associate an album with a particular version of a track. What you want is an *n-way relationship*, one that connects more than two nodes. The model in Figure 4-4 would be ideal, but in graph databases such as Neo4j, a relationship must have exactly two nodes—one on either end.

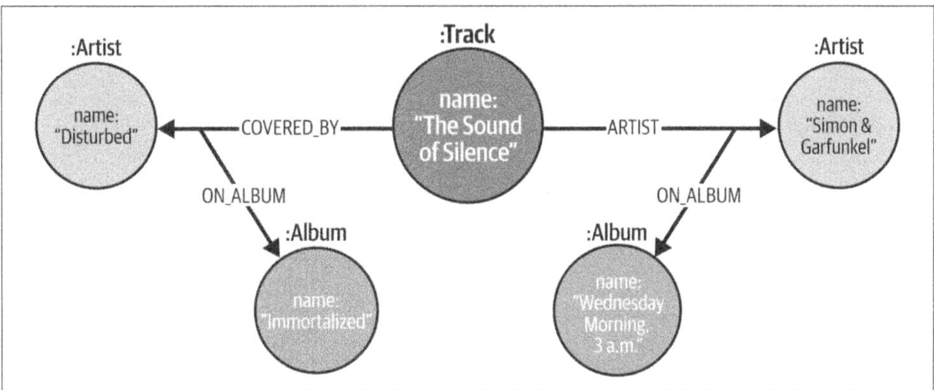

Figure 4-4. An n-way relationship, which is not supported

The solution here is to capture the shared context at the junction of the n-way relationship into a node called a *hyperedge*. This hyperedge is bound to its related nodes, and the data it holds is only applicable in this local context.

The new intermediate nodes in Figure 4-5 are represented by the label `Recording`. Every time a new version of a track is created by the ingestion process, a new `Recording` node must be created to hold context for that particular recording. What's nice about this model is that it can be extended to model other concepts that are specific to the hyperedge, such as whether the track won any rewards or recognitions.

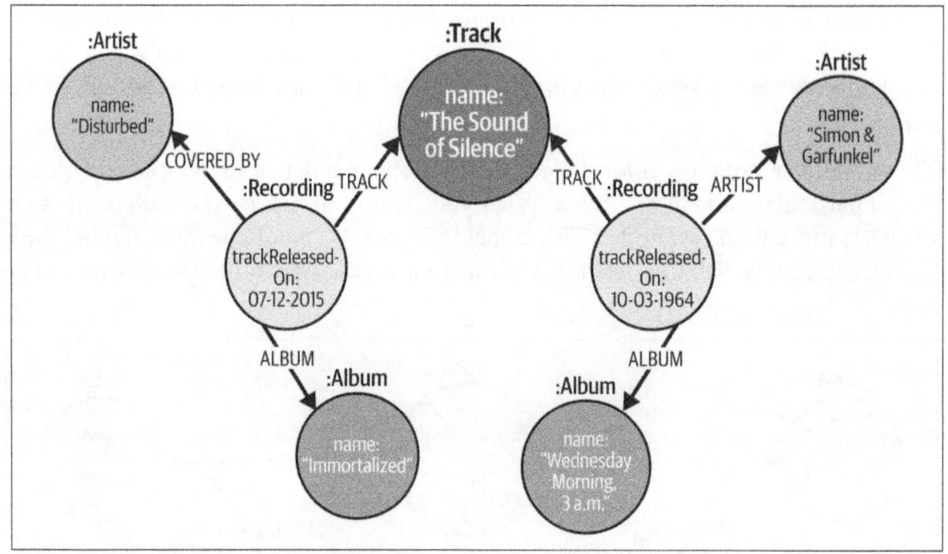

Figure 4-5. Introducing the `Recording` node

In Figure 4-6, the graph makes it clear via the `Establishment` node that the Simon & Garfunkel version was inducted into the Grammy Hall of Fame in 2004. The previous models would have obscured this information.

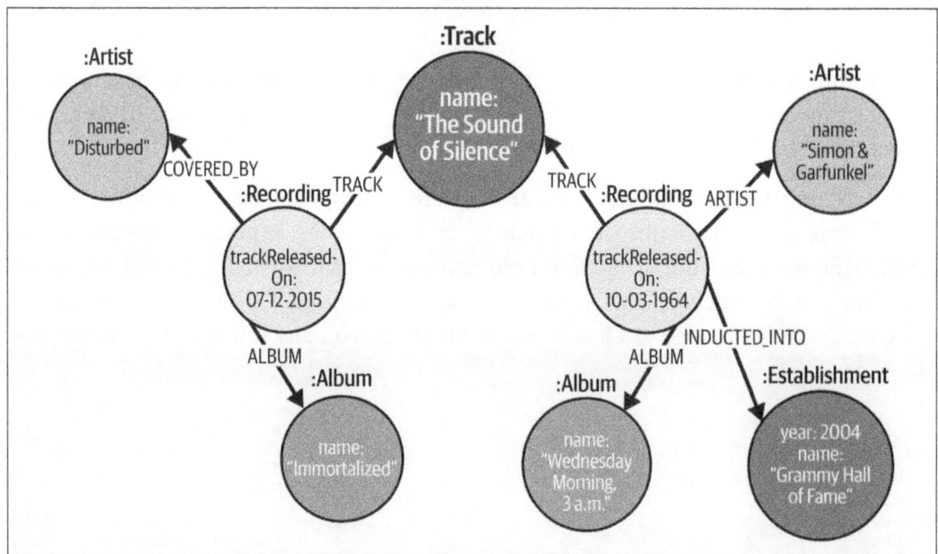

Figure 4-6. Adding context to the `Recording` node with new relationships such as `INDUCTED_INTO`

The model can also represent performances, since graphs' schema-free nature supports exceptions and variations with ease. Figure 4-7 depicts how not every track has an `Album`.

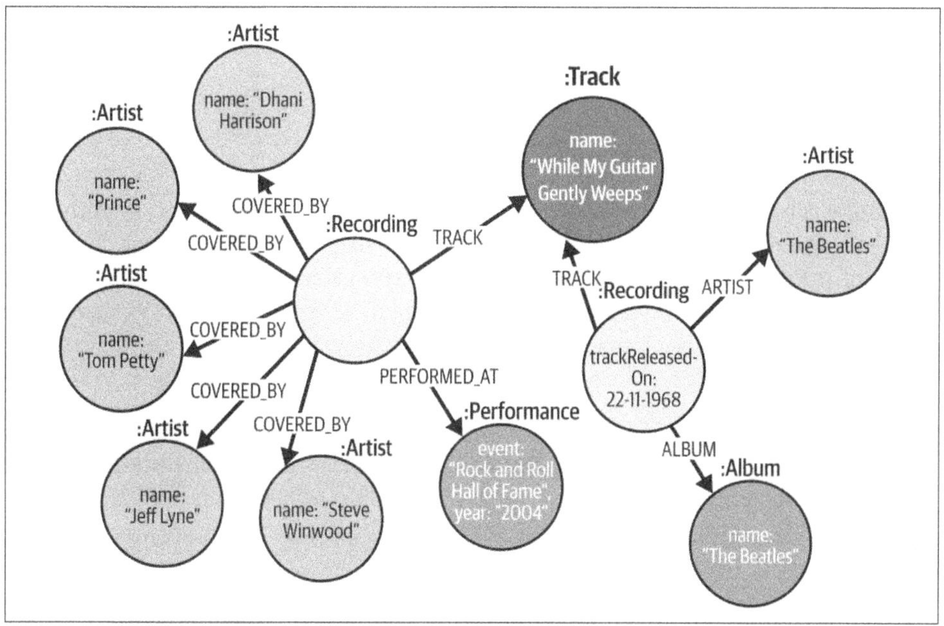

Figure 4-7. Neo4j's schema-free nature lets you attach additional information to the graph where it is available, such as on the `Performance` node.

Usually, intermediate nodes emerge to be entities themselves that were previously undiscovered. If that's not the case, consider carefully whether you want to use them: remember, they add more nodes to the graph and, consequently, more hops during traversal.

Key Takeaways

Use intermediate nodes in place of n-way relationships when your graph would otherwise lose context that cannot be represented clearly by two nodes and the relationship that connects them. If you find yourself needing to start a traversal at a relationship, that's a hint that these might be a good idea. Weigh the trade-offs of introducing more nodes into the graph that will also have to be created or updated during data ingestion flows.

Time-Based Versioning

A few business domains, such as infrastructure and retail, have use cases to version their graphs over time.[1] Applications of this concept include:

- Determining how the network changed over time
- Tracking behavior changes
- Updating entities without affecting past records

This section applies a variation of the *time-based versioning* pattern to a simplified use case for ElectricHarmony: versioning a user's "Favorites" playlist to track the music tastes of the user over time. This feature will be especially useful by applying *time decay* to artists and genres—applying lower weights to artists and genres that a user might have loved in the past, but not as much now, to improve the relevance of recommendations.

Every user has a default `Favorites` playlist which contains their favorite songs, as shown in Figure 4-8. Over time, they add or remove tracks from this playlist. To apply the principles of time-based versioning, you'll separate the object from the state: here, the object is the `Favorites` playlist, and the state is its contents at various points in time.

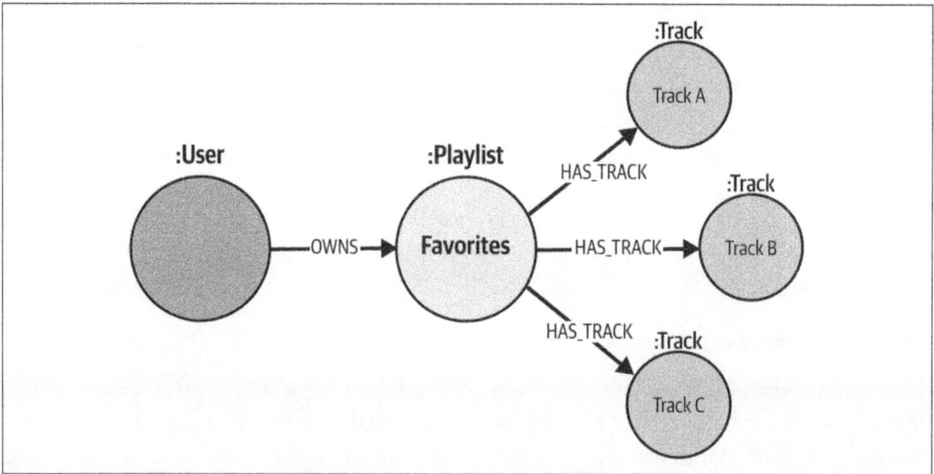

Figure 4-8. The default `Favorites` playlist for every user

1 A common modeling pattern for this was first introduced by Ian Robinson (*https://oreil.ly/960CK*); although the original article appears to have vanished, the topic has subsequently been covered by Ljubica Lazarevic (*https://oreil.ly/ad_Ay*).

After some debate about time-period granularity, ElectricHarmony settles on six months to detect if a user's listening preference has changed. This means that their application will create and maintain a new state for six months. You decide to capture this timeframe as a property of relationships between the objects and their states, as pictured in Figure 4-9.

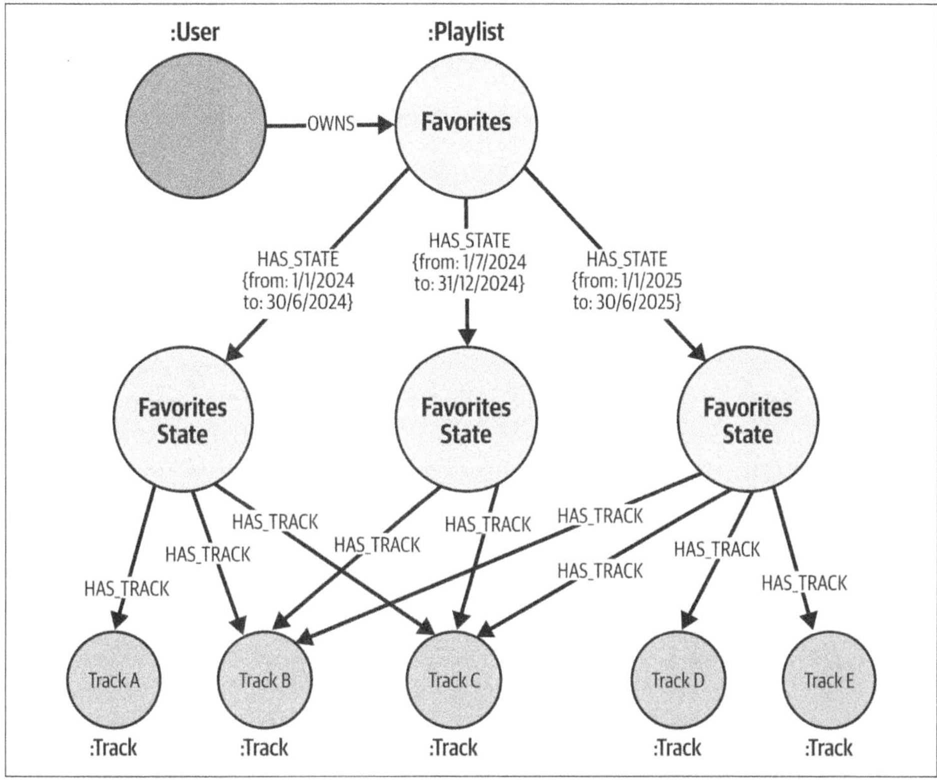

Figure 4-9. Separating the object and its state

Every time a track is added or removed from the Favorites playlist, the `HAS_TRACK` relationship is created or deleted between the `Track` and the active `FavoritesState` node for the current time period, which is matched with a condition in the query, such as:

```
MATCH (u:User {id:"100"})-[:OWNS]->(p:Playlist {name:"Favorites"})
        -[r:HAS_STATE]->(f:FavoritesState)
WHERE r.from <= timestamp() <=r.to
RETURN f
```

It's worth familiarizing yourself with the *temporal instant* types (*https://oreil.ly/bqGEp*) available in Neo4j. In this case, you have two main options. One is to represent time as a `Timestamp` in milliseconds past the epoch (midnight UTC on January 1, 1970). The other is to represent it as a `DateTime` or other fitting temporal type. Timestamps are integers, which are compact and straightforward to compare. However, timestamps for dates before the epoch will be represented as negative integers. A `DateTime` is a richer object, making it easier to calculate durations, convert formats, or extract components (such as the day or month). For time versioning in this example, a timestamp does the job.

Introducing time-based versioning brings its own trade-offs—the model is more complex, you need to adjust your queries, and writing data to the graph is more involved. One way of reducing complexity in the main graph is to offload *all states except the active state* to another database. Chapter 10 explains how to do this with composite databases.

Another avenue to explore is encoding the time period into the relationship type. This is helpful for cases where you want to capture when relationships were created or when they were valid or applicable. Recall the section "Bucketed Relationships" on page 97—the relationship from the Favorites playlist to a track could also be recorded as `FAVORITE_2024_H1` for the time period of the first half of the year.

Key Takeaways

Time-based versioning is useful when you want to track or audit changes made to the graph or go backward in time to compare the states of the graph. It adds complexity, however, so consider carefully.

Representing Sequences

Recall that, in Chapter 1, you learned that `Playlists` are related to their tracks via the `HAS_TRACK` relationship, which includes a `position` property representing the order of the tracks (see Figure 4-10).

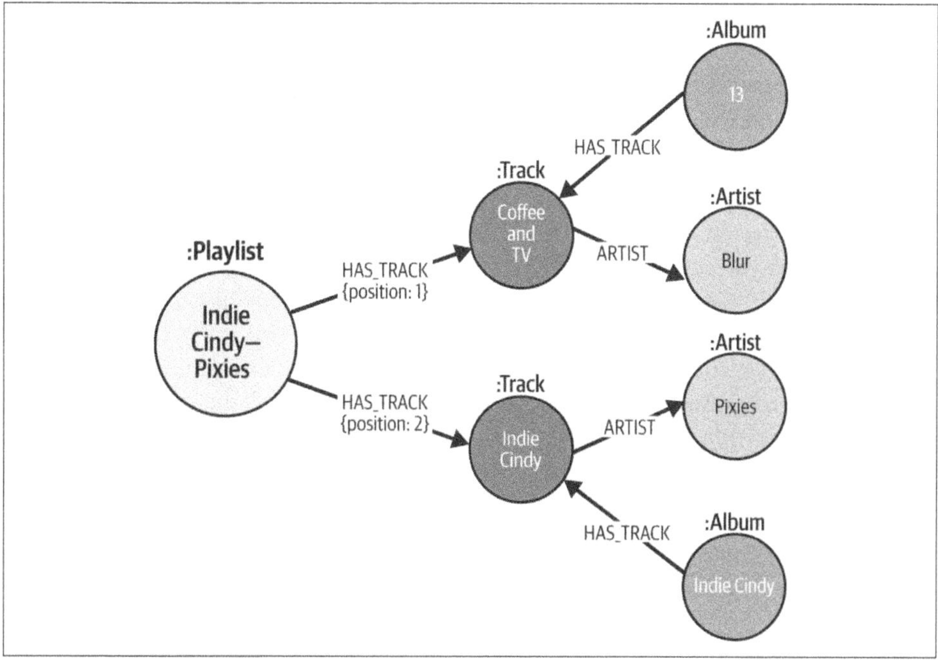

Figure 4-10. The graph model for playlists and their tracks

Although this did the job for your proof-of-concept model, while working with it, the team has uncovered some disadvantages:

Finding the last track in a playlist
: The recommendation query in the proof-of-concept model is based on the last track in a playlist, which is queried in an awkward way. Neo4j traverses every `HAS_TRACK` relationship from the playlist to inspect the `position` property and compare it to the total number of tracks on the playlist (determined by the `COUNT` subquery):

```
MATCH (p)-[r:HAS_TRACK]->(t)
WHERE r.position = COUNT { (p)-[:HAS_TRACK]->() }
WITH p AS playlist, t AS lastTrack
```

It also assumes that all `position` properties are correct and sequential, with no holes, since the last track position must match the count of all tracks. This brings us to the next problem.

Maintaining track order
: Users frequently reorder tracks in a playlist: new tracks are added, others are removed. Every time one of these operations takes place, your code must recalculate the positions of all tracks in the playlist.

You can make that happen by writing a procedure that extends Neo4j (*https://oreil.ly/rrp53*). The disadvantage of going down this route is that you have to write procedures in a JVM language (such as Java or Scala) and compile them into Java archive (JAR) files, which you must then deploy as plugins to the Neo4j database server.

Since you're working with a graph, there is a more natural way to model sequences—whether they are tracks in a playlist, episodes in a TV series, or jobs in your employment history: linked lists. You'll also find linked lists to be especially useful when splitting text into chunks and linking them in order to represent the original document—Chapter 13 on generative AI, will refer to this concept. *Linked lists* are fundamental data structures where each element maintains a reference or pointer to the next. The graph fetches the elements in sequence by simply following the pointer to the next element in the list. The complexity of insertion and deletion is, at best, `O(1)` and, at worst, `O(n)`.

In a graph, the pointers are implicitly represented by relationships, and traversing across relationships is the sweet spot for graph databases. Figure 4-11 shows a playlist modeled as a linked list.

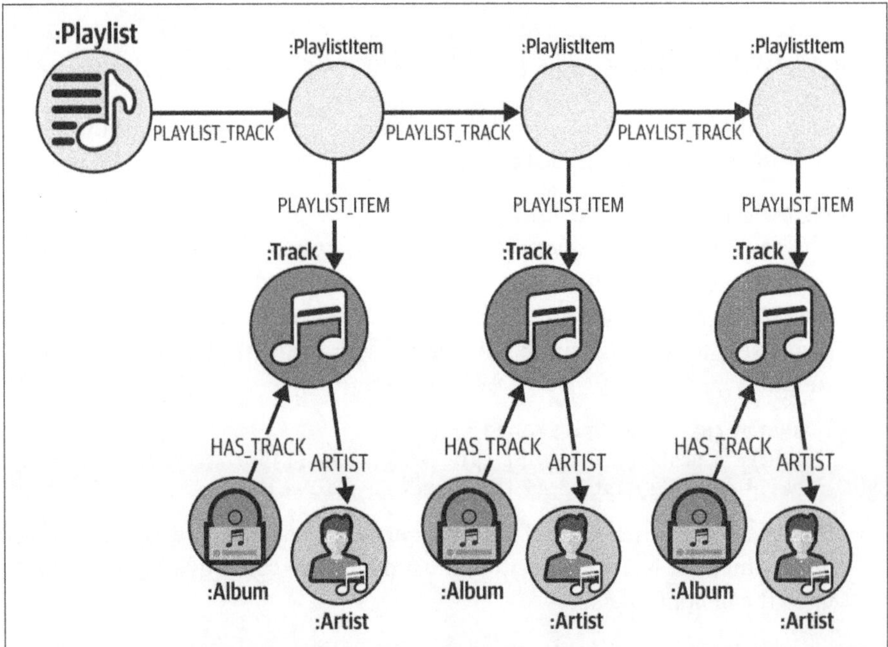

Figure 4-11. Modeling tracks in a playlist as a linked list

Let's connect some of the concepts you've read in Chapter 3. The coarse-grained `HAS_TRACK` relationship from the `Playlist` to a `Track` has been replaced with a more specific relationship, `PLAYLIST_TRACK` (the `PLAYLIST_TRACK` relationship can also be called `NEXT`—it's just a matter of preference).

Consider Figure 4-12. Can you tell which tracks are part of which playlist?

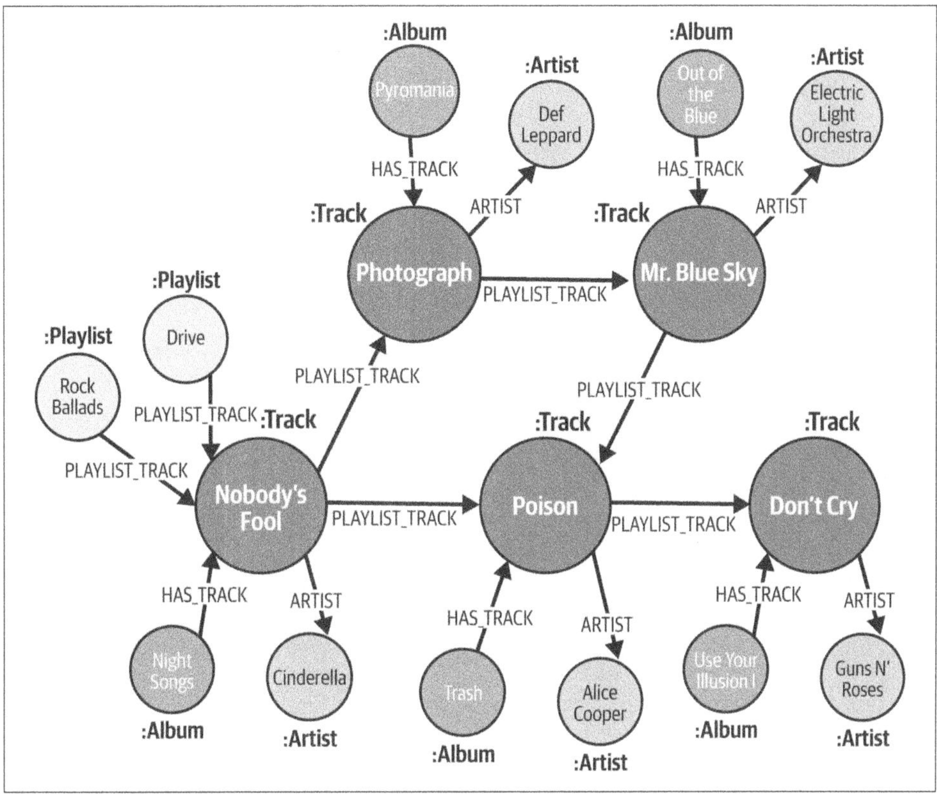

Figure 4-12. A linked list of tracks directly related to each other via a `PLAYLIST_TRACK` relationship

You can probably tell that "Nobody's Fool" is the first track of two playlists, "Rock Ballads" and "Drive," but the tracks that follow it in each playlist are unclear.

To avoid losing context about how tracks are related to playlists, let's introduce a new node: `PlaylistItem`. The `PlaylistItem` node makes it much easier for the graph to traverse the playlist and to modify its order.

Figure 4-13 contains one more modification you can make. Since finding the last track of any `Playlist` is a top use case for ElectricHarmony, instead of traversing all tracks in the sequence, you can give the graph a shortcut and send it straight to the last track by adding a `LAST_PLAYLIST_TRACK` relationship. Only add this relationship, however, if it's useful for the majority of your use cases or if it shows a substantial performance advantage when traversing over extremely long playlists. Premature optimization in the form of adding the `LAST_PLAYLIST_TRACK` leads to issues in other areas—you increase complexity because the pointer to the tail of the linked list has to be maintained, especially when the list is updated frequently.

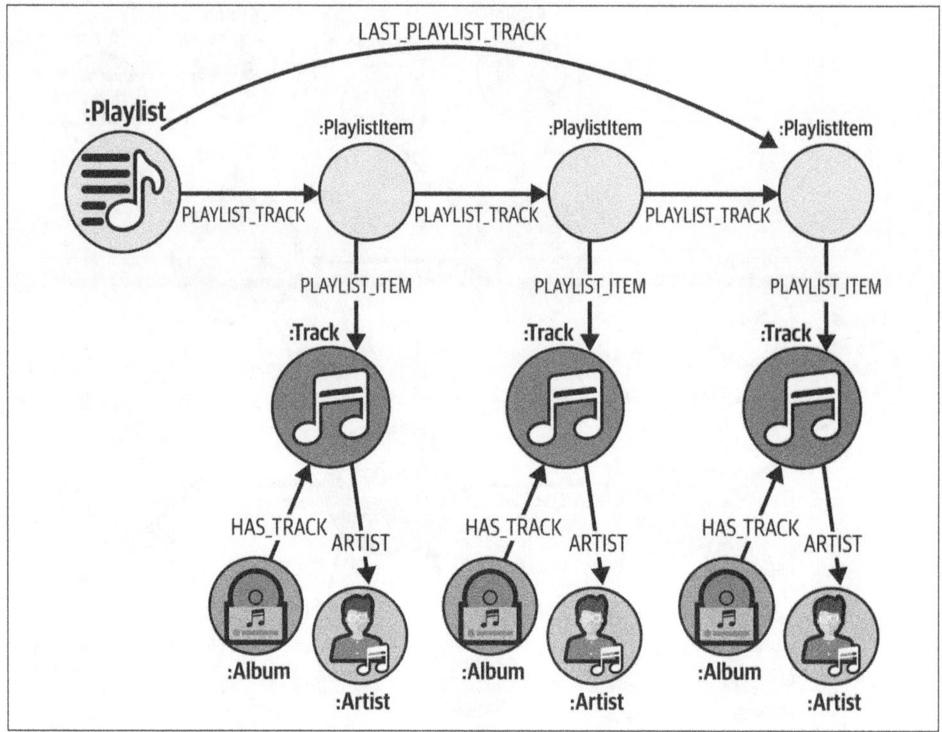

Figure 4-13. The `LAST_PLAYLIST_TRACK` navigates directly to the last track on a playlist.

The recommendation query you wrote on Day 4 in Chapter 1 contained the following segment to find the last track:

```
// Find the last track
MATCH (p)-[r:HAS_TRACK]->(t)
WHERE r.position = COUNT { (p)-[:HAS_TRACK]->() }
WITH p AS playlist, t AS lastTrack, popularTracks
```

With the introduction of the `LAST_PLAYLIST_TRACK` relationship, this part of the query reduces to:

```
MATCH (p)-[:LAST_PLAYLIST_ITEM]->()<-[:PLAYLIST_ITEM]-(lastTrack)
```

In the next section, you will refactor the graph you created in Chapter 1 to this enhanced model.

Be careful not to model a doubly linked list data structure by introducing a `PREVIOUS_PLAYLIST_TRACK` relationship to navigate the playlist in reverse, as shown in Figure 4-14.

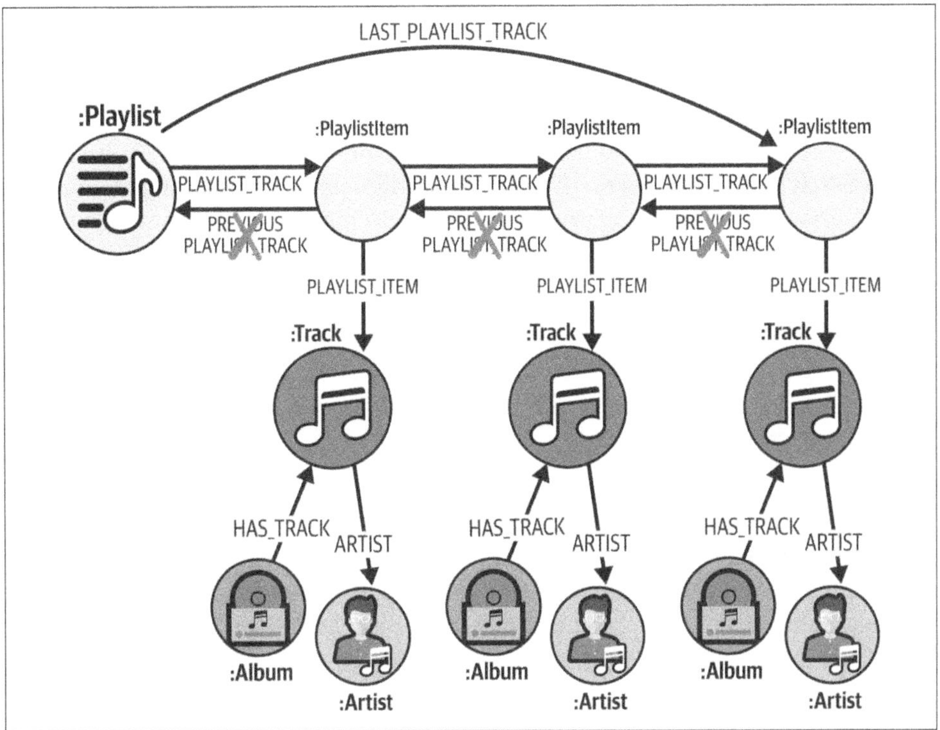

Figure 4-14. Do not model doubly linked lists in a graph.

As you learned in the section on bidirectional relationships, these are redundant and bad practice. Remember that Neo4j can traverse the relationship in either direction without any performance penalty.

Key Takeaways

When you encounter sequences in your domain, think about whether you can model them as linked lists for easier modification and faster traversal through the sequenced nodes. Weigh the pros and cons of query complexity against the frequency of updates to the list.

Refactoring Patterns

At some point, you'll need to enhance your graph model for performance or new data or new use cases, and that means refactoring your graph data. There are two basic ways to refactor:

Reingest all data
: This method assumes that the graph can be completely reconstructed from original sources. Here, you modify the ingestion queries or scripts to write data to the graph as per the new model. The benefit of this approach is that ingestion scripts are always current. The downside is that replacing the graph in production will require some minimal downtime.

Refactor live
: When you can't reconstruct your graph or when it's quite small, live refactoring is the way to go—refactor queries are executed directly on the live graph. Typically, you'll do this on a backup of the graph and validate it before applying the refactor in production.

You can also combine these two approaches. If data is constantly streaming into the graph, refactoring will feel like a never-ending quest. One way of tackling this problem is to first update the ingestion scripts or queries to write new data to the graph in accordance with the refactored model. This serves to stop propagating the current graph model. Then you can perform a live refactor to address the current graph.

In most cases, you can maintain backward compatibility. The current and refactored version of the graph and applications can coexist provided they are not in conflict (for example, due to a changed property data type or removed label), which lets you migrate queries gradually with no downtime. However, you need to plan what to do in case things go wrong. For example, if the graph is too large to apply the refactor in a single transaction, you run the risk of applying a partial refactor until you can reattempt the rest of the transactions that have failed. This is why we advise keeping both versions of the graph in place until you've verified the success of the operation. Then you can remove the previous version.

A huge benefit of graph refactoring is that it lets dependent applications catch up and migrate over time. You can phase out the "old" graph model once all queries and applications have switched over to the new one. This is similar to Martin Fowler's description of the Strangler Fig Application (*https://oreil.ly/p6N9k*) (You will see this in action in the following sections.)

You've already performed the first type of refactoring: in Chapter 1, you converted the data type of the `position` property of the `HAS_TRACK` relationship from a string to an integer by updating the LOAD CSV query and reingesting the data. You also removed the redundant SIMILAR relationship in the previous chapter.

The next three sections describe a few more refactoring patterns that you're likely to come across, all of which use live refactoring.

Refactoring to Change the Type of a Relationship

After you read the section on relationship granularity in Chapter 3, you decide to refactor the graph to replace the HAS_TRACK relationship between Playlists and Tracks with a ON_PLAYLIST relationship from Tracks to Playlists.

Continue to use the graph from Chapter 3 which built upon the first graph named chapter01.

Neo4j does not support changing the type of a relationship, so you need to delete the HAS_TRACK relationship type and create ON_PLAYLIST. Since you want to keep the graph backward compatible until ElectricHarmony's engineering team updates their recommendation queries, you'll refactor in the following stages.

Stage 1

Match all HAS_TRACK relationships from a Playlist to a Track. For each pair of Track and Playlist matches, create an ON_PLAYLIST relationship from the Track to the Playlist and set the position on the new relationship. At this point, both models coexist in the same graph; the recommendation query will not break.

First, count how many relationships need to be refactored in the graph you ended with from Chapter 1:

```
MATCH (:Playlist)-[r:HAS_TRACK]->(:Track)
RETURN count(r)
```

There are 73,153 relationships to be refactored. This is not a large number; Neo4j can refactor these relationships in a single transaction.

Execute the following query to refactor the graph:

```
//001-rel-type-refactor-1.cypher
//Step 1
MATCH (p:Playlist)-[hastrack:HAS_TRACK]->(t:Track)
//Step 2
MERGE (t)-[onplaylist:ON_PLAYLIST]->(p)
SET onplaylist.position = hastrack.position;
```

If you pause here and inspect a playlist in the graph, you'll see that both versions of the model are maintained, like the example in Figure 4-15.

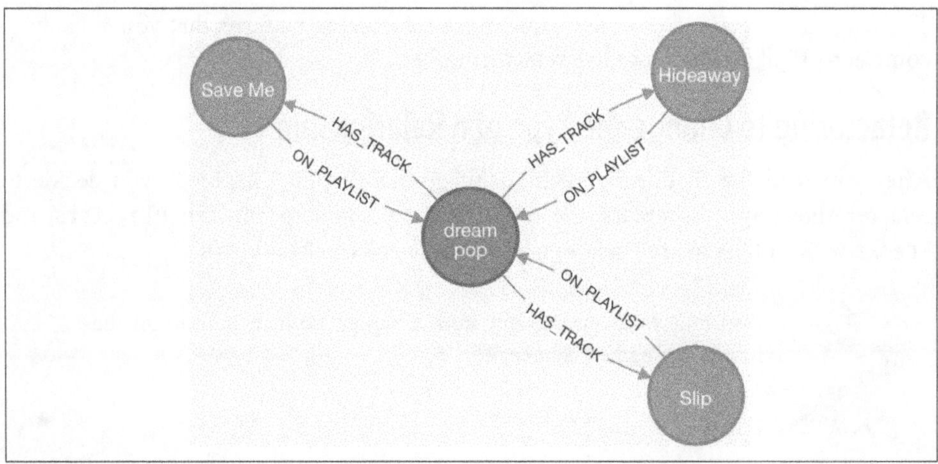

Figure 4-15. The old and new relationship types coexist in the graph.

Stage 2

Update all queries that depend on the `HAS_TRACK` relationship to use the new `ON_PLAYLIST` relationship.

Here's the updated recommendation query that you can test:

```
//002-recommendation-1.cypher
//Find popular tracks
MATCH (popularTrack:Track)-[:ON_PLAYLIST]-(:Playlist)
WITH popularTrack, count(*) as playlistCount
 ORDER BY playlistCount DESC
 LIMIT 10
WITH collect(elementId(popularTrack)) as popularTracks
// For a given Playlist
MATCH (p:Playlist) WHERE p.name = "all that jazz"
// Find the last track
MATCH (p)<-[r:ON_PLAYLIST]-(t)
 WHERE r.position = COUNT { (p)<-[:ON_PLAYLIST]-()}
WITH p AS playlist, t AS lastTrack, popularTracks
// Get the previous tracks
WITH playlist, lastTrack, popularTracks, COLLECT {
MATCH (playlist)<-[:ON_PLAYLIST]-(previous)
 WHERE previous <> lastTrack
RETURN elementId(previous)
} AS previousTracks
// Find other playlists that have the same the last track
MATCH (lastTrack)-[:ON_PLAYLIST]->(otherPlaylist)-[:SIMILAR]-(playlist)
// Find other tracks which are not in the given playlist
MATCH (otherPlaylist)<-[:ON_PLAYLIST]-(recommendation)
```

```
WHERE NOT elementId(recommendation) IN previousTracks
AND NOT elementId(recommendation) IN popularTracks
// Score them by how frequently they appear
RETURN recommendation.id as recommendedTrackId,
  recommendation.name AS recommendedTrack,
  otherPlaylist.name AS fromPlaylist, count(*) AS score
ORDER BY score DESC
LIMIT 5
```

Note that the `WHERE` clause from the original query has been dropped:

```
// Find other playlists that have the same the last track
MATCH (lastTrack)<-[:HAS_TRACK]-(otherPlaylist)-[:SIMILAR]-(playlist)
WHERE otherPlaylist <> playlist
```

This is because the graph now has a single `SIMILAR` relationship between any pair of playlists

Stage 3

Delete the `HAS_TRACK` relationship:

```
//003-rel-type-refactor-2.cypher
//Step 3
MATCH (p:Playlist)-[hastrack:HAS_TRACK]->(t:Track)
DELETE hastrack
```

Refactoring to Create a Node from a Property

To see this refactoring pattern in action, you'll first add a property to a few `Artist` nodes that represents `genre`. Then you'll refactor the graph to extract genres as nodes.

The accompanying GitHub repository contains a CSV file of genres for a limited number of artists, which you can import into the graph using `LOAD CSV`. Since this data source does not contain artist IDs, you will match artists by their names. Adding an index on artist name will speed up the `MATCH` and hence the import:

```
//004-artistNameIndex.cypher
CREATE INDEX artist_name FOR (n:Artist) ON n.name;
```

The data source isn't particularly clean and contains a slash-delimited set of genres for each artist. The following query will split the genres on the / delimiter, trim spaces, convert them to lowercase, and store them as a list of strings on the `Artist` node:

```
//005-loadGenres.cypher
LOAD CSV WITH HEADERS FROM "file:///genres.csv" AS row
WITH row
WITH row.Artist as artist, split(row.Genre,"/") AS genreList
UNWIND genreList AS genre
WITH artist, collect(trim(toLower(genre))) AS genres
```

```
MATCH (a:Artist {name:artist})
SET a.genres=genres
```

Figure 4-16 shows a sampling of artist-genre pairs after this data has been ingested.

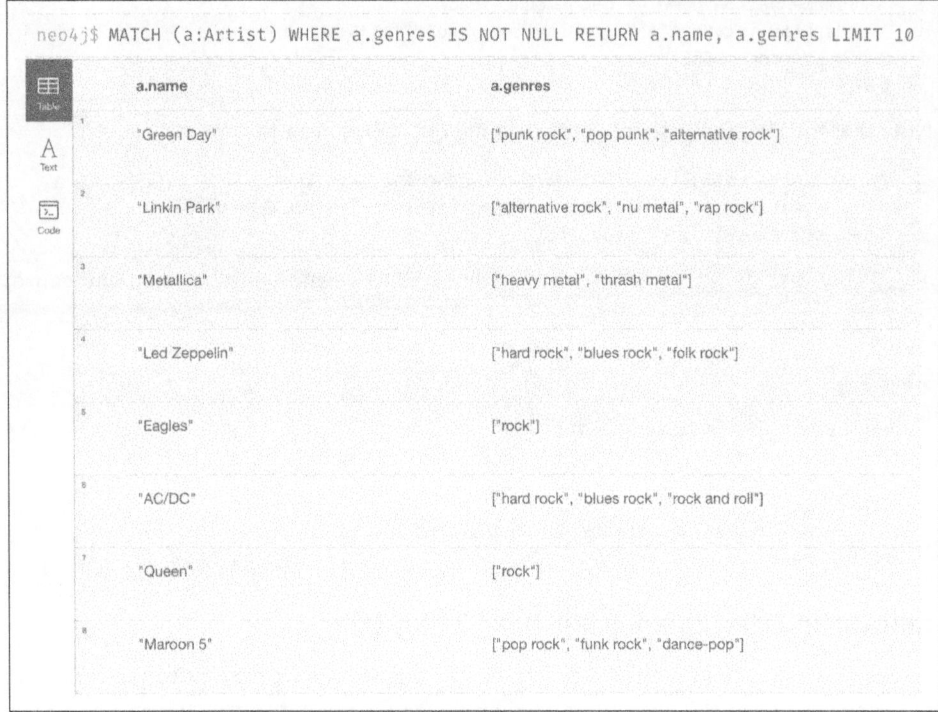

Figure 4-16. The `genres` property on `Artist` nodes

Your next task is to create `Genre` nodes from the `genres` property. Since you don't want duplicate `Genre` nodes, you will use `MERGE`. This will result in a single `Genre` node for "alternative rock," even though this genre is repeated across the artists listed in Figure 4-16.

The best practice is to create the constraint first:

```
//006-genreConstraint.cypher
CREATE CONSTRAINT genre_name
FOR (genre:Genre) REQUIRE genre.name IS UNIQUE
```

The following steps will complete the refactor:

1. Match all `Artist` nodes that have a `genres` property.
2. `UNWIND` the genres, which will convert the list of genres into individual rows.
3. Merge a `Genre` node for each unwound genre name.
4. Merge a `GENRE` relationship from the `Artist` to each `Genre` node from the previous step.
5. Now both models coexist in the graph. Once you have refactored all queries that use `genres` property on an `Artist` to traverse the `GENRE` relationship, drop the property.

Here's the Cypher query to execute on your graph:

```
//007-refactor-genre.cypher
//Step 1
MATCH (a:Artist)
WHERE a.genres IS NOT NULL
//Step 2
WITH a
UNWIND a.genres as genreName
//Step 3
MERGE (g:Genre {name:genreName})
//Step 4
MERGE (a)-[:GENRE]->(g)
//Step 5
REMOVE a.genres
```

Figure 4-17 depicts the refactored graph.

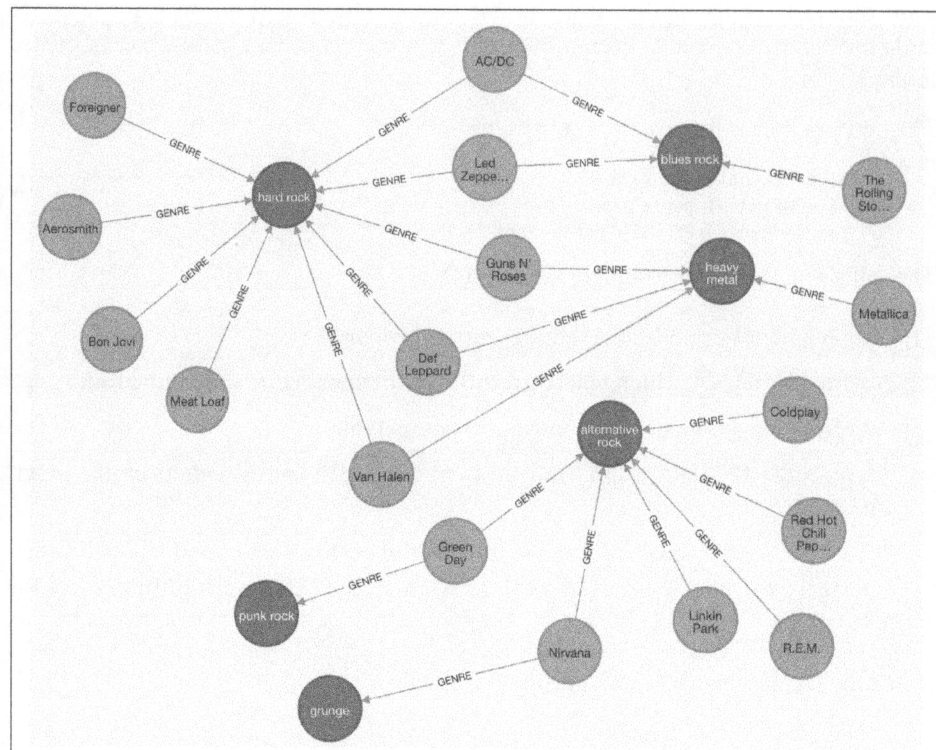

Figure 4-17. `Genre` nodes extracted from the `genres` property

Refactoring to Create a Node from a Relationship

Now it's time to refactor the `ON_PLAYLIST` relationships into new `PlaylistTrack` nodes and create linked lists, following the model described in the section "Representing Sequences" on page 114.

> This refactoring pattern is also handy when you're creating intermediate nodes.

Refresh your memory using Figure 4-18, which shows the transformation required to accomplish this.

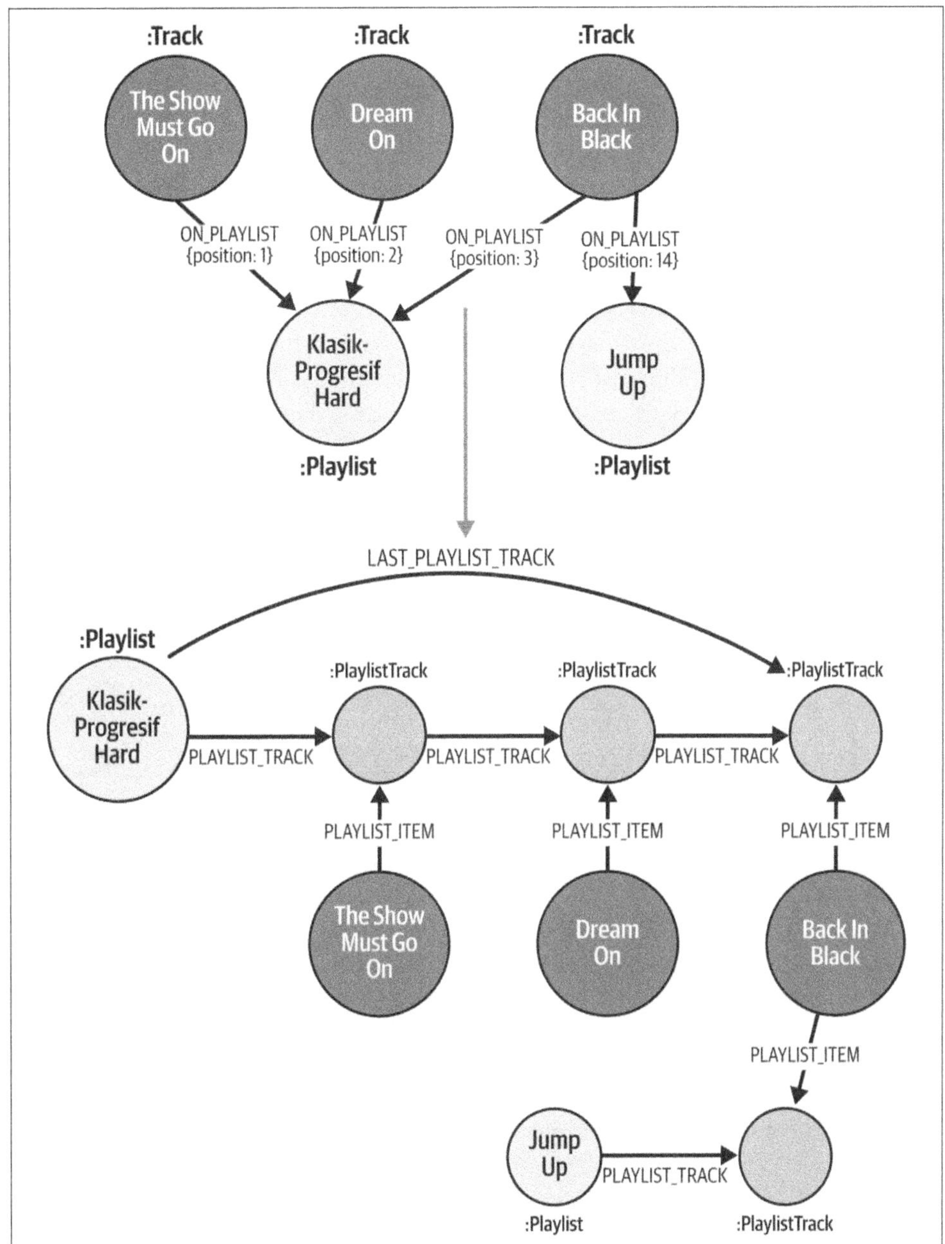

Figure 4-18. Refactoring the `ON_PLAYLIST` relationship into `PlaylistTrack` nodes and connecting them sequentially

Use realistic examples to expose potential problems with your refactoring early. The graph in Figure 4-18 includes "Back in Black," a track that is on two playlists.

While creating a node from a relationship looks complicated, breaking the process up into stages makes it more manageable.

Stage 1

Before getting into the creation of the linked list, you'll first create `PlaylistTrack` nodes. Remember that the `PlaylistTrack` nodes are nodes that represent a track at a particular spot in the playlist. The result should look like Figure 4-19.

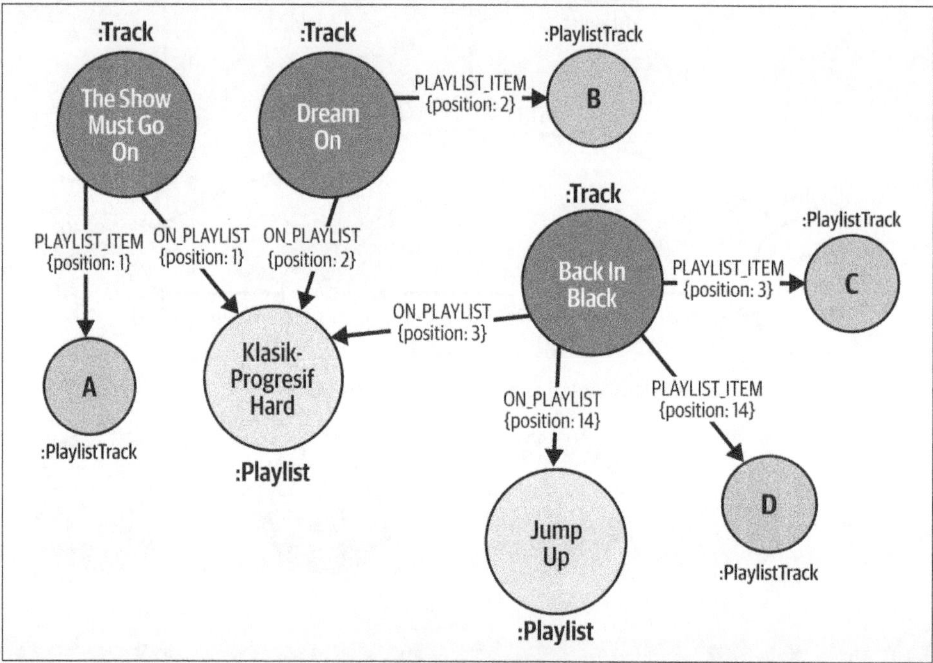

Figure 4-19. The state of the graph after creating `PlaylistTrack` nodes

Can you spot the problem with this new graph? Look closely at the new `PlaylistTrack` nodes. How will you sequence them in a linked list later on?

The lists to create are `Klasik-Progresif-Hard -> A -> B -> C` and `Jump Up -> D`.

Introducing the `PlaylistTrack` nodes has muddied the waters, and it is not clear how to figure out which `PlaylistTrack` for "Back in Black" belongs to which playlist, except by correlating its position numbers on the `ON_PLAYLIST` and `PLAYLIST_ITEM` relationships. If the same track is at the same position in multiple playlists, then the problem is magnified.

Don't be afraid to use temporary relationships during refactoring to help you write simple but predictable queries—you'll delete these relationships when they've done their job of assisting with the refactor.

Here, try introducing a temporary `TRACK_ITEM_TEMP` relationship between the `Playlist` and the `PlaylistTrack` (as shown in Figure 4-20). This relationship is essentially a copy of the `ON_PLAYLIST` relationship, but it terminates at the new `PlaylistTrack` nodes and will help reconstruct the sequence for the linked list.

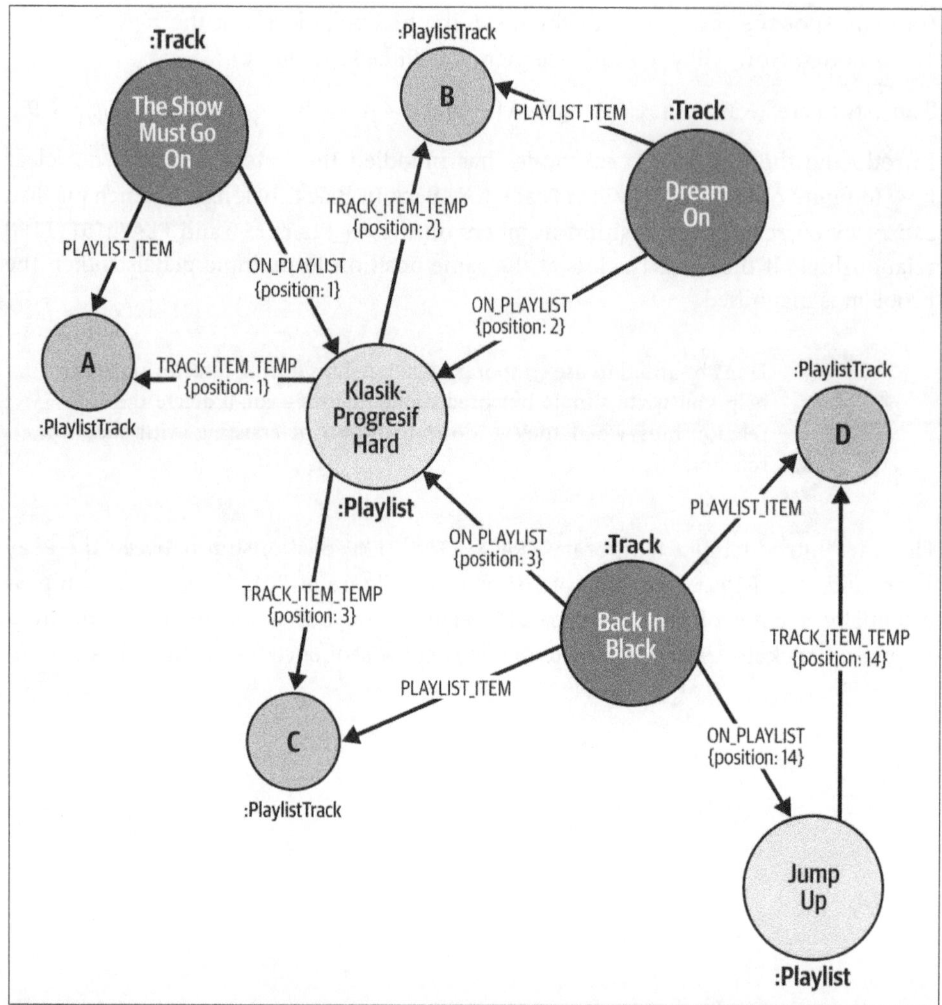

Figure 4-20. Adding a temporary helper relationship, `TRACK_ITEM_TEMP`

Now it's time to write the Cypher query for this stage. It consists of three steps. First, find all tracks and the playlists they're on. Then, create a `PlaylistTrack` node for every `Track` in the `Playlist`. Finally, create the `TRACK_ITEM_TEMP` relationship from the `Playlist` to the `PlaylistTrack`, recording the `position` of the track in the playlist on the relationship.

Since the number of playlists and tracks are fairly large, you'll execute this in transactions, with a default batch size of 1,000:

```
//008-refactor-playlist-linked-1.cypher
//Stage 1
//Step 1
:auto
MATCH (p:Playlist)
CALL {
  WITH p
  MATCH (t:Track)-[r:ON_PLAYLIST]->(p:Playlist)
  //Step 2
  CREATE (pt:PlaylistTrack)
  CREATE (t)-[:PLAYLIST_ITEM]->(pt)
  //Step 3
  CREATE (p)-[:TRACK_ITEM_TEMP {position:r.position}]->(pt)
} IN TRANSACTIONS
```

Stage 2

This stage simply links the `Playlist` to the head and tail `PlaylistTrack` nodes:

```
//009-refactor-playlist-linked-2.cypher
//Stage 2
:auto
MATCH (p:Playlist)
CALL {
  WITH p
  MATCH (p)-[:TRACK_ITEM_TEMP {position:1}]->(firstTrack:PlaylistTrack)
  CREATE (p)-[:PLAYLIST_TRACK]->(firstTrack)
  WITH p
  MATCH (p)-[r:TRACK_ITEM_TEMP]->(lastTrack:PlaylistTrack)
    WHERE r.position = COUNT {()-[:ON_PLAYLIST]->(p)}
  CREATE (p)-[:LAST_PLAYLIST_TRACK]->(lastTrack)
} IN TRANSACTIONS
```

Stage 3

This is where the linked list is produced by creating relationships between `PlaylistTrack` nodes. You'll use the `position` property on the `TRACK_ITEM_TEMP` relationship to maintain the playlist's track order.

One way to do this in Cypher is to collect a playlist's `PlaylistTrack` nodes, in order. Then use a combination of `RANGE` and `UNWIND` (*https://oreil.ly/lw1Jm*) to obtain a pair of adjacent tracks and create the relationship between them:

```
//010-refactor-playlist-linked-3.cypher
//Stage 3
//Step 1
:auto
MATCH (p:Playlist)
CALL {
  WITH p
  MATCH (p)-[r:TRACK_ITEM_TEMP]->(t:PlaylistTrack)
  WITH r,t
  ORDER BY r.position
  WITH COLLECT(t) AS playlistTracks
  UNWIND RANGE(0,SIZE(playlistTracks) - 2) as idx
  WITH playlistTracks[idx] AS t1, playlistTracks[idx+1] AS t2
  MERGE (t1)-[:PLAYLIST_TRACK]->(t2)
} IN TRANSACTIONS
```

The apoc library contains a handy list of refactoring procedures (*https://oreil.ly/jFLH6*), such as apoc.nodes.link (*https://oreil.ly/Cq1Ng*) to create a linked list—this would simplify the query you just wrote.

Next, drop the temporary relationships as they've done their job. You can batch the deletes in transactions to avoid running out of memory:

```
//011-refactor-playlist-linked-4.cypher
//Stage 3
//Step 2
:auto
MATCH ()-[r:TRACK_ITEM_TEMP]-()
CALL {
    WITH r
    DELETE r
}
IN TRANSACTIONS
```

Now both models coexist in the same graph, as can be seen in Figure 4-21.

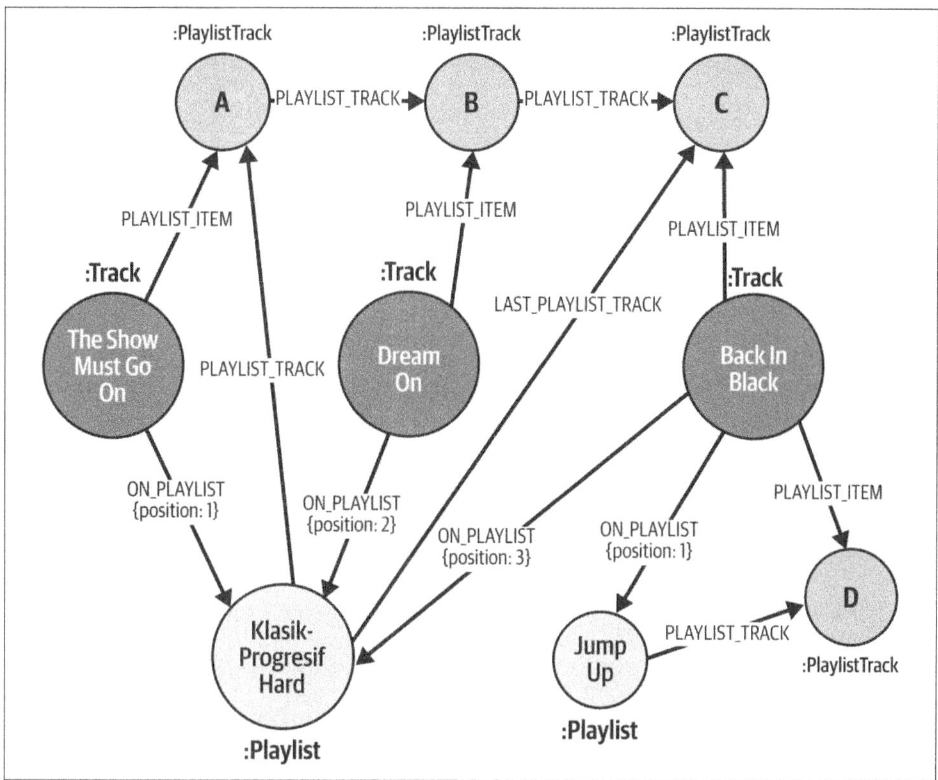

Figure 4-21. The playlist is refactored into a linked list, and the old `ON_PLAYLIST` relationship is maintained till it is no longer in use.

Stage 4

To use the linked list, rework the recommendation query from Chapter 1 as follows:

```
//012-recommendation-2.cypher
//Stage 4
//Find popular tracks
MATCH (popularTrack:Track)-[:PLAYLIST_ITEM]->()
WITH popularTrack, count(*) as playlistCount
ORDER BY playlistCount DESC
LIMIT 10
WITH collect(popularTrack) as popularTracks

// For a given Playlist
MATCH (playlist:Playlist) WHERE playlist.name = "all that jazz"
// Find the last track
MATCH (playlist)-[:LAST_PLAYLIST_TRACK]->(lastTrackItem)
// Get the previous tracks
WITH playlist, lastTrackItem, popularTracks, COLLECT {
MATCH (playlist) (()-[:PLAYLIST_TRACK]->()) {1,100} (previousTrackItem)
WHERE previousTrackItem <> lastTrackItem
RETURN previousTrackItem
} AS previousTrackItems

// Find other playlists that have the same the last track
MATCH (playlist)-[:SIMILAR]-(otherPlaylist:Playlist)-
[:LAST_PLAYLIST_TRACK]->(otherLastTrack)<-[:PLAYLIST_ITEM]-(:Track)-
[:PLAYLIST_ITEM]->()<-[:LAST_PLAYLIST_TRACK]-(playlist)

// Find other tracks which are not in the given playlist
MATCH (otherPlaylist) (()-[:PLAYLIST_TRACK]->()) {1,100} (recommendationItem)
<-[:PLAYLIST_ITEM]-(recommendation)
WHERE NOT recommendationItem IN previousTrackItems
AND NOT recommendationItem IN popularTracks

// Score them by how frequently they appear
RETURN recommendation.id as recommendedTrackId,
recommendation.name AS recommendedTrack,
otherPlaylist.name AS fromPlaylist,
count(*) AS score
ORDER BY score DESC
LIMIT 5
```

Finally, drop the ON_PLAYLIST relationships:

```
//013-refactor-playlist-linked-5.cypher
//Stage 4
:auto
MATCH ()-[r:ON_PLAYLIST]-()
CALL(r) {
  DELETE r
}
IN TRANSACTIONS
```

Key Takeaways

Refactoring is a normal part of graph modeling. You can refactor a live graph or reingest all the data to comply with an updated model. A model's old and new versions of the model can often coexist in the same graph: this provides backward compatibility and eases the query migration process.

Sometimes refactoring can result in more complex queries, such as with the recommendation query. Always consider the cost and benefits, taking the principles of modeling into account.

Summary

You can now recognize when specific modeling patterns such as linked lists and hyperedges can be applied. Most domains are straightforward to model and, with experience, you'll find yourself using these patterns intuitively. You've also practiced refactoring your graph. Soon this will be second nature.

Chapter 5 addresses query analysis and tuning: we'll show you how queries are executed and how your modeling decisions affect it.

CHAPTER 5

Query Analysis and Tuning

Any graph application in production relies on performant queries and an effective use of resources. This is even more important in mission-critical applications, where the difference between an efficient query and a slow one can sometimes bring dire consequences, such as financial loss, security compromise, or even loss of life. Instead of only providing ready solutions, this chapter focuses on *why* queries perform efficiently (or not). Its goal is to give you enough depth of understanding to be able to reason about your own queries when you need to tune them.

As Neo4j consultants, we've encountered a myriad of Cypher queries in all sorts of domains, and the good news is that the majority of those queries can be tweaked to perform better if you have a strong grasp of the fundamentals. In this chapter, you will learn how the query planner operates and how to read and understand the execution plan it produces. We'll explore concepts such as anchor selectivity and row cardinality, which are core to writing good queries, as well as the use of indexes for performance.

Query Execution

A Cypher query starts off as a string that describes the pattern(s) you want to match in the graph, the conditions to apply, and any transformations to be applied to the results. Figure 5-1 shows the steps involved at a high level, which take your Cypher query string through its execution to produce results.

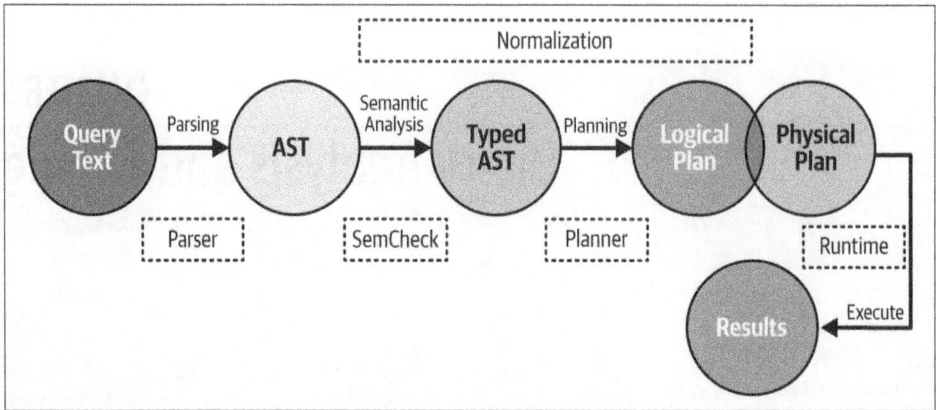

Figure 5-1. Cypher's query processing pipeline (https://oreil.ly/anirI)

The query is first parsed into an abstract syntax tree (AST). Then it goes through a series of normalization steps, including semantic analysis. The query optimizer, or *query planner*, uses database statistics as well as the current state of indexes and constraints to produce an imperative logical plan. This plan usually represents the most efficient way of executing the query against the current database state. It contains the steps to execute the query and consists of a binary tree of operators.

Next, the Cypher runtime turns this plan into a physical plan and executes it against the database. The Cypher planner and runtimes are constantly improving, with newer versions of Neo4j resulting in more and more efficient query executions. As we write this book, Cypher has three available runtimes: *slotted*, *pipelined*, and *parallel*. The default runtime (currently the pipelined runtime in Neo4j Enterprise) is generally the best for overall performance, especially for transactional workloads with a large number of queries running in parallel. Each runtime has its own characteristics. You may decide to override the runtime for a specific query, as you come to understand the advantages and disadvantages of doing so. We'll revisit runtimes later in this chapter. Now let's look at how the query planner works.

Pattern Anchors

The next concept to grasp is the sequence of steps the query planner uses to match patterns in the graph. Briefly stated, the planner must:

1. Identify suitable anchors in the pattern (nodes or relationships that serve as entry points for the query to be matched in the graph).
2. Locate these anchors and load them into memory if they aren't already in the page cache.

3. Expand from the anchors, following pointers to traverse the graph and find occurrences of the patterns specified in the Cypher query.

Along the way, the planner evaluates predicates, aggregations, and other transformations and operations.

It is important to understand why anchors are the key to query planning and execution. Follow along as we explore this through the following set of queries.

Global graph query

The first query is very broad: it matches all nodes in the graph:

```
MATCH (n)
RETURN n
```

In the absence of any anchor, there is no clear place in the graph to start. The planner must load all nodes from the nodes store. This type of query is known as a *global graph query* because it utilizes the whole graph and places the burden of consuming these results on the client application—this will be expensive on nontrivial graphs.

Querying based on labels

The next query is a bit more specific—it matches all artists and their tracks:

```
MATCH (a:Artist)<-[:ARTIST]-(t:Track)
RETURN a,t
```

The query planner has more information now. It doesn't need to scan the whole graph, which contains other nodes, such as playlists. It can use any of three anchors: nodes with the label `Artist`, nodes with the label `Track`, or relationships of type `ARTIST`.

Here is where the database statistics come into play. Neo4j maintains a variety of statistics about the graph. One is the *count store*, which holds count metadata about:

- The number of nodes with a certain label
- The number of relationships by type
- The number of relationships by type starting from or ending with a node with a specific label
- The selectivity per index (the ratio of unique values to the total entries in the index)

Since the query planner gets counts from the count store in constant time, this is a really quick way for it to make an informed choice about the query plan. In this case, it finds that the smallest set is artists. It designates these artists, identified as `a`, as the anchors for this query.

You can inspect the count store by running this procedure:

```
CALL db.stats.retrieve('GRAPH COUNTS')
```

Once these artist nodes are loaded into the page cache, if they weren't there already, the planner traverses the `ARTIST` relationship rapidly to locate the `Track` nodes on the other end, matching the pattern.

If the number of pattern matches for artists and their tracks remains constant, this query matching artists and their tracks will execute in constant time, even if the total graph might be much larger than the nodes and relationships specified in our pattern, such as playlists or genres. In Neo4j, the idea of a *graph local query* refers to a query whose scope is intentionally limited to a portion of the graph—typically the neighborhood around a set of starting nodes—instead of scanning or aggregating information from the entire graph. This is why it is important to make your patterns (and therefore your anchors) as specific as possible, including labels, relationship types, and directions (when known). If this were a global graph query, as in the first example, query execution time would grow as the size of the graph grows.

Let's look at one more query.

A more selective query

Our third query is even more specific: match artists with songs that have the exact title "Tonight":

```
MATCH (t:Track {name:"Tonight"})-[:ARTIST]->(a:Artist)
RETURN a.name
```

Where do you think the planner will choose to start its traversal?

The graph counts show that there are fewer artist nodes than tracks. However, the presence of a property on the `Track` indicates that the track has chances of higher selectivity than the artist. That is, instead of locating every `Artist` in the graph, which would be a very large set, locating the number of tracks with the name "Tonight" is likely to result in a smaller set of matches.

If you've set up an index on the `name` property for `Track`, then the anchors will be the `Track` nodes named "Tonight"—so the planner simply looks them up from the index. Once it obtains that smaller set, it continues traversing by expanding from these nodes through the `ARTIST` relationship to find artists.

The absence of an index, however, forces the planner to scan *all* track nodes (which become the anchors) and then filter them by name to retain only the tracks named "Tonight." From there, it expands as before. As the number of tracks in your graph grows, this query gets less and less performant because it must progressively load *all* tracks into memory. You can see why indexing properties that are identity values or business keys or are frequently queried is critical to making queries performant.

Fortunately, you can view the query execution plan, which will help you identify areas that need tuning.

Query Profiling

There are two ways to view the query execution plan: the `EXPLAIN` command and the `PROFILE` command:

`EXPLAIN`
: Prepend your Cypher query with `EXPLAIN`. This does not run the query; instead, it uses estimates based on the logical plans to create the execution plan. Since it does not run the query, using `EXPLAIN` is safe: it does not modify your database and produces no results. What it does is show you the tree of operators that will be used to produce results when the query is executed.

`PROFILE`
: The `PROFILE` command produces a similar query plan, but it actually runs the query. This produces results or modifies the database, depending on the query. In addition to the information produced by `EXPLAIN`, `PROFILE` shows you the total cost of running the query plan. It will track, for each operator, the runtime, how much memory is used, how many rows pass through it, and how each operator needs to interact with the storage layer to retrieve data.

Since it actually runs the query, using `PROFILE` is more resource-intensive. When you're attempting to tune a very long-running query, use `EXPLAIN` to identify key bottlenecks quickly. Just remember that because `EXPLAIN` uses database statistics and estimates, the actual cost of the query is only precisely known with `PROFILE`.

Now, we'll look at the execution plans for some of the example queries to correlate the explanation with actual numbers. This chapter uses a much larger graph than previous chapters: it contains over 18 million nodes and 100 million relationships. To run the queries in this chapter, refer to the README (*https://oreil.ly/mmXol*) for Chapter 5 in the GitHub repository (*https://github.com/neo4j-the-definitive-guide/book*).

Start with example query 1, the global graph query, to return all nodes. You know this is going to be expensive, so use `EXPLAIN`:

```
//001-explain-global
EXPLAIN MATCH (n)
RETURN n
```

Run this in your browser, and you'll see that the view in the result frame switches to "Plan" and the operators in the execution plan are displayed, as in Figure 5-2.

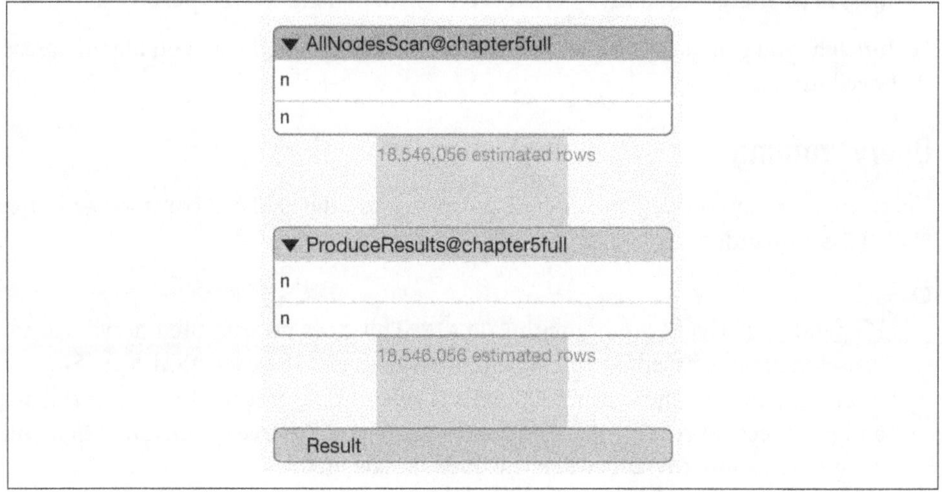

Figure 5-2. Query plan results for the first example, the global graph query

This plan uses two operators before terminating at the result. The first is an `AllNodesScan`, using the variable or identifier `n` in the query. This tells you that `n` will contain all nodes that are read from the node store. The planner can estimate that the query will produce 18,546,056 rows without running it. It does so by looking up the count of all nodes from the count store. These "rows" are intermediate results passed between the processing units, the operators. You can verify this by running the following:

```
call db.stats.retrieve('GRAPH COUNTS')
```

The results contain the following:

```
"nodes": [
    {
      "count": 18546056
    },....
```

The query then simply returns all of the nodes, and the next operator prepares for that. `ProduceResults` is part of every query that produces some results; there's nothing to optimize for here.

Now that you can begin to think like the planner, you can also infer that the more nodes in the graph, the longer a query that uses an `AllNodesScan` will take to execute. Execution time is directly proportional to the number of nodes in the graph.

If you prefer to read the text version of an execution plan, you can download it as text from the result frame in your browser or, more conveniently, via the Cypher Shell.

Cypher Shell (*https://oreil.ly/X6P7f*) is a command-line tool that ships with your Neo4j distribution, although it can also be downloaded separately. You can perform administrative tasks or run queries against your graph and do some lightweight scripting. We find it very handy when tuning queries—the time to render the visualization in the browser is eliminated. This book will use the text versions of query plans as much as possible to aid readability. The Neo4j documentation (*https://oreil.ly/5-Pjt*) explaining operators also uses this version, so it is worth getting familiar with.

If you run the `EXPLAIN` command for the third query in the Cypher Shell, you will see output as in Figure 5-3:

```
//002-explain-tonight.cypher
EXPLAIN
MATCH (t:Track {name:"Tonight"})-[:ARTIST]->(a:Artist)
RETURN a.name
```

```
+-------------------+----+---------------------------+----------------+---------------------+
| Operator          | Id | Details                   | Estimated Rows | Pipeline            |
+-------------------+----+---------------------------+----------------+---------------------+
| +ProduceResults   |  0 | `a.name`                  |         873580 |                     |
| |                 +----+---------------------------+----------------+                     |
| +Projection       |  1 | a.name AS `a.name`        |         873580 |                     |
| |                 +----+---------------------------+----------------+                     |
| +Filter           |  2 | a:Artist                  |         873580 |                     |
| |                 +----+---------------------------+----------------+                     |
| +Expand(All)      |  3 | (t)-[anon_0:ARTIST]->(a)  |         873580 |                     |
| |                 +----+---------------------------+----------------+                     |
| +Filter           |  4 | t.name = $autostring_0    |         664100 |                     |
| |                 +----+---------------------------+----------------+                     |
| +NodeByLabelScan  |  5 | t:Track                   |       13282008 | Fused in Pipeline 0 |
+-------------------+----+---------------------------+----------------+---------------------+

Total database accesses: ?

0 rows
```

Figure 5-3. A plan produced by EXPLAIN

The text version contains the same tree of operators, but you read it from the bottom up. A unique ID is assigned to each operator (as shown in the `Id` column). This ID decreases in value from leaf operators, such as `NodeByLabelScan`, till it reaches the root, typically at the results stage. The `Details` column describes the task the operator is performing: in this simple query, it is processing nodes identified by `n`. Finally, `Estimated Rows` is an approximation of the number of rows passing through each operator. This is calculated based on statistical information; it doesn't know the *actual* number of times the database was accessed. The total number of rows is 0—which makes sense, because `EXPLAIN` doesn't really run the query.

Try using `PROFILE` for the next query:

```
//003-profile-tonight.cypher
PROFILE
MATCH (t:Track {name:"Tonight"})-[:ARTIST]->(a:Artist)
RETURN a.name
```

The plan produced with Cypher Shell is shown in Figure 5-4.

Operator	Id	Details	Estimated Rows	Rows	DB Hits	Memory (Bytes)	Page Cache Hits/Misses	Time (ms)	Pipeline
+ProduceResults	0	`a.name`	873580	2385	0	0			
+Projection	1	a.name AS `a.name`	873580	2385	4770				
+Filter	2	a:Artist	873580	2385	4770				
+Expand(All)	3	(t)-[anon_0:ARTIST]->(a)	873580	2385	15331				
+Filter	4	t.name = $autostring_0	664100	1999	26564018				
+NodeByLabelScan	5	t:Track	13282008	13282008	13282009	240	4583478/10	3988.677	Fused in Pipeline 0

```
Total database accesses: 39870898, total allocated memory: 320

2385 rows
ready to start consuming query after 64 ms, results consumed after another 3995 ms
```

Figure 5-4. The query plan produced with `PROFILE` using Cypher Shell

Remember to read from the bottom to the top.

This plan validates our reasoning about how the query will execute: the track nodes are identified as anchors. A `NodeByLabelScan` operator loads all tracks in the graph from the node label index. The `Rows` column tells you that this number is around thirteen million and these are input to the next operator. The `Filter` operator takes over to filter all tracks that have a name property with the value "Tonight." This discards a vast portion of the rows—notice that from the 13 million, only 1,999 match the track name. Next, `Expand(All)` iteratively traverses out from the 1,999 track nodes supplied to it, following the outgoing `ARTIST` relationship to arrive at the node on the other end. Here, another `Filter` checks that the end node has an `Artist` label.

Finally, the `Projection` step evaluates what we've asked it to return—in this case, just the `name` property—and returns the final set of 2,385 rows. Since `PROFILE` executes the query and produces results, we now have the total number of database accesses, total allocated memory, number of rows returned, and how long it takes before any results are ready to be consumed.

There are some extra pieces of information in this plan as compared to `EXPLAIN`: rows, database hits, and page cache hits and misses. Let's look at each in turn.

Rows

A *row* is basically a processing unit—often a path that corresponds to the pattern matched by the query—but sometimes it can simply be a set of literal values. In the very first query, `MATCH (n)`, you're matching a pattern `n`, which is simply a node. So, every match of a node in the graph is a row. If the graph contains 1 million nodes, then the number of pattern matches is 1 million and the number of rows is 1 million.

The query you just profiled has a more specific pattern:

```
MATCH (t:Track {name:"Tonight"})-[:ARTIST]->(a:Artist)
```

The query plan produced by `PROFILE` shows you how it matches parts of the pattern. For the anchors, the pattern was "all nodes with label `Track`"—roughly 13 million nodes—and so you see that number of rows listed by the `NodeByLabelScan` operator. These rows form the input to the next operator, where most of them are discarded by the filter, resulting in 1,999 rows that represent tracks with name "Tonight." The next operator takes all those rows and expands from them to reach the nodes on the other end of each `ARTIST` relationship, increasing the number of rows to 2,385.

Why is this? If you examine the graph, you'll find that some tracks have multiple artists. Each of these `Track-Artist` permutations counts as a pattern match, and hence as a row. Figure 5-5 makes this easier to understand. The pattern `(:Track)-[:ARTIST]->(:Artist)` for this particular track shows that while the track is just one node, it has three artists, and each of these three patterns matches generate a row.

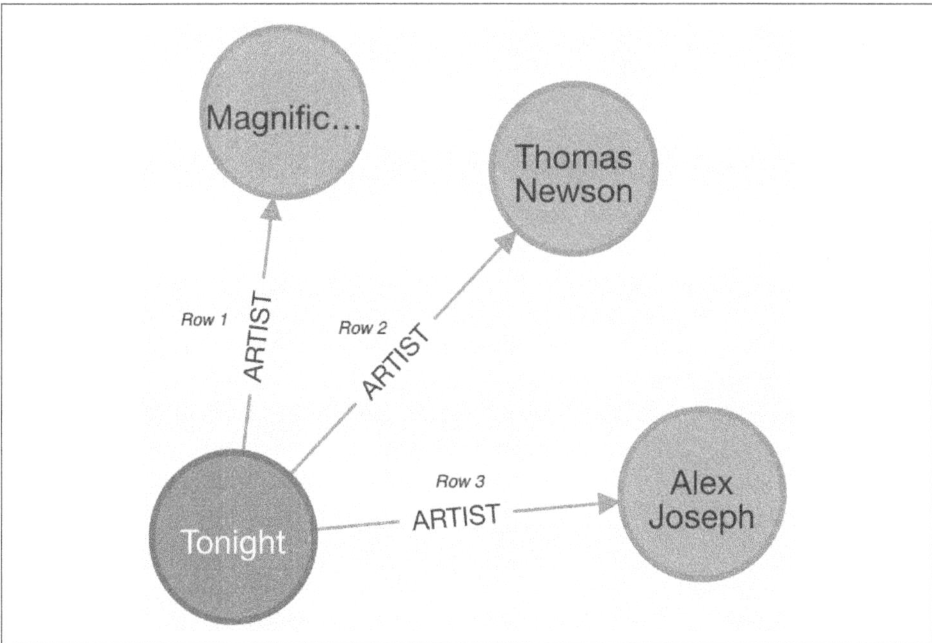

Figure 5-5. A single track node with three artists, resulting in three matches for the pattern `(:Track)-[:ARTIST]->(:Artist)`

For the purpose of memory consumption, a *row* is a single object on the heap. The size of each row varies (depending on the length of the pattern, for example), but this explains why some queries, like global graph queries, can cause Neo4j to run out of memory if the heap allocated is too small. In most cases, though, rows are streamed through and aggregations and eager operations (see the section "Don't Be Eager!" on page 165) allocate data on the heap.

Database hits

The next column you see in the plan is `DB Hits` (database hits). A *DB hit* is an abstract unit of storage-engine work that represents a request from an operator to the storage engine to store or retrieve data and may cause an IO operation to occur. One or more DB hits occur for requests such as getting a node by its ID, getting the label of a node, getting a property or finding a node through an index seek, creating or deleting nodes or relationships, and so on. The full list of operations that result in DB hits can be found in the documentation (*https://oreil.ly/Xvngf*).

Page cache hits/misses

The page cache is an off-heap area of memory that Neo4j uses to cache data stored on disk. Disk access is relatively expensive, and optimal performance is achieved by caching graph data and indexes into the page cache. Initially, upon database startup, the page cache is empty. Neo4j loads graph data on demand from disk when queries need it.

In Figure 5-4, you can see that when we ran the query, all tracks were not yet loaded into the page cache, causing 10 page cache misses (or faults). As data is loaded into the cache, the page faults reduce, since it is likely that the data the queries need is already in the cache. This is good to monitor, since a sustained or increasing number of page cache misses across queries can indicate that you need to tune your queries or that the size of your page cache is inadequate. When the page cache is full, Neo4j will replace the page that was not accessed for the longest time with a new page. If the page cache is too small, this thrashing leads to increased IO waiting time as new blocks are read from disk and then are evicted quickly. The ideal case would be for your entire graph, or at the very least the most frequently accessed portion, to fit into the page cache.

You can configure the amount of memory allocated to the page cache using the parameter `server.memory.pagecache.size`.

Neo4j Enterprise has a setting called `db.memory.pagecache.warmup.enable` that is enabled by default. It is used to warm the page cache up faster. When the database is running, cache profiles that contain information about what data is (and is not) in memory are periodically recorded. If Neo4j were to be restarted, instead of empty page caches, it would use these profiles to load the same data that was in memory at the time the profiles were created. This helps to get the page cache warm faster and more predictably than a cold start, where query execution forces the loading of data from disk into the cache.

Row Cardinality

Cypher operations execute on a stream of rows coming into an operator and produce a stream of rows to the next operator. Cypher's streaming, or "lazy," nature contributes to its speed and efficiency. This means that most operators pipe their output to the next operator as soon as rows are produced and that one operator doesn't have to exhaust all its rows before the next operator can start executing.

There are exceptions to this laziness: notably, the "eager" operators, sorts, and aggregations, which must aggregate all their rows before passing the output onward. This is covered in the section "Don't Be Eager!" on page 165.

The more rows that stream to an operator, the more the operator must be called, resulting in more work to be done. The cost of the operator is the `number of rows × number of DB hits per row`. Not only has the cost increased, but the number of rows that flow onwards to the next operator has also increased, leading to cascading impact. Ideally, you want to reduce the cardinality of these intermediate rows as early as possible. For example, perhaps your query includes many filtering conditions. If you have them run at the end, you'll incur the cost of DB hits and execution times only to discard large volumes of rows. Instead, move the most specific filters to run as early as possible in your query. Some operators, such as aggregations, `Distinct` and `Limit`, reduce row cardinality; others, such as `Expand(All)` and `Unwind`, increase cardinality—be aware of this when writing your query and try to order them optimally as much as possible.

Now that you understand how queries are executed and how to read a plan, you should follow these principles to get your queries as performant as possible:

- Help the Cypher planner choose the smallest possible anchor set by using indexes and specifying labels and relationship types and directions.
- Keep row cardinality in mind. Reduce the number of rows passed from operator to operator by filtering data as early as possible, to decrease the wasteful work done later in the query.

- Ensure, as much as possible, that you're only retrieving necessary data from the graph.

The next set of queries will demonstrate how to aim for these goals. Remember to refer back to Chapters 3 and 4 frequently to correlate how modeling decisions can affect the performance of your queries.

Matching Disconnected Patterns

Even though Neo4j is a graph, focusing on connections, you can write Cypher that queries across disconnected patterns. Run the following `EXPLAIN`:

```
//004-explain-disconnected.cypher
EXPLAIN
MATCH (a:Artist),(t:Track)
RETURN a,t
```

Do not `PROFILE` or run this query directly on your graph. It is extremely memory-intensive! Only use `EXPLAIN`.

You will see the dreaded `CartesianProduct` operator. Figure 5-6 shows the plan.

```
+---------------------+----+----------+----------------+----------------+
| Operator            | Id | Details  | Estimated Rows | Pipeline       |
+---------------------+----+----------+----------------+----------------+
| +ProduceResults     |  0 | a, t     | 17142583009296 |                |
| |                   +----+----------+----------------+                |
| +CartesianProduct   |  1 |          | 17142583009296 | In Pipeline 2  |
| |\                  +----+----------+----------------+----------------+
| | +NodeByLabelScan  |  2 | t:Track  |    16748612088 | In Pipeline 1  |
| |                   +----+----------+----------------+----------------+
| +NodeByLabelScan    |  3 | a:Artist |        1290662 | In Pipeline 0  |
+---------------------+----+----------+----------------+----------------+

Total database accesses: ?

0 rows
```

Figure 5-6. The `CartesianProduct` operator in the query plan

A *Cartesian product* of two inputs (also called a *cross join*) is where each row from the left operator is combined with all rows from the right operator, producing an explosive set of permutations on a nontrivial graph size. The `Pipeline` column in Figure 5-6 shows that the operators have been divided into three pipelines. Operators in a pipeline (in this case, there is just one operator in pipelines 0 and 1) operate on batches of rows and are fused together so the runtime can execute them as a single task. This also demonstrates the disconnectedness of the query.

The visual query plan in Figure 5-7 will help you picture how those two pipelines deal with nodes with labels `Artist` and `Track`, respectively, and then supply those rows to the next pipeline, `CartesianProduct`.

Figure 5-7. The visual representation of the same plan, obtained by running `EXPLAIN` *in the Neo4j browser.*

The query in this section attempts to combine *every* artist in the graph with *every* track in the graph (irrespective of whether there is a relationship at all between the artist and the track).

Why would you attempt such a query on a graph database that champions connectedness? What would the use case really be? The first way to fix the problem is to not create it at all. If you do for some reason need to execute this sort of query, think about its purpose once again. If you're convinced, then try to reduce the row cardinality as much as possible. For example, instead of combining about 1.2 million artists with 16.7 million tracks, use an aggregating function such as `COLLECT` to reduce row cardinality after matching artists to 1. Now that single row is combined with every track:

```
//005-disconnected-collect.cypher
EXPLAIN
MATCH (a:Artist)
```

```
WITH COLLECT(a) as artists
MATCH (t:Track)
WITH artists, COLLECT(t) as tracks
RETURN artists,tracks
```

The tracks are then aggregated. Finally, the query returns a collection of tracks and a collection of artists, as in Figure 5-8.

```
+-------------------+--+------------------------------+--------------+-------------------+
|Operator           |Id|Details                       |Estimated Rows|Pipeline           |
+-------------------+--+------------------------------+--------------+-------------------+
|+ProduceResults    | 0|artists, tracks               |          3644|In Pipeline 3      |
||                  +--+------------------------------+--------------+-------------------+
|+EagerAggregation  | 1|artists, collect(t) AS tracks |          3644|                   |
||                  +--+------------------------------+--------------+                   |
|+Apply             | 2|                              |      13282008|                   |
||\                 +--+------------------------------+--------------+                   |
|| +NodeByLabelScan | 3|t:Track                       |      13282008|Fused in Pipeline 2|
||                  +--+------------------------------+--------------+-------------------+
|+EagerAggregation  | 4|collect(a) AS artists         |             1|                   |
||                  +--+------------------------------+--------------+                   |
|+NodeByLabelScan   | 5|a:Artist                      |       1290662|Fused in Pipeline 0|
+-------------------+--+------------------------------+--------------+-------------------+

Total database accesses: ?

0 rows
```

Figure 5-8. The query plan with an early aggregation of artists to reduce the row cardinality

If you want to squeeze out a little more performance, you need to understand the shape of your graph well. At ElectricHarmony, you know the number of tracks will always exceed the number of artists. This means it's better to collect the tracks first, so that the number of combinations with the smaller set, that of artists, reduces the overall combinations as compared to the other way round:

```
//006-disconnected-tracks.cypher
EXPLAIN
MATCH (t:Track)
WITH COLLECT(t) as tracks
MATCH (a:Artist)
WITH tracks, COLLECT(a) as artists
RETURN artists,tracks
```

While this eliminates the `CartesianProduct`, notice the appearance of the `Eager Aggregation` operator in the query plan in Figure 5-8. Due to the presence of the aggregating function `COLLECT`, Cypher can no longer lazily stream artists or tracks to the result consumer. Instead, it has to eagerly pull in the required data (tracks and artists) and hold its state, which in turn puts pressure on memory. In addition, the returned collections will be huge.

The bottom line is: if you feel the need for such a query, question it—hard. The workaround does not solve every problem for this kind of undesired use case.

Increasing Anchor Selectivity

As you read earlier in this chapter, every query starts with an *anchor*, which may be one or more nodes or relationships. One of the goals of query tuning is to help the Cypher planner locate anchors as quickly and efficiently as possible. If you don't have any predicates, your best bet is to provide enough information in the query to aid the Cypher planner in consulting the graph counts. Recall that Neo4j collects statistics about the following:

- The number of nodes with a certain label
- The number of relationships by type
- The number of relationships by type starting with or ending at a node with a specific label

The following query, to find all artists that have tracks on playlists, does very little in the way of helping the planner:

```
MATCH (a)-[:ARTIST]-(t)-[:ON_PLAYLIST]-(p)
RETURN a.name AS artistName, count(p) as playlistCount
```

It specifies no labels for the nodes and no relationship directions, either. The only information that it gives the planner is the relationship types involved. If you run the following, you can make a guess about which graph element will form the anchor for this query:

```
CALL db.stats.retrieve("GRAPH COUNTS")
```

The planner cannot use the information about nodes because the query doesn't specify any labels. You haven't set up any indexes or constraints yet, either. In the relationships section, you must ignore all counts such as the following, because there are no labels:

```
{
      "relationshipType": "HAS_TRACK",
      "count": 13282006,
      "endLabel": "Track"
}
```

The only counts it can use are:

```
{
        "relationshipType": "HAS_TRACK",
        "count": 13282006
    },
    {
        "relationshipType": "ARTIST",
        "count": 17471590
    },
  {
        "relationshipType": "ON_PLAYLIST",
        "count": 125451006
    }
```

`ARTIST` is more selective than `ON_PLAYLIST`, so those relationships will anchor the query. Verify your assumption by prefixing the query with `EXPLAIN`.

Operator	Id	Details	Estimated Rows	Pipeline
+ProduceResults	0	artistName, playlistCount	21742	In Pipeline 1
+EagerAggregation	1	cache[a.name] AS artistName, count(p) AS playlistCount	21742	
+Expand(All)	2	(t)-[anon_1:ON_PLAYLIST]-(p)	472732001	
+CacheProperties	3	cache[a.name]	34943180	
+UndirectedRelationshipTypeScan	4	(a)-[anon_0:ARTIST]-(t)	34943180	Fused in Pipeline 0

Figure 5-9. The `ARTIST` relationship anchors the query.

Figure 5-9 shows that, indeed, the `ARTIST` relationships are the starting point of the query. They're loaded from their relationship index, which Neo4j creates and maintains automatically. Once it locates the anchors, traversal and expansion take place as usual.

If you try to execute this query or check the actual execution plan with `PROFILE`, you will find that it is extremely slow—if it returns at all. We threw more memory at it to help it along. The result is pictured in Figure 5-10.

Operator	Id	Details	Estimated Rows	Rows	DB Hits
+ProduceResults	0	artistName, playlistCount	21742	1193310	0
+EagerAggregation	1	cache[a.name] AS artistName, count(p) AS playlistCount	21742	1193310	0
+Expand(All)	2	(t)-[anon_1:ON_PLAYLIST]-(p)	472732001	161011964	382443726
+CacheProperties	3	cache[a.name]	34943180	34943180	70166576
+UndirectedRelationshipTypeScan	4	(a)-[anon_0:ARTIST]-(t)	34943180	34943180	17471591

Total database accesses: 470081893, total allocated memory: 202431560

Figure 5-10. The `PROFILE` of the query with actual rows and DB hits, anchored on the `ARTIST` relationship

Are you wondering why the graph counts show around 17 million `ARTIST` relationships but the profile shows around 34 million? The operator name gives you a clue—

the query does not specify any directions, so each relationship is matched twice, once in either direction.

This is definitely not the kind of query you want in production. Based on your understanding of graph counts, what can you do to make this query more performant? Add in all the information you have—labels and relationship directions:

```
//007-selective-1.cypher
EXPLAIN
MATCH (a:Artist)<-[:ARTIST]-(:Track)-[:ON_PLAYLIST]->(p:Playlist)
RETURN a.name AS artistName, count(p) as playlistCount
```

Use EXPLAIN with this query to see how the plan changes (see Figure 5-11).

```
+--------------------+----+-------------------------------------------------------+----------------+----------------------+
| Operator           | Id | Details                                               | Estimated Rows | Pipeline             |
+--------------------+----+-------------------------------------------------------+----------------+----------------------+
| +ProduceResults    |  0 | artistName, playlistCount                             |          12846 | In Pipeline 1        |
| |                  +----+-------------------------------------------------------+----------------+----------------------+
| +EagerAggregation  |  1 | cache[a.name] AS artistName, count(p) AS playlistCount |         12846 |                      |
| |                  +----+-------------------------------------------------------+----------------+                      |
| +Filter            |  2 | p:Playlist                                            |      165022378 |                      |
| |                  +----+-------------------------------------------------------+----------------+                      |
| +Expand(All)       |  3 | (anon_1)-[anon_2:ON_PLAYLIST]->(p)                    |      165022378 |                      |
| |                  +----+-------------------------------------------------------+----------------+                      |
| +Filter            |  4 | anon_1:Track                                          |       17471590 |                      |
| |                  +----+-------------------------------------------------------+----------------+                      |
| +Expand(All)       |  5 | (a)<-[anon_0:ARTIST]-(anon_1)                         |       17471590 |                      |
| |                  +----+-------------------------------------------------------+----------------+                      |
| +CacheProperties   |  6 | cache[a.name]                                         |        1290662 |                      |
| |                  +----+-------------------------------------------------------+----------------+                      |
| +NodeByLabelScan   |  7 | a:Artist                                              |        1290662 | Fused in Pipeline 0  |
+--------------------+----+-------------------------------------------------------+----------------+----------------------+

Total database accesses: ?
```

Figure 5-11. A more performant query when Cypher has more information about labels and relationship directions, resulting in a better choice of anchor

In comparison with the previous plan in Figure 5-9, the anchor is now more selective—about 1 million `Artist` nodes with the `NodeByLabelScan` operator, as opposed to the 34 million relationships. Once the artist nodes are anchored, the graph is traversed along the specified relationships: `ARTIST` and `ON_PLAYLIST`.

Eliminating Redundant Filter Operations

While the anchor set is smaller, did you notice that if you profile the previous query, the number of DB hits is higher in the plan, shown in Figure 5-12, as compared to the earlier profile in Figure 5-10?

Operator	Id	Details	Estimated Rows	Rows	DB Hits
+ProduceResults	0	artistName, playlistCount	12846	1193310	0
+EagerAggregation	1	cache[a.name] AS artistName, count(p) AS playlistCount	12846	1193310	0
+Filter	2	p:Playlist	165022378	161011964	322023928
+Expand(All)	3	(anon_1)-[anon_2:ON_PLAYLIST]->(p)	165022378	161011964	229635828
+Filter	4	anon_1:Track	17471590	17471590	35223518
+Expand(All)	5	(a)<-[anon_0:ARTIST]-(anon_1)	17471590	17471590	18824302
+CacheProperties	6	cache[a.name]	1290662	1290662	2893360
+NodeByLabelScan	7	a:Artist	1290662	1290662	1290663

Total database accesses: 609891599, total allocated memory: 202408600

Figure 5-12. A high count of DB hits due to additional operators in the execution plan

Go through the operators to see what is different in both profiles. The new profile has two `Filter` operators that filter the labels of the nodes matched after traversing each relationship.

Here's where you have to apply your understanding of the domain. You may be able to remove some labels from the query and get rid of the redundant `Filter` operators *if* you know for a fact that there is no possibility that a node with a different label is on the end of those relationships, as pictured in Figure 5-13. Are you *sure* that this model represents your domain?

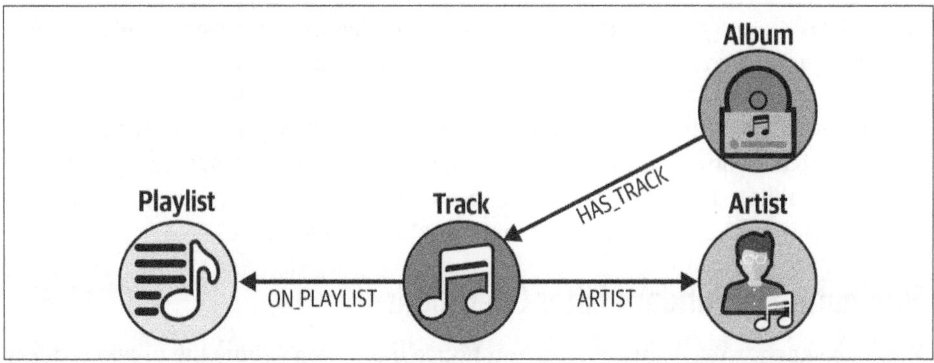

Figure 5-13. Playlists can have only tracks on them, and artists only record tracks.

Or might your graph have some variations, such as the one in Figure 5-14?

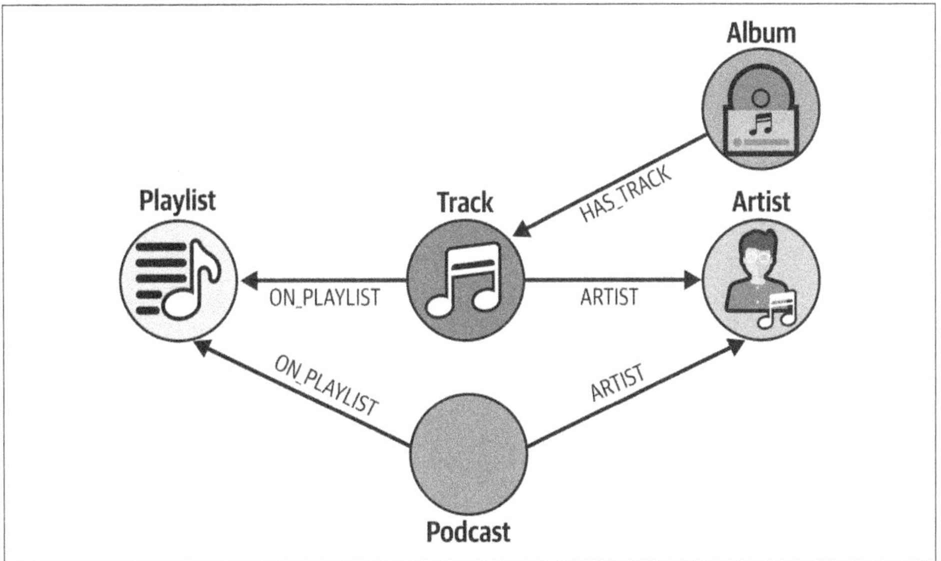

Figure 5-14. Playlists can contain podcasts in the future, and artists may record both tracks and podcasts.

If indeed your graph extends to podcasts and is modeled like this, then dropping the label `Track` isn't a good idea, because your query will also start to match podcasts. But if you're confident about your domain and you will remember to revisit your queries if the model evolves, then go ahead and drop the two labels that Cypher filters on after traversing the relationships:

```
//008-selective-2.cypher
PROFILE
MATCH (a:Artist)<-[:ARTIST]-()-[:ON_PLAYLIST]->(p)
RETURN a.name AS artistName, count(p) as playlistCount
```

Check the profile of this query. The `Filter` operations are gone, the anchor `Artists` retains its selectivity, and the total DB hits have dropped to around 252 million, as shown in Figure 5-15. Much better than the first query without any labels and relationship directions!

Operator	Id	Details	Estimated Rows	Rows	DB Hits
+ProduceResults	0	artistName, playlistCount	10871	1193310	0
+EagerAggregation	1	cache[a.name] AS artistName, count(p) AS playlistCount	10871	1193310	0
+Expand(All)	2	(anon_1)-[anon_2:ON_PLAYLIST]->(p)	118183000	161011964	229635828
+Expand(All)	3	(a)<-[anon_0:ARTIST]-(anon_1)	17471590	17471590	18824302
+CacheProperties	4	cache[a.name]	1290662	1290662	2893360
+NodeByLabelScan	5	a:Artist	1290662	1290662	1290663

Total database accesses: 252644153, total allocated memory: 202408600

Figure 5-15. Remove filters only if you understand your domain very well and the performance gain is significant.

Once again, you can see how your graph model and use cases are intrinsically linked to your Cypher queries. Carefully considering all these aspects allows you to extract the best performance possible.

Improving Anchor Selectivity in Queries with Predicates

When your queries have at least one condition, you have more options to increase the selectivity of the query anchors. You decide to modify the previous query to add one simple condition—to match only playlists that have at least 5,000 followers:

```
//009-selective-3.cypher
EXPLAIN
MATCH (a:Artist)<-[:ARTIST]-()-[:ON_PLAYLIST]->(p)
WHERE p.followers > 5000
RETURN a.name AS artistName, count(p) as playlistCount
```

Before you run the `EXPLAIN`, refer to the graph counts again and try to sketch out the execution plan yourself. Did you change the anchor? Did you add a `Filter` operator? Figure 5-16 shows what the plan looks like.

Operator	Id	Details	Estimated Rows	Pipeline
+ProduceResults	0	artistName, playlistCount	5954	In Pipeline 1
+EagerAggregation	1	a.name AS artistName, count(p) AS playlistCount	5954	
+Filter	2	a:Artist	35454900	
+Expand(All)	3	(anon_1)-[anon_0:ARTIST]->(a)	35454900	
+Expand(All)	4	(p)<-[anon_2:ON_PLAYLIST]-(anon_1)	37635302	
+Filter	5	p.followers > $autoint_0	5563817	
+AllNodesScan	6	p	18546056	Fused in Pipeline 0

Figure 5-16. The query plan after adding a condition

Figure 5-16 shows that the anchor isn't very selective at all! The `AllNodesScan` operator reads *all nodes* from the node store. The reason it does this is because it sees the predicate on `p.followers` and assumes that its best bet is filtering on this condition early to prevent wasteful expansions. Now, put the `Playlist` label back in to prevent loading all nodes for no reason:

```
//010-selective-4.cypher
EXPLAIN
MATCH (a:Artist)<-[:ARTIST]-()-[:ON_PLAYLIST]->(p:Playlist)
WHERE p.followers > 5000
RETURN a.name AS artistName, count(p) as playlistCount
```

The `$autoint_0` in operator 5 is the first integer parameter in the query: 5,000, in this case.

Check the plan in Figure 5-17. It's far better: the anchor set is now just playlists. In the very next step, you'll discard all playlists with fewer than 5,000 followers, so the query will expand only to the ones that matter and will be included in the results.

Operator	Id	Details	Estimated Rows	Pipeline
+ProduceResults	0	artistName, playlistCount	5954	In Pipeline 1
+EagerAggregation	1	a.name AS artistName, count(p) AS playlistCount	5954	
+Filter	2	a:Artist	35454900	
+Expand(All)	3	(anon_1)-[anon_0:ARTIST]->(a)	35454900	
+Expand(All)	4	(p)<-[anon_2:ON_PLAYLIST]-(anon_1)	37635302	
+Filter	5	p.followers > $autoint_0	316481	
+NodeByLabelScan	6	p:Playlist	1054935	Fused in Pipeline 0

Figure 5-17. The `Playlist` label provides enough information to the planner to anchor on playlists, apply the filter, and only then expand to artists from the smaller, filtered set of playlist nodes.

But you can do better still. In Chapter 1, you created indexes to speed up data ingestion. These same indexes are invaluable to evaluate query filters efficiently and provide quick access to the anchors in your query.

Recall that an index is a copy of specific data in your graph, such as nodes, relationships, or properties, in a data structure that is optimized for fast access. Cypher will automatically use the available indexes to evaluate a particular predicate as efficiently as possible. It uses indexes primarily at the start of the query, to load the anchors, not during traversal. Recall that indexes are not required during traversal, since pointers are followed instead of using indexes, like in relational databases.

We used *token lookup* indexes in the queries earlier in this section. These indexes are generated by default when you create a database in Neo4j. They store copies of node labels and relationship types and only solve these kinds of predicates. `NodeByLabelScan` is one operator that uses this type of index to speed up the query. Without the token index, an `AllNodesScan` operator would have been used to read all nodes from the database.

The *range index* is the default index type. You will need to create these indexes yourself, as you come to understand what conditions you'll be using frequently in your queries. Create one now for the `followers` property on nodes with label `Playlist`:

```
//011-selective-index-1.cypher
CREATE INDEX playlist_followers_range
FOR (n:Playlist)
ON (n.followers)
```

You've named this index `playlist_followers_range`. It's a single-property index for nodes with label `Playlist`, on the property `followers`. The index will be populated in the background. It's a pretty fast operation, however, and you can confirm that it has completed by running `SHOW INDEXES`. The state of the index will be `ONLINE` when it is ready.

Rerun the `EXPLAIN` and examine how the plan has changed, now that the Cypher planner can consult the index you just created. Now it can quickly locate nodes with a range condition, instead of having to load all `Playlist` nodes and then filter on the `followers` property. The `NodeIndexSeekByRange` in Figure 5-18 shows how only playlists with more than 5,000 followers directly form the anchors for this query, without loading any other irrelevant nodes.

```
+-----------------------+----+--------------------------------------------------------------+----------------+----------------------+
| Operator              | Id | Details                                                      | Estimated Rows | Pipeline             |
+-----------------------+----+--------------------------------------------------------------+----------------+----------------------+
| +ProduceResults       |  0 | artistName, playlistCount                                    |           1882 | In Pipeline 1        |
| |                     +----+--------------------------------------------------------------+----------------+----------------------+
| +EagerAggregation     |  1 | a.name AS artistName, count(p) AS playlistCount              |           1882 |                      |
| |                     +----+--------------------------------------------------------------+----------------+                      |
| +Filter               |  2 | a:Artist                                                     |        3541172 |                      |
| |                     +----+--------------------------------------------------------------+----------------+                      |
| +Expand(All)          |  3 | (anon_1)-[anon_0:ARTIST]->(a)                                |        3541172 |                      |
| |                     +----+--------------------------------------------------------------+----------------+                      |
| +Expand(All)          |  4 | (p)<-[anon_2:ON_PLAYLIST]-(anon_1)                           |        3758946 |                      |
| |                     +----+--------------------------------------------------------------+----------------+                      |
| +NodeIndexSeekByRange |  5 | RANGE INDEX p:Playlist(followers) WHERE followers > $autoint_0 |          31610 | Fused in Pipeline 0 |
+-----------------------+----+--------------------------------------------------------------+----------------+----------------------+
```

Figure 5-18. Use an index for properties that are frequently queried on. The filter step is discarded and only the exact set of nodes are fetched from the index.

As before, if you want to make this query even more performant and you're *sure* that the only label possible on the end node of `ARTIST` relationships is an `Artist`, you may drop the `Artist` label from the query and eliminate the `Filter` operator.

Range indexes are used for most predicates, including equality, existence, list membership and prefix, in addition to the range search you just saw in action and ordering (addressed later in this chapter). The other types of indexes are *text indexes*, for filtering and searching string values (covered in Chapter 7), and *point indexes*, for spatial `POINT` property types. These indexes optimize queries that filter on spatial distance, for example.

Creating constraints, such as uniqueness constraints or node and relation keys, implicitly adds indexes on the properties involved. You will not be allowed to create an index (except a full text index) on that set of properties for the label or relationship type you use in the constraint. Cypher uses these implicitly added indexes just like it would any index you create yourself. Remember, though, that when you delete a constraint, you also delete the index that was created with it. If you still require that index, you'd then need to create it manually. Also, attempting to drop an index that was created implicitly by constraint creation will result in an "Unable to drop index" error.

It's good practice to check the query plan to ensure that the indexes you intend to be used are *actually* used. One common issue is defining the index on a misspelled property. The query plan simply will not show usage of this index, so you should verify that the correct index has been set up.

Another good practice is to check the usage of your indexes. `SHOW INDEXES` returns the time the index was last read. If this looks suspicious to you, then you should check whether your index was set up as you expected and why the index isn't used by your queries.

Another common misunderstanding is expecting multiple indexes to be used when your query specifies multiple predicates for the same label. To see what we mean, go ahead and create another index for `playlist` nodes, this time on the `name` property:

```
//012-selective-index-2.cypher
CREATE INDEX playlist_name_range
FOR (n:Playlist)
ON (n.name)
```

Profile this query, which matches playlists that have more than 5,000 followers and a name that starts with "Sound":

```
//013-selective-5.cypher
PROFILE
MATCH (n:Playlist)
WHERE n.followers > 5000 AND n.name STARTS WITH "Sound"
RETURN n
```

You might have expected that both indexes—one on `followers` and one on `name`—would be used, but only a single index is selected to locate the query anchors. The index used in this query (see Figure 5-19) is the index on `name`.

Neo4j maintains statistics about indexes and their selectivity, which it uses to determine which index it should pick to be most performant. In this case, it has decided that the selectivity of the playlist `name` is higher than that of `followers`.

Operator	Id	Details	Estimated Rows	Rows	DB Hits
+ProduceResults	0	n	95	1	5
+Filter	1	n.followers > $autoint_0	95	1	1418
+NodeIndexSeekByRange	2	RANGE INDEX n:Playlist(name) WHERE name STARTS WITH $autostring_1	3165	709	710

Total database accesses: 2133, total allocated memory: 304

Figure 5-19. The more selective index, on playlist `name`, is selected as the anchor.

If you change the `followers` condition to be quite specific, you'll find that it may choose the followers index instead:

```
//014-selective-6.cypher
PROFILE
MATCH (n:Playlist)
WHERE n.followers = 5574 AND n.name STARTS WITH "Sound"
RETURN n
```

Indeed, the query plan in Figure 5-20 has now changed to use the other index, because the value 5574 is highly specific (it matches a single row).

Operator	Id	Details	Estimated Rows	Rows	DB Hits
+ProduceResults	0	n	1	1	5
+Filter	1	n.name STARTS WITH $autostring_1	1	1	2
+NodeIndexSeek	2	RANGE INDEX n:Playlist(followers) WHERE followers = $autoint_0	180	1	2

Total database accesses: 9, total allocated memory: 304

1 row

Figure 5-20. The planner chooses the index on playlist `followers` now since the selectivity of the follower value is more specific.

If querying by followers and the names of playlists is a very frequent use case, it would be beneficial to use a *composite index* to fulfill all predicates in one go, rather than partially. A range index on multiple properties is called a composite index.

Composite indexes are created in Neo4j like so:

```
//015-selective-index-3.cypher
CREATE INDEX playlist_name_followers_range
FOR (n:Playlist)
ON (n.name,n.followers)
```

Now try the query again:

```
//013-selective-5.cypher
PROFILE
MATCH (n:Playlist)
WHERE n.followers > 5000 AND n.name STARTS WITH "Sound"
RETURN n
```

The composite index is now used as shown in the query plan (see Figure 5-21) because it can fulfill both conditions simultaneously.

Operator	Id.	Details	Estimated Rows	Rows	DB Hits
+ProduceResults	0	n	95.	1	3.
+Filter	1	cache[n.followers] > $autoint_0	95	1	0
+NodeIndexSeek	2	RANGE INDEX n:Playlist(name, followers) WHERE name STARTS WITH $autostring_1 AND followers IS NOT NULL, cache[n.name], cache[n.followers]	3161.	709	710

Total database accesses: 713, total allocated memory: 312

Figure 5-21. Usage of a composite index for multiple properties in a condition

In fact, since the `followers` property is stored in the index, there's no need to retrieve it from the graph—the value from the index is already at hand, so Cypher uses that instead. Remember that the indexed value and graph value will always be consistent because Neo4j is ACID transactional.

Indexing Guidelines

Why not index *everything*, then? That would give Cypher plenty of options to choose from!

The first disadvantage of this approach is that it greatly increases the storage space used. Since indexes contain copies of the values on which graph elements are indexed, the space these properties occupy is doubled in the worst case where all values are unique: one copy in the graph storage, one in the index.

The second factor to consider is decreased write throughput. Every write to the graph for nodes or relationships that are indexed necessitates a write to the index as well. There is no straightforward formula to achieve a perfect balance between read and write performance and which indexes to maintain, but the general rules of thumb are:

- Frequently queried or filtered properties are good cases for indexing.
- If a certain set of critical queries runs slowly, consider indexing on the properties that can contribute to speeding them up, even if they are not frequently used in other queries.
- Properties that are used to filter and have high cardinality, such as identifiers or fairly distinct values, will benefit from high index selectivity.

It bears repeating: *do not optimize prematurely*. Start off with frequently filtered, high-cardinality properties; only consider adding other indexes, or composite ones, when performance is an issue. Revisit your graph model as your domain expands or changes to make sure the model is still suitable and to avoid overusing indexes to hide a modeling problem.

Accessing Properties

A general tip to wring out more performance in your queries is to defer reading properties of nodes and relationships to as late as possible. Accessing properties of nodes can be more expensive than it should be. If the properties are inlined with the node in storage or already in the page cache, then this is of no consequence, but it's impossible for you to know this beforehand. Typically, good reasons to access a property in a query come at the end, when returning a subset of properties or applying a predicate to a property value. We've seen that Cypher query writers tend to access properties very early in the query and pass them on through further stages using `WITH`. An example is:

```
//016-access-1.cypher
EXPLAIN
MATCH (a:Artist)<-[:ARTIST]-(t:Track)
RETURN a.name, count(t) as trackCount
ORDER by trackCount DESC
LIMIT 10;
```

The purpose of this query is to return the 10 artists that have the most tracks. The plan (see Figure 5-22) shows approximately 1.29 million artist names retrieved right at the start by operator ID 5, but you were only ever interested in 10.

Operator	Id	Details	Estimated Rows	Ordered by	Pipeline
+ProduceResults	0	`a.name`, trackCount	10		
+Top	1	trackCount DESC LIMIT 10	10	trackCount DESC	In Pipeline 2
+EagerAggregation	2	cache[a.name] AS `a.name`, count(t) AS trackCount	4180		
+Filter	3	t:Track	17471590		
+Expand(All)	4	(a)<-[anon_0:ARTIST]-(t)	17471590		
+CacheProperties	5	cache[a.name]	1290662		
+NodeByLabelScan	6	a:Artist	1290662		Fused in Pipeline 0

Figure 5-22. Retrieving the artist name property too early

Instead, you can use the artist node as the aggregating key and defer accessing the name property until much later, when the limit has been applied:

```
//017-access-2.cypher
EXPLAIN MATCH (a:Artist)<-[:ARTIST]-(t:Track)
WITH a, count(t) as trackCount
ORDER by trackCount DESC
```

```
LIMIT 10
RETURN a.name, trackCount
```

Now, the plan (see Figure 5-23) changes.

```
+-----------------------+----+-----------------------------+----------------+-----------------+---------------------+
| Operator              | Id | Details                     | Estimated Rows | Ordered by      | Pipeline            |
+-----------------------+----+-----------------------------+----------------+-----------------+---------------------+
| +ProduceResults       |  0 | `a.name`, trackCount        |             10 |                 |                     |
| |                     +----+-----------------------------+----------------+                 |                     |
| +Projection           |  1 | a.name AS `a.name`          |             10 |                 |                     |
| |                     +----+-----------------------------+----------------+                 |                     |
| +Top                  |  2 | trackCount DESC LIMIT 10    |             10 | trackCount DESC | In Pipeline 2       |
| |                     +----+-----------------------------+----------------+-----------------+---------------------+
| +OrderedAggregation   |  3 | a, count(t) AS trackCount   |           4180 |                 | In Pipeline 1       |
| |                     +----+-----------------------------+----------------+                 +---------------------+
| +Filter               |  4 | t:Track                     |       17471590 |                 |                     |
| |                     +----+-----------------------------+----------------+                 |                     |
| +Expand(All)          |  5 | (a)<-[anon_0:ARTIST]-(t)    |       17471590 |                 |                     |
| |                     +----+-----------------------------+----------------+                 |                     |
| +NodeByLabelScan      |  6 | a:Artist                    |        1290662 | a ASC           | Fused in Pipeline 0 |
+-----------------------+----+-----------------------------+----------------+-----------------+---------------------+
```

Figure 5-23. Deferring access of the artist name to as late as possible

Operator 1, the projection, only accesses the names of 10 artists, as intended. To summarize, on large graphs, be conscious of accessing a high number of property values when they're not necessary, and look for ways to delay this step as much as possible.

Node Degrees

Let's say your use case is to find tracks that are on more than `n` playlists. To do this, your query needs to count how many playlists a track is related to, via the `ON_PLAYLIST` relationship. This is the query that your colleague has written:

```
//018-degrees-1.cypher
PROFILE
MATCH (t:Track)-[:ON_PLAYLIST]->(p)
WITH t, count(p) as playlistCount
WHERE playlistCount > 2500
RETURN t.name
```

First, while this looks like a reasonable query, it is the relationships that are important, not really the playlist nodes `(p)` on the end. Second, running this query takes a really long time, especially considering that it only returns 1,505 rows. The profile of this query plan is shown in Figure 5-24.

```
+-----------------------+----+-----------------------------------+----------------+-----------+-----------+
| Operator              | Id | Details                           | Estimated Rows | Rows      | DB Hits   |
+-----------------------+----+-----------------------------------+----------------+-----------+-----------+
| +ProduceResults       |  0 | `t.name`                          |           3360 |      1505 |         0 |
| |                     +----+-----------------------------------+----------------+-----------+-----------+
| +Projection           |  1 | t.name AS `t.name`                |           3360 |      1505 |      3010 |
| |                     +----+-----------------------------------+----------------+-----------+-----------+
| +Filter               |  2 | playlistCount > $autoint_0        |           3360 |      1505 |         0 |
| |                     +----+-----------------------------------+----------------+-----------+-----------+
| +OrderedAggregation   |  3 | t, count(p) AS playlistCount      |          11200 |  13282008 |         0 |
| |                     +----+-----------------------------------+----------------+-----------+-----------+
| +Expand(All)          |  4 | (t)-[anon_0:ON_PLAYLIST]->(p)     |      125451006 | 125451006 | 169768574 |
| |                     +----+-----------------------------------+----------------+-----------+-----------+
| +NodeByLabelScan      |  5 | t:Track                           |       13282008 |  13282008 |  13282009 |
+-----------------------+----+-----------------------------------+----------------+-----------+-----------+

Total database accesses: 183053593, total allocated memory: 25328

1505 rows
ready to start consuming query after 37 ms, results consumed after another 15982 ms
```

Figure 5-24. Tracks are expanded through the `ON_PLAYLIST` relationship to calculate the number of playlists that each track is on.

What you see in Figure 5-24 is an expansion through the `ON_PLAYLIST` relationship, which costs around 169 million DB hits, to be able to count the playlists for a track.

There is a more efficient way to do this: with the `getDegree` function. The *degree* of a node is the number of edges incident to it.

In graph theory, a node is *incident* to a relationship if the node is one of the two nodes that the relationship connects. In other words, it is the number of relationships from or to a node.

To count the number of playlists that a track is on, you need the degree of the track node for the `ON_PLAYLIST` relationship type. Neo4j stores these degrees (by relationship type and direction) with the node, and the function `getDegree` accesses this value without the need to traverse the graph.

The performance of queries that require node degrees vastly improves when you write the queries that `COUNT` like this:

```
//019-degrees-2.cypher
PROFILE
MATCH (t:Track)
WHERE COUNT {(t)-[:ON_PLAYLIST]->() } > 2500
RETURN t.name
```

In the query profile shown in Figure 5-25, the `COUNT` function in this form uses the `getDegree` function in the `Filter` operator.

```
+-----------------+----+------------------------------------------------+----------------+----------+----------+
| Operator        | Id | Details                                        | Estimated Rows | Rows     | DB Hits  |
+-----------------+----+------------------------------------------------+----------------+----------+----------+
| +ProduceResults |  0 | `t.name`                                       |        9961506 |     1505 |        0 |
| |               +----+------------------------------------------------+----------------+----------+----------+
| +Projection     |  1 | t.name AS `t.name`                             |        9961506 |     1505 |     3010 |
| |               +----+------------------------------------------------+----------------+----------+----------+
| +Filter         |  2 | getDegree((t)-[:ON_PLAYLIST]-()) > $autoint_0  |        9961506 |     1505 | 13282008 |
| |               +----+------------------------------------------------+----------------+----------+----------+
| +NodeByLabelScan|  3 | t:Track                                        |       13282008 | 13282008 | 13282009 |
+-----------------+----+------------------------------------------------+----------------+----------+----------+

Total database accesses: 26567027, total allocated memory: 304

1505 rows
ready to start consuming query after 6 ms, results consumed after another 4668 ms
```

Figure 5-25. Instead of expanding through all `ON_PLAYLIST` relationships, the highly efficient `getDegree` function is used.

As compared to the previous plan, with 183 million DB hits, this one, which is optimized by making use of `getDegree`, reduces the DB hits to 26 million.

However, not every `COUNT` function implies the use of `getDegree`. Try an `EXPLAIN` on the following query:

```
//020-degrees-3.cypher
EXPLAIN
MATCH (t:Track)
WHERE COUNT {(t)-[:ON_PLAYLIST]->(:Playlist)} > 2500
RETURN t.name
```

If you attempt to make the pattern more specific, for instance by specifying the `Playlist` label, you'll get a plan that once again traverses the graph with `Expand` instead of `getDegree`.

This is because node degrees are not maintained on labels on the other end. Adding the `Playlist` label will require a `Filter` operator.

Thus, `getDegree` is a cheap way to obtain node degrees. Use it whenever you need to query for the degrees of nodes.

Don't Be Eager!

Cypher tries to execute queries in a *lazy* fashion, which means that as operators fetch values from the graph, they are streamed to subsequent operators and finally to the client. If the client can consume this stream efficiently at the same speed, then Neo4j effectively requires no extra memory allocation to hold results. Figure 5-26 illustrates this.

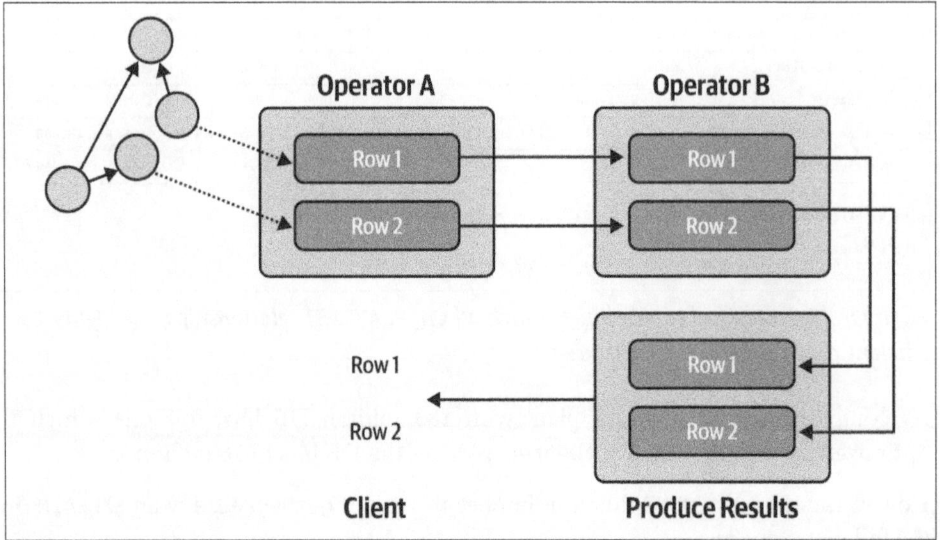

Figure 5-26. Operators lazily stream rows to the next in the chain.

Operator A fetches row 1 from the graph. It does not need to wait for other rows to be fetched before streaming it to Operator B, the final results operator, and to the client. Meanwhile, Operator A has fetched row 2, which is streamed in a similar manner.

Two types of eagerness can trip up this efficient laziness. The first is *implicit eagerness*, which occurs when queries contain both reads and writes on interdependent elements. This query illustrates implicit eagerness:

```
//021-eager-1.cypher
EXPLAIN
MATCH (p:Playlist) WHERE p.followers = 100
DELETE p
MERGE (p2:Playlist) SET p2.followers = 100
```

If Cypher were to execute this query lazily, it would create an infinite loop, because every matched row is deleted but then generates another row to be matched. Instead, the planner has to read all nodes that satisfy the predicate before progressing to update the predicate. This keeps the two operations isolated and prevents updates to the graph from influencing the pattern matches to be read. Instead of fetching one playlist from the graph, deleting it, and then merging a new one, it fetches and deletes all playlists that have 100 followers before executing any `MERGE`, as depicted in Figure 5-27.

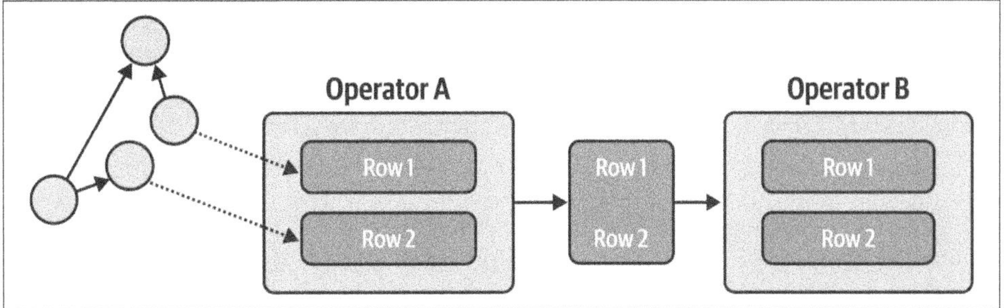

Figure 5-27. `Eager` execution where Operator A must wait for all rows before passing them to the next Operator B

The planner will also insert an `Eager` operator when it detects such a situation. The query plan in Figure 5-28 shows this operator along with the conflicting property, `followers`.

```
+--------------------+----+--------------------------------------------------------------------+----------------+
| Operator           | Id | Details                                                            | Estimated Rows |
+--------------------+----+--------------------------------------------------------------------+----------------+
| +ProduceResults    |  0 |                                                                    |            180 |
| |                  +----+--------------------------------------------------------------------+----------------+
| +EmptyResult       |  1 |                                                                    |            180 |
| |                  +----+--------------------------------------------------------------------+----------------+
| +SetProperty       |  2 | p2.followers = $autoint_1                                          |            180 |
| |                  +----+--------------------------------------------------------------------+----------------+
| +Apply             |  3 |                                                                    |            180 |
| |\                 +----+--------------------------------------------------------------------+----------------+
| | +Merge           |  4 | CREATE (p2:Playlist)                                               |            180 |
| | |                +----+--------------------------------------------------------------------+----------------+
| | +NodeByLabelScan |  5 | p2:Playlist                                                        |      189713678 |
| |                  +----+--------------------------------------------------------------------+----------------+
| +Eager             |  6 | read/delete conflict for variable: p2 (Operator: 7 vs 5)           |            180 |
| |                  +----+--------------------------------------------------------------------+----------------+
| +Delete            |  7 | p                                                                  |            180 |
| |                  +----+--------------------------------------------------------------------+----------------+
| +NodeIndexSeek     |  8 | RANGE INDEX p:Playlist(followers) WHERE followers = $autoint_0     |            180 |
+--------------------+----+--------------------------------------------------------------------+----------------+
```

Figure 5-28. The `Eager` operator inserted by the planner when it detects that implicit eagerness is required

This can lead to a lot of memory usage. Why is this a problem? The first line of reasoning is that the heap space is exhausted, causing database panic. But there are other impacts, too. The JVM may stop the world to reclaim space on the heap, which causes a pause in service for a single server. This might appear as a transient failure to a cluster, causing a repair to happen, which takes perhaps a second where the database isn't accepting any writes.

When creating large volumes of data, especially through ingestion, aim to isolate the reads from the writes. Instead of writing one complex query that both reads and writes dependent data to the graph, consider breaking it up into separate simple queries—for example, splitting the nodes and relationships—even if it involves multiple passes over the same set of input data.

The second scenario is *explicitly eager*. Certain operations require that data be pulled in eagerly to execute over the entire set. Examples of these are aggregating functions, such as `avg()`, `min()`, `max()`, or `collect()`; a `sort` operation if not using an index; and a `DISTINCT`. Here's an example of an explicitly eager aggregation:

```
//022-eager-2.cypher
EXPLAIN
MATCH (t:Track)-[:ARTIST]->(a:Artist)
RETURN a.name as artistName, avg(t.duration) as avgDuration
ORDER BY avgDuration
```

The `EXPLAIN`, in Figure 5-29, shows the query plan.

Operator	Id	Details	Estimated Rows	Ordered by	Pipeline
+ProduceResults	0	artistName, avgDuration	4180		
+Sort	1	avgDuration ASC	4180	avgDuration ASC	In Pipeline 2
+EagerAggregation	2	cache[a.name] AS artistName, avg(t.duration) AS avgDuration	4180		
+Filter	3	t:Track	17471590		
+Expand(All)	4	(a)<-[anon_0:ARTIST]-(t)	17471590		
+CacheProperties	5	cache[a.name]	1290662		
+NodeByLabelScan	6	a:Artist	1290662		Fused in Pipeline 0

Figure 5-29. The `EagerAggregation` operator must consume all rows from the previous operators in order to calculate the average duration of all tracks.

The anchors in this query are the `Artist` nodes. If there was no `avg` function in this query, the artist-track expansions could have been lazy. However, the query requires the average track duration for an artist. This results in the `EagerAggregation` operator, which forces this data to be materialized in memory to be able to calculate the average. After this, the `Sort` operator also must wait for all the rows evaluated before it can sort on average, resulting in increased memory pressure. If the query operates over a trivial set of data, though, this is still a fast operation.

`EagerAggregation` is slightly less memory intensive than the `Eager` operator; however, you will find that as the volume of rows grows past the tens of millions, this query starts to get inefficient and Neo4j may run out of memory.

Sorting

The `Sort` operator in an execution plan sorts rows by a key and is a result of an `ORDER BY` in the query. It is an eager operator: it pulls in all rows to be sorted and holds them in memory, resulting in increased memory usage. Examine the execution plan for this query, which sorts tracks based on their duration:

```
//023-sorting-1.cypher
EXPLAIN
MATCH (a:Artist)<-[:ARTIST]-(t:Track)
```

```
RETURN a.name as artistName, t.duration as trackDuration
ORDER BY trackDuration
```

Operator 2, `Sort`, in Figure 5-30, must wait for the expansion of all tracks from all artists before it can do its work.

```
+-------------------+----+------------------------------+-----------------+--------------------+
| Operator          | Id | Details                      | Estimated Rows  | Ordered by         |
+-------------------+----+------------------------------+-----------------+--------------------+
| +ProduceResults   |  0 | artistName, trackDuration    |        17471590 |                    |
| |                 +----+------------------------------+-----------------+                    |
| +Projection       |  1 | cache[a.name] AS artistName  |        17471590 |                    |
| |                 +----+------------------------------+-----------------+                    |
| +Sort             |  2 | trackDuration ASC            |        17471590 | trackDuration ASC  |
| |                 +----+------------------------------+-----------------+--------------------+
| +Projection       |  3 | t.duration AS trackDuration  |        17471590 |                    |
| |                 +----+------------------------------+-----------------+--------------------+
| +Filter           |  4 | t:Track                      |        17471590 |                    |
| |                 +----+------------------------------+-----------------+--------------------+
| +Expand(All)      |  5 | (a)<-[anon_0:ARTIST]-(t)     |        17471590 |                    |
| |                 +----+------------------------------+-----------------+--------------------+
| +CacheProperties  |  6 | cache[a.name]                |         1290662 |                    |
| |                 +----+------------------------------+-----------------+--------------------+
| +NodeByLabelScan  |  7 | a:Artist                     |         1290662 |                    |
+-------------------+----+------------------------------+-----------------+--------------------+
```

Figure 5-30. The `Sort` operator is also eager. To be able to sort all tracks by their duration, it must eagerly pull in all rows from the previous stages.

Try adding a limit of 5 and see how the plan changes (see Figure 5-31):

```
//024-sorting-2.cypher
EXPLAIN
MATCH (a:Artist)<-[:ARTIST]-(t:Track)
RETURN a.name as artistName, t.duration as trackDuration
ORDER BY trackDuration LIMIT 5
```

```
+-------------------+----+------------------------------+-----------------+--------------------+
| Operator          | Id | Details                      | Estimated Rows  | Ordered by         |
+-------------------+----+------------------------------+-----------------+--------------------+
| +ProduceResults   |  0 | artistName, trackDuration    |               5 |                    |
| |                 +----+------------------------------+-----------------+                    |
| +Projection       |  1 | a.name AS artistName         |               5 |                    |
| |                 +----+------------------------------+-----------------+                    |
| +Limit            |  2 | 5                            |               5 |                    |
| |                 +----+------------------------------+-----------------+                    |
| +Filter           |  3 | a:Artist                     |               5 |                    |
| |                 +----+------------------------------+-----------------+                    |
| +Expand(All)      |  4 | (t)-[anon_0:ARTIST]->(a)     |               5 |                    |
| |                 +----+------------------------------+-----------------+                    +
| +Sort             |  5 | trackDuration ASC            |               4 | trackDuration ASC  |
| |                 +----+------------------------------+-----------------+--------------------+
| +Projection       |  6 | t.duration AS trackDuration  |        13282008 |                    |
| |                 +----+------------------------------+-----------------+--------------------+
| +NodeByLabelScan  |  7 | t:Track                      |        13282008 |                    |
+-------------------+----+------------------------------+-----------------+--------------------+
```

Figure 5-31. Introducing a `Limit` in the query results in the `Sort` being planned earlier so that the `Artist` expansion is not wasteful and operates on fewer rows.

Now, the planner decides that it need not expand artists and tracks, since you only want 5 tracks sorted by their duration. The anchor changes to tracks (operator 7), and `Sort` eagerly pulls 13 million rows and keeps them in query state to sort them. Five are then input to the next operator, which expands them to fetch their artists.

There is a way to avoid some of these expensive queries. Since range indexes store their properties in ascending order, Cypher can benefit from using them instead of the `Sort` operator. Create an index on the track duration, the property to be sorted on:

```
//025-sorting-3.cypher
CREATE INDEX track_duration
FOR (n:Track)
ON (n.duration)
```

Wait for the index to populate before rerunning the query. `SHOW INDEXES` will list the indexes, and the `state` column will indicate whether it is populating or online.

Now rerun the `EXPLAIN`. You'll see that the plan is the same as in Figure 5-29. Indeed, if you check the `track_duration` index in the table produced by `SHOW INDEXES`, you will see that the `readCount` is 0 and the `lastRead` time is null, confirming that your new index was not used.

The reason it was not picked up is that there is no predicate and no type constraint on this property, so the planner decides that it will use the `token lookup` index for artists. Here's where you can nudge the planner into using the `track_duration` index to back the sorting. Since the track duration is expected to be positive, add a condition that won't affect your results:

```
//026-sorting-4.cypher
EXPLAIN
MATCH (a:Artist)<-[:ARTIST]-(t:Track)
WHERE t.duration > 0
RETURN a.name as artistName, t.duration as trackDuration
ORDER BY trackDuration
```

Now the plan (see Figure 5-32) is far better! The `Sort` operator has vanished, and instead, the planner is using the new index to retrieve already sorted track durations (which were fetched from the index in the `NodeIndexSeekByRange` stage). It then traverses the `ARTIST` relationship to retrieve the artist names. It preserves the sort order and returns the results.

Operator	Id	Details	Estimated Rows	Ordered by
+ProduceResults	0	artistName, trackDuration	524147	
+Projection	1	a.name AS artistName, cache[t.duration] AS trackDuration	524147	trackDuration ASC
+Filter	2	a:Artist	524147	
+Expand(All)	3	(t)-[anon_0:ARTIST]->(a)	524147	
+NodeIndexSeekByRange	4	RANGE INDEX t:Track(duration) WHERE duration > $autoint_0, cache[t.duration]	398459	t.duration ASC

Figure 5-32. An index-backed `Sort` is far more efficient than the eager `Sort` operator.

In this case, the heuristics result in an estimation of 398,459 rows. In reality, due to the condition that matches every track, the number of actual rows will be around 13 million. You can verify this by running `PROFILE`. We recommend doing this via Cypher Shell instead of the Neo4j browser, since it will execute much faster to stream 13 million rows to the shell.

What about adding a limit? Let's add the predicate on track duration and rerun the earlier query:

```
//027-sorting-5.cypher
EXPLAIN
MATCH (a:Artist)<-[:ARTIST]-(t:Track)
WHERE t.duration > 0
RETURN a.name as artistName, t.duration as trackDuration
ORDER BY trackDuration LIMIT 5
```

The `LIMIT` does make a huge difference. Since the sort is now backed by the index, the planner is smart enough to stream up to 5 tracks from the index and expand them. Unlike the situation when there was no index, there is now no expansion. Figure 5-33 confirms this.

Operator	Id	Details	Estimated Rows	Ordered by
+ProduceResults	0	artistName, trackDuration	5	
+Projection	1	a.name AS artistName, cache[t.duration] AS trackDuration	5	trackDuration ASC
+Limit	2	5	5	
+Filter	3	a:Artist	5	
+Expand(All)	4	(t)-[anon_0:ARTIST]->(a)	5	
+NodeIndexSeekByRange	5	RANGE INDEX t:Track(duration) WHERE duration > $autoint_0, cache[t.duration]	4	t.duration ASC

Figure 5-33. Since the index on track duration is sorted, only 5 nodes need to be fetched from it, massively cutting down on query time.

While properties in a range index are stored in ascending order, `ORDER BY property DESC` can also take advantage of the index, because it can be read efficiently in reverse too.

Sorting can be an expensive operation due to its eagerness. Always evaluate your queries that use an `ORDER BY` to see if an index can make them more performant.

Where sorting is the last part of the query and it is particularly expensive, consider sending the unsorted data to the client and let it do the sorting job.

I Want to Break Free (of the Planner)

The Cypher planner improves constantly, and the cases where you might think you know better than the planner get more rare with every new release of Neo4j. In those rare cases where you need to squeeze out every last millisecond of performance, you can provide hints to the planner. Look at the following query:

```
//028-planner-1.cypher
PROFILE
MATCH (t:Track)-[:ON_PLAYLIST]->(p:Playlist)
WHERE t.duration > 8000000 and p.followers > 5000
RETURN p.name, t.name
```

There are indexes on track duration and playlist followers, so the planner can use either index to anchor the query. Figure 5-34 shows the profile for this query.

Operator	Id	Details	Estimated Rows	Rows	DB Hits	Memory (Bytes)
+ProduceResults	0	`p.id`, `t.name`	112768	3	0	0
+Projection	1	cache[p.id] AS `p.id`, t.name AS `t.name`	112768	3	6	
+Filter	2	t.duration > $autoint_0 AND t:Track	112768	3	1157816	
+Expand(All)	3	(p)<-[anon_0:ON_PLAYLIST]-(t)	3758946	578905	583287	
+CacheProperties	4	cache[p.id]	31610	2511	5022	
+NodeIndexSeekByRange	5	RANGE INDEX p:Playlist(followers) WHERE followers > $autoint_1	31610	2511	2512	240

Total database accesses: 1748643, total allocated memory: 320

Figure 5-34. The Cypher planner has chosen the playlist duration index to anchor the query based on database statistics.

The planner has picked the playlist follower index over the track duration index. This is a good choice, because the selectivity of the playlists index is higher, based on the ratio of unique values to total size.

However, because you know your graph really well, you know that very few tracks are longer than 3 hours. Verify this by counting the number of tracks with this particular duration, as well as the number of playlists with more than 5,000 followers:

```
//029-planner-2.cypher
MATCH (t:Track)
WHERE t.duration > 8000000
RETURN count(t);

MATCH (p:Playlist)
WHERE p.followers > 5000
RETURN count(p);
```

The number of tracks is 252, while the number of playlists is 2,511. Expanding 2,511 playlists to find all tracks produces more than 500,000 rows, only to discard all but 3 tracks that meet the duration criteria. Wouldn't it be better to expand 252 tracks to their playlists instead?

The planner will be forced to use the track index if you direct it to do so with an index hint:

```
//030-planner-3.cypher
PROFILE
MATCH (t:Track)-[:ON_PLAYLIST]->(p:Playlist)
USING INDEX t:Track(duration)
WHERE t.duration > 8000000 and p.followers > 5000
RETURN p.name, t.name
```

The planner uses the track index as directed and continues using the playlist index as well. Figure 5-35 shows that there are two starting points now; their branches join together in a `NodeHashJoin` operator. This operator is one of the variants of a hash join operator and executes based on node IDs efficiently.

Operator	Id	Details	Estimated Rows	Rows	DB Hits	Memory (Bytes)
+ProduceResults	0	\`p.name\`, \`t.name\`	112768	3	0	0
+Projection	1	cache[p.name] AS \`p.name\`, t.name AS \`t.name\`	112768	3	6	
+NodeHashJoin	2	p	112768	3	0	731352
+Expand(All)	3	(t)-[anon_0:ON_PLAYLIST]->(p)	3763523	521	1296	
+NodeIndexSeekByRange	4	RANGE INDEX t:Track(duration) WHERE duration > $autoint_0	398459	252	253	368
+CacheProperties	5	cache[p.name]	31610	2511	5022	
+NodeIndexSeekByRange	6	RANGE INDEX p:Playlist(followers) WHERE followers > $autoint_1	31610	2511	2512	368

Total database accesses: 9089, total allocated memory: 731944

Figure 5-35. The index hint provided in the query forces the planner to use the track duration as well, resulting in a `NodeHashJoin` to merge the two branches, tracks and playlists.

The smaller input is called the *build input* and is pulled in eagerly, producing a *probe table*. The larger input branch is called the *probe input*. The planner checks the probe table against every row of the probe input. The visual query plan in Figure 5-36 shows this better.

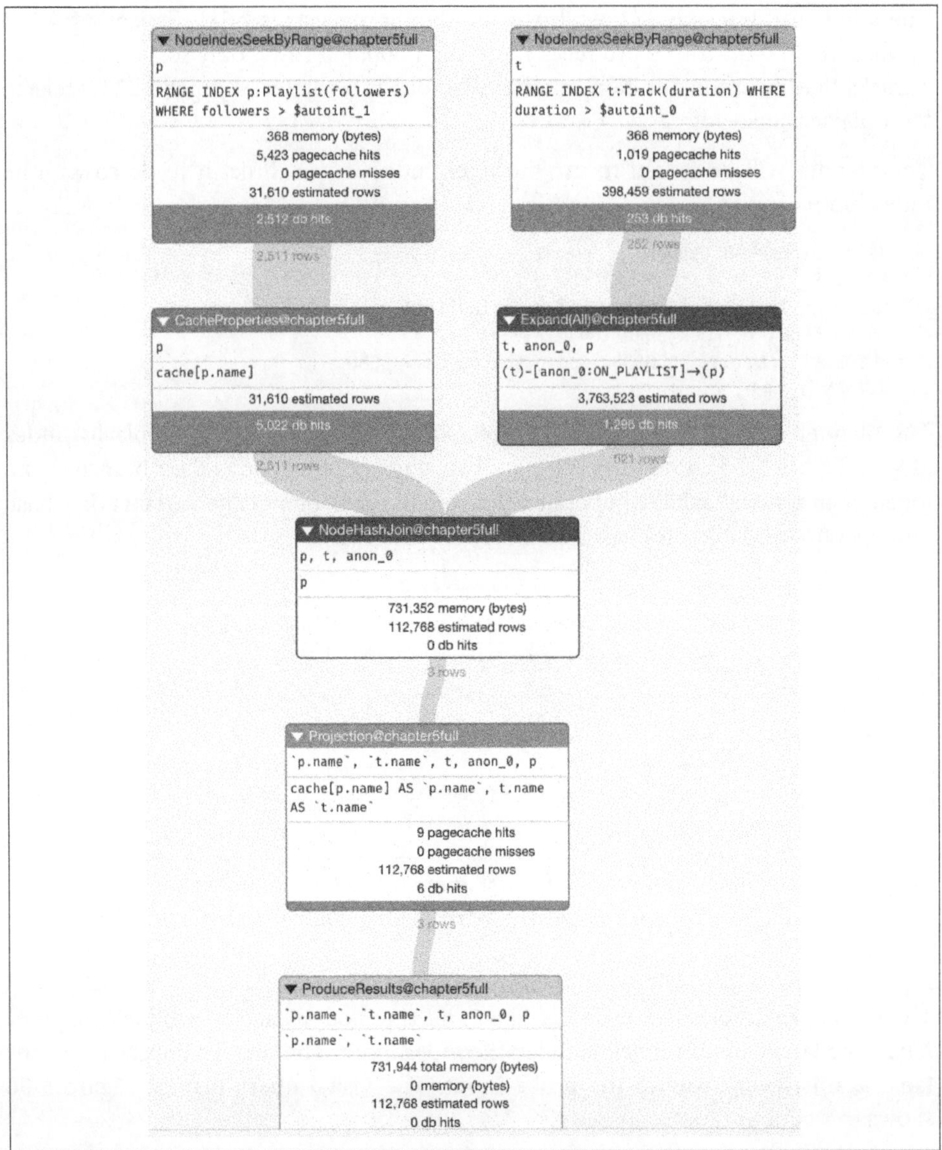

Figure 5-36. The visual query plan better illustrates both indexes being used and then the branches merged at the `NodeHashJoin` operator.

The DB hits for this query are 9,089, which is a big improvement over the previous 1.7 million hits. You'll notice, though, that the join that's now part of the plan is more expensive in terms of memory. This is something to watch out for; you'll need to evaluate whether the trade-off is still worth it.

In some cases, you may be able to eliminate the join as well. This example shows how you could try to manipulate the query, though it's very rarely worth doing, as you'll see with this query:

```
//031-planner-4.cypher
PROFILE
MATCH (t:Track)-[:ON_PLAYLIST]->(p:Playlist)
USING INDEX t:Track(duration)
WHERE t.duration > 8000000
MATCH (t)-[:ON_PLAYLIST]->(p)
WHERE p.followers > 5000
RETURN p.name, t.name
```

The corresponding plan is shown in Figure 5-37.

Operator	Id	Details	Estimated Rows	Rows	DB Hits	Memory (Bytes)
+ProduceResults	0	`p.name`, `t.name`	1	3	0	0
+Projection	1	p.name AS `p.name`, t.name AS `t.name`	1	3	9	
+Expand(Into)	2	(t)-[anon_0:ON_PLAYLIST]->(p)	1	3	19	1368
+Filter	3	p.followers > $autoint_1 AND p:Playlist	112768	3	1048	
+Expand(All)	4	(t)-[anon_1:ON_PLAYLIST]->(p)	3763523	521	1296	
+NodeIndexSeekByRange	5	RANGE INDEX t:Track(duration) WHERE duration > $autoint_0	398459	252	253	240

Total database accesses: 2625, total allocated memory: 1576

Figure 5-37. The `NodeHashJoin` has been eliminated with a double match on the `ON_PLAYLIST` relationship. This sort of trick is rarely worth it.

The trick here is to match the `ON_PLAYLIST` relationship *twice*, to get around the join. The total number of DB hits is a bit higher, though better than the original query, and the memory consumption is lower than the one with the `NodeHashJoin`. However, it won't be easy to remember why you wrote the query this way. You'll have to monitor it as your graph evolves and when you upgrade Neo4j for performance degradation—one reason we don't recommend extreme or clever hacks like this.

Other types of query hints include *label scan hints*, which force the planner to use a different index for a `NodeByLabelScan` or a `RelationshipByTypeScan`, and *join hints*, which enforce a hash join at a certain point between two branches. These are rarely required for the majority of queries you will write.

Use hints cautiously and measure if they're really worth it. If the shape of your graph changes significantly, or a new version of Neo4j optimizes the planner, your hint could be rendered ineffective or even detrimental.

Cypher Runtimes

The runtime executes query plans from the planner. Knowing the characteristics of each of these runtimes will help you understand whether you want to override the default for a particular query, so let's look at each in turn:

Pipelined
: The pipelined runtime is the default runtime for Neo4j Enterprise edition. This runtime allows operators to produce and consume batches of rows, which are written into buffers containing both the data and the tasks in the pipeline. The *pipeline* is a sequence of operators executed together, in the same task, by the runtime. This model makes better use of CPU caches, enables direct use of CPU registers, and avoids the cost of the virtual function calls used in traditional models like the slotted runtime. It is well suited for transactional use cases and in systems where large numbers of queries are being executed in parallel.

Parallel
: The pipelined and slotted runtimes both execute queries in a single thread assigned to one CPU core. The parallel runtime can execute one query over many cores, typically resulting in a performance boost for graph analytics queries. It thus produces more pipelines than the pipelined runtime. It contains the *partitioned operators*, which can segment the data and then operate on the segments in parallel.

  Long-running queries and systems with multiple cores can benefit from the parallel runtime, but you're unlikely to see a large performance boost on queries that execute in less than 500ms. Graph global queries, where there is no specific anchor node, are good candidates for the parallel runtime. So are queries that anchor on dense nodes or supernodes and queries that expand from the anchor to a very large portion of the graph.

  The parallel runtime currently only supports read queries. It does not take advantage of property indexes for sorting, so queries that use `ORDER BY` can perform worse than with the pipelined runtime.

  Monitor your system if you begin using the parallel runtime heavily, because increased concurrency can decrease the overall throughput and increase CPU load. As such, transactional systems are ideal with queries that must support workloads with high throughput. However, an analytics system with few queries but expensive and long-running ones would also benefit. You may also want to consider larger provisioned read-replicas for parallel analytical queries.

Slotted
: The slotted runtime follows traditional database models and is the default planner for Neo4j's Community edition. It is directly mapped to the logical plan,

where the logical operators match a physical operator and the operators are processed row by row. This runtime has a short planning phase, so it can be useful for rarely executed but planning-intensive queries. The disadvantages of the slotted runtime are slower execution and less efficient use of CPU caches. But it is more efficient than the previous runtime, as it uses preallocated arrays (which sit in the CPU cache) instead of maps for the query state rows.

The following query uses the default pipelined runtime and takes 201ms to have results ready to start consuming (see Figure 5-38):

```
//032-runtime-1.cypher
PROFILE
MATCH (a:Artist)<-[:ARTIST]-(t:Track)
WHERE t.duration > 0 AND a.name="Pink Floyd"
RETURN t.name as trackName, t.duration as trackDuration
```

Runtime PIPELINED

Runtime version 5.19

Batch size 1024

Operator	Id	Details	Estimated Rows	Rows	DB Hits	Pipeline
+ProduceResults	0	trackName, trackDuration	26207	1423	0	
+Projection	1	t.name AS trackName, cache[t.duration] AS trackDuration	26207	1423	1423	
+Filter	2	a.name = $autostring_1 AND a:Artist	26207	1423	34945964	
+Expand(All)	3	(t)-[anon_0:ARTIST]->(a)	524147	17471559	98807516	
+NodeIndexSeekByRange	4	RANGE INDEX t:Track(duration) WHERE duration > $autoint_0, cache[t.duration]	398459	13281980	13281981	Fused in Pipeline 0

Total database accesses: 147036884, total allocated memory: 320

1423 rows
ready to start consuming query after 201 ms, results consumed after another 47129 ms

Figure 5-38. The default pipelined runtime with pipeline 0 being the only one, using a single core

While this is not a graph-global query, you can still see a boost when you use the parallel runtime. Prefix the query with `CYPHER runtime = parallel` to force the usage of this runtime:

```
//033-runtime-2.cypher
CYPHER runtime = parallel
PROFILE
MATCH (a:Artist)<-[:ARTIST]-(t:Track)
WHERE t.duration > 0 AND a.name="Pink Floyd"
RETURN t.name as trackName, t.duration as trackDuration
```

You can see the introduction of the `PartitionedNodeIndexSeekByRange` in Figure 5-39. The results are available faster due to parallel processing.

Planner COST

Runtime PARALLEL

Runtime version 5.19

Batch size 1024

Operator	Id	Details	Estimated Rows	Rows	DB Hits	Pipeline
+ProduceResults	0	trackName, trackDuration	26207	1423	0	In Pipeline 2
+Projection	1	t.name AS trackName, cache[t.duration] AS trackDuration	26207	1423	1423	
+Filter	2	a.name = $autostring_1 AND a:Artist	26207	1423	34945964	
+Expand(All)	3	(t)-[anon_0:ARTIST]->(a)	524147	17471559	98807516	Fused in Pipeline 1
+PartitionedNodeIndexSeekByRange	4	RANGE INDEX t:Track(duration) WHERE duration > $autoint_0, cache[t.duration]	398459	13281988	13281988	In Pipeline 0

Total database accesses: 147036891, total allocated memory: 4849664

1423 rows
ready to start consuming query after 98 ms, results consumed after another 5536 ms

Figure 5-39. `PartitionedNodeIndexSeekByRange` is an operator used when the parallel runtime is in play.

The parallel runtime is very effective for certain kinds of queries, especially graph-global ones, but keep in mind that it is not a drop-in substitute for the default runtime.

Parameterizing Queries

There is a cost associated with producing an optimal query plan. In order to keep planning to a minimum, Neo4j maintains a set of query caches per database; the default number of cached queries is 1,000. When your query plan is retrieved from the query cache, the cost of planning is zero.

Parameterizing your queries enables them to be cached, leading to faster execution times.

Parameters can be used for node and relationship IDs as well as literals and expressions, and these values are substituted at execution time. Always parameterize your queries. Here's an example:

```
MATCH (a:Artist)<-[:ARTIST]-(t:Track)
WHERE t.duration > $duration AND a.name = $artistName
RETURN t.name as trackName, t.duration as trackDuration
ORDER BY trackDuration
```

In this query, `$duration` and `$artistName` are parameters, with values supplied by the client. The following query, which supplies literals, is not recommended, because it may not be cached, leading to query planning on every execution:

```
MATCH (a:Artist)<-[:ARTIST]-(t:Track)
WHERE t.duration > 0 AND a.name="Pink Floyd"
RETURN t.name as trackName, t.duration as trackDuration
ORDER BY trackDuration
```

Since Neo4j version 5, Cypher has attempted to autoparameterize queries, meaning that it infers parameters and then substitutes them. However, we still don't recommend relying on this behavior. Parameterization also helps guard against Cypher injection (*https://oreil.ly/PU_NS*) and aids query readability, so there is no reason to not parameterize your queries.

Monitoring and Measuring Query Times

It is good practice to monitor your queries' performance and measure how long they take to execute before putting them into production. There are many ways to measure query times, ranging from trivial to more advanced.

One of the critical aspects is the graph on which you execute the query. Query performance can vary significantly, depending on the shape of the graph. You want your test graph to mirror your graph in production so that the database statistics are as similar as possible. It might be easy to generate a test graph with a uniform distribution of nodes and relationships, but it will not represent the performance of your queries in production. If you have access to your production graph, you have the best test graph (you may obfuscate some properties or other sensitive information). If not, the next option is to gather statistics and use them to generate the same shape of graph.

Once you have a test graph, then the trivial way to test query time is to profile your expensive queries and record the number of DB hits and memory usage. As with any performance testing system, the infrastructure and resources you use should mirror production as much as possible.

You can also do load testing of Cypher queries via JMeter (*https://oreil.ly/9Qq1B*). These test plans can be recorded and rerun at intervals or before upgrading the application or Neo4j. Tools such as this give you a consistent way to test, and you can version-control plans as well as test reports.

Neo4j's query log is another valuable source of information about how your queries are performing in production. To turn on query logging, edit the *neo4j.conf* file to set `db.logs.query.enabled` to `VERBOSE` (the default) or `INFO` (if you set it to `OFF`, nothing is logged).

Another configuration, `db.logs.query.threshold`, is used in `INFO` mode and will log any queries that exceed this threshold (in seconds). This configuration is ignored in `VERBOSE` mode.

This gives you the flexibility to monitor everything or just the long-running queries. The query log can provide a wealth of information, including query planning time, page hits and faults, CPU time, the user executing the query, and the query plan itself. Here is an example of what you might find in the *query.log*:

```
2024-06-07 20:01:27.083+0000 INFO  id:13 - transaction id:3 - 110 ms:
(planning: 29, waiting: 0) - 731944 B - 6264 page hits, 187 page faults -
bolt-session    bolt    neo4j-browser/v5.15.0        client/127.0.0.1:55902
server/127.0.0.1:7687>    chapter5full - neo4j - MATCH
(t:Track)-[:ON_PLAYLIST]->(p:Playlist)
                    USING INDEX t:Track(duration)
                    WHERE t.duration > 8000000 and p.followers > 5000
                    RETURN p.name, t.name; - {} - runtime=pipelined - {app:
'neo4j-browser_v5.15.0', type: 'user-direct'}
```

Monitoring the log and setting up alerts is a good way to capture poorly performing or expensive queries. We discuss how to do this in Chapter 11.

Summary

You've learned to use `EXPLAIN` and `PROFILE`, and you now understand the work that the query planner does under the hood. Indexes are critical to anchor selectivity and to the efficiency of most queries and should be the starting point when you examine your queries. To get more comfortable with query tuning, we recommend that you profile your queries frequently and analyze the plans. Revisit Chapters 3 and 4 as well to gain a fresh perspective of how your graph model can impact query performance. In Chapter 8, we'll discuss subqueries that can help performance, as well as quantified path patterns.

CHAPTER 6
Securing Your Database

Securing Neo4j (and any other database, for that matter) is of paramount importance. Your database is likely to contain business-critical and sensitive data, including personal, financial, and tactical information. A security breach by data thieves can reveal information that could damage your business's reputation and financial stability. Securing Neo4j is usually necessary to meet regulatory and compliance standards—a breach could even lead to a legal censure. Graph databases, in particular, can reveal crucial patterns and insights; unauthorized or malicious modification of the data may lead to misleading or incorrect predictions or results.

Security is always a top priority at Neo4j. We advise that you keep aware of the latest features in this area by visiting the release notes (*https://oreil.ly/OqUAZ*) frequently.

As part of its compliance process, ElectricHarmony has brought in a team of security experts to conduct a threat analysis study of their system. They will adopt the STRIDE (*https://oreil.ly/KGFAV*) threat-assessment model, a structured framework for identifying and mitigating security threats. STRIDE is a mnemonic for security threats in six categories: spoofing, tampering, repudiation, information disclosure, denial of service, and elevation of privilege. This chapter is structured along that framework, assessing each type of threat in turn. You will represent the Neo4j database team at ElectricHarmony and tag along with the experts to help them identify and mitigate potential threats.

Spoofing

Spoofing is the first threat category in the STRIDE model. It occurs when an attacker illegally accesses the system using a legitimate user's credentials.

Authentication

Verifying a user's identity in order to gain access to the database is called *authentication* (often shortened to *auth*). Neo4j supports many authentication providers (*https://oreil.ly/qd6T8*), including custom plugins, Lightweight Directory Access Protocol (LDAP), and single sign-on (SSO) integration with services such as Okta and Google; consult the relevant documentation (*https://oreil.ly/6L1e-*) for setup instructions. Neo4j's default is the native auth provider that stores user and role information in the system database. In our experience, serious enterprise deployments almost always disable the native auth provider in favor of others, such as LDAP or SSO. To disable the native provider and thus the native user, modify the configuration file *dbms.security.authentication_providers* and set it to your preferred provider.

Using the native auth provider

You must set a password for the native user `neo4j` before starting Neo4j for the first time. If you don't set one, it will use the default password `neo4j` and prompt you to change it on first login. The best practice is to set this password yourself before you start Neo4j, using the `set-initial-password` command of the `neo4j-admin` tool. You can also force this password to be changed upon first login to the database. An example of this command is:

```
neo4j-admin dbms set-initial-password be4Hw%qi9 --require-password-change
```

The default minimum length of passwords in Neo4j is eight characters. This can be changed with the configuration setting `dbms.security.auth_minimum_password_length`.

Using the LDAP provider

Consider the following configuration settings if you're using the LDAP provider:

`dbms.security.ldap.authentication.cache_enabled`
: If `true` (the default), then the result of authentication via the LDAP server will be cached. Your security policies may dictate otherwise, in which case, turn this cache off.

`dbms.security.auth_cache_ttl`
: Another way to turn off the cache is to set its time to live (TTL) to 0. If you do, or if you set it to a very small value, be aware that reauthentication and reauthorization will be required more frequently, which could affect performance. On the other hand, a long TTL would mean that changes on the LDAP server (such as those to user settings) won't be reflected quickly in Neo4j's authorization behavior.

`dbms.security.auth_cache_use_ttl`
: This related setting is a boolean; if set to `false`, the TTL setting is ignored and the cache lives forever or is evicted when the maximum capacity of the authentication cache is reached. The maximum capacity of the authentication and authorization cache is configured by `dbms.security.auth_cache_max_capacity` and the default is 10000.

Securing Access via the Neo4j browser

By now, you're very familiar with the Neo4j browser as one of the mechanisms to access the data stored in your Neo4j database. You want to be sure that if users leave their machines unattended for long periods with the Neo4j browser open in a tab, it does not provide unauthenticated users an unintended route to access Neo4j. By default, Neo4j keeps the browser session to the database alive while the tab is open; the default timeout for an idle session is 0 seconds (which means there is no time limit). Change this configuration to log the user out after a set period of idleness.

You can configure browser credential timeouts using `browser.credential_timeout`. The timeout is reset when the user interacts with the browser.

The Neo4j browser caches unencrypted user credentials in its local storage, where they are governed by the `browser.credential_timeout` settings. If the browser tab is closed and reopened within the timeout period, it uses the cached credentials to reestablish its database connection. We recommend turning this behavior off for users who share workstations.

Set the Neo4j browser configuration `browser.retain_connection_credentials` to `false` to disable credential caching.

Best Practices

To improve protection against spoofing, review your Neo4j deployment and implement lockout mechanisms and activity monitoring.

You can configure the maximum number of unsuccessful authentication attempts allowed with `dbms.security.auth_max_failed_attempts`. The default is 3 attempts. Setting this number higher makes it easier for an attacker to brute-force the password. Once the maximum number of attempts are reached, the user's account will be locked until the time specified in `dbms.security.auth_lock_time` expires, even if they provide correct credentials.

It is important to log authentication attempts and review these logs periodically. Neo4j logs security-related events to a file called *security.log* (located by default in the *<NEO4J_HOME>/logs* directory) if the configuration setting `dbms.security.auth_enabled` is set to `true`, which is its default setting. The security log contains:

- Successful and unsuccessful login attempts
- Authorization failures from role-based access control
- All administration commands run against the system database, such as creating users or granting and revoking roles
- LDAP server communication events and failures
- Some cases of misconfiguration

As with any other system, you'll want to set up alerts for suspicious activity, such as multiple failed login attempts, and periodically review user accounts and access levels.

Tampering

Tampering refers to the unauthorized and malicious modification of data, either directly in the database or by manipulating queries.

Securing Communication Channels

Securing data in transit involves enabling SSL/TLS for communication channels between Neo4j and client applications or administrative tools, such as backups or cluster communication. Table 6-1 lists the default ports Neo4j uses. However, it is a best practice to change these ports to reduce the attack surface.

Table 6-1. Neo4j default communication ports

Channel	Default port
bolt	7687
https	7473
cluster	5000, 6000, 7000, 7688
backups	6362

Neo4j uses the Netty (*https://netty.io*) library, which supports OpenSSL derivatives and the native JDK SSL provider. Remote access to Neo4j—including client applications and APIs—should use only encrypted Bolt or HTTPS. If your system permits loading data via the `LOAD CSV` command, enforce that this is also done securely, over HTTPS. Follow the manual to ensure that the relevant channels are configured correctly. Use SSL certificates from a trusted certificate authority.

If your Neo4j deployment is clustered, configure intra-cluster communication (*https://oreil.ly/-UMrS*) to use encryption.

Securing Data at Rest

You can set up volume encryption to protect your Neo4j database on disk. Vormetric Data Security Manager (*https://oreil.ly/sMJsO*) from Thales is one option to configure full-disk encryption. If you use Neo4j Aura, data is encrypted at rest using the underlying cloud provider's encryption mechanism. You can go a step further with Aura and use customer-managed keys. These are managed using a supported cloud key management service. All data at rest is encrypted with this key.

Don't forget to protect access to the backups of your database, too, to prevent unauthorized users from making copies of your database. Apart from configuring the backup server to use SSL/TLS, make sure that no external access is allowed to the backup port. The backup port is configured in the setting `server.backup.listen_address`.

Neo4j uses several files and directories for configuration, logs, and data. Ensure that the correct file permissions are set up for these. Only the data, logs, run, and metrics directories require write permissions; the rest should be read only, with the bin directory also requiring execute permissions.

Using Consistency Checks

The `check` command in the `neo4j-admin` tool performs a consistency check on your database, dump, or backups. It can be included in general housekeeping routines to verify the integrity of the graph and its indexes and counts. However, you can't execute a consistency check on a running database and shouldn't need to.

To run a consistency check, run the following at the command line:

```
neo4j-admin database check <database_name>
```

By default, this checks consistency between nodes, relations, properties, types, and tokens. If the tool finds inconsistencies, it produces a report; otherwise, the process exits cleanly. If there are inconsistencies, you can try to make a copy of the database using the `neo4j-admin copy` command. The copy command performs a couple of actions while copying a database: it defragments (and therefore compacts) it by reclaiming unused space, creates the node and relationship lookup indexes, and can fix inconsistencies. In the rare event that all inconsistencies are not fixed, you'll need to reach out to Neo4j Support to get help to resolve them.

Defending Against Cypher Injection Attacks

You've likely heard of SQL injection attacks. Cypher injection attacks apply the same concept to the Cypher query language. In a Cypher injection attack, a Cypher query is "injected" with new or changed pieces or with complete queries that terminate the original via the input data from the client. This dynamically modified query, if successful, can have severe effects. Attackers can tamper with existing data, spoof identities, access sensitive information, and elevate their privileges.

Here's an example of a Cypher query that uses string concatenation to create a new node:

```
String query = "CREATE (u:User) SET u.name = '" + username + "'";
```

If an attacker wants to delete all nodes and relationships in your graph, they could supply the username string as the following:

```
"Bob' WITH 1 as nothing MATCH (n) DETACH DELETE n //"
```

The `WITH` provides the bridge for the next part of the query to execute, and the trailing // serves to comment out anything that remains of the original query.

This is why you should always use parameters in your Cypher query. Here's how you could rewrite the earlier query creating a new node:

```
String query = "CREATE (u:User) SET u.name = $username";
```

This method supplies the username by mapping key-value pairs. Recall from Chapter 5 that the query is compiled into an executable plan. Once compiled, nothing that is supplied later with the parameter map can alter or hijack the query. Apart from protecting against Cypher injection on literals, such as the username string in the example, parameterizing your query is also important for query caching. In short, there's no reason not to always use parameters.

Don't forget to examine APOC library usage. Supply the parameters, via a parameter map, to the procedures that allow you to execute a Cypher statement. For example, the procedure `apoc.periodic.submit` allows you to provide a Cypher statement and creates a background job which runs the Cypher statement once:

```
CALL apoc.periodic.submit("create-user",
"CREATE (u:User) SET u.name = '" + $username + "', {})
```

Even though we've used a parameter for the username here, the string concatenation still makes this code vulnerable to attacks. Use a parameter map instead:

```
CALL apoc.periodic.submit("create-user",
"CREATE (u:User) SET u.name =  $name"', {name: $username })
```

Not only can such literal injections compromise the integrity of your database, but they can also result in information disclosure, if the injected text includes a further `MATCH` clause to return sensitive data.

Never return database errors directly to your users. They should always be mapped or sanitized by your application to return a more generic error. This is because attackers can inject syntax errors into a Cypher query that return in the query to the attacker, exposing any information used in it, such as labels, properties, and relationships.

Starting from Neo4j 5.26, the error codes that Neo4j returns to indicate the unsuccessful outcome of a query or command execution also contain a GQL status object. The `GQLSTATUS` codes (*https://oreil.ly/C4AmH*) can be reliably used to map to generic error messages by your application.

From the example above, simply guessing an invalid identifier and injecting `Bob' RETURN x //` will reveal the entire query:

```
Variable `x` not defined (line 1, column 43 (offset: 42))
"CREATE (u:User) SET u.name = 'Bob' RETURN x //"
```

Wherever parameterization is not supported and string concatenation is used, it is always a good idea to sanitize user input. This involves using backticks around labels, relationship types and property keys, escaping quotes, and removing delimiters that could be interpreted as the end of the string literal or identifier.

Finally, ensure that your application runs with the fewest privileges required to do the job. This adds another layer of security against an attack: the database will reject any operations that the application is not allowed to perform.

Implementing Role-Based Access Control

After authentication, authorization is the next line of defense. *Authorization* determines the actions that authenticated users are allowed to perform against the database. Neo4j uses *role-based access control* (RBAC) for this. A *role* is a collection of privileges that enable users to perform certain actions on the data or database.

Multiple roles can be assigned to a single user. Roles simplify user management and reduce complexity when combinations of privileges are assigned directly to users.

The next track recommendations at ElectricHarmony are ready to go to production. You're going to work with your team to set up the right authorization.

First, you need to think through the kinds of users who will need access to the graph at a macro level. Which labels, relationship types, and properties will they need? Your team members come up with a list:

- The recommendation application needs read access to all labels and relationships in the graph. However, it should only be able to access the `id` property on the `User` node. All other properties, such as their name and email, should be hidden.
- Paul and John from the data science team need read access to playlists, artists, tracks, albums, and the relationships between them. They also need the ability to create `SIMILAR` relationships.
- Angus from the content team needs access to albums, artists, and tracks. He should not have access to users or playlists.

> ### Using Service Accounts
>
> To illustrate RBAC concepts in this chapter, the recommendation application will use a *service account*. This is a specific user account set up solely for use by the recommendation application's driver. While service accounts are easier to manage than individual accounts (which are typically configured to use SSO or LDAP), they have several drawbacks. Generally, service accounts tend to be assigned more privileges than individual accounts. If a service account is compromised, attackers gain broader access to the database than should have been possible with better configured individual accounts. Secondly, while a service account creates a clear audit trail of the application's actions, this is also a disadvantage, since malicious actions can no longer be attributed to a specific user. Furthermore, if you have a multitenant application where data separation is critical and therefore each tenant must be restricted to its own database, using a service account that spans all tenant databases gets complex.

Start by creating these user accounts:

```
CREATE USER reco
SET PASSWORD 'password' CHANGE NOT REQUIRED;

CREATE USER paul
SET PASSWORD 'password';

CREATE USER john
SET PASSWORD 'password';
```

```
CREATE USER angus
SET PASSWORD 'password';
```

Paul, John, and Angus will be prompted to change their passwords when they first log into Neo4j.

Now go ahead and try logging in as the `reco` user. Then, in the Neo4j browser, run `:server disconnect` to log out. You will see that simply having a user account does not grant you access to any of the nodes or relationships in the graph. The users you just created have all been granted the `PUBLIC` role by default. This is one of the built-in roles; it allows users to access the home database, load data, and execute procedures and functions.

Run `SHOW USER PRIVILEGES` to see what actions your user can perform.

In addition to `PUBLIC`, Neo4j has five other built-in roles: *reader*, *editor*, *publisher*, *architect*, and *admin*. The combination of roles assigned to a user determines that user's full set of privileges. These roles are hierarchical: the reader role has the fewest privileges, while admin has them all. These roles' privileges apply across all databases. Though the default roles can be modified, we recommend using custom roles unless your application is fairly trivial.

Create the following roles:

```
CREATE ROLE content_manager;
CREATE ROLE data_scientist;
CREATE ROLE reco_app;
```

Now you'll grant the appropriate roles to each user:

```
GRANT ROLE reco_app TO reco;
GRANT ROLE content_manager TO angus;
GRANT ROLE data_scientist TO paul, john;
```

In Figure 6-1, the `SHOW USERS` command verifies that these roles have been granted.

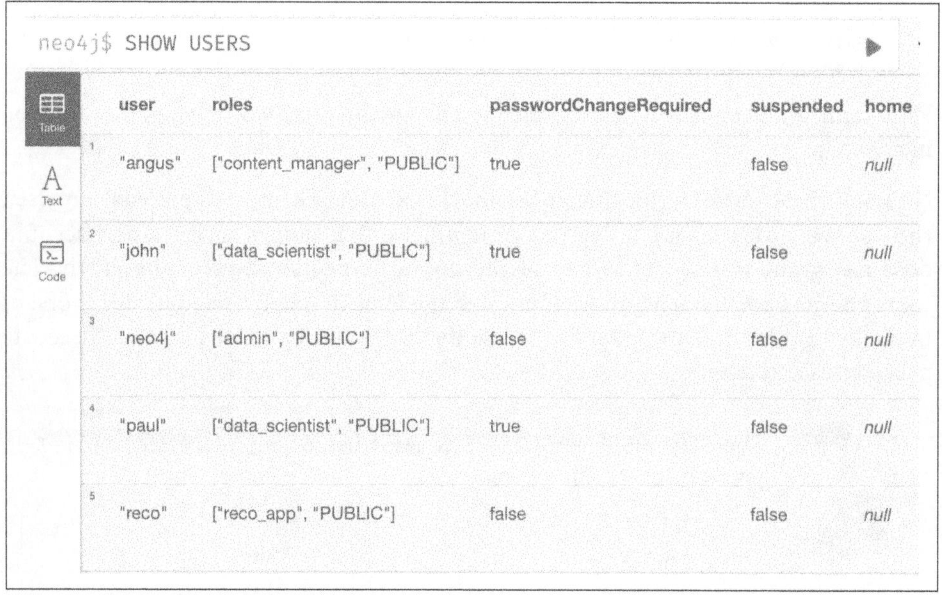

neo4j$ SHOW USERS

	user	roles	passwordChangeRequired	suspended	home
1	"angus"	["content_manager", "PUBLIC"]	true	false	*null*
2	"john"	["data_scientist", "PUBLIC"]	true	false	*null*
3	"neo4j"	["admin", "PUBLIC"]	false	false	*null*
4	"paul"	["data_scientist", "PUBLIC"]	true	false	*null*
5	"reco"	["reco_app", "PUBLIC"]	false	false	*null*

Figure 6-1. List users and their roles

Now you can grant privileges. First, tackle the privileges that the recommendation application needs. The read privileges that can be assigned are:

`TRAVERSE`
: Traversing the graph does not require access to properties of nodes or relationships. The `TRAVERSE` privilege enables specific nodes or relationships to be found by their label(s) or relationship type and then traversed. When you don't want to give certain users access to nodes with a particular label or relationships of a particular type, simply do not grant those users the `TRAVERSE` privilege.

  This privilege is also useful when you want users to be able to traverse a subgraph—for example, to find the shortest path between two nodes—but you do not want to reveal any information from the properties of nodes lying along that path.

`READ`
: The `READ` privilege enables users to read property values on nodes and relationships, provided they can find them in the first place (thanks to the `TRAVERSE` privilege).

`MATCH`
: The `MATCH` privilege conveniently grants both `TRAVERSE` and `READ` privileges, allowing users to find elements such as nodes or relationships, traverse them, and access their properties.

The recommendation application requires MATCH privileges on all labels and relationships, but this privilege should not be allowed to access any property on the User nodes except for id.

To secure access to the User nodes, you'll grant only the rights to read the id property on them:

```
GRANT MATCH {id} ON GRAPH neo4j NODES User TO reco_app;
```

You don't know yet how the properties on these User nodes will evolve, so at the beginning, it's wiser to grant access only to named properties. Then, as new properties are added to the User nodes, you don't have to revisit the user's privileges to deny access to them.

Contrast this to the strategy of granting access to all properties on User nodes, but denying access to name and email. This looks like:

```
GRANT MATCH {*} ON GRAPH neo4j NODES User TO reco_app;
DENY READ {name,email} ON GRAPH neo4j NODES User TO reco_app;
```

The drawback to this is that as new properties are added, such as the user's date of birth, the role reco_app will have access to it unless you remember to go back and deny that access. We've worked with several organizations where the use of DENY is forbidden. It results in overly complex management and violates the principle of least privilege (*https://oreil.ly/FYztq*).

Thus, granting access only to named properties is the strategy you should adopt for any labels or relationships that are likely to contain sensitive information.

Finish setting up the reco_app role by granting MATCH privileges on the other labels and relationship types:

```
GRANT MATCH {*} ON GRAPH neo4j NODES Album, Artist, Track, Playlist TO reco_app;
GRANT MATCH {*} ON GRAPH neo4j RELATIONSHIPS * TO reco_app;
```

Go ahead and set up privileges for the content_manager and data_scientist roles yourself. Once you're done, try logging in as those users to verify that you have access to the right elements. You can check your work against these Cypher statements:

```
GRANT MATCH {*} ON GRAPH neo4j NODES Album,Artist,Track TO content_manager;
GRANT MATCH {*} ON GRAPH neo4j RELATIONSHIPS HAS_TRACK,ARTIST TO
  content_manager;
GRANT MATCH {*} ON GRAPH neo4j NODES Album,Artist,Track,Playlist TO
  data_scientist;
GRANT MATCH {*} ON GRAPH neo4j RELATIONSHIPS HAS_TRACK,ARTIST,ON_PLAYLIST,
  SIMILAR TO data_scientist;
GRANT MERGE {*} ON GRAPH neo4j RELATIONSHIP SIMILAR TO data_scientist;
```

You've likely found that everything looks okay. If not, go over the privileges you set up and compare them against this list to see what was missing.

Now log in as Paul. Paul has come up with a new similarity score that's based on whether the tracks in playlists are performed live or not. He informs the recommendations team that there'll be a new property called `similar_liveness` on the `SIMILAR` relationships. To help the team start incorporating this new property into their queries, he decides to initialize it to 1 on all `SIMILAR` relationships:

```
MATCH (a:Playlist)-[r:SIMILAR]-(b:Playlist)
WHERE id(a) < id(b)
CALL (r) {
    SET r.similar_liveness=1
} IN TRANSACTIONS
```

Paul's set operation is denied due to a `Neo.ClientError.Security.Forbidden` error: `Creating new property name on database 'neo4j' is not allowed for user 'paul' with roles [PUBLIC, data_scientist].`

This is a current limitation in Neo4j. When you authorize a user to perform an action, only the privileges for existing properties, labels, and relationship types are applied. Since the `similar_liveness` property is new—that is, it doesn't exist in the graph—the privilege cannot be applied to it. Thus, Paul's set operation is denied.

There are two ways around this. The first is to have an admin create the property in the database using this procedure:

```
CALL db.createProperty('similar_liveness');
```

The drawback of this is that every time the data science team needs access to a new property, they'll need to find an admin to grant it.

The other option is to grant the data scientists the ability to create new properties in the database:

```
GRANT CREATE NEW PROPERTY NAME ON DATABASE neo4j TO data_scientist;
```

While this makes the data scientists more independent, it also implies that they are now allowed to create any property in the database on *any* elements to which they have write access, not just on the `SIMILAR` relationships. You'll need to pick one approach over the other depending on your organization policies. ElectricHarmony decided to choose the second option and allow their data scientists to create new properties on any elements that they can write to.

Write Privileges

These privileges aren't applicable to your use case now. However, here is the list of other write privileges that exist in Neo4j:

`CREATE`
: Granting this privilege allows the user to create nodes and relationships.

`DELETE`
: This privilege allows deleting of nodes and relationships.

`SET LABEL`
: The `SET LABEL` privilege allows a label to be set using the SET clause.

`REMOVE LABEL`
: Labels can be removed from nodes using the `REMOVE` clause if the `REMOVE LABEL` privilege is granted.

`SET PROPERTY`
: In order to set properties on nodes and relationships, the `SET PROPERTY` privilege must be granted.

Compound privileges combine commonly used privileges together. `MERGE` allows `MATCH`, `CREATE`, and `SET PROPERTY` so that you can run `MERGE` commands. `WRITE` allows all writes across the graph. Finally, `ALL GRAPH PRIVILEGES` combine all `READ` and `WRITE` operations on the entire graph.

By setting up these privileges, you've guarded your graph against accidental or malicious data tampering by unauthorized users. We recommend you follow the principle of least privilege to reduce the risk and surface area of damage should a tampering attempt take place.

Using the Load CSV Command

Loading data via the `LOAD CSV` command is very convenient when you're starting out and need to get datasets into the graph quickly, like you did in Chapter 1. However, it also presents a vulnerable entry point into the system that you should consider when evaluating possible tampering threats. The `LOAD` privilege can be used with this command to allow or disallow certain roles from importing data. However, this privilege applies to the whole system, not just a specific database; if it's granted, users can use the `ALL DATA` command to load files from all sources. For example:

```
GRANT LOAD ON ALL DATA TO dataloaders;
```

The other option is to restrict loading to a certain range of IP addresses specified as Classless Inter-Domain Routing (CIDR) (*https://oreil.ly/_jxcE*) notation. To do this, use the `ON CIDR` clause instead.

Denying the `LOAD` privilege works similarly. Here, loading files is denied from the single localhost IP:

```
DENY LOAD ON CIDR "127.0.0.1/32" TO dataloaders;
```

Audit Logs

As we mentioned in the spoofing section, it's important to audit the security log regularly. Let's look at how the security log captures the moment when Paul inadvertently tries to create a new property on `Album` nodes:

```
ERROR [paul]: Set property for property 'something_new' on database 'neo4j' is
not allowed for user 'paul' with roles [PUBLIC, data_scientist].
```

We'll explore monitoring in more depth in Chapter 11.

Constraints

Neo4j supports various types of database constraints (*https://oreil.ly/xJxuM*). To preserve the integrity of the database and reduce tampering threats, you can set up the following constraints:

Uniqueness
: Both nodes and relationships support property uniqueness on both a single property and a combination of properties.

Property existence
: This constraint ensures that a specific property exists on nodes or relationships and cannot be deleted.

Property type
: This constraint mandates a data type for the specified property on nodes or relationships.

Node/Relationship key
: Akin to a primary key, these constraints are defined for a set of properties on either a label or relationship type and ensure that all properties exist and that the combination of their values is unique.

Defining property uniqueness constraints or node/relationship keys implicitly adds an index on the property or set of properties. These indexes are used for fast lookups at query time, as you learned in Chapter 5.

Backups

While backups do not prevent tampering, they aid in data recovery after an incident. You can back up both online and offline Neo4j databases. Designing a robust backup-and-restore strategy, which we cover in Chapter 9, is vital to ensuring that your database is operational again as quickly as possible, preventing another threat—the system becoming unavailable for users and critical functions.

Repudiation

Repudiation is a threat that occurs when a user denies having performed an action and there is no way to prove otherwise. *Nonrepudiation* refers to the system's ability to provide evidence as a counterclaim. Preventing repudiation is essential to maintaining accountability, traceability, and legal compliance.

Make sure that all logs are configured to provide a trail of all actions performed. We covered logging earlier in this chapter and will revisit it in Chapter 11, but for now, Table 6-2 summarizes the various types of logs Neo4j produces.

Table 6-2. Types of logging in Neo4j

Type of log	Purpose	Filename
General	General functioning of the database, configuration issues, startup and shutdown, and errors	*neo4j.log*
Debug	More detailed information about errors, useful for debugging and as a source of information when contacting Neo4j Support	*debug.log*
Query	Queries, including parameters, literals (can be obfuscated), query plans, and queries that run longer than a specified threshold	*query.log*
Security	Information about security-related events	*security.log*
Garbage collection	Garbage-collection information provided by the JVM	*gc.log*
Http	HTTP API information	*http.log*

By configuring the logs, you can control what types of events and information are written to the log files, as well as their level of granularity and how long to keep them. We highly recommend planning and documenting your log-retention strategy for any production-grade system. Neo4j's logs are not tamperproof, though, so if you need very strong nonrepudiation guarantees, plan to integrate Neo4j with a secure logging infrastructure that can provide cryptographic integrity and access control.

When using a service account for applications, remember that, by default, queries executed by the application cannot be traced back to individual user accounts. To achieve nonrepudiation, you'll want to attach extra metadata to the query transaction via the application: for example, the logged-in user's name or ID, or some other identifying characteristics. The built-in procedure `CALL tx.setMetadata` accepts a map of information, which is logged to the query log with the query transaction, providing a clear audit trail.

Information Disclosure

Information disclosure occurs when sensitive information is disclosed to unauthorized parties. In previous sections, we've covered several preventive mechanisms to secure your graph data at rest via encryption and in transit, as well as database configuration files and backups. This section discusses a few more precautions you can take.

Query Logs

Be aware that the query log can reveal information to those who can access it. By default, all queries are logged, along with their parameter values. This means that viewers of the log file can see which users ran queries and what they were looking for. If you want to turn off parameter logging, set `db.logs.query.parameter_logging_enabled` to `false`. Another setting, `db.logs.query.obfuscate_literals`, goes a step further and obfuscates any literals in Cypher queries. By default, this is set to `false`.

Fine-Grained Access Control

Your graph may contain sensitive information in the form of property values on nodes and relationships. These should always be protected by appropriate read or write privileges (as you did for the `User` nodes in the RBAC section) to ensure that they are not inadvertently disclosed through something like a path traversal. In addition to protecting certain properties for all nodes with a given label or all relationships of a specific type, Neo4j allows for *property-based access control*, in which the value of the property determines if the element should be accessible or not.

For example, ElectricHarmony's European marketing team should only be able to access user information for users who reside in the EU. This is indicated by the property `zone` on the `User` nodes. To enforce this, you use a privilege such as:

```
GRANT TRAVERSE ON GRAPH neo4j FOR (n:User) WHERE n.zone = "EU" TO marketing_eu
```

Keep in mind that with the current version of Neo4j, 5.2, using property-based access control can incur significant performance overhead. We cover how property-based and label-based access control affect performance in Chapter 8.

Property Encryption

Your application can encrypt the values of sensitive properties to further protect revealing them in the event of an information disclosure event. Choose a strong encryption algorithm and encrypt sensitive property values in the application layer before storing them in Neo4j and decrypt them after they're read back by the application. Keep in mind that typically, encrypted properties are not searchable and therefore should not be indexed unless it is an exact search and the encryption of the search term produces the same string as the encryption of the property value.

Denial of Service

The purpose of a *denial-of-service* (DoS) attack is to render a system unusable to legitimate users. Attackers typically achieve this in databases by causing resource starvation, leading to an eventual crash. Some strategies for mitigating or preventing DoS attacks include:

Transaction configuration
: You can configure the maximum time a transaction should run before timing out. The default for the setting `db.transaction.timeout` is 0 seconds, which means that the setting is disabled. We always recommend changing this to prevent multiple very long transactions from hogging system resources. In addition to timeouts, you can control the maximum number of concurrent transactions with `db.transaction.concurrent.maximum`. The default is 1,000. This configuration also protects against DoS attacks that attempt to overwhelm the database by initiating a large number of simultaneous, long-running transactions.

Memory limits
: Recall that transactions in execution consume on-heap memory for the running state and for uncommitted data. Long-running queries and some very complex queries tend to occupy more memory. To prevent rogue queries from draining enough memory to bring the system down, limit the total memory that a single transaction can consume by changing the value of `dbms.memory.transaction.max` from the default of 0 (the largest possible value of memory available). You can constrain memory consumption for an entire set of transactions by setting a value for `dbms.memory.transaction.total.max`. The default is 70% of the heap size limit.

Query monitoring
: Not all DoS incidents have malicious causes. Inadvertent DoS incidents can occur if, for example, your system has several unoptimized queries that are causing high workloads and exhausting memory. Review the query logs routinely to monitor for and fix any poorly performing queries.

  There are two configuration settings you can combine to find your optimal query-logging strategy. The first is `db.logs.query.enabled`. Its default value is `VERBOSE`, which logs the entire query at the beginning and end of its execution, irrespective of the `db.logs.query.threshold` setting, which specifies a duration. `INFO` logs only queries that have exceeded the threshold. `OFF` does not log any queries (we do not recommend that you use this value). If a query executes longer than the threshold value, it is logged once completed, provided that the `db.logs.query.enabled` setting is `INFO`.

The second setting to know is `db.logs.query.transaction.enabled`. The default value here is `OFF` (nothing is logged). Like the previous setting, the other two values are `VERBOSE` and `INFO`, which log the start and end of the transaction to the query log. `INFO` depends on the threshold you set in `db.logs.query.transaction.threshold`.

Clustering

Operating Neo4j in clustered mode makes it resilient and highly available. The primary-mode database servers provide the fault tolerance for transaction execution, by staying available when a simple majority of primary servers are functional. Secondary-mode servers provide read availability at scale. Neo4j also supports multidatacenter clusters, which are key to disaster-recovery planning. Clustering strategies are covered in Chapter 10.

Elevation of Privilege

In an *elevation of privilege* attack, an attacker gains higher privileges than intended. This is generally used to facilitate access to carry out other kinds of attacks. To avoid or mitigate elevation of privilege attacks, we recommend the following strategies.

Immutable Privileges

Setting *immutable privileges* is useful to restrict the actions of users who have the rights to administer privileges. Suppose that you want to prevent all users (they have the `PUBLIC` role) from executing procedures, such as `db.schema.visualization`. As an admin, you could execute the following:

```
DENY EXECUTE PROCEDURE db.* ON DBMS TO PUBLIC
```

Now users cannot execute any database procedures.

However, if Steven is an admin, he could revoke this `DENY`:

```
REVOKE DENY EXECUTE PROCEDURE db.* ON DBMS FROM PUBLIC
```

To prevent this, immutable privileges can be granted. Immutable privileges can only be added or removed when auth is disabled. When you're doing this, make sure that other mechanisms are preventing access to the database. Disable auth by setting `dbms.security.auth_enabled` to `false` and restart Neo4j. Then add the immutable privilege:

```
DENY IMMUTABLE EXECUTE PROCEDURE db.* ON DBMS TO PUBLIC
```

Change the config to set `dbms.security.auth_enabled` to `true` and restart Neo4j. You'll find that Steven can no longer revoke your `DENY`.

Least Privileges

The principle of least privileges applies to this threat as well as tampering. You can also explicitly deny privileges to protect against anyone accidentally or intentionally granting broad access. Neo4j will grant access to a resource in the presence of a `GRANT` and the absence of an explicit `DENY` rule.

Extensions

Neo4j allows you to write your own extensions in the form of custom code that can be invoked directly from Cypher. Always review and validate these extensions to ensure they expose no sensitive data and are not susceptible to security breaches.

The principle of least privileges applies to procedures and functions, too, whether they're shipped with Neo4j or you've developed them yourself. Procedures and functions that use Neo4j's internal APIs are disabled by default. Remove the restrictions on these only on a case-by-case basis, via the configurations setting `dbms.security.procedures.unrestricted`. The value is a comma-separated list of procedures and functions to unrestrict.

The APOC set of procedures is quite vast and versatile, so you will likely want to restrict which procedures are exposed to users. You can specify an allow list using the configuration setting `dbms.security.procedures.allowlist`. This also applies to any third-party packages of procedures or functions you might wish to use.

By default, all procedures are allowed in Neo4j. The default setting of `dbms.security.procedures.allowlist` is `*`. If you do not change it or if you give it no value, all procedures in the plugins directory will be loaded.

User and Privilege Reviews

As with any system, periodically review all users, roles and privileges. Review Neo4j configuration files, too. Carry out additional audits when users join or leave the system as well.

We recommend granting DBMS privileges only as needed. DBMS privileges include the ability to manage users, roles, and privileges and to create and drop databases. The built-in *admin* role is very powerful, so consider restricting users who have this role and instead assigning them only a subset of admin privileges.

File Permissions

To prevent an attacker from elevating their privileges by modifying procedure allow lists and the like, protect Neo4j's directories and files by granting the minimum permissions required. The manual (*https://oreil.ly/avdRt*) includes a complete list of directories; the `bin`, `conf`, `plugins`, and `import` directories are especially important to review periodically to make sure that no broad access has been granted.

Patches

Always upgrade Neo4j to the latest patch available (*https://oreil.ly/DSeRq*). The patch release notes (*https://oreil.ly/e9P1D*) contain a section on security and begin with an advisory section noting any critical issues. Patch versions are backward compatible.

If you're running a standalone server, simply stop it, install the new version, and start it up again. You can upgrade clusters in a rolling fashion (see Chapter 10).

Summary

This chapter introduced you to some very important aspects of securing your Neo4j database. Many of these aspects frequently appear in requests for proposals (RFPs), so you can use this chapter as a handy guide to help you fill them out accurately. We also introduced you to the STRIDE threat model, a practical tool that you can use to identify and mitigate potential threats early on.

CHAPTER 7

Search

The winter holidays are coming, and your team at ElectricHarmony decides to run a challenge for the whole month of December to drive user engagement. You run a brainstorming workshop, then vote for the best idea. This year, the winning idea is a 30-day song challenge (see Figure 7-1)!

30-DAY SONG CHALLENGE

DAY 1	DAY 2	DAY 3	DAY 4	DAY 5	DAY 6
A song you like with a color in the title	*A song you like with a number in the title*	*A song that reminds you of summertime*	*A song that reminds you of someone you'd rather forget*	*A song that needs to be played loud*	*A song that makes you want to dance*
DAY 7	**DAY 8**	**DAY 9**	**DAY 10**	**DAY 11**	**DAY 12**
A song to drive to	*A song about drugs or alcohol*	*A song that makes you happy*	*A song that makes you sad*	*A song you never get tired of*	*A song from your preteen years*
DAY 13	**DAY 14**	**DAY 15**	**DAY 16**	**DAY 17**	**DAY 18**
A song you like from the 70s	*A song you'd love to be played at your wedding*	*A song you like that's a cover by another artist*	*A song that's a classic favorite*	*A song you'd sing a duet with someone on karaoke*	*A song from the year you were born*
DAY 19	**DAY 20**	**DAY 21**	**DAY 22**	**DAY 23**	**DAY 24**
A song that makes you think about life	*A song that has many meanings to you*	*A song you like with a person's name in the title*	*A song that moves you forward*	*A song you think everybody should listen to*	*A song by a band you wish were still together*
DAY 25	**DAY 26**	**DAY 27**	**DAY 28**	**DAY 29**	**DAY 30**
A song you like by an artist no longer living	*A song that makes you want to fall in love*	*A song that breaks your heart*	*A song by an artist whose voice you love*	*A song you remember from your childhood*	*A song that reminds you of yourself*

Figure 7-1. The 30-day song challenge

The goal of the challenge is trivial—every day has a theme tag, and users share songs associated with it on social media. While the challenge is fun, your team is hoping to gather an understanding of users' personalities, since the meanings of songs differ for everyone. It's also interesting to note how tags such as "childhood" can reveal personal associations with music: someone might tag a Led Zeppelin song that way because it was part of their early memories, regardless of when the song was released.

To test the idea, you decide to run the challenge internally. You immediately encounter some issues related to finding tracks in your database. For example:

- Searching for a partial track name like `heaven` doesn't find the track "Stairway to Heaven."
- Variations in English dialect: searching for `colour` doesn't find `color`.
- Search is case-sensitive, so users need to know exactly how the track name is stored in the database. First letter uppercase? Lowercase? All lowercase? So many possible variations!

This chapter will teach you all the ins and outs of how to store and query textual data for maximum relevance of search results. It is a fascinating topic because providing accurate and relevant results to users based on simple textual input is both a highly challenging and immensely rewarding endeavor. This chapter will walk you through different kinds of data structures and algorithms used for search and how they add their own value to a powerful search system. While this book is about Neo4j, much of the content is foundational to Apache Lucene-based search technologies, such as Solr and Elasticsearch, so users of those technologies will find familiar concepts here.

What Is Search?

Picture yourself in a vinyl record store. The racks are each marked with a letter, to indicate that it contains records by artists whose names start with that letter. You head to the "L" rack for "letter" and start crate-digging vinyls until you finally find your favorite band: Led Zeppelin.

This whole experience is a kind of search! Let's say you enter the store with a query. The store has a system in place to help you find things efficiently. You either find the record you wanted or leave empty-handed. And if you do find the artist, you might notice other albums by the same band—suggestions that align with your original intent.

Text

What text elements will you want to make searchable? Not every text is eligible for search, in contrast to lookups. Your team is looking for texts that are stored as properties on nodes or relationships. The track identifier in your graph, by contrast, is probably not something you will want to make searchable. Users are unlikely to want to retrieve the value `1FTSo4v6BOZH9QxKc3MbVM` by typing just three or four characters in a search bar.

However, the track title contains text that must be found, even if the user's query contains only a portion of it. For example, typing `start` in the search bar should return "Start Me Up" by the Rolling Stones, "Let's Get It Started" by the Black Eyed Peas, or "Firestarter" by Prodigy.

The following use cases identify text that is eligible for search:

- Finding texts that start, contain, end with, or are equal to the search query. For example: Typing "Love" returns "Love Me Do" (starts with), "All You Need Is Love" (ends with), and "Crazy Little Thing Called Love" (contains).
- Finding texts that match the search query. Matches should account for common typing and grammar mistakes. For example: Typing "Stairway To Heven" (misspelling "Heaven") should still return "Stairway to Heaven" by Led Zeppelin. Typing "Smels Like Teen Spirit" (missing an "l" in "Smells") should return "Smells Like Teen Spirit" by Nirvana. Typing "dont stop belivin" (missing apostrophe and "e") should return "Don't Stop Believin'" by Journey.

Not all identifiers are equal. While the track identifier is a good example of text that shouldn't be searchable, other identifiers have some parts with a logical meaning that could be used to find results in groups. For example, part of an International Standard Book Number (ISBN) indicates the book's publisher; in some countries, the two last letters of car license plate numbers indicate the province; in other countries, a national ID number may have a suffix that indicates if a person is a citizen of the country or not. Techniques for handling such identifiers are detailed later in this chapter.

Indexes

Text indexes are the backbone of search. They utilize specialized indexing structures to efficiently organize and retrieve text property values. In Neo4j, three types of indexes are available:

Text index
: Optimized for queries using the operators `STARTS WITH`, `ENDS WITH`, and `CONTAINS`. This type of index is *case sensitive*: it differentiates between uppercase and lowercase letters, such as "top" and "Top."

Full-text index
: Optimized for more complex search use cases, including proximity search and relevance ranking; can index larger texts, like full song lyrics or PDF texts.

Vector index
: Optimized for storing mathematical representations of texts in the form of embeddings; they use similarity functions to compare vectors in a higher-order geometric space.

Understanding the capabilities of each type of index and using each in well-thought-out ways is key to building a successful search experience.

The rest of this chapter will guide you through advanced text search techniques, helping you make the most of what Neo4j offers.

This chapter uses a full dataset listing 13 million tracks. You can download it from the book's GitHub repository (*https://oreil.ly/fH6C8*).

Searching for Data

You start by trying out the first day's challenge, which is to share a song that contains a color in its title. Without hesitation, you decide on "Purple Rain" by Prince. You execute the following query in the Neo4j browser:

```
//001-match-track.cypher
MATCH (n:Track)
WHERE n.name = "purple rain"
RETURN n
```

The query is stuck in the browser as indicated by the permanent spinning icon. Your knowledge from the previous chapters suggests that an index is missing, so you look up the Neo4j documentation for the right syntax (*https://oreil.ly/B59cz*) and create an index:

```
//002-create-constraint.cypher
CREATE INDEX track_name
FOR (n:Track)
ON n.name
```

Now the query is very fast, but it still doesn't return any result. The reason is simple: the text was not transformed when you stored it in the index. This leads to case sensitivity: your query `purple rain` doesn't match anything stored as "Purple Rain" in the index.

You find a potential solution in the Cypher syntax: the `toLower()` function, which can convert the indexed texts to all lowercase letters to match your query. This transformation occurs only in memory during the query execution and does not alter the underlying data:

```
//003-match-lower.cypher
MATCH (n:Track)
WHERE toLower(n.name) = "purple rain"
RETURN n
```

The query takes approximately 4–5 seconds to execute, which is too slow. Instead, you decide to profile the query and look at the query plan (see Figure 7-2).

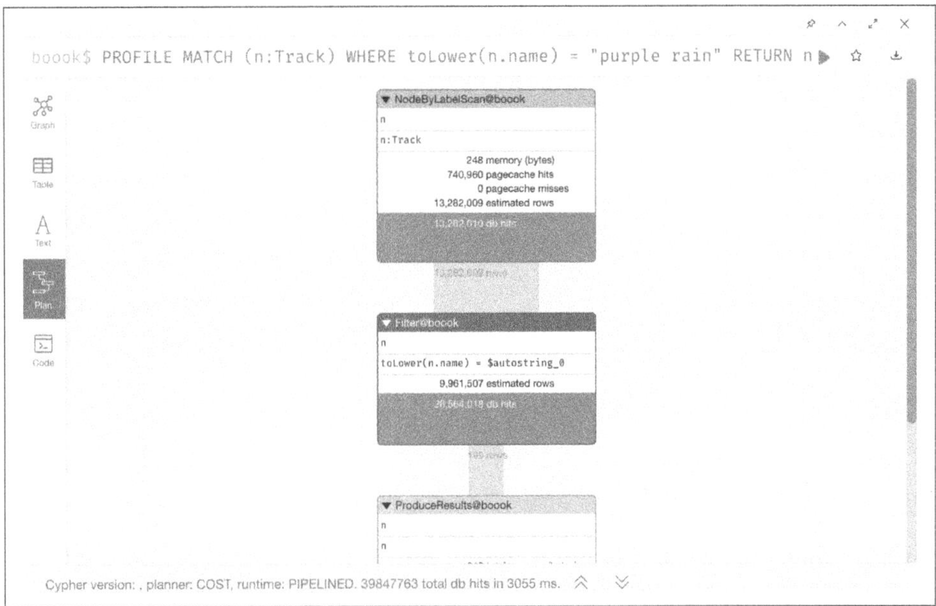

Figure 7-2. Cypher query plan using the `toLower()` function on the node property

The `NodeByLabelScan` operator indicates that no index is used. That means the query will iterate over all 13 million tracks, converting each track name to all lowercase characters and comparing it to your query. Indeed, when you use transformation functions on the values stored in Neo4j, it *can't* use the index.

The solution is to transform the text into the right case *before* storing it in the database and the index, which is what you will do now:

```
//004-transform-text.cypher
:auto
MATCH (n:Track)
CALL (n) {
    SET n.name = toLower(n.name)
} IN TRANSACTIONS OF 50_000 ROWS
```

Figure 7-3 shows the query plan, this time omitting the transformation of the name value. The text is now stored in the same case as your query. The plan indicates 1,935 database hits—a grain of sand compared to the previous plan's 39 million database hits.

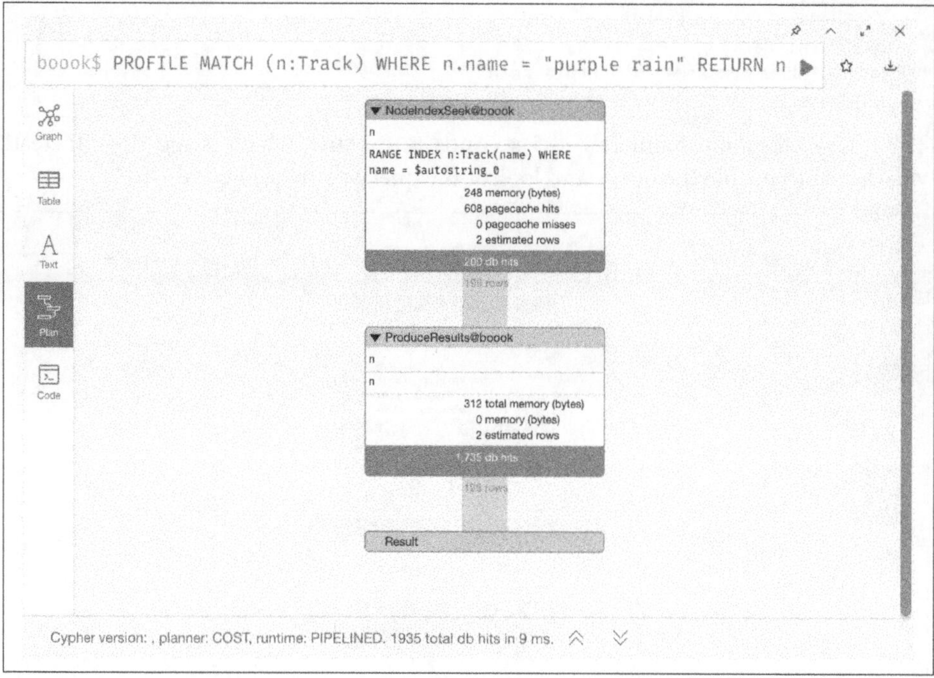

Figure 7-3. Cypher query plan showing the correct usage of the index

Transforming the case of the input doesn't prevent Neo4j from using the index. For example, the following query will produce the same very optimized query plan as in Figure 7-3:

```
//005-match-lower-b.cypher
MATCH (n:Track)
WHERE n.name = toLower("Purple RAIN")
RETURN n
```

The case in which the text is stored in the database plays a critical role in search query performance. For this reason, you'll often want to store the same text with two different properties: one version optimized for search and the original value for screen-display purposes or human readability, as shown in Figure 7-4.

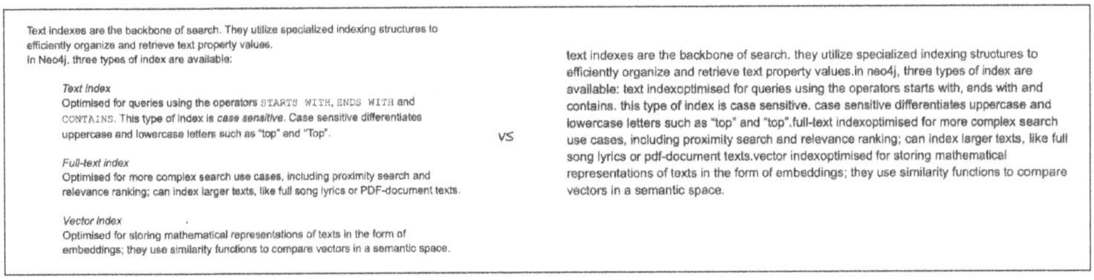

Text indexes are the backbone of search. They utilize specialized indexing structures to efficiently organize and retrieve text property values.
In Neo4j, three types of index are available:

Text Index
Optimised for queries using the operators `STARTS WITH`, `ENDS WITH` and `CONTAINS`. This type of index is *case sensitive*. Case sensitive differentiates uppercase and lowercase letters such as "top" and "Top".

Full-text index
Optimised for more complex search use cases, including proximity search and relevance ranking; can index larger texts, like full song lyrics or PDF-document texts.

Vector index
Optimised for storing mathematical representations of texts in the form of embeddings; they use similarity functions to compare vectors in a semantic space.

VS

text indexes are the backbone of search. they utilize specialized indexing structures to efficiently organize and retrieve text property values.in neo4j, three types of index are available: text indexoptimised for queries using the operators starts with, ends with and contains. this type of index is case sensitive. case sensitive differentiates uppercase and lowercase letters such as "top" and "top".full-text indexoptimised for more complex search use cases, including proximity search and relevance ranking; can index larger texts, like full song lyrics or pdf-document texts.vector indexoptimised for storing mathematical representations of texts in the form of embeddings; they use similarity functions to compare vectors in a semantic space.

Figure 7-4. Human-readable version of a text (left) versus the same text converted for search engine performance (right)

Partial Searches

You know that your `purple rain` query should return more results, such as live versions and remixes. The = operator finds only exact matches, but you can use additional operators to find track names that include your search term anywhere in their text. These include:

`CONTAINS`
: The track name contains your search term anywhere in the text.

`STARTS WITH`
: The track name must start with your search term.

`ENDS WITH`
: The track name must end with your search term.

You use the `CONTAINS` operator to find all tracks that have `purple rain` in their names:

```
//006-contains.cypher
MATCH (n:Track)
WHERE n.name CONTAINS "purple rain"
RETURN n
```

All the relevant tracks are returned correctly this time. However, it takes longer than a second to return the results. That's still slow, so you analyze the query plan (see Figure 7-5).

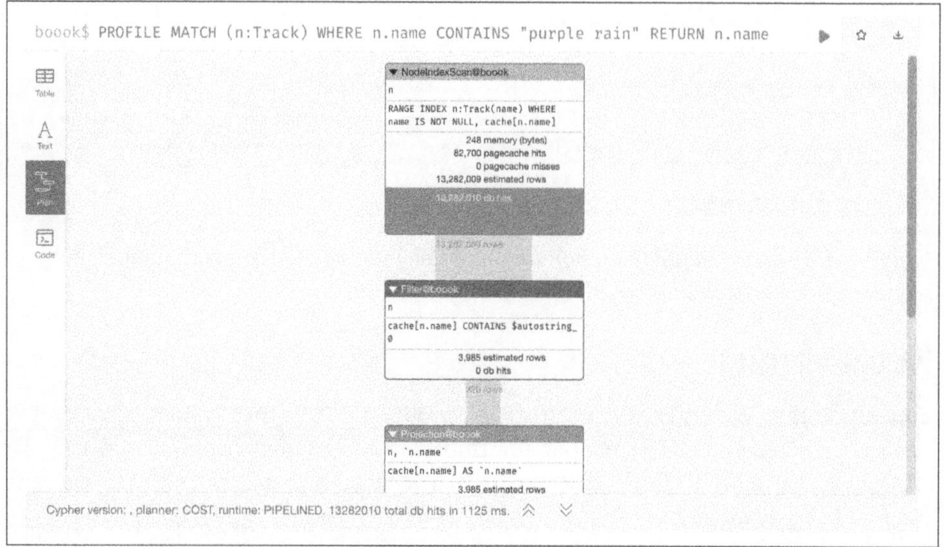

Figure 7-5. Cypher query plan for a query using `CONTAINS` *with a* `RANGE` *index*

This query plan indicates 13 million database hits, which seems excessive. Why? It turns out that the type of index you created is not suitable for partial searches. Let's see why in the next section, which dives into how to use specialized `TEXT` indexes.

TEXT Indexes

`TEXT` indexes sometimes take up more disk space—a trade-off for faster data retrieval. To index text, they use a specialized data structure called an *n-gram*: a sequence of *n* adjacent letters in a particular order. In Neo4j, the value for *n* is 3, so it's commonly known as a *trigram index*. Let's look at the trigram for the word *purple*:

`purple`	`pur, urp, rpl, ple`

Texts are indexed in trigrams alongside sequences. When Neo4j executes a query, it decomposes the input into trigrams. The search engine then locates corresponding trigrams and retrieves documents that contain those trigrams in the same sequence as in the search query.

To see how this works, you drop the previous index and create a specialized `TEXT` index for the track names:

```
//007-recreate-index.cypher
DROP INDEX track_name;
CREATE TEXT INDEX track_name FOR (n:Track) ON n.name;
```

You then run the same CONTAINS query, and this time it performs only 961 database hits (see Figure 7-6). The query time also drops from 1 second to 21 milliseconds.

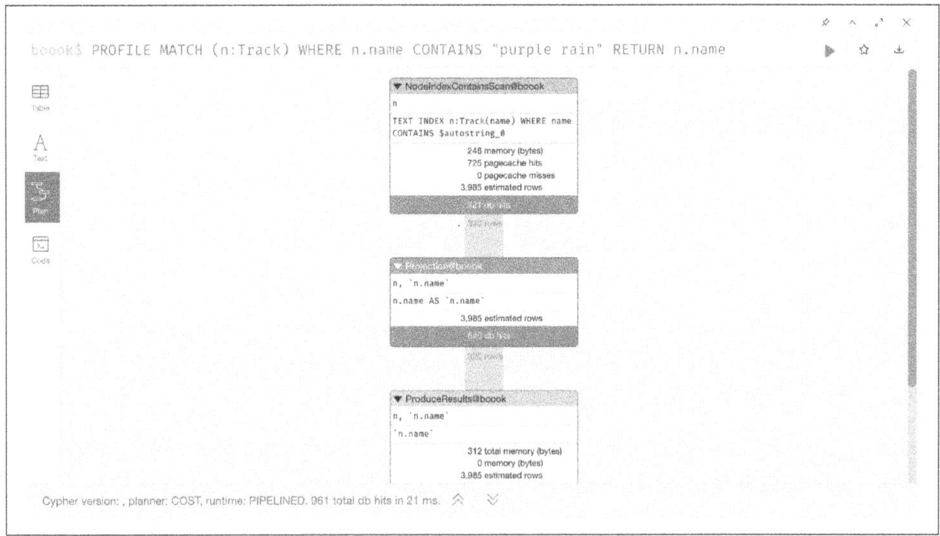

Figure 7-6. Cypher query plan for a query using CONTAINS and a TEXT index

Try it out. You can experiment with other combinations, too, like `ENDS WITH "rain"` or `STARTS WITH "purple"`.

TEXT indexes are limited to texts with a maximum size of 32KB. However, that's not always equivalent to 32K characters: some Unicode characters take more than 1 byte, such as emojis and certain letters with diacritical marks, such as in the French alphabet. Attempting to index a text larger than that will result in an error. You can simulate this effect by using an APOC function (see Chapter 2) to generate the large value of the `track_name` property:

```
//008-text-limit-reached.cypher
CREATE (t:Track {id: "test_id_large"})
SET t.name = apoc.text.repeat('hello', 10_000)
```

The query results in an error, as shown in Figure 7-7.

ERROR **Neo.DatabaseError.Statement.ExecutionFailed**

```
Property value is too large to index, please see index documentation for limitations. Index: Index( id=3,
name='track_name', type='TEXT', schema=(:Track {name}), indexProvider='text-2.0' ), entity id: 13174675, property
size: 50000, value:
[String("hellohellohellohellohellohellohellohellohellohellohellohellohellohellohellohellohellohellohelloh....
```

Figure 7-7. Cypher returns an error when you try to index a text larger than 32KB.

A *string-based index*, like the TEXT index, treats the entire text as one unit for searching. These indexes are especially powerful in use cases where exact matches are important. Table 7-1 shows examples of when search queries do not return results.

Table 7-1. Search queries that do and do not return results

Query	Text in database	Results
`n.name = "the beatles"`	`beatles, the`	No
`n.name ENDS WITH "beatles"`	`beatles, the`	No
`n.name STARTS WITH "beatles"`	`beatles, the`	Yes
`n.name CONTAINS "eatl"`	`beatles, the`	Yes

Because the Cypher query planner is aware of TEXT indexes and can leverage them during the query-planning phase, this type of index is the best suited for queries that combine text search with graph patterns.

Let's say you have a TEXT index on artist names. To retrieve `purple rain` songs from an artist named `Prince`, you could run the following query:

```
//009-combined-match.cypher
PROFILE
MATCH (n:Track)-[:ARTIST]->(a:Artist)
WHERE n.name CONTAINS "purple rain"
AND a.name = "prince"
RETURN n
```

The Cypher planner will not only leverage the index but also determine that the fastest query plan would start from the label with the lowest cardinality—that is, the one associated with the fewest nodes (as depicted in Figure 7-8). If you're unfamiliar with cardinality and how it impacts query performance, refer to Chapter 5, where this concept is explained in more detail.

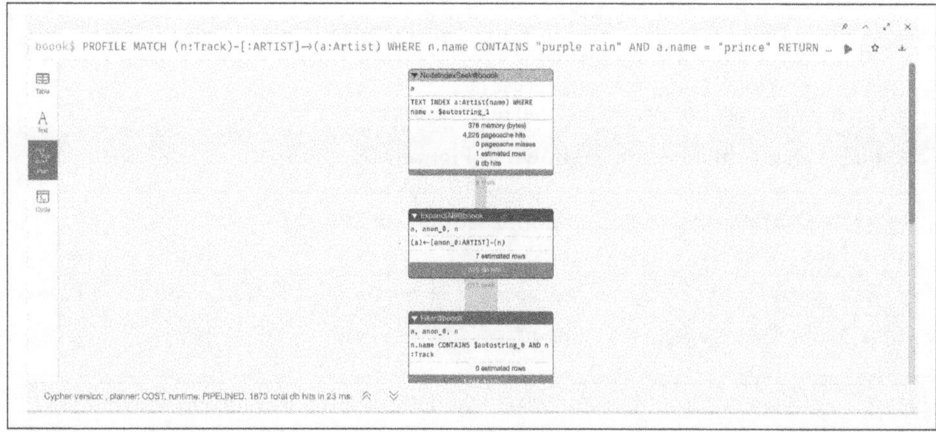

Figure 7-8. A Cypher query plan that uses both a TEXT index and a graph pattern

In summary, TEXT indexes consider the whole text string when searching, are optimized for queries using inexact match operators, and are limited to texts of 32K bytes or less.

Next, we'll look at another type of index that's capable of circumventing limitations such as spelling and grammar mistakes.

Full-Text Indexes

Full-text indexes are specialized, token-based indexes designed for more flexible and powerful search capabilities. Unlike string-based indexes, which treat the entire value as a single unit, *token-based indexes* break text into individual tokens (typically words) and index each one separately. This allows for advanced search features such as fuzzy matching, wildcard searches, and range queries. Neo4j's full-text indexes are built on Apache Lucene's inverted index (*https://oreil.ly/NGG0J*), the same foundation used by popular search engines like Elasticsearch and Solr.

Look at the FULLTEXT index creation command syntax. What differences from the TEXT index can you identify?

```
CREATE FULLTEXT INDEX my_index
FOR (n:Label1|Label2)
ON EACH [n.prop1, n.prop2, n.prop3...]
OPTIONS {
  indexConfig: {
    `fulltext.analyzer`: 'english',
    `fulltext.eventually_consistent`: false
  }
}
```

In a nutshell, you index objects as "documents" containing one or more fields, generally the text properties of your nodes. Thus, when you search for purple, you're searching not on a particular property but on all the properties that are part of the document.

The most notable differences you might have spotted, also highlighted in Table 7-2, are:

- You can create an index for nodes with different labels.
- You can create an index for more than one property.
- Neo4j uses an analyzer to analyze your texts.
- The indexing process can be *eventually consistent* (asynchronous) and can run in the background.

Table 7-2. FULL-TEXT and TEXT indexes

	FULL TEXT	TEXT
Case	insensitive	sensitive
Maximum length	none	32KB
Efficient with graph patterns	no	yes
Order by backed by index	no	yes
Prefix wildcard	yes	no
Suffix wildcard	yes	yes (using `CONTAINS`)
Phrase search	yes	yes
Fuzzy matching	yes	no
Stemming	yes	no

Stemming helps match different forms of a word by reducing it to its root, while fuzzy search allows for matching results despite typos or small mistakes in the query.

The analysis phase of the indexing process consists of a series of steps that transform the text into smaller, more precise units for the sake of searching. The specific steps will depend on your choice of analyzer. Choosing the right analyzer based on the type of text at hand is crucial when designing your search capability, because it directly affects how the text is processed and indexed—which, in turn, affects the search engine's relevance, performance, and overall effectiveness.

You can find the list of all available analyzers in Neo4j with the following command:

```
CALL db.index.fulltext.listAvailableAnalyzers
```

The analyzer `standard-no-stopwords` is the default in Neo4j. Figure 7-9 shows how the default analyzer transforms the texts before storing them.

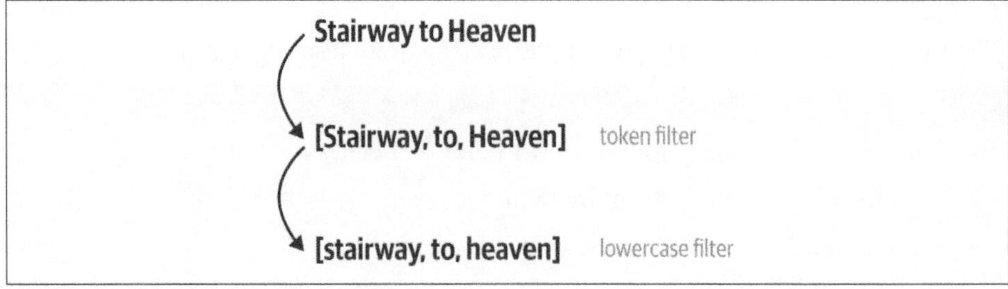

Figure 7-9. Simple text analysis phase

Using a different analyzer, such as the English analyzer, would lead to different steps optimized for the English language (see Figure 7-10).

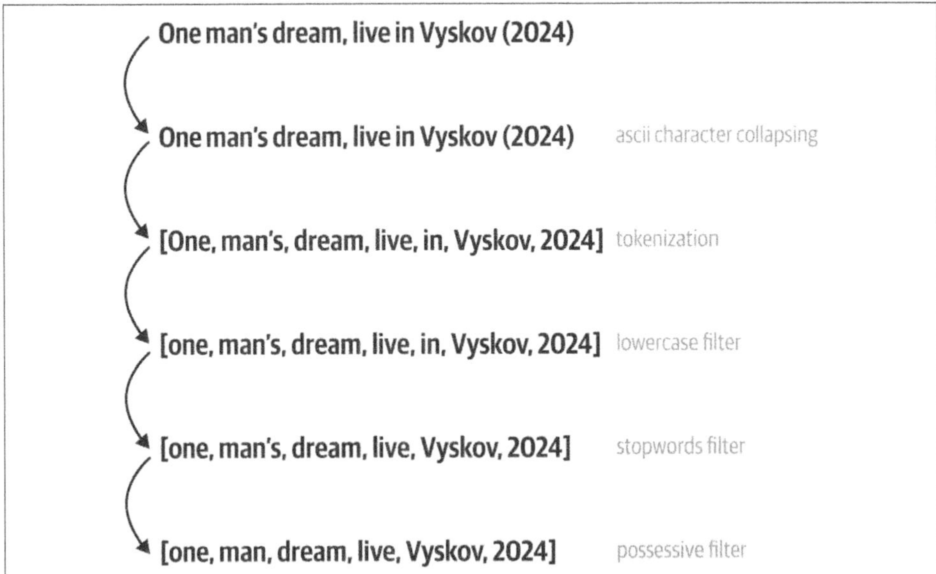

Figure 7-10. A more complex text-analysis phase

Here is an explanation of the steps:

Tokenization
: Tokenization involves using a tokenizer to parse the text and split it into tokens based on certain rules and delimiters. The tokenizer identifies boundaries where the text should be divided, such as spaces, punctuation, or other nonletter characters.

ASCII character collapsing
: The ASCII character-collapsing step in Lucene is a process used to normalize characters by converting them to their ASCII equivalents. This is particularly useful for improving search functionality by reducing variations of characters that may look different but are essentially the same for search purposes, such as *é*, *è*, and *ê* all being collapsed to *e*.

Lowercase filter
: The lowercase filter step in Lucene is a token filter that converts all characters in the tokens to lowercase. This is a common and essential step in text analysis for search engines. It helps ensure that searches are case-insensitive.

Stopwords filter
: The stopwords filter step is a token filter that removes stopwords from the token stream during text analysis. *Stopwords* are common, insignificant words that occur frequently in a language but carry little meaningful information in the context of search queries (for instance, *and*, *the*, and *is* are stopwords). By

removing these words, the stopwords filter helps to improve search relevance and efficiency.

Possessive filter
: The possessive filter step in Lucene is a token filter that removes possessive endings from tokens in the token stream. This step is particularly useful for normalizing text by handling possessive forms of words, making search queries more effective by treating possessive forms as their base forms. The most common possessive ending in English is *'s* (apostrophe-s).

Full-text indexes are token-based; they use an inverted index consisting of two main elements. The first is a *term dictionary*: a sorted list of all terms that occur in a given field across the corpus. It assigns a unique identifier to each term. The second is a *postings list*, which maps each term (referenced by ID) to the list of documents in which it appears (see Figure 7-11).

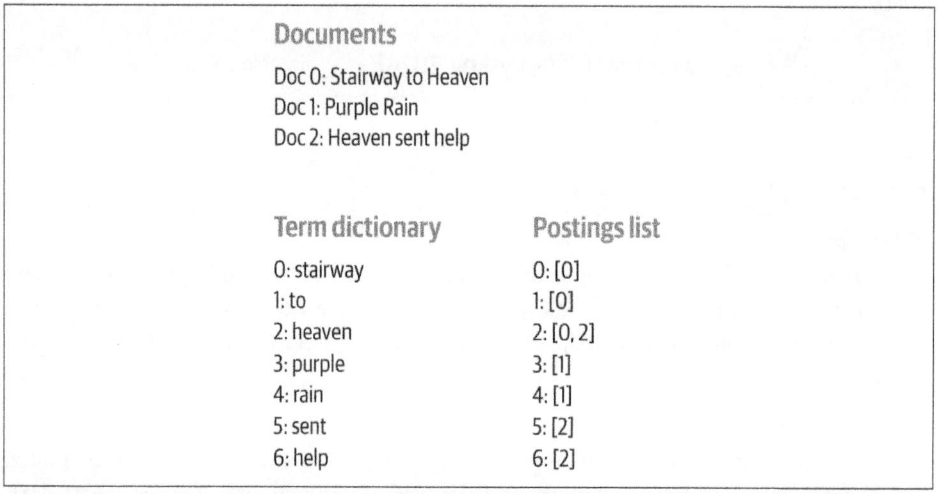

Documents

Doc 0: Stairway to Heaven
Doc 1: Purple Rain
Doc 2: Heaven sent help

Term dictionary	Postings list
0: stairway	0: [0]
1: to	1: [0]
2: heaven	2: [0, 2]
3: purple	3: [1]
4: rain	4: [1]
5: sent	5: [2]
6: help	6: [2]

Figure 7-11. Structure of a Lucene inverted index

You create a `FULLTEXT` index for the tracks:

```
//010-create-fts-index.cypher
CREATE FULLTEXT INDEX Track
FOR (n:Track)
ON EACH [n.name]
```

Next, you execute a search query with the full-text procedure and the Lucene simple query syntax (*https://oreil.ly/8cryM*):

```
//011-query-fts-index.cypher
CALL db.index.fulltext.queryNodes('Track', 'purple', {limit: 10})
YIELD node, score
RETURN node.name AS trackName, score
```

The procedure call takes two or more arguments:

- The name of the index to search on (`Track`)
- The search query (`purple`)
- Optional parameters, such as a cap on the number of results to return (here, 10)

The procedure call returns 10 track names along with a *score*. The score is a numerical statistic that reflects how important a word is to a document in a collection or corpus. It's computed by Lucene with an algorithm named *term frequency–inverse document frequency* (tf–idf), which is the most common similarity-computation function used in information retrieval. *Term frequency* is the raw count of how many times a term appears in a document (in the equation below, the number of times the term t appears in document d). *Inverse document frequency* is a measure of how much information the word provides, based on whether it's common or rare across the corpus.

In the formula for the idf, N is the total number of documents in the corpus and $|d \in D: t \in d|$ is the number of documents where the term t appears:

$$\mathrm{idf}(t, D) = \log \frac{N}{|\{d \in D: t \in d\}|}$$

The tf-idf is calculated with this formula:

$$\mathrm{tfidf}(t, d, D) = \mathrm{tf}(t, d) \cdot \mathrm{idf}(t, D)$$

There are some variations and adaptations in the concrete implementation of tf–idf in Lucene, but you have the basic idea. For a detailed explanation, you can refer to its Javadocs (*https://oreil.ly/-AnEb*).

To illustrate the concept, let's create two random nodes and a simple query using the full-text index:

```
//012-create-test-fts-index.cypher
CREATE FULLTEXT INDEX Test FOR (n:Test) ON EACH [n.text];
CREATE (a:Test {text: "this is a sample"});
CREATE (b:Test {text: "this is a sample in a longer text"});

//013-query-test-fts-index.cypher
CALL db.index.fulltext.queryNodes("Test", "sample");
```

Table 7-3 shows the results.

Table 7-3. Full-text index query results with TF/IDF scores

Node	Score
`This is a sample`	0.0959
`This is a sample in a longer text`	0.0729

As you can see, the importance of the term `sample` is higher in the first result because the text is shorter than the second result—this is the effect of the tf formula.

Now let's create 100 additional `Test` nodes with a similar text and run the search query again:

```
//014-more-test-data.cypher
UNWIND range(1,100) AS i
CREATE (n:Test {text: "this is a sample in a longer text " + i});

//015-query-more-test-data.cypher
CALL db.index.fulltext.queryNodes("Test", "sample");
```

Table 7-4. Full-text index query results with 100 more nodes, again with tf–idf scores

Node	Score
`This is a sample`	0.00285
`This is a sample in a longer text 100`	0.00221

Table 7-4 shows the results. The difference in similarity increases between the first result and all other results for the term `sample` because it appears frequently in many documents.

Multitoken Searches

Searching for `purple rain` in the music database using this technique yields some results, as shown in Figure 7-12:

```
//016-multi-token-search.cypher
CALL db.index.fulltext.queryNodes("Track", "purple rain")
YIELD node, score
MATCH (node)-[:ARTIST]->(artist)
RETURN node.name AS track, artist.name AS artist, score
```

Figure 7-12. FULLTEXT query results with track title and score

However, if you scroll down the list, you will also find results where the track name consists of the single word `purple`. Recall that the index is token-based; the query is also decomposed into tokens, in this case two: `purple` and `rain`. The default behavior of the Lucene query syntax is to do an `OR` query that effectively translates to "Find me tracks with `purple` OR `rain` in the name":

```
//017-or-query.cypher
CALL db.index.fulltext.queryNodes("Track", "purple OR rain")
YIELD node, score
RETURN node.name, score
```

You can change the query to use an `AND` operator for the tokens if you want to ensure that both tokens are part of the name:

```
//018-and-query.cypher
CALL db.index.fulltext.queryNodes("Track", "purple AND rain")
YIELD node, score
RETURN node.name, score
```

This returns 320 results, compared to more than 3,000 with the original query (see Figure 7-13).

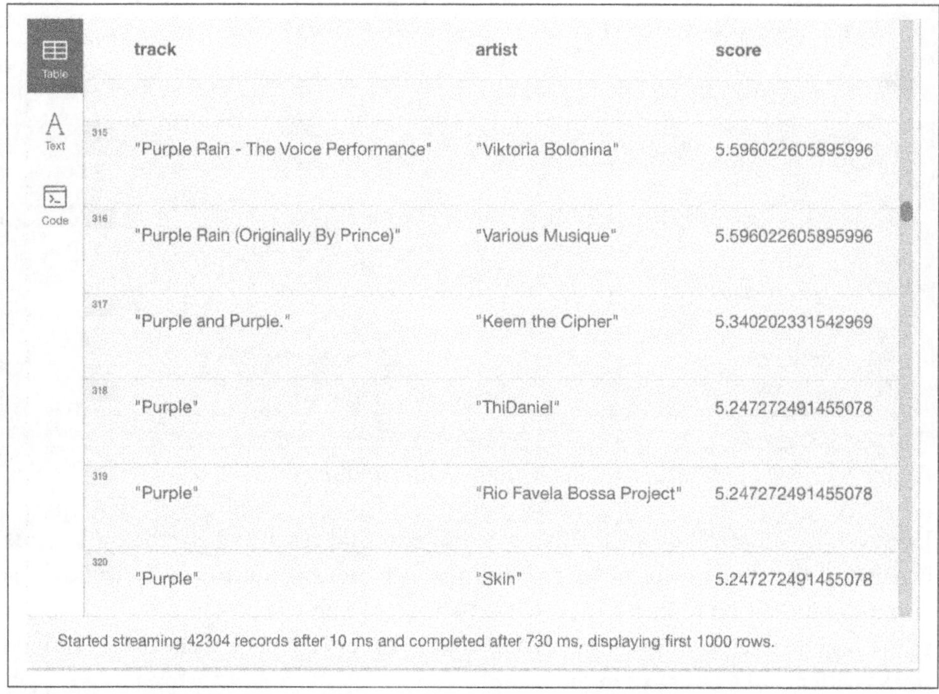

	track	artist	score
315	"Purple Rain - The Voice Performance"	"Viktoria Bolonina"	5.596022605895996
316	"Purple Rain (Originally By Prince)"	"Various Musique"	5.596022605895996
317	"Purple and Purple."	"Keem the Cipher"	5.340202331542969
318	"Purple"	"ThiDaniel"	5.247272491455078
319	"Purple"	"Rio Favela Bossa Project"	5.247272491455078
320	"Purple"	"Skin"	5.247272491455078

Table
Text
Code
Started streaming 42304 records after 10 ms and completed after 730 ms, displaying first 1000 rows.

Figure 7-13. FULLTEXT query results using multiple tokens and the AND operator

Phrase Searches

Token-based searches like the ones you've just seen do not take into account each token's position in the text. The following search query would return the exact same results as the previous query:

```
CALL db.index.fulltext.queryNodes("Track", "rain AND purple")
YIELD node, score
RETURN node.name, score
```

When the order of tokens is important, enclose the tokens inside double quotation marks to tell the Lucene syntax parser to execute a *phrase search* instead: a search query that looks for a specific sequence of words appearing together in the same order within a document. Unlike simple term searches, where each term is searched independently, a phrase search ensures that the exact phrase, with words in the specified order and typically adjacent to each other, is found in the documents. For example:

```
//019-phrase-search.cypher
CALL db.index.fulltext.queryNodes('Track', ' "rain purple" ')
YIELD node, score
RETURN node.name, score
```

No results would be returned from the query, because there are no tracks with names that contain `rain` and `purple` in that order.

Wildcard Searches

You probably don't want your users to have to type the full tokens in a search bar to get results. Simply typing `pur` should start to return results, including `purple rain`. In applications with search-as-you-type inputs, it is very common to internally append a wildcard to what the user is typing. Wildcard searches find tokens ending with anything after the partial token given in the query, so the query `pur*` would find tracks where the name contains, for example, `purple`, `purity`, or `purse`. Thus, if the user queries `pur rai`, your application might retype it as `pur* AND rai*`:

```
//020-wildcard-search.cypher
CALL db.index.fulltext.queryNodes('Track', 'pur* AND rai*')
YIELD node, score
RETURN node.name, score
```

Wildcards aren't limited to suffixes. You can also use prefix wildcards (e.g., `*rock`) to find tokens that end with a certain string. These are typically more expensive, since the index must scan more broadly, but they can be useful in specific use cases. For instance, if a user searches for genres or subgenres with a common suffix like *-rock* (think *punk-rock*, *indie-rock*, *hard-rock*), a query like this might help:

```
//021-wildcard-prefix.cypher
CALL db.index.fulltext.queryNodes('Genre', '*rock')
YIELD node, score
RETURN node.name, score
```

Next, let's look at fuzzy search.

Fuzzy Search

Fuzzy search queries retrieve results even if the query doesn't exactly match the original text; for example, if users make spelling mistakes or write the same query term differently according to regional spellings, like `color` and `colour`.

To execute a fuzzy search, you use the ~ (tilde) character at the end of the query term, along with a coefficient that specifies the minimum percentage of similarity there should be between the query and the original data stored in the index.

The following query includes results that contain the word `colour` in its count, even if the query itself was `color`:

```
//022-fuzzy-search.cypher
CALL db.index.fulltext.queryNodes('Track', 'color~0.7')
YIELD node, score
WITH node WHERE node.name CONTAINS 'colour'
RETURN count(*) AS count
```

In this section, we've explored various query possibilities in Lucene, including wildcard searches, phrase searches, keyword searches, and fuzzy searches. Each of these query types offers unique capabilities for tailoring search results to meet specific needs. Wildcard searches allow for flexible pattern matching, phrase searches ensure the retrieval of exact sequences of words, and keyword searches facilitate precise term matching. These tools enhance the robustness and accuracy of search functionalities, providing powerful mechanisms to extract relevant information from large datasets.

Additional Index and Query Considerations

Let's look at a few more important factors to consider when dealing with indexes.

Tokenization

Token-based indexes can lead to surprising effects, especially when you're analyzing documents before storing them. It's important to consider these effects before configuring your indexes in order to ensure that you're using the right analyzer. This section provides some examples of common patterns.

Tokenization is definitely one of the most important factors to consider in choosing your analyzer. The way a text is broken down into tokens can lead to undesired effects if not done properly. A practical example will be worth a thousand words.

In a test database, create two `Person` nodes, each with an email address:

```
//023-test-persons-db.cypher
CREATE DATABASE persons WAIT;
:use persons ;
CREATE (:Person {name: "John Doe", email: "john.doe@example.com"});
CREATE (:Person {name: "Bob Green", email: "bob.green@example.com"});
```

We will create an index with the `` `stop` `` analyzer, whose documentation tells us that it "tokenizes at nonletter characters and filters out English stop words. This differs from the 'classic' and 'standard' analyzers in that it makes no effort to recognize special terms, like likely product names, URLs or email addresses":

```
//024-persons-fts-index.cypher
CREATE FULLTEXT INDEX test
FOR (n:Person)
ON EACH [n.email]
OPTIONS {
  indexConfig: {
    `fulltext.analyzer`: 'stop',
    `fulltext.eventually_consistent`: false
  }
}
```

This will ultimately break down the email addresses into tokens as nonletter characters, producing the following tokens for John Doe's email address:

"[john, doe, example, com]"

Querying for "bob.green@example.com" would lead to both Person nodes being returned, because the breakdown of [bob, green, example, com] has at least one token matching those from John Doe's email address tokens.

To circumvent this issue, choose an analyzer that preserves emails as single tokens, such as the whitespace analyzer.

Special Characters: Hashtags and Mentions

If you're combining your own data with data from social media, it might include certain special characters. For example, on many platforms, users can *mention* an artist using the "@" symbol, like "jekyll & hyde - live @ wiesbaden" or add a hashtag with the name of a song, like #HighwayToHell.

As previously mentioned, special characters are removed before data is stored, which yields tokens like HighwayToHell. This makes it impossible for users to search for data that *must* be a hashtag or a mention. Even if they type the "#" in their query, the query analyzer will remove it.

To circumvent this behavior, it's important to choose the right analyzer for the particular type of text in question. You can create your own analyzer (*https://oreil.ly/W_gdV*) with a Neo4j extension. You can also combine full-text indexes with normal text indexes, like in the following query:

```
//025-fts-and-normal-search.cypher
CALL {
    CALL db.index.fulltext.queryNodes('Track', '#highwayToHell')
    YIELD node
    RETURN node AS track

    UNION DISTINCT
    // DISTINCT ensures the same node
    // found by the two queries will be returned
    // only once

    MATCH (n:Track)
    WHERE n.name CONTAINS '#highwayToHell'
    RETURN n AS track
}
RETURN track
```

Next, let's look at how analyzers handle nonword terms.

Identifiers, IP Addresses, and Other Nonword Terms

Look at the following identifier:

```
V-1234
```

Neo4j's default analyzer, `standard-no-stopwords`, will tokenize this text on nonletter boundaries, producing two tokens: `V` and `1234`. Lucene doesn't index single-letter tokens, so it will only index `1234`.

This means that if you query `V-*` in hopes of finding all identifiers starting with `V-`, you'll get no results, because no such thing exists in the index. The solution is to use an analyzer that breaks the strings into tokens at the whitespace character rather than at nonletter boundaries, such as the `whitespace` analyzer.

IP addresses (for instance, 127.0.0.1) often yield unwanted results in search engines because applications tend to separate tokens using the dot character (period). In IP addresses, this produces four tokens. Fortunately, you can leverage the same solution as for the identifiers. It is also very common to convert IP addresses to full numbers instead so they can be compared with `lower than` and `greater than` operators.

Stopwords: To Be or Not to Be

Did you ever imagine you would use this speech from Shakespeare's *Hamlet* in your professional career? Well, here you are. This line is special because it consists entirely of *stopwords*: words that are too common to be meaningful to language-specific analyzers, such as the English analyzer. The analyzers thus consider them noise and remove them from the text before analyzing it.

In English, words like *the*, *at*, and *and* are stopwords. So are *to*, *be*, and *not*. Therefore, as Figure 7-14 shows, analyzing the phrase "to be or not to be" with the English analyzer produces an empty token set and stores nothing in the index.

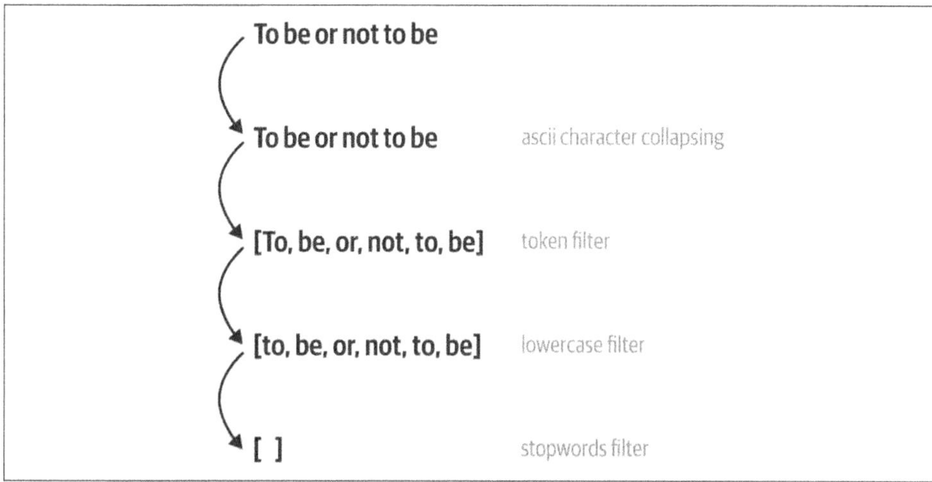

Figure 7-14. Analysis of the "to be or not to be" speech using the English analyzer

Analyzers vary widely, so it may take long hours of experimentation to find the right analyzer for your use case.

Performance with Graph Patterns

The Cypher query planner does not perform as well with full-text indexes in combination with graph patterns as it does with text indexes. While this isn't apparent with a simple search query, writing a Cypher query to include a graph pattern and multiple search queries on different indexes is quite complex. For example:

```
//026-artist-search.cypher
CALL db.index.fulltext.queryNodes('Track', 'purple rain')
YIELD node AS track
MATCH path=(track)-[:ARTIST]->(a:Artist)
WHERE a IN COLLECT {
  CALL db.index.fulltext.queryNodes('Artist', 'prince')
  YIELD node
}
RETURN path
LIMIT 10
```

Try it. If you're adventurous enough, attempt to rewrite this query so that it optionally matches "`Prince`"; results matching both conditions should be scored higher. The complexity lies in combining optional path matching with multiple full-text searches. You can find the solution in the GitHub repository (*https://github.com/neo4j-the-definitive-guide/book*) accompanying this book.

As a last thing to say, Neo4j allows you to inspect when an index was last used and how many times it has been hit. As shown in Figure 7-15, this can be a valuable indicator for identifying unused indexes or spotting queries that aren't making effective use of indexing. If the hit count is far below what you'd expect, it could suggest redundant indexes or unoptimized queries. Monitoring these metrics regularly helps you refine both your indexing strategy and query performance:

```
SHOW FULLTEXT INDEXES YIELD lastRead, readCount
```

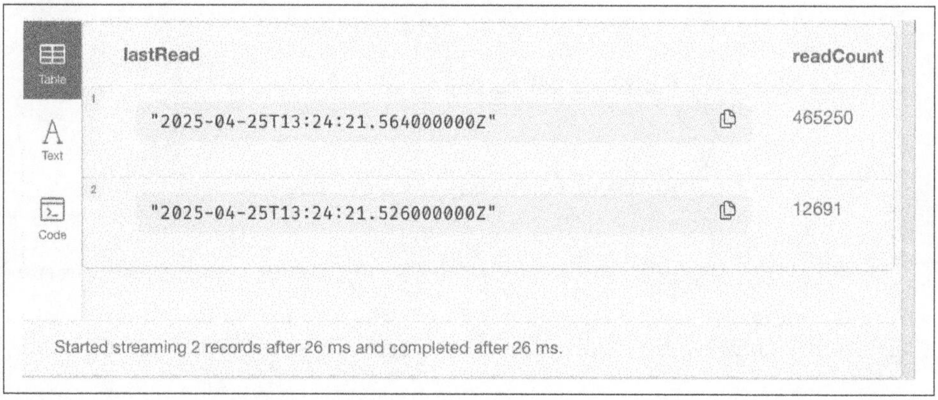

	lastRead	readCount
1	"2025-04-25T13:24:21.564000000Z"	465250
2	"2025-04-25T13:24:21.526000000Z"	12691

Started streaming 2 records after 26 ms and completed after 26 ms.

Figure 7-15. Statistics of the index usage

Summary

In this chapter, you learned the characteristics of the two main types of indexes used for searching textual data. Text indexes are simple, efficient indexes for case-sensitive search queries. They work best with text no bigger than 32KB and combine well with graph pattern queries. Full-text indexes allow far more complex ways of handling text and search; they're great for finding the starting point in your graph but can't be efficiently combined with complex graph patterns.

The next chapter will delve into the topic of advanced graph patterns.

CHAPTER 8

Advanced Graph Patterns

This chapter explores advanced graph patterns that are useful to know as a Neo4j expert. The topics here touch on modeling techniques for security as well as entity resolution, more efficient queries, dealing with node degrees, and the more recent quantified path patterns. You've seen some usage of subqueries in previous chapters—now you'll learn more about them.

To try the queries, continue using the `chapter5` database, or, recreate it following the README (*https://oreil.ly/s_m9b*) in the GitHub repository.

Subqueries

Subqueries in Cypher are nested queries that execute within a nested scope of the outer query. The `CALL` subquery executes per row that arrives from the outer query. This is an important point: since the subquery operates in its own scope, it does not need to hold onto any data structures that were created while it executes over a row before it moves on to the next incoming row, thus reducing memory overhead. Subqueries are used both when reading from and writing to the graph.

CALL Subqueries

In Chapter 5, you imported a large set of data, which resulted in a graph with 18 million nodes and 100 million relationships. This graph is ideal to examine the effects of using a subquery. The first version of the query asks Neo4j to return every track in the graph along with the playlists that they're on, and it uses a regular `MATCH` with path expansion:

```
//001-explain-all-tracks.cypher
EXPLAIN
```

```
MATCH (t:Track)-[:ON_PLAYLIST]->(p:Playlist)
RETURN t as track, COLLECT(p) as playlists
```

There are about 13 million tracks in this graph, and this query is going to traverse them all to collect the playlists they're on. Run an `EXPLAIN` of this query (don't try to `PROFILE` it, or you could be waiting a very long time for the query to actually execute). The plan, as shown in Figure 8-1, shows the `EagerAggregation` operator (refer to Chapter 5 for a refresher about eager operations).

```
+-------------------+----+-------------------------------------+----------------+---------------------+
|Operator           |Id  | Details                             | Estimated Rows | Pipeline            |
+-------------------+----+-------------------------------------+----------------+---------------------+
|+ProduceResults    | 0  | track, playlists                    |          11200 | In Pipeline 1       |
||                  +----+-------------------------------------+----------------+---------------------+
|+EagerAggregation  | 1  | t AS track, collect(p) AS playlists |          11200 |                     |
||                  +----+-------------------------------------+----------------+                     |
|+Filter            | 2  | t:Track                             |      125451006 |                     |
||                  +----+-------------------------------------+----------------+                     |
|+Expand(All)       | 3  | (p)<-[anon_0:ON_PLAYLIST]-(t)       |      125451006 |                     |
||                  +----+-------------------------------------+----------------+                     |
|+NodeByLabelScan   | 4  | p:Playlist                          |        1054935 | Fused in Pipeline 0 |
+-------------------+----+-------------------------------------+----------------+---------------------+
```

Figure 8-1. The `EXPLAIN` plan for the query to return all tracks and their playlists

The `MATCH` must fully execute over all tracks and playlists to allow the `COLLECT` aggregation to be processed correctly. These aggregated results are kept in memory till the operator completes, and then the streaming of results proceeds. This can stress the heap, leading to potential `Out of Memory` exceptions or increased garbage collection (GC) pauses. This type of query is ideal for demonstrating the power of subqueries. Since the results of the query (the actual tracks and playlists) aren't of interest, we've simplified the query to only return a count:

```
//002-count.cypher
MATCH (t:Track)-[:ON_PLAYLIST]->(p:Playlist)
WITH t as track, COLLECT(p) as playlists
RETURN count(*)
```

Before you run this query, check your memory settings in *neo4j.conf*. If they were generous, you can reduce them to see the effect more easily. The settings we used are:

```
dbms.memory.heap.max_size=1G
server.memory.heap.initial_size=512m
dbms.memory.transaction.total.max=256m
db.memory.transaction.max=16m
```

Run the query and monitor *debug.log*. You'll start to see stop-the-world GC pauses, like these:

```
WARN  [o.n.k.i.c.VmPauseMonitorComponent] Detected VM stop-the-world pause:
        {pauseTime=337, gcTime=476, gcCount=7}
WARN  [o.n.k.i.c.VmPauseMonitorComponent] Detected VM stop-the-world pause:
        {pauseTime=542, gcTime=666, gcCount=7}
WARN  [o.n.k.i.c.VmPauseMonitorComponent] Detected VM stop-the-world pause:
        {pauseTime=214, gcTime=363, gcCount=8}
```

```
WARN  [o.n.k.i.c.VmPauseMonitorComponent] Detected VM stop-the-world pause:
        {pauseTime=344, gcTime=398, gcCount=3}
```

A *stop-the-world pause* is a period of time when all application threads are suspended to allow the Java virtual machine (JVM) to perform certain operations, usually garbage collection. These pauses affect Neo4j by making the database unresponsive for the duration of this pause. They're typically caused by pressure on the heap when many objects are created too rapidly and not enough space is available, triggering garbage collection cycles. While stop-the-world pauses in themselves are not a problem, very frequent and long ones are. The JVM is constantly improving garbage collection, though, so over time, the impact of these stop-the-world pauses will continue to decrease.

As Figure 8-2 explains, your query has most likely failed as well, as it hit the configured memory limit for the transaction.

ERROR **Neo.TransientError.General.MemoryPoolOutOfMemoryError**

```
The allocation of an extra 2.0 MiB would use more than the limit 716.8 MiB. Currently using 716.0 MiB.
dbms.memory.transaction.total.max threshold reached
```

Figure 8-2. The query's high memory requirements have caused it to fail.

Now use a subquery to find the playlists that each track is on:

```
//003-subquery.cypher
EXPLAIN
MATCH (t:Track)
CALL (t) {
MATCH (t)-[:ON_PLAYLIST]->(p:Playlist)
RETURN collect(p) as playlists
}
RETURN count(*)
```

Before you run it, look at the `EXPLAIN` plan. Figure 8-3 is now different, thanks to the introduction of the `CALL` subquery.

```
+---------------------+----+-----------------------------------+----------------+----------------------+
| Operator            | Id | Details                           | Estimated Rows | Pipeline             |
+---------------------+----+-----------------------------------+----------------+----------------------+
| +ProduceResults     |  0 | `count(*)`                        |              1 |                      |
| |                   +----+-----------------------------------+----------------+                      |
| +EagerAggregation   |  1 | count(*) AS `count(*)`            |              1 | In Pipeline 3        |
| |                   +----+-----------------------------------+----------------+----------------------+
| +Apply              |  2 |                                   |       13282008 |                      |
| |\                  +----+-----------------------------------+----------------+----------------------+
| | +EagerAggregation |  3 | collect(p) AS playlists           |       13282008 |                      |
| | |                 +----+-----------------------------------+----------------+                      |
| | +Filter           |  4 | p:Playlist                        |      125451006 |                      |
| | |                 +----+-----------------------------------+----------------+                      |
| | +Expand(All)      |  5 | (t)-[anon_0:ON_PLAYLIST]->(p)     |      125451006 |                      |
| | |                 +----+-----------------------------------+----------------+                      |
| | +Argument         |  6 | t                                 |       13282008 | Fused in Pipeline 1  |
| |                   +----+-----------------------------------+----------------+----------------------+
| +NodeByLabelScan    |  7 | t:Track                           |       13282008 | In Pipeline 0        |
+---------------------+----+-----------------------------------+----------------+----------------------+
```

Figure 8-3. Each track is now processed in pipeline 1. The subquery executes in its own scope, expands only to the playlists of the single track, and performs the `Eager Aggregation` collect on a much smaller number of rows. The memory consumed by this operation is released before the next track is processed.

When you run this query, you should have a result and fewer to no GC pauses in your *debug.log*. `CALL` subqueries are an effective way to allow large queries to scale and be more performant.

What is the difference between the `CALL` subquery and pattern comprehension? *Pattern comprehension* is a construct to create a list from a pattern, optionally based on predicates. It closely resembles an `OPTIONAL MATCH` and collect. The previous query can be rewritten to use pattern comprehension:

```
//004-pattern-comprehension.cypher
MATCH (t:Track)
WITH [(t)-[:ON_PLAYLIST]->(p:Playlist) | p] AS playlists
RETURN count(*)
```

The `EXPLAIN` plan in Figure 8-4 is similar to that in Figure 8-3.

```
+--------------------+---+----------------------------------+----------------+--------------------+
| Operator           |Id | Details                          |Estimated Rows  |Pipeline            |
+--------------------+---+----------------------------------+----------------+--------------------+
|+ProduceResults     | 0 | `count(*)`                       |              1 |                    |
||                   +---+----------------------------------+----------------+                    |
|+EagerAggregation   | 1 | count(*) AS `count(*)`           |              1 |In Pipeline 3       |
||                   +---+----------------------------------+----------------+--------------------+
|+Apply              | 2 |                                  |       13282008 |                    |
||\                   +---+----------------------------------+----------------+--------------------+
|| +EagerAggregation | 8 | collect_all(anon_0) AS playlists|       13282008 |                    |
|| |                 +---+----------------------------------+----------------+                    |
|| +Projection       | 3 | p AS anon_0                      |      125451006 |                    |
|| |                 +---+----------------------------------+----------------+                    |
|| +Filter           | 4 | p:Playlist                       |      125451006 |                    |
|| |                 +---+----------------------------------+----------------+                    |
|| +Expand(All)      | 5 | (t)-[anon_1:ON_PLAYLIST]->(p)    |      125451006 |                    |
|| |                 +---+----------------------------------+----------------+                    |
|| +Argument         | 6 | t                                |       13282008 |Fused in Pipeline 1|
||                   +---+----------------------------------+----------------+--------------------+
|+NodeByLabelScan    | 7 | t:Track                          |       13282008 |In Pipeline 0       |
+--------------------+---+----------------------------------+----------------+--------------------+
```

Figure 8-4. The query plan of the query with pattern comprehension

Apart from having the same execution benefits as the CALL subquery, pattern comprehension is more succinct. However, it cannot be used for other types of aggregations, and it's less versatile than subqueries when you also need to limit, skip, or sort results.

Post-Union Processing

Subqueries are very handy when you want to aggregate the results of a union. Say you want to sum the number of artists who have really long tracks and the number of artists whose tracks are on more than 500 playlists. You might start with a query like this:

```
//005-post-union-a.cypher
MATCH (a:Artist)<-[:ARTIST]-(t)
WHERE t.duration > 2000000
RETURN COUNT(a) AS artistCount
UNION
MATCH (a:Artist)<-[:ARTIST]-(t)
WHERE COUNT { (t)-[:ON_PLAYLIST]->(:Playlist) } > 500
RETURN COUNT(a) as artistCount
```

The UNION used in the query above will eliminate duplicates from the combined result. If an artist falls into both categories, they will be counted only once. If you want duplicates to be retained, use UNION ALL.

Unfortunately, this does not return the sum of artists across both parts of the query. Instead, you see a row returned for each. Subqueries are the answer to post-union processing:

```
//006-post-union-b.cypher
MATCH (a:Artist)
```

```
CALL (a) {
MATCH (a)<-[:ARTIST]-(t)
WHERE t.duration > 2000000
RETURN COUNT(a) AS artistCount
UNION ALL
MATCH (a)<-[:ARTIST]-(t)
WHERE COUNT { (t)-[:ON_PLAYLIST]->(:Playlist) } > 500
RETURN COUNT(a) as artistCount
}
RETURN SUM(artistCount)
```

Here, the sums of artists from both parts of the union are processed after the subquery executes, resulting in a whopping 48,632 artists.

Concurrent Transactions with CALL

`CALL {} IN CONCURRENT TRANSACTIONS` is also a subquery. By default, `CALL {} IN TRANSACTIONS` executes on a single core. But adding `CONCURRENT` to it will allow batches to execute in parallel, utilizing the number of cores you specify or the number of CPU cores available by default.

With concurrent transactions in play, the now-familiar `LOAD CSV` looks like this:

```
LOAD CSV WITH HEADERS FROM "file:///track_artist1.csv" AS row
CALL (row) {
MATCH (t:Track {id: row.track_id})
MATCH (a:Artist {id: row.artist_id})
MERGE (t)-[:ARTIST]->(a)
} IN 4 CONCURRENT TRANSACTIONS OF 1000 ROWS
```

If you skipped over Chapter 2, revisit it to understand more about high-volume imports and concurrent transactions.

Fine-Grained Relationship Types

Before diving into relationship-type granularity, let's refresh your understanding of *node degree.*

In Neo4j, a node's *degree* represents the number of relationships connected to it. This measure indicates how interconnected the node is with its neighbors within the graph and plays a crucial role in query performance and optimization.

Neo4j internally tracks the degree of a node based on relationship type and direction. For example, the `Track` node shown in Figure 8-5 has a degree of 9 for incoming `HAS_TRACK` relationships.

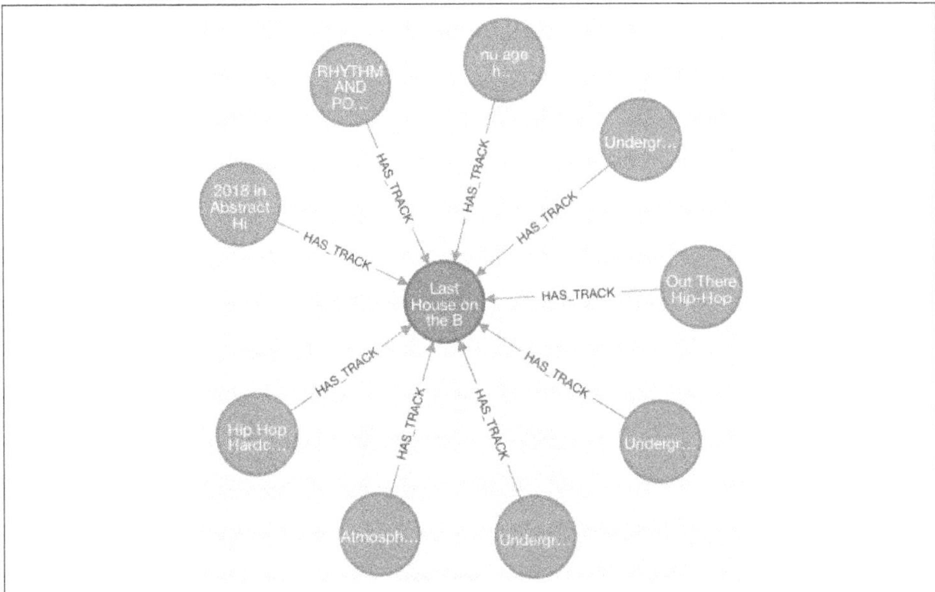

Figure 8-5. The track node has an in-degree of 9.

As we discussed in Chapter 2, a node's internal structure maintains references to its connected relationships. That's why retrieving the degree for a specific relationship type is as straightforward as using the `COUNT` subquery:

```
//007-degree.cypher
PROFILE
MATCH (n:Track) WHERE n.track_id = '0qbV8TfCN7gTESOxixV2SI'
RETURN COUNT { (n)<-[:HAS_TRACK]-() } AS degreeInHasTrack
```

Figure 8-6 shows a profile of the same query, in which you can identify the usage of the **`GetDegree`** operator. (For more information about operators in the profile, see Chapter 5.)

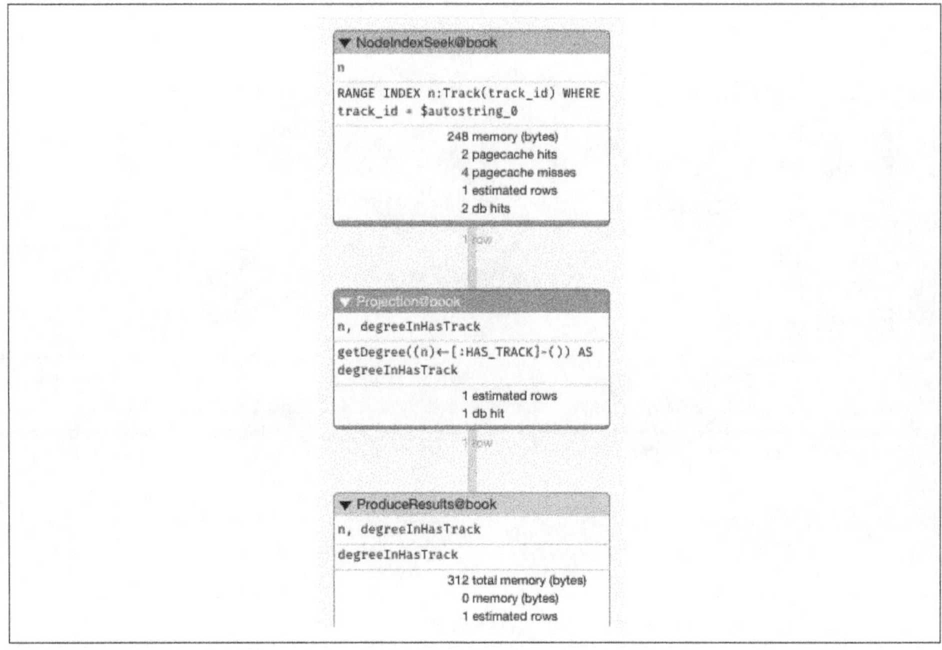

Figure 8-6. The `GetDegree` operator is an optimal way to get the degree of a node.

Modifying the query to include the `Playlist` label in the `COUNT` pattern prevents Neo4j from using the `GetDegree` operator, as you'll notice in Figure 8-7. As a result, the query requires more database accesses, leading to increased overhead and reduced performance:

```
//008-degree-broken.cypher
PROFILE
MATCH (n:Track) WHERE n.track_id = '0qbV8TfCN7gTESOxixV2SI'
RETURN COUNT { (n)<-[:HAS_TRACK]-(:Playlist) } AS degreeInHasTrack
```

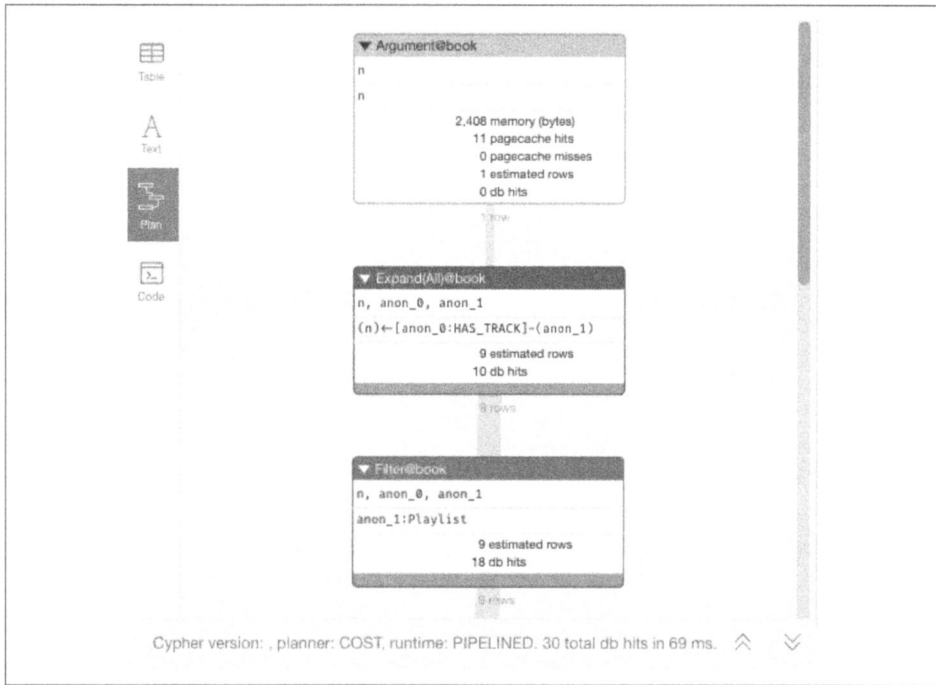

Figure 8-7. Specifying the `Playlist` label prevents you from using the `GetDegree` operator.

In this case, Neo4j must traverse all incoming `HAS_TRACK` relationships, filter the connected nodes to check if they have the `Playlist` label, and then count the matches. This approach is less efficient than directly retrieving the degree, because it requires additional traversal and filtering steps. Experienced Neo4j developers often refer to this as the "HAS-everywhere" relationship-type antipattern (see Figure 8-8).

The node-degree example illustrates how avoiding label-specific filtering on relationships can improve performance. The same principle applies when traversing the graph. For instance, if you start from a `Track` node to retrieve its associated playlists and their users, you may also encounter `HAS_TRACK` relationships from other sources, such as `WeeklyChart` nodes that track the top 50 tracks per week. In such cases, specifying only the relationship type without filtering by node labels allows for more efficient traversal.

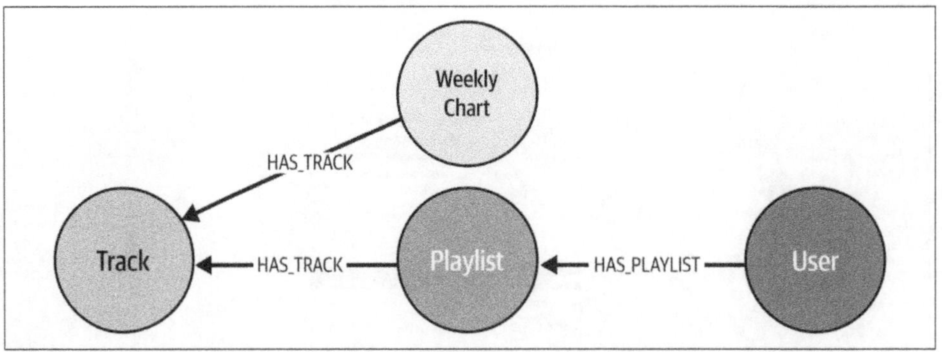

Figure 8-8. An example of a HAS-everywhere relationship antipattern

The query starts from a `Track` node but is immediately penalized because it must traverse all incoming `HAS_TRACK` relationships, filter out those connected to `Weekly Chart`, *and* retain only those linked to `Playlist`. This additional filtering increases query complexity and reduces performance (see Figure 8-9).

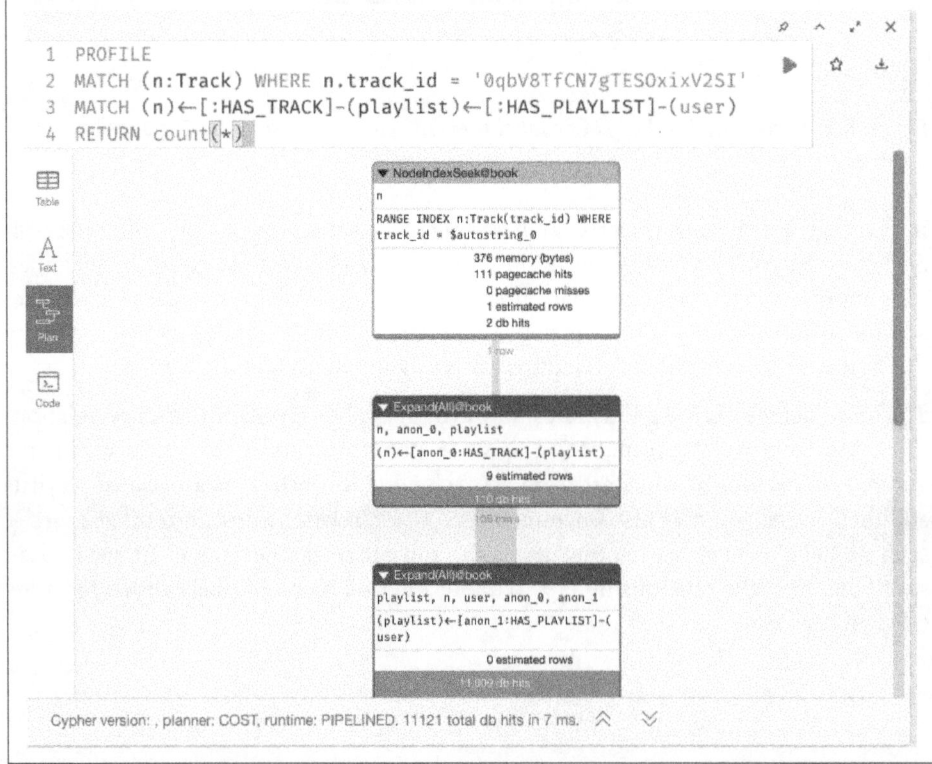

Figure 8-9. The query traverses to `WeeklyChart` labels via the HAS_TRACK relationship, but they are then filtered out.

Refactoring the relationship type between `WeeklyChart` and `Track` from `HAS_TRACK` to `INCLUDES_TRACK`, as shown in Figure 8-10, significantly improves performance. Running the same query with this adjustment reduces the number of database hits by a factor of 10, making the adjusted query far more efficient.

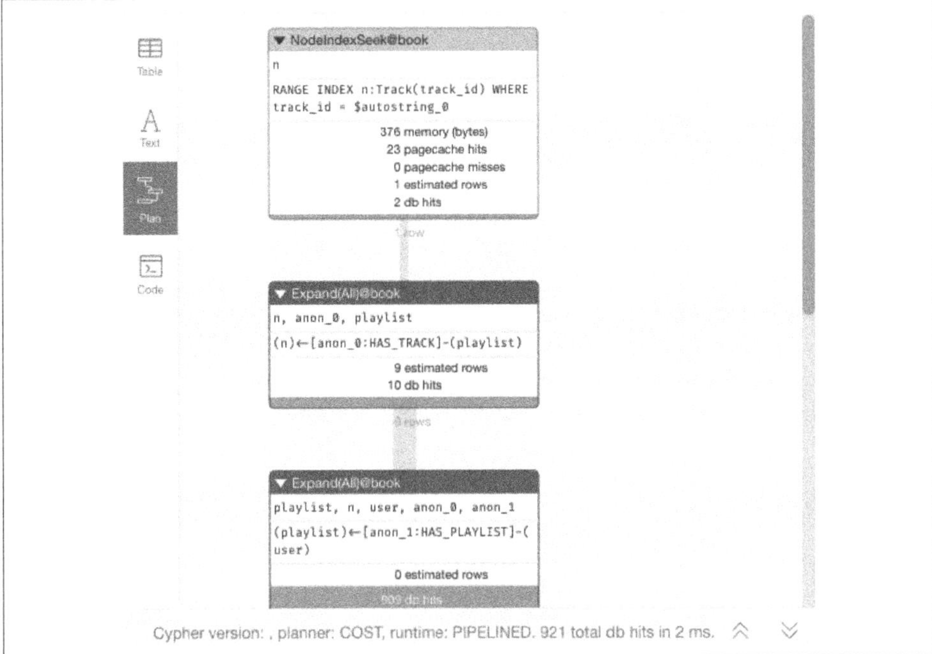

Figure 8-10. The query plan is more efficient with a specific relationship type.

To achieve maximum performance, it's best to ensure that for a given node label, each relationship type and direction corresponds to a unique target node label. This eliminates the need to filter by the other node's label, allowing Neo4j to optimize traversal efficiency.

Other factors also impact traversal efficiency, such as using a generic relationship type combined with a subtype property (see Figure 8-11).

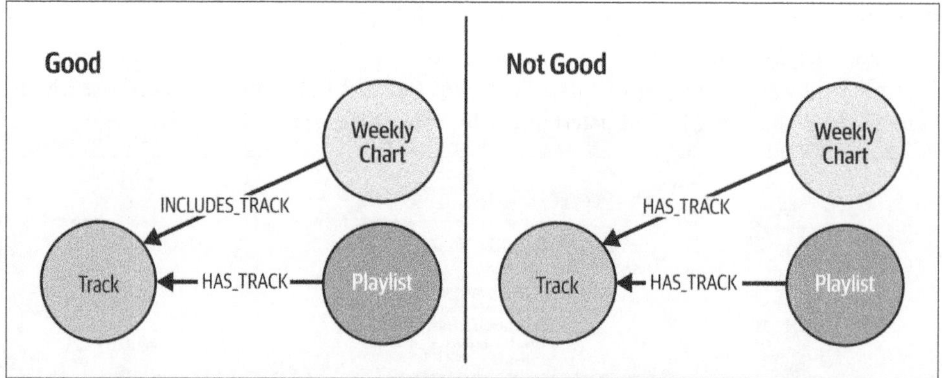

Figure 8-11. Avoid general relationship types where possible: be specific.

The HAS_TRACK example has a parallel in modern knowledge graphs, where entities are extracted from text and linked to their source documents. In ElectricHarmony's domain, this could involve extracting entities from track lyrics and linking mentions to people, cities, or other relevant concepts (see Figure 8-12).

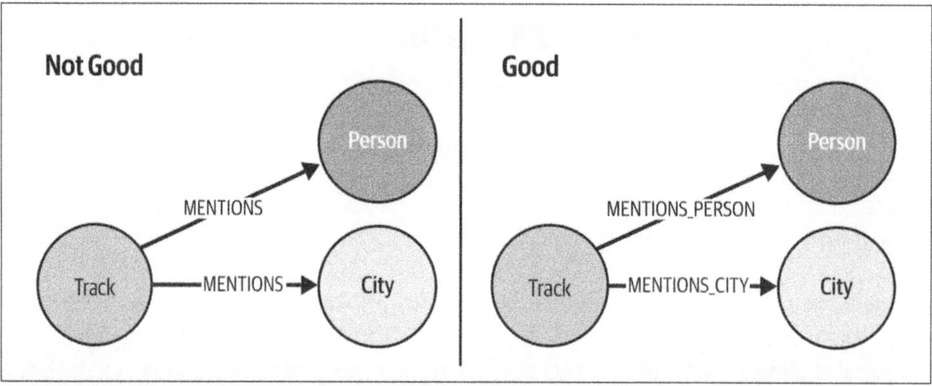

Figure 8-12. Entity extraction benefits from specific relationships in knowledge graphs to enable more efficient querying and better understanding of the graph

You might question whether performance at the level of a single node is significant. While it's true that the impact is minimal for a node with only a few relationships, the situation changes as nodes become *dense*, accumulating thousands of relationships. At that point, performance optimization becomes crucial.

Another scenario where node degree efficiency matters is when analyzing the overall structure of the graph: for example, when gathering statistics such as the number of nodes per label or counting relationships per type from a given label.

A typical query for counting all incoming HAS_TRACK relationships for the Track label would look like Figure 8-13.

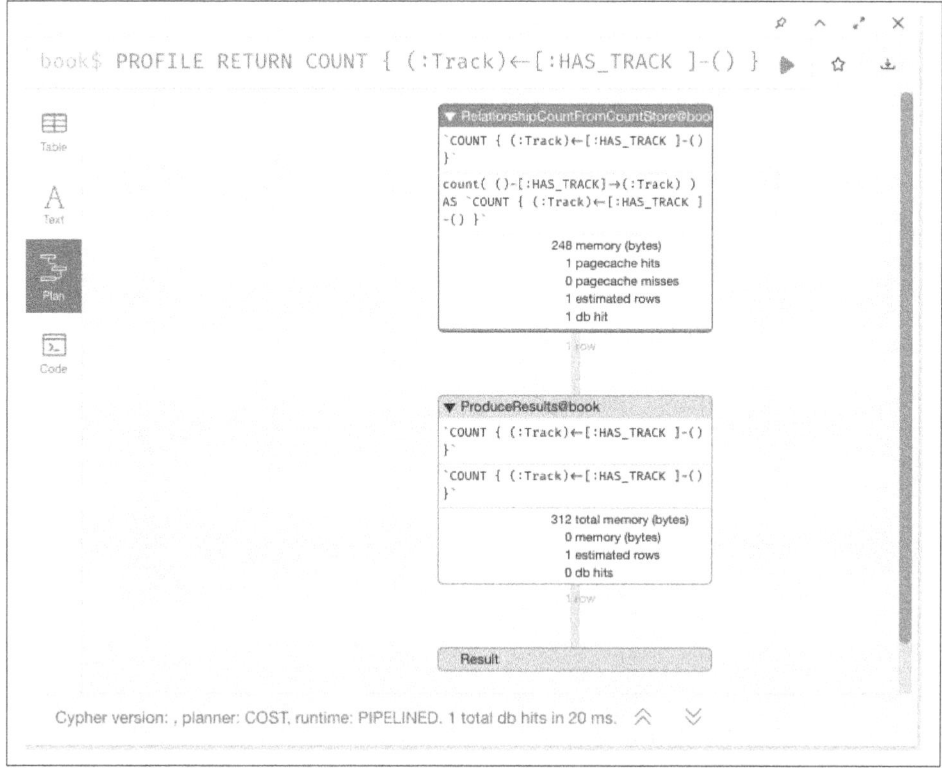

Figure 8-13. A `COUNT` subquery is typically used to gather statistics about nodes and relationships.

The query uses the `RelationshipCountFromCountStore` operator, which is highly efficient because Neo4j maintains these counts separately in its *counts store* (see Chapter 5). However, if you need to constrain the incoming relationship to only those originating from the `Playlist` label, the query becomes significantly less efficient.

As shown in Figure 8-14, Neo4j must traverse all 13 million `Track` nodes, iterate through their relationships, filter by the end node's label, and then compute the count. This approach drastically increases execution time and computational cost, making it highly inefficient.

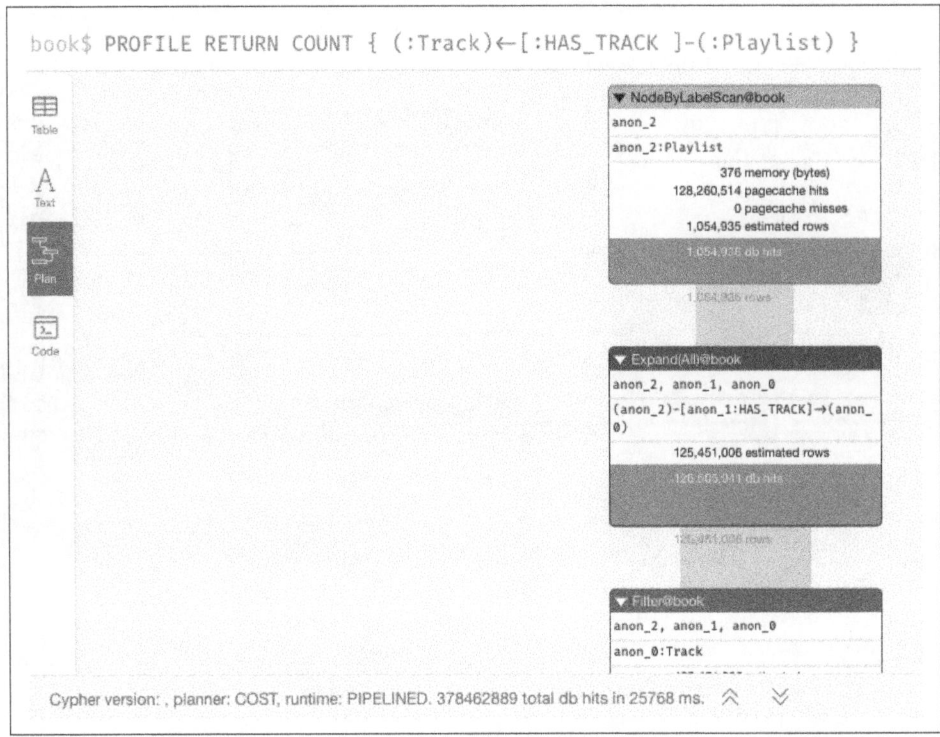

Figure 8-14. When the `Playlist` label is included, the count store cannot be used.

In summary, selecting relationship types in graph modeling carefully is crucial for both performance and maintainability. By ensuring that each relationship type has a clear and distinct semantic meaning, you can avoid unnecessary filtering, reduce traversal overhead, and help Neo4j's query engine to optimize its execution.

Modeling Resolved Entities

ElectricHarmony's success is growing, and they've acquired a smaller regional streaming service. But in their enthusiasm to merge their newly acquired catalog into the graph quickly, they've added artists and tracks (many of them misspelled) without checking if they were already there. Users are finding their quality of experience degraded when their search results find multiple artists that are actually the same artist but are now repeated in the graph with minor variations. Guns N' Roses is, as you'd expect, a bit of a jungle, as shown in Figure 8-15.

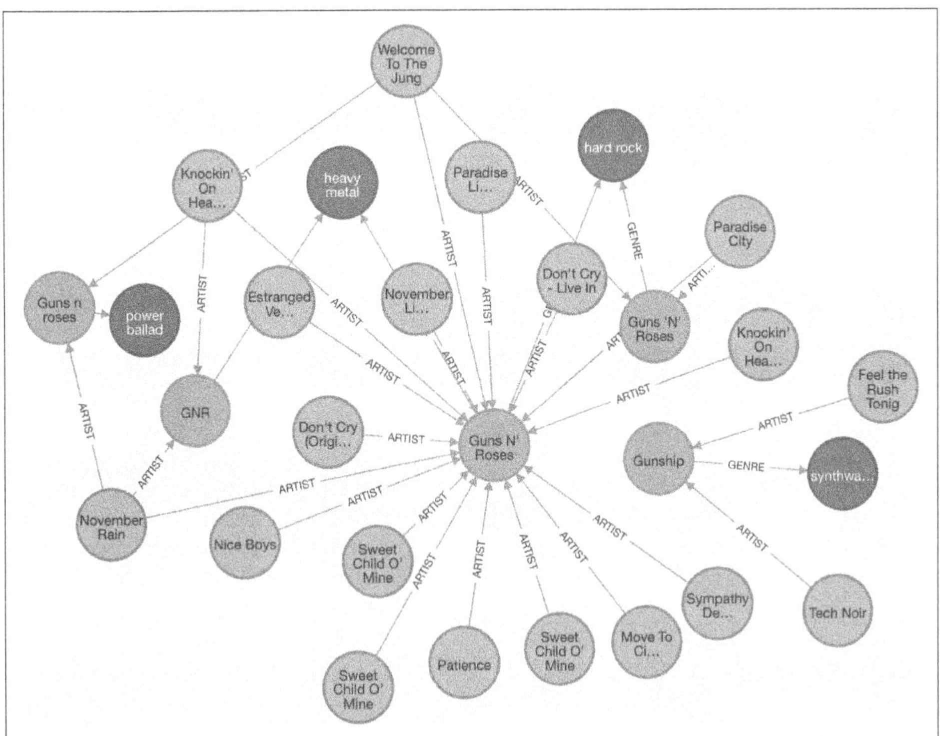

Figure 8-15. Possible representation of multiple instances of the same artist, Guns N' Roses

Users can flag duplicates, so the music curators at ElectricHarmony now have a long queue of flagged content to work through. Since resolving duplicates is a tedious affair, they decide to get help from Claude.ai (*http://claude.ai*), an AI assistant. They give Claude the set of possibly similar artists, along with extra context in the form of their genres and tracks, and instruct it to resolve the duplicate artist entities.

This book does not cover entity resolution techniques; the example used here is to illustrate how resolved entities are modeled in a graph.

You can find the CSV of artists (and additional context) that the curators supplied to the chatbot in the code repository (*https://oreil.ly/Jpb7m*), or you can export it yourself using the following Cypher code and then download the results as CSV from the Neo4j browser:

```
//009-genres-export.cypher
MATCH (n:Artist)
```

```
WHERE toLower(n.name) STARTS WITH "guns" OR
toLower(n.name) STARTS WITH "gnr"
RETURN n.id as `ID`,
n.name as `Music Artist`,
COLLECT {MATCH (n)-[:GENRE]->(g:Genre) return g.name} AS `Genre`,
COLLECT {MATCH (n)<-[:ARTIST]-(t:Track) return t.name} AS `Tracks`
```

The COLLECT subquery creates a list from a set of rows produced by the subquery.

The resulting CSV will look like Table 8-1.

Table 8-1. Duplicate artists

ID	Music artist	Genre	Tracks
3qm84nBOXUEQ2vnTfUTTFC	Guns N' Roses	[hard rock, heavy metal]	[Paradise City - Live, Knockin' On Heaven's Door - Live In London / 1992, Estranged - Live Version, Welcome To The Jungle, Paradise City, Move To The City, Knockin' On Heaven's Door, November Rain - Live In Japan / 1992, Sweet Child O' Mine - Live In Paris / 1992, Sweet Child O' Mine, November Rain, Nice Boys, Sympathy For The Devil, Patience, Don't Cry (Original), Don't Cry - Live In Japan / 1992, Sweet Child O' Mine]
3PALZKWkpwjRvBsRmhlVSS	Gunship	[synthwave]	[Tech Noir, Feel the Rush Tonight]
b7f3a2c9e5d1x8k6m4n0p2q9r	Guns 'N' Roses	[hard rock]	[Paradise City, Welcome To The Jungle]
t5k9j2h7f1w6m3n8p4q0r2s6x	Guns n roses	[power ballad]	[Welcome To The Jungle, November Rain]
z6r4k9n2h7p3m1j5f8x0w2d4q	GNR	[heavy metal]	[Knockin' On Heaven's Door, November Rain]

Along with the CSV file they attach, they supply Claude.ai with the following prompt:

```
This is a CSV of music artists, their IDs, the genres they belong to and some
of their tracks.
You have to resolve the artist entities and produce results in this format:
Primary ID, Duplicate Entity ID, Confidence Level, Reason
```

The answer they receive is displayed in Table 8-2 for easier reading (and your results may vary).

Table 8-2. Results returned by Claude.ai

Primary ID	Duplicate entity ID	Confidence level	Reason
3qm84nBOXUEQ2vnTfUTTFC	b7f3a2c9e5d1x8k6m4n0p2q9r	0.95	Matching tracks (Paradise City, Welcome To The Jungle) and similar name with minor punctuation difference, same genre (hard rock)
3qm84nBOXUEQ2vnTfUTTFC	t5k9j2h7f1w6m3n8p4q0r2s6x	0.90	Matching tracks (Welcome To The Jungle, November Rain) and similar name with different capitalization
3qm84nBOXUEQ2vnTfUTTFC	z6r4k9n2h7p3m1j5f8x0w2d4q	0.85	Matching tracks (Knockin' On Heaven's Door, November Rain) and common acronym GNR, overlapping genre (heavy metal)

Claude also says: "Note: Gunship (3PALZKWkpwjRvBsRmhlVSS) is not included in the results as it's a different artist with different genre (synthwave) and completely different tracks."

Armed with a faster way to process flagged content, the curators ask the engineering team to improve the graph using this information.

Before you proceed, you'll need to have the right graph data set up. Follow the instructions in the GitHub section "Modeling Resolved Entities" of the *chapter 08 README*.

Entity Groups

Entity groups are one way to show that two or more entities in the graph might be the same. We've seen this mechanism used more than often in places where resolved entities must not be merged, as their sources must be maintained distinctly. A node with the label `EntityGroup` (and optionally, the label of the entity being resolved) represents these resolved entities. Different graph visualization tools use this to visually "group" them to help with exploratory analysis (see Figure 8-16).

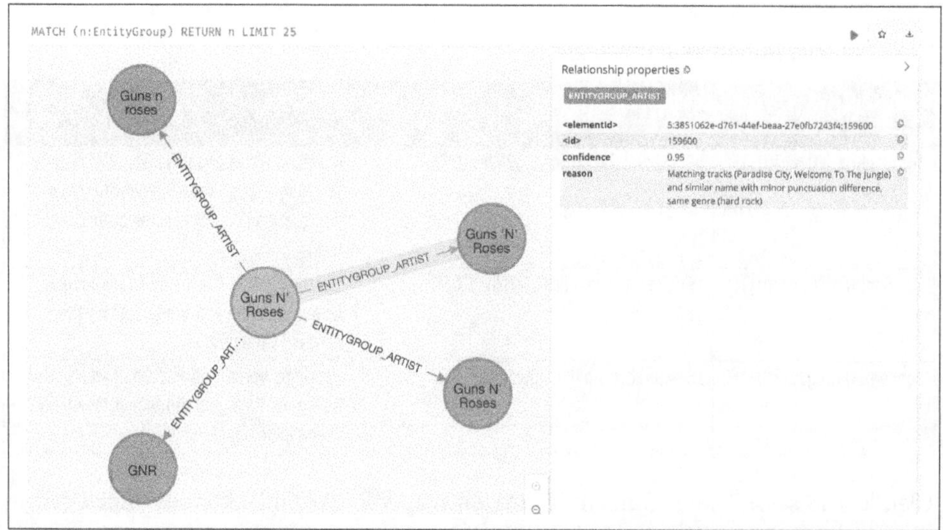

Figure 8-16. An `EntityGroup` node created to represent the group of resolved Guns N' Roses `Artist` entities. The confidence level and reason for resolution are stored as properties on the `ENTITYGROUP_ARTIST` relationship.

This model preserves the original `Artist` entities. You can immediately trace a path from the entity group to its component entities; depending on the domain you're in, traceability and preserving the original data may be an important factor. If you expand each individual artist, you'll see that none of the original relationships are affected.

As your graph grows more complex and richer, especially with new relationships adding context to entities, rerunning entity resolution may actually result in new and more precise groupings. With this model, adjusting or updating the entities in the group is straightforward. Since you're now a pro at graph modeling, the drawback of this approach is exactly what you're thinking: the entity group introduces an extra hop in your queries, adding complexity.

Fused Entities

Another approach is to actually resolve the entities—or *fuse* them (*https://oreil.ly/AcO3j*)—into a single one. Start again with the variations of Guns N' Roses, as shown in Figure 8-17.

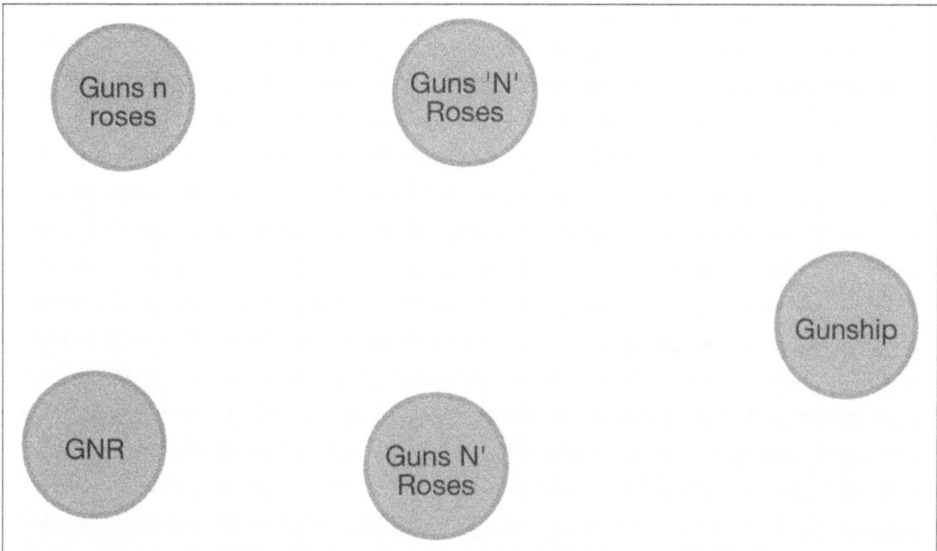

Figure 8-17. Leaving aside Gunship, the other four `Artist` nodes all represent the same artist, Guns N' Roses.

The first variation of the fused entity is to merge all four nodes and their relationships into one single fused node, resulting in a single `Artist` node that represents Guns N' Roses.

Drawing on the response of the AI chatbot, the artist with the name *Guns N' Roses* is the primary node, and we want to retain this node's name and ID in the fused entity. There are quite a few ways to go about it in Cypher; let's look at one of the most straightforward.

First, temporarily mark the primary node:

```
//010-primary-artist.cypher
MATCH (n:Artist {id: '3qm84nBOXUEQ2vnTfUTTFC'})//Guns N' Roses
SET n.primary=true
```

Then gather all four nodes and use the `mergeNodes` procedure (*https://oreil.ly/7lQgx*) from the APOC library, which takes care of merging the nodes and their relationships and removing the duplicate `Artist` nodes. This handy procedure lets you specify strategies for how properties and relationships should be merged. This example sticks to the defaults and asks the procedure to combine the values of properties into an array if they are different across nodes. In addition, the name and ID of the primary node are retained, and the alternate names of the artist, as recorded on the original nodes, are written into a `namesAlias` property for future reference:

```
//011-resolve-artist.cypher
MATCH (n:Artist)
```

```
WHERE n.id IN ['3qm84nBOXUEQ2vnTfUTTFC','t5k9j2h7f1w6m3n8p4q0r2s6x',
'b7f3a2c9e5d1x8k6m4n0p2q9r','z6r4k9n2h7p3m1j5f8x0w2d4q'] ❶
WITH n ORDER BY n.primary ❷
WITH collect(n) as nodes ❸
WITH nodes, head(nodes).name AS primaryName, head(nodes).id AS primaryId ❹
CALL apoc.refactor.mergeNodes(nodes,{properties:"combine", mergeRels:true}) ❺
YIELD node
WITH node, primaryName, primaryId
SET node.nameAlias=node.name, node.name=primaryName, node.id=primaryId ❻
REMOVE node.primary ❼
RETURN node
```

❶ Find the four artists to merge

❷ Sort so that the primary node appears first

❸ Collect all nodes into a list, the primary is first

❹ Extract the artist name and id from the primary node for subsequent use

❺ Merge all four nodes and combine the property values into an array if the values from all 4 nodes differ

❻ Set the aliases, name and id

❼ Clean up the temporary primary property

The resulting node and its merged properties are shown in Figure 8-18.

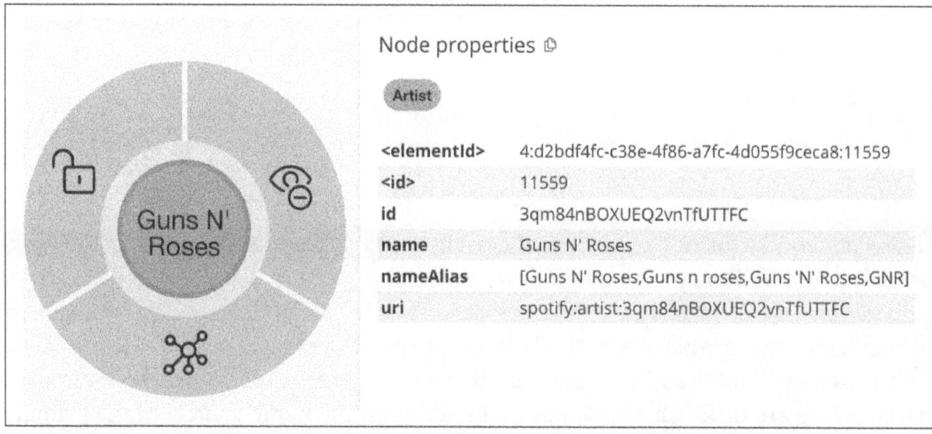

Figure 8-18. The ID and name property of the primary node are retained, and the `nameAlias` property contains all the possible values that existed in the graph for this artist.

Now, if you query again for all artists whose names start with "gun" or "gnr," you'll see only Gunship and a single Guns N' Roses node see (Figure 8-19), which now also has relationships to the tracks previously associated with "GNR" and the other variations:

```
//012-match-resolved.cypher
MATCH (n:Artist)-[r]-(m)
WHERE toLower(n.name) STARTS WITH "guns" OR
toLower(n.name) STARTS WITH "gnr" return n,r,m
```

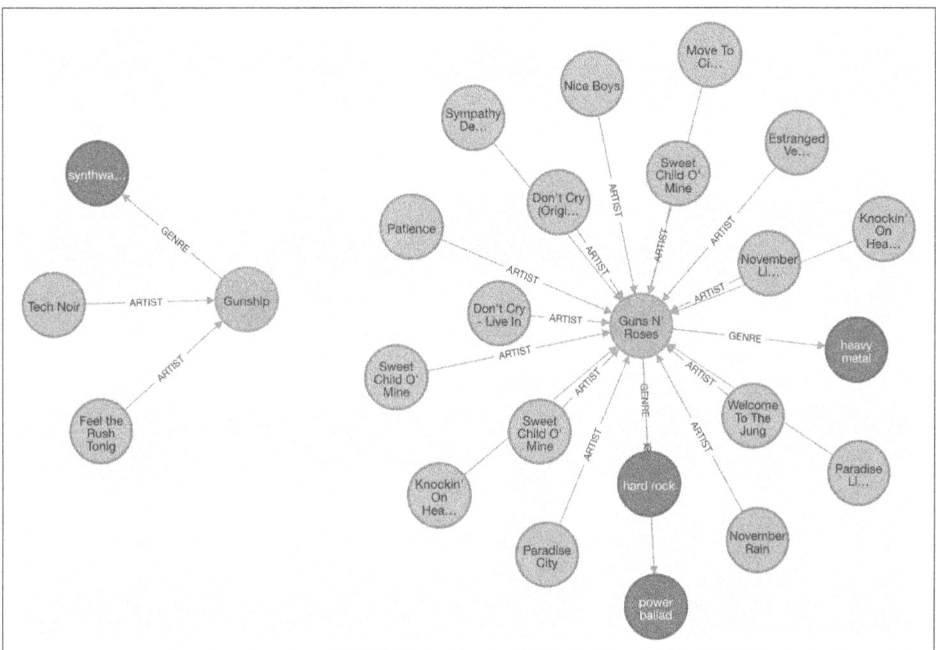

Figure 8-19. A single fused entity for Guns N' Roses

This method results in a model that is the same as the original graph model—there are no extra hops as with the entity group. However, depending on the merging strategy you choose, keep in mind that you may end up with lists as property values on these nodes. That can make your Cypher queries harder to write, since they now have to deal with nodes that have either single values or lists. You've also lost any paper trail documenting what those original entities were and who added them. In some domains that's not a problem, but if it matters to you, read on.

Maintaining the original entities, or facts, can be important for auditing, data lineage, and reporting. A *fact* is a record of information about something that existed, whether it is entirely accurate or not. In the example we've been using, each `Artist` node that represents Guns N' Roses is a fact. To enhance the previous fused entity model, you would not delete the facts, but instead you'd link them to the fused entity.

How is this different from the entity group? The fused entity carries merged properties from the facts. Whether this is done automatically or through human intervention, the fused entity and its properties represent a single "resolved" view of the facts. The facts' relationships are *also* merged onto the fused entity so that, in the absence of the facts, the fused entity complies with the graph model and is traversable. An entity group, however, simply serves to link the underlying facts and is not a substitute for any of them.

Start over and create a fused entity—but this time, don't delete the facts. If you want to try this, you'll need to re-create the graph since you fused the entity already in the previous query. Follow the instructions in the README. You do not have to download the backup again if you have it already. Either drop the database of Chapter 5 with `DROP DATABASE chapter5` and restore the backup, or restore the backup into a new database, say `chapter8`.

Reimport the genres and then proceed. We will use plain Cypher, without APOC:

```
//013-resolve-no-apoc.cypher
MATCH (primary:Artist {id:"3qm84nBOXUEQ2vnTfUTTFC"})
WITH primary ❶
MERGE (fused:Artist {id:"fused-3qm84nBOXUEQ2vnTfUTTFC"})
SET fused.name = primary.name, fused.uri = primary.uri, ❷
fused.aliases=[] ❸
SET fused:$(labels(primary)) ❹
WITH fused
MATCH (fact:Artist)
WHERE fact.id IN ['3qm84nBOXUEQ2vnTfUTTFC','t5k9j2h7f1w6m3n8p4q0r2s6x',
'b7f3a2c9e5d1x8k6m4n0p2q9r','z6r4k9n2h7p3m1j5f8x0w2d4q']
SET fused.aliases=fused.aliases + fact.name ❺
WITH fused, fact
OPTIONAL MATCH (fact)-[factRelOut]->(otherOut)
MERGE (fused)-[fusedRelOut:$(type(factRelOut))]->(otherOut) ❻
SET fusedRelOut=factRelOut ❼
WITH fact, fused
OPTIONAL MATCH (fact)<-[factRelIn]-(otherIn) ❽
MERGE (fused)-[fusedRelIn:$(type(factRelIn))]->(otherIn)
SET fusedRelIn=factRelIn
WITH fact, fused
MERGE (fused)-[:FACT]->(fact) ❾
```

❶ This is our primary Guns N' Roses node, which will serve as the base of the fused entity.

❷ Copies all properties from the primary node to the fused node.

❸ Here is where you can customize what you want to store on the fused entity. In this case, we want to maintain the names of all the facts in the `aliases` property.

❹ Sets any additional labels the primary node might have had.

❺ Adds the fact name to the aliases list on the fused entity.

❻ Copies all outgoing relations from the facts to the fused node.

❼ Copies the relationship properties as well.

❽ Copies all incoming relations from the facts to the fused node.

❾ Creates a relationship from the fused entity to the facts.

Figure 8-20 shows the final state after the query is run.

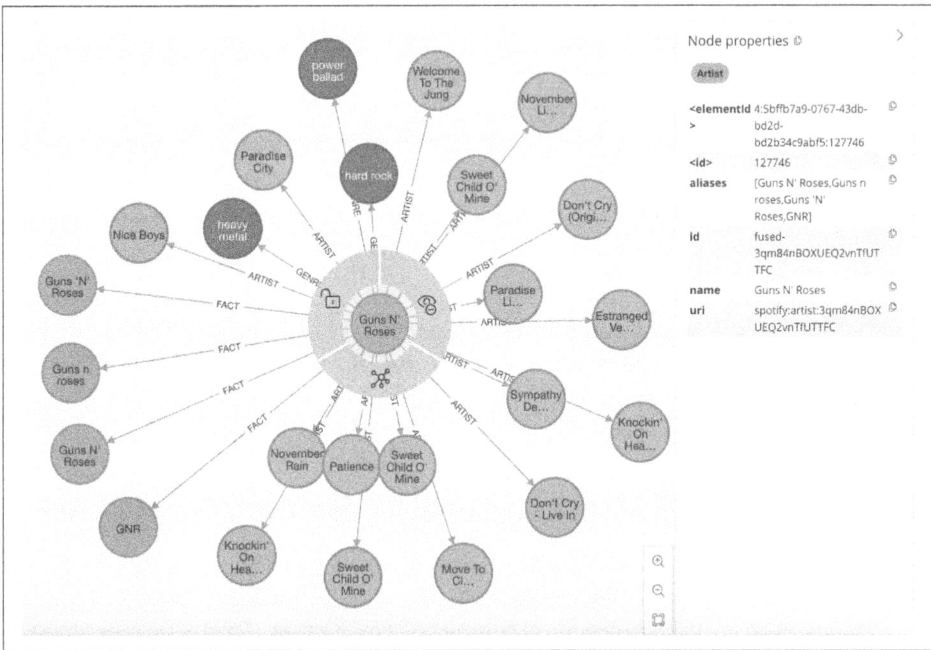

Figure 8-20. The new fused entity, which preserves relationships to its facts

Dynamic Labels and Types

Prior to Neo4j v5.26, labels, dynamic relationship types, and property keys could not be dynamically created or set via parameters or variables. If you wanted to construct a query without knowing the label, relationship type, or property key beforehand, you had to either build the query string at runtime, risking potential Cypher injections, or use APOC procedures, such as those from the `apoc.refactor` package.

Cypher v5.26 introduced the ability to use dynamic labels and types. The previous query uses these. Callout ❹ sets all the labels from the primary node on the fused entity. Callouts ❻ and ❼ set the relation type dynamically: the new relationship type is the type of the relationship between the fact and the other entity.

While this is a great addition to Cypher, at the time of writing this book, the planner isn't as efficient when it encounters any of these dynamic expressions. This means that these queries will be less efficient while executing. Since the planner uses static query information when planning, as you will recall from Chapter 5, a dynamic label or property key results in an `AllNodesScan` because it can't leverage an index. Do not use dynamic expressions indiscriminately. If you know these values, help the planner and specify them up front.

Now, the fused entity retains its usefulness, as in the previous model, but it also allows you to drill down through to the facts, which is helpful for curators, analysts, and data scientists who want to understand why fused entities are created. However, this model now suffers from the same problem as entity groups, affecting node expansions and path finding. One mitigation is to change the labels of the `Fact` nodes so that they no longer participate in queries as their original entity (in this case, they would no longer be artists). Apart from this, `Fact` nodes can clutter the graph visualization when you perform exploratory analysis.

The final variation on the fused entity model is to offload facts to another graph database and start using a composite database, as we explain in Chapter 10. With composite databases, you get the best of both worlds: you have a fused entity (with a traceable lineage) in the main graph, but you avoid the clutter of the `Fact` nodes by moving them to a composite database where you can analyze them.

Quantified Path Patterns: An Entity-Resolution Use Case

Quantified path patterns (QPP) solve the problem of matching repeated parts of a path without the need to write multiple distinct queries joined with `UNION`. Instead, they let you extract the repeating part of a path pattern into parentheses and apply a quantifier that specifies the allowed number of repetitions. This leads to more concise and expressive Cypher queries, especially when dealing with variable-length path segments that follow a common structure. They're the perfect solution for traversing entities that are resolved into entity groups, where a common pattern connects members of the same group in a repetitive structure.

Consider the scenario illustrated in Figure 8-21. We start from an `Artist` node and resolve it as equivalent to other `Artist` nodes with different spellings. Without QPP, the query would not account for these variations, so attempting to find tracks belonging to the artist would result in a single `Track` match.

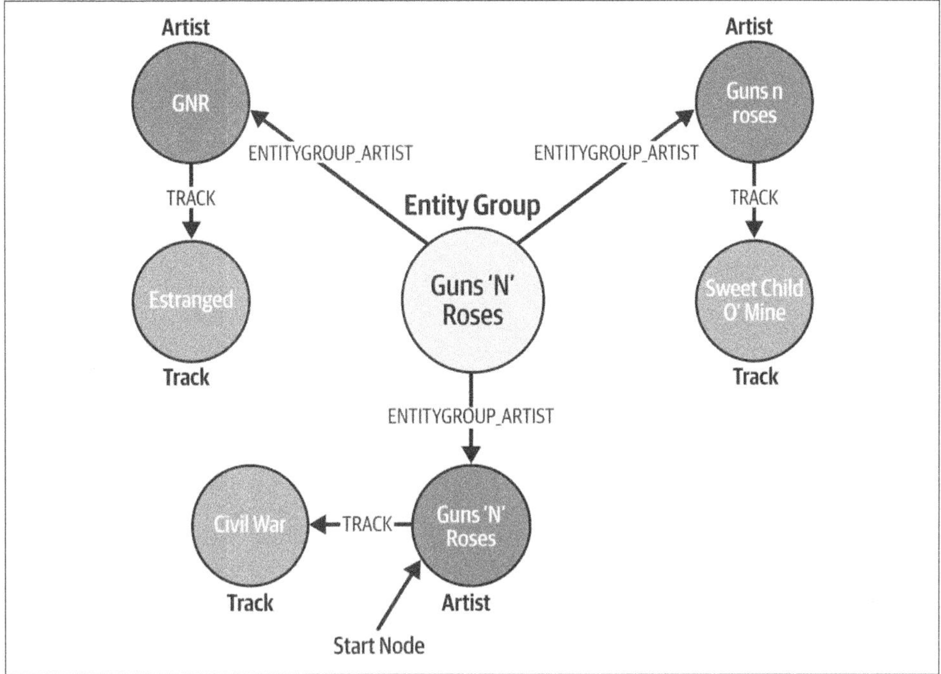

Figure 8-21. Entity group linking variations of the same artist

With the help of QPP, we have the option to take the entity-resolved group into account as we traverse the graph.

The following QPP query will return the tracks correctly. The query file, *014-qpp-one.cypher* in the GitHub repository, contains the necessary sample data creation in order to execute this query:

```
//014-qpp-one.cypher
MATCH
  (n:Artist {name: "Guns'N' Roses"})
  (()-[:ENTITYGROUP_ARTIST]->()<-[:ENTITYGROUP_ARTIST]-()){0,1}
  ()-[:TRACK]-(track)
RETURN track
```

To clarify, this query begins from the starting node, the `Artist`, as shown in Figure 8-21. Then an additional pattern is introduced to represent possible connections between artist entities:

```
()-[:ENTITYGROUP_ARTIST]--()--[:ENTITYGROUP_ARTIST]-() .
```

This pattern is wrapped in parentheses to ensure it is treated as a single unit. A *quantifier* (the quantified name in QPP), similar to a regular expression quantifier, is added at the end, specifying that the pattern can appear 0 or 1 times—effectively making it optional. Finally, the query continues with the relationship to the `Track` nodes to complete the traversal. The result is illustrated in Figure 8-22.

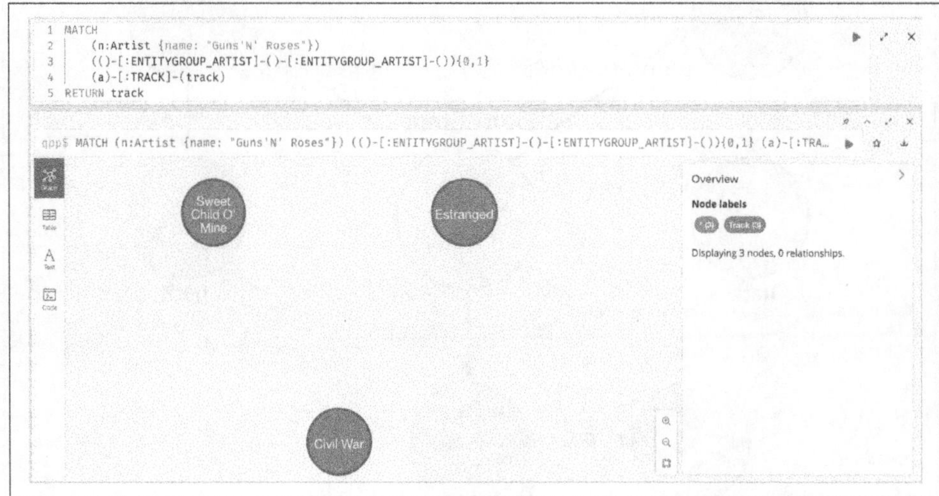

Figure 8-22. QPP query to traverse from the artist to its tracks through the entity group

In Figure 8-23, we take the concept further, also resolving tracks with entity groups.

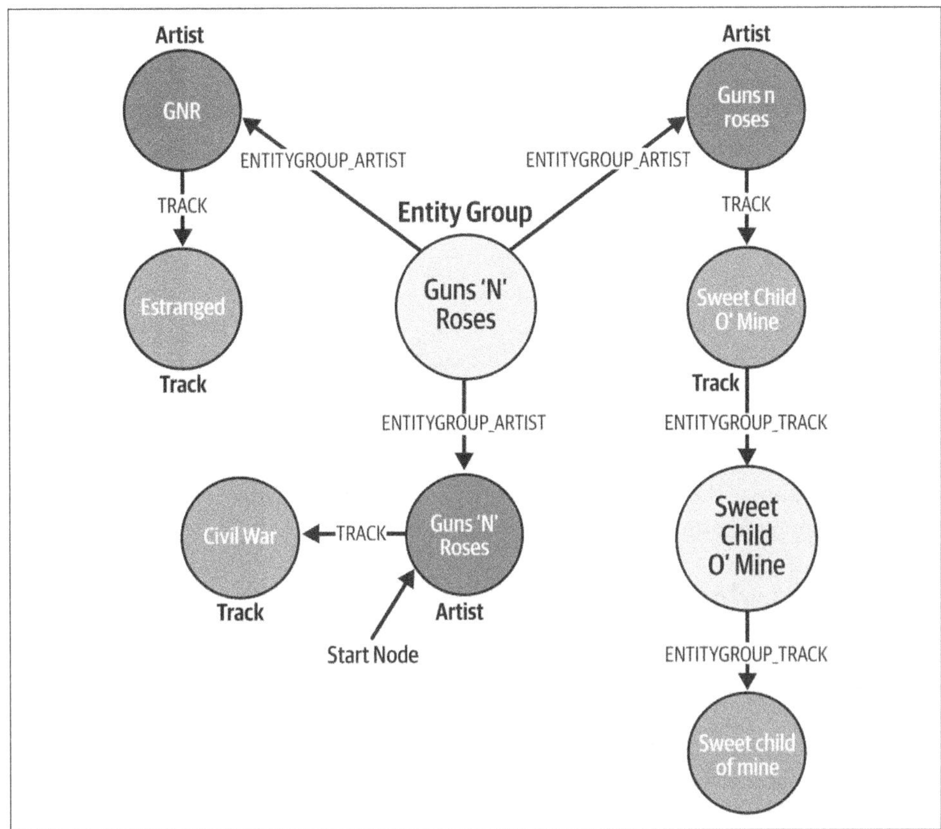

Figure 8-23. Entity groups for both resolved artists and tracks

This query can be easily extended to take the optional new pattern into account:

```
//015-qpp-two.cypher
MATCH p =
(n:Artist {name: "Guns'N' Roses"})
(()-[:ENTITYGROUP_ARTIST]-()-[:ENTITYGROUP_ARTIST]-()){0,1}
()-[:TRACK]-()
(()-[:ENTITYGROUP_TRACK]-()-[:ENTITYGROUP_TRACK]-()){0,1}
RETURN p
```

Figure 8-24 shows the result.

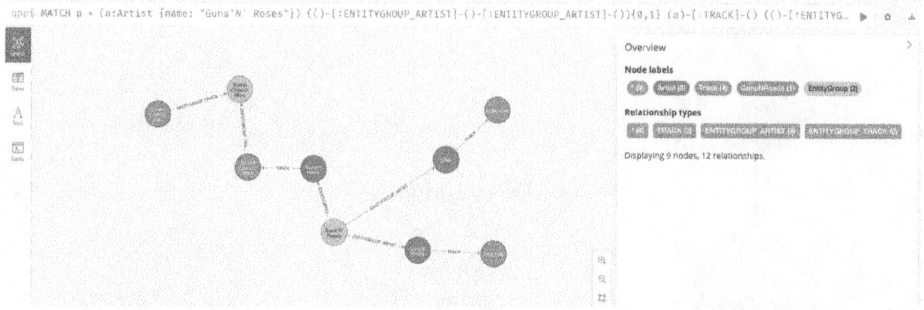

Figure 8-24. Query result showing how QPP can traverse through multiple entity groups

QPP originates from GQL, and Cypher is gradually transforming into GQL while maintaining backward compatibility. This means you can still use your existing queries and knowledge about Cypher. You can find more information about QPP in the Neo4j documentation (*https://oreil.ly/e9NnF*).

Security Modeling: Labels Versus Properties

As you previously learned in Chapter 6, Neo4j offers two primary mechanisms for controlling access:

Label-based access control (LBAC)
: Restricts access based on node labels and relationship types, making it easy to enforce role-based access control (RBAC) at a high level.

Property-based access control (PBAC)
: Allows fine-grained restrictions by defining property-level visibility rules on nodes and relationships, enabling more dynamic and flexible access policies.

To illustrate these approaches, we modeled a multiregional graph shown in Figure 8-25. A few things to notice here:

- Europe and Latin America have distinct datasets.
- Some users have access to only one of these two regions (such as the EU or Latin America) and non-region-specific data.
- Some users can access both regions *and* non-region-specific data.
- Data tied to specific regions includes `Customer`, `Profile`, `Payment`, and other types of nodes and relationships.

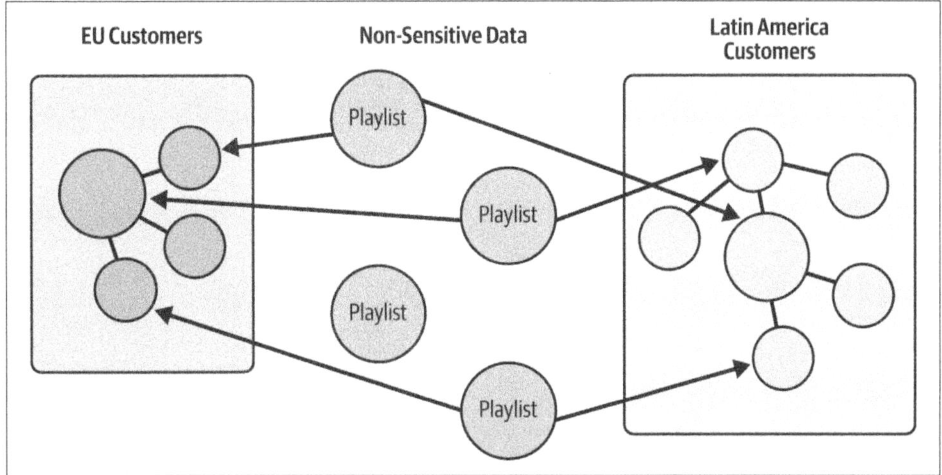

Figure 8-25. Multiregional graph

Now, let's consider the following users:

Alice
: Alice is part of the European marketing team. She is preparing to launch a campaign offering Taylor Swift tickets to users who have the greatest number of her tracks in their playlists.

Bob
: Bob works in the Latin American (LATAM) customer-retention team. His role involves identifying whether customers approaching their renewal date are still active on the platform.

Charlie
: Charlie is a senior customer support agent responsible for handling support requests from sensitive customers, such as influencers and high-value artists. Support requests are classified into four levels (1 to 4). While all agents can access requests up through level 3, only senior agents like Charlie have permission to view level 4 requests.

Drew
: Drew is a junior customer support agent and has access to requests up through level 3.

Privileges cannot be assigned directly to users, only to roles, so let's create a role for each of them. We'll also need to create a role that can only access generic data, such as playlists and tracks. The roles we'll create are:

- marketing_europe
- sales_latam
- senior_customer_support
- junior_customer_support
- music_info

The code for this is:

```
//016-security-setup-a.cypher
CREATE ROLE marketing_europe IF NOT EXISTS;
CREATE ROLE sales_latam IF NOT EXISTS;
CREATE ROLE senior_customer_support IF NOT EXISTS;
CREATE ROLE junior_customer_support IF NOT EXISTS;
CREATE ROLE music_info IF NOT EXISTS;

CREATE USER alice IF NOT EXISTS SET PASSWORD 'password' CHANGE NOT REQUIRED;
CREATE USER bob IF NOT EXISTS SET PASSWORD 'password' CHANGE NOT REQUIRED;
CREATE USER charlie IF NOT EXISTS SET PASSWORD 'password' CHANGE NOT REQUIRED;
CREATE USER drew IF NOT EXISTS SET PASSWORD 'password' CHANGE NOT REQUIRED;

GRANT ROLE marketing_europe TO alice;
GRANT ROLE music_info TO alice;
GRANT ROLE sales_latam TO bob;
GRANT ROLE music_info TO bob;
GRANT ROLE senior_customer_support TO charlie;
GRANT ROLE music_info TO charlie;
GRANT ROLE junior_customer_support TO drew;
GRANT ROLE music_info TO drew;
```

Right now, none of our users can access the database. Let's give the role `music_info` access to the database:

```
GRANT ACCESS ON DATABASE electric_harmony TO music_info;
```

Playlists and tracks are visible to all users, making them both strong candidates for granting access under the `music_info` role. To simplify access control, we will also grant this role permissions to all relationships. However, relationships will only be traversable if the user has access to *both* connected nodes:

```
GRANT MATCH {*} ON GRAPH electric_harmony NODES Playlist, Track TO music_info;
GRANT MATCH {*} ON GRAPH electric_harmony RELATIONSHIPS * TO music_info;
```

To grant the EU marketing team access to European customers, we need to determine the best way to model this access control. Should we use a label, such as `Europe`, on customer nodes, or a property, like `region="eu"`?

From a performance standpoint, label-based privileges are significantly more efficient than property-based ones. Neo4j optimizes label-based access control by leveraging its label index, making it faster to evaluate and enforce permissions. In contrast, property-based privileges require scanning node properties, which can introduce performance overhead (*https://oreil.ly/mFLJl*), especially at scale.

Given these considerations, we recommend assigning a `Europe` label to relevant customer nodes for efficient and scalable access control:

```
GRANT MATCH {*} ON GRAPH electric_harmony NODES Europe TO marketing_europe;
```

Note that we didn't grant the privilege on the `Customer` label itself, since that would grant access to *all* customers, regardless of their region.

Now, let's define access privileges for Bob, who needs access to only those LATAM customers whose subscription renewal date falls on or before April 1, 2025 (including late renewals).

Granting Bob access based on the `Latam` label alone won't be sufficient, because we also need to restrict his access based on the renewal date. While one option would be to introduce labels like `Expiration202503` or `Expiration202504`, maintaining such a system would quickly become cumbersome and unmanageable due to the continuous need for new labels.

A more practical approach is to use property-based privileges, allowing Bob access to `Customer` nodes with the `Latam` label only if their `subscriptionRenewal` property is on or before April 1, 2025. Although property-based privileges come with a performance cost compared to label-based ones, in this case, they provide the necessary granularity without introducing label sprawl.

A well-sized page cache could alleviate the cost of property access. With the block storage format, if this property were inlined with the node, then the cost would be insignificant.

Let's implement that approach:

```
GRANT MATCH {*}
ON GRAPH electric_harmony
FOR (n:CustomerLatam)
WHERE n.subscriptionRenewal <= date('2025-04-01') TO sales_latam;
```

One key consideration from the command above is that Neo4j does *not* support label-based privileges that require multiple labels on the same node. This means you cannot create a rule that enforces access only when *both* the `Customer` and `Latam` labels are present. Granting access based on the `Latam` label alone would apply to all nodes with that label, regardless of whether they also have the `Customer` label.

Charlie and Drew need access to the same types of nodes, but with different security levels. Let's start with the junior customer support role and grant Drew access to `SupportRequest` nodes where the security level is lower than or equal to 3:

```
GRANT MATCH {*}
ON GRAPH electric_harmony
FOR (n:SupportRequest)
WHERE n.securityLevel <= 3 TO junior_customer_support;
```

We'll do the same for Charlie's senior customer support role, simply changing the `3` to a `4`:

```
GRANT MATCH {*}
ON GRAPH electric_harmony
FOR (n:SupportRequest)
WHERE n.securityLevel <= 4 TO senior_customer_support;
```

A best practice is to ensure that the properties used for security checks actually exist on the nodes. We will do this by creating a property existence constraint for the `subscriptionRenewal` and `securityLevel` properties:

```
CREATE CONSTRAINT customer_renewal_date_exist
FOR (n:Customer)
REQUIRE n.subscriptionRenewal IS NOT NULL;

CREATE CONSTRAINT support_request_security_level_exist
FOR (n:SupportRequest)
REQUIRE n.securityLevel IS NOT NULL;
```

You have learned that label-based privileges are more efficient than property-based privileges in Neo4j due to the label index, which optimizes access control. While labels should be used whenever possible for better performance, property-based privileges provide finer granularity when labels alone are insufficient. Additionally, always ensuring that the properties used in access rules exist can prevent unintended access.

Summary

You'll almost certainly encounter subqueries on your path to production with Neo4j. Now you've learned why they're important and when to use them. Quantified path patterns continue to improve with newer releases of Neo4j, so getting the hang of them is very beneficial. When you start to tackle fine-grained access control and entity resolution, you'll now be familiar with the pros and cons of the various approaches to handling them.

CHAPTER 9

Backup and Restore

ElectricHarmony's journey with Neo4j has been nothing short of transformative. What started as an experimental graph database to map artists, albums, and user preferences has quickly become a core component of their recommendation engine. The team has successfully built real-time music discovery, playlist curation, and artist relationship mapping, all powered by Neo4j's ability to traverse complex connections at lightning speed.

But success comes with scale, and scale comes with risk.

As ElectricHarmony's user base explodes, so does its graph database. Millions of relationships are created and updated daily, and downtime is no longer an option. Their engineering team has optimized queries, tuned indexes, and deployed Neo4j into production, yet one critical piece remains: a robust backup and recovery strategy.

The Write Path

Before diving into backup strategies, it's essential to understand how Neo4j writes and persists data. The transaction lifecycle in Neo4j follows a structured sequence to ensure durability and consistency.

Figure 9-1 shows a high-level overview of the sequence.

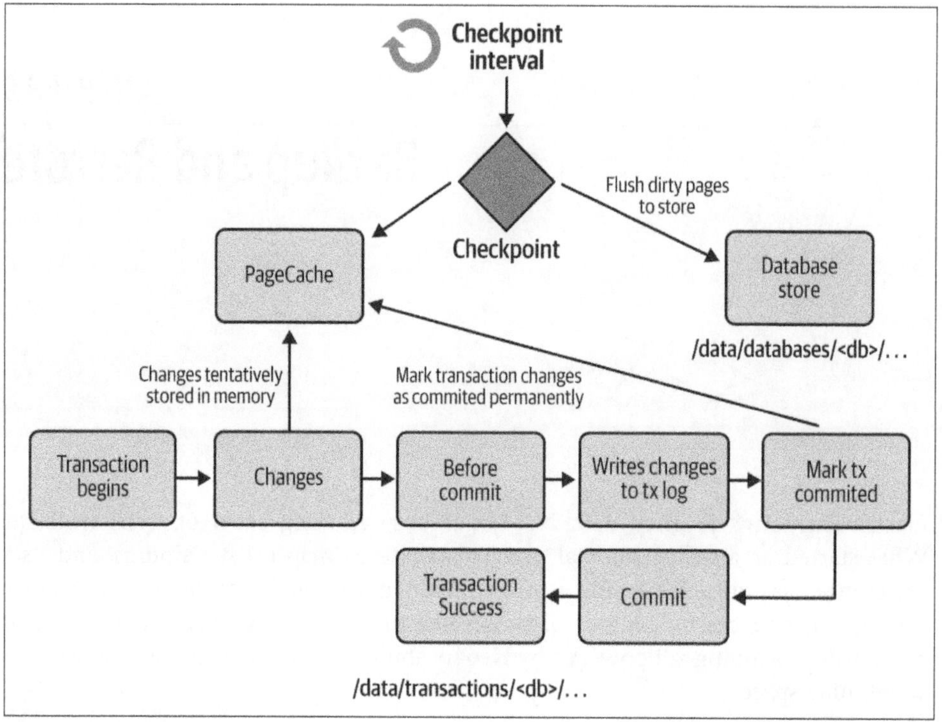

Figure 9-1. Transaction lifecycle

Recall from Chapter 2 that a *transaction* starts when changes are made in the database. These changes are initially applied in memory and stored in the page cache, which acts as an intermediary layer before the data is eventually written to disk.

Before a transaction is committed, its changes must be written to the *transaction log*, also called *write-ahead logging* (WAL). This step ensures durability by recording modifications in a separate, sequential log file located under the transaction directory.

Once the transaction log entry is durably written to disk, the system marks the transaction as committed. This guarantees that the changes are recoverable in case of failure. The commit operation finalizes the transaction, making its changes officially visible and allowing the system to proceed with subsequent requests.

Checkpoints

Checkpoints in Neo4j are part of the database's housekeeping process. While transaction logs guarantee durability by recording all changes, checkpoints help optimize recovery time by flushing dirty pages (those modified by committed transactions) from the page cache to the store files. During a checkpoint, Neo4j records the latest log position up to which all changes are reflected in the store files. This allows the system to discard older parts of the transaction log and restart more quickly after a crash, without needing to replay the entire log.

Checkpoints serve two primary purposes:

Optimizing crash recovery
: In the event of a crash, Neo4j replays transaction logs starting from the *last checkpoint*. The more recent the checkpoint, the less work the database must do to recover. Without checkpoints, the database would have to replay the entire transaction history, resulting in longer recovery times.

Truncating transaction logs
: Once a checkpoint confirms that data has been fully persisted, any transaction log entries preceding that checkpoint become redundant for recovery. This enables Neo4j to safely rotate and delete old logs, freeing up disk space and keeping the log directory manageable.

Checkpoints are triggered by:

- Time-based or volume-based intervals, which are defined in the configuration (such as in `db.checkpoint.interval.time`)
- Manual triggers, such as `CALL db.checkpoint()` in administrative operations
- Full backups

While committed transactions exist in the page cache, they are not immediately written to the store files. Instead, a checkpoint mechanism is responsible for flushing dirty pages from the page cache to persistent storage at predefined intervals. This ensures that data in memory is persisted to disk gradually, optimizing write performance while maintaining system integrity.

In the event of a crash, Neo4j can recover committed transactions because they have already been flushed to disk in the transaction log, fulfilling the durability guarantee of ACID. Upon restart, Neo4j replays the transaction log to reapply any changes that were not yet reflected in the store files. Checkpoints enhance this process by marking safe log positions and allowing truncation of older log entries, reducing recovery time.

This structured write path plays a crucial role in defining a robust backup strategy, as understanding the interplay between transaction logs, page cache, and store files allows you to make informed decisions about backup frequency, log retention, and recovery processes.

Transaction-Log Retention

Neo4j physically maintains a series of transaction logs to ensure durability and recoverability. These logs record all write operations in the database and are essential for crash recovery, replication, and backup. However, depending on their configuration, transaction logs can grow indefinitely if not managed. To avoid exhausting your disk space and improve manageability, Neo4j rotates its transaction logs, splits them into manageable chunks, and removes or archives older segments based on your configuration.

The rotation typically occurs when a configured threshold is reached (for example, size or time) or when a new checkpoint is written.

A well-defined log rotation strategy balances several needs, including:

Durability
: Recent transaction logs will be needed for recovery in case of a crash. Retaining enough history ensures minimal data loss.

Backup and replication
: Logs are also used by tools like `neo4j-admin` backup and for syncing with replicas in clusters. Rotating them too aggressively may break these processes.

Disk usage
: Without rotation, logs will consume unbounded disk space. Rotating them too conservatively may leave you accumulating logs that are no longer useful.

Performance
: Keeping logs smaller and well-rotated improves efficiency during recovery and reduces I/O overhead.

How Aggressive Is Aggressive?

Transaction logs are used by tools like `neo4j-admin backup` and for syncing state across cluster members. If logs are rotated before a backup completes or before a replica has had a chance to consume them, the process can fail. As a rule of thumb, "too aggressive" means:

- Retaining less than three files in a high-write environment
- Using a `db.tx_log.rotation.retention_policy` that's time-based but shorter than your full and incremental backup cycles
- Not retaining logs for at least as long as it takes for all replicas in a cluster to catch up

A Guided Example

Now it's time for you to put these principles into practice. First, configure Neo4j with the following settings:

```
db.checkpoint=VOLUME
db.checkpoint.interval.volume=250MB
db.tx_log.rotation.size=1MB
db.tx_log.rotation.retention_policy=3 files
```

These settings define that:

- A checkpoint should occur after 250MB of transaction log data.
- Transaction logs will be rotated after 1MB of data.
- Only the last three log files will be retained.

These are definitely not production-ready settings, but they will help you perform operations manually without being interrupted by automated database operations.

You can now start the Neo4j server:

```
./bin/neo4j start
```

While we use Docker throughout most of this book, for this particular chapter, it would have made the commands unnecessarily verbose. To keep things clear and focused, the examples here are shown without Docker. If you're working with Docker, you'll find equivalent commands provided in the GitHub companion repository.

Create a new database named `staging`:

```
//001-create-staging-db.cypher
CREATE DATABASE staging WAIT
:use DATABASE staging
```

Neo4j stores data and logs in two separate directories. For the staging database:

- Transaction logs are in *data/transactions/staging*.
- Database files are in *data/databases/staging*.

Check the contents of the transaction log directory:

```
//002-list-tx-logs.txt
ls -l data/transactions/staging
```

You should see something like:

```
checkpoint.0 neostore.transaction.db.0
```

These files contain the write-ahead log entries used for durability and crash recovery.

To inspect the database store directory:

```
//003-list-db-stores.txt
ls -lha data/databases/staging
```

This will list a variety of `.db` files that represent Neo4j's internal data structures (nodes, relationships, tokens, schema, etc.). Here's a sample:

```
block.token.label.db
block.schema.db
block.relationship.map.db
database_lock
quarantine_marker
```

Now create one random node in the database:

```
//004-random-node.cypher
CREATE (n:Node {id: randomUuid()})
```

Inspect the transaction logs directory again:

```
ls -lha data/transactions
```

The first transaction log is now present:

```
-rw-r--r--@  1 cwillemsen  staff   360B  4 Apr 09:17 checkpoint.0
-rw-r--r--@  1 cwillemsen  staff   1.5K  4 Apr 09:17 neostore.transaction.db.0
```

Since we created one node only, it does not reach the 1MB threshold for transaction log rotation.

If you inspect the databases directory, you'll see that nothing has changed, as expected. Since no checkpoint has occurred yet, the dirty pages in the page cache have not been flushed to the store files, but the transactions themselves are already safely persisted in the transaction log.

Now create 20,000 random nodes:

```
//005-20k-random.cypher
UNWIND range(1,20000) AS i
CREATE (n:Node {id: randomUuid()})
```

Inspect the transaction logs again:

```
-rw-r--r--@  1 cwillemsen  staff   360B  4 Apr 09:19 checkpoint.0
-rw-r--r--@  1 cwillemsen  staff   1.1M  4 Apr 09:19 neostore.transaction.db.0
-rw-r--r--@  1 cwillemsen  staff   128B  4 Apr 09:19 neostore.transaction.db.1
```

A single transaction creating 20,000 nodes will take up approximately 1.1MB of space. Even though the rotation threshold is 1MB, you cannot divide a transaction across multiple files, so this transaction is kept in the *db.0* transaction log. The next transaction will be logged in the *db.1* transaction log:

```
CREATE (n:Node {id: randomUuid()})
```

Again, if you inspect the database store, nothing has changed yet:

```
-rw-r--r--@  1 cwillemsen  staff   360B  4 Apr 09:19 checkpoint.0
-rw-r--r--@  1 cwillemsen  staff   1.1M  4 Apr 09:19 neostore.transaction.db.0
-rw-r--r--@  1 cwillemsen  staff   252B  4 Apr 09:21 neostore.transaction.db.1
```

Repeat the random 20,000-node creation ten times, to create 10 additional transaction logs of approximately at 1.1MB each:

```
// do this 10 times
UNWIND range(1,20000) AS i
CREATE (n:Node {id: randomUuid()})
```

Inspect the transaction logs again:

```
-rw-r--r--@  1 cwillemsen  staff   360B  4 Apr 09:19 checkpoint.0
-rw-r--r--@  1 cwillemsen  staff   1.1M  4 Apr 09:19 neostore.transaction.db.0
-rw-r--r--@  1 cwillemsen  staff   1.1M  4 Apr 09:28 neostore.transaction.db.1
-rw-r--r--@  1 cwillemsen  staff   1.1M  4 Apr 09:28 neostore.transaction.db.10
-rw-r--r--@  1 cwillemsen  staff   128B  4 Apr 09:28 neostore.transaction.db.11
-rw-r--r--@  1 cwillemsen  staff   1.1M  4 Apr 09:28 neostore.transaction.db.2
-rw-r--r--@  1 cwillemsen  staff   1.1M  4 Apr 09:28 neostore.transaction.db.3
-rw-r--r--@  1 cwillemsen  staff   1.1M  4 Apr 09:28 neostore.transaction.db.4
-rw-r--r--@  1 cwillemsen  staff   1.1M  4 Apr 09:28 neostore.transaction.db.5
-rw-r--r--@  1 cwillemsen  staff   1.1M  4 Apr 09:28 neostore.transaction.db.6
-rw-r--r--@  1 cwillemsen  staff   1.1M  4 Apr 09:28 neostore.transaction.db.7
-rw-r--r--@  1 cwillemsen  staff   1.1M  4 Apr 09:28 neostore.transaction.db.8
-rw-r--r--@  1 cwillemsen  staff   1.1M  4 Apr 09:28 neostore.transaction.db.9
```

You will observe that even though Neo4j is configured to retain only three transaction log files, it is smart enough to not prune older transaction logs if those transactions have not been flushed to the data store by a checkpoint.

You can manually perform a checkpoint by running this query in the Neo4j browser:

```
//006-checkpoint.cypher
CALL db.checkpoint()
```

Now inspect the transaction logs directory, and you'll observe that the logs have been pruned:

```
-rw-r--r--@  1 cwillemsen  staff   592B  4 Apr 09:31 checkpoint.0
-rw-r--r--@  1 cwillemsen  staff   1.1M  4 Apr 09:28 neostore.transaction.db.10
-rw-r--r--@  1 cwillemsen  staff   128B  4 Apr 09:28 neostore.transaction.db.11
-rw-r--r--@  1 cwillemsen  staff   1.1M  4 Apr 09:28 neostore.transaction.db.8
-rw-r--r--@  1 cwillemsen  staff   1.1M  4 Apr 09:28 neostore.transaction.db.9
```

Additionally, the data directory has now changed:

```
total 56664
drwxr-xr-x@ 31 cwillemsen  staff   992B  4 Apr 09:34 ./
drwxr-xr-x@ 12 cwillemsen  staff   384B  4 Apr 09:34 ../
1 cwillemsen  staff     0B  4 Apr 09:34 block.big_values.db
```

```
1 cwillemsen  staff   40K  4 Apr 09:36 block.big_values.db.id
1 cwillemsen  staff   48K  4 Apr 09:36 block.counts.db
1 cwillemsen  staff   40K  4 Apr 09:36 block.huge.db
1 cwillemsen  staff   48K  4 Apr 09:36 block.indexstats.db
1 cwillemsen  staff   48K  4 Apr 09:36 block.metadata.db
1 cwillemsen  staff    0B  4 Apr 09:34 block.node.xd.db
1 cwillemsen  staff   40K  4 Apr 09:36 block.node.xd.db.id
1 cwillemsen  staff   40K  4 Apr 09:36 block.relationship.degrees.db
1 cwillemsen  staff   40K  4 Apr 09:36 block.relationship.dense.db
1 cwillemsen  staff    0B  4 Apr 09:34 block.relationship.map.db
1 cwillemsen  staff   40K  4 Apr 09:36 block.relationship.map.db.id
1 cwillemsen  staff    0B  4 Apr 09:34 block.relationship.xd.db
1 cwillemsen  staff   40K  4 Apr 09:36 block.relationship.xd.db.id
1 cwillemsen  staff   40K  4 Apr 09:36 block.schema.db
1 cwillemsen  staff   40K  4 Apr 09:36 block.schema.db.id
1 cwillemsen  staff   48K  4 Apr 09:36 block.token.label.db
1 cwillemsen  staff   40K  4 Apr 09:36 block.token.label.db.id
1 cwillemsen  staff   48K  4 Apr 09:36 block.token.property_key.db
1 cwillemsen  staff   40K  4 Apr 09:36 block.token.property_key.db.id
1 cwillemsen  staff   40K  4 Apr 09:36 block.token.relationship_type.db
1 cwillemsen  staff   40K  4 Apr 09:36 block.token.relationship_type.db.id
1 cwillemsen  staff   27M  4 Apr 09:36 block.x1.db
1 cwillemsen  staff   64K  4 Apr 09:36 block.x1.db.id
1 cwillemsen  staff    0B  4 Apr 09:34 database_lock
1 cwillemsen  staff    0B  4 Apr 09:34 id-buffer.tmp.0
drwxr-xr-x@ 27 cwillemsen  staff   864B  4 Apr 09:35 profiles/
1 cwillemsen  staff  1.0K  4 Apr 09:34 quarantine_marker
drwxr-xr-x@  3 cwillemsen  staff    96B  4 Apr 09:34 schema/
```

You can also find traces of these Neo4j operations in the *debug.log* file:

```
...
2025-04-04 07:35:51.945+0000 INFO  [o.n.k.d.Database] [staging/bebc7d3a] Rotated
to transaction log [/Users/cwillemsen/dev/_graphs/book-db-data/transactions/
staging/neostore.transaction.db.11] version=10, last append index in previous
log=16, rotation took 5 millis, started after 653 millis.
2025-04-04 07:36:04.791+0000 INFO  [o.n.k.i.t.l.c.CheckPointerImpl]
[staging/bebc7d3a] Checkpoint triggered by "Call to db.checkpoint() procedure"
@ txId: 16, append index: 16 checkpoint started...
2025-04-04 07:36:05.037+0000 INFO  [o.n.k.i.t.l.c.CheckPointerImpl]
[staging/bebc7d3a] Checkpoint triggered by "Call to db.checkpoint() procedure"
@ txId: 16, append index: 16 checkpoint completed in 246ms. Checkpoint flushed
3500 pages (0% of total available pages), in 2064 IOs. Checkpoint performed with
IO limit: 600, paused in total 1 times( 41 millis).
2025-04-04 07:36:05.040+0000 INFO  [o.n.k.i.t.l.p.LogPruningImpl]
[staging/bebc7d3a] Pruned log versions 0 through 7. The strategy used was
'3 files'.
```

Go ahead and add more random nodes:

```
// do this 10 times
UNWIND range(1,20000) AS i
CREATE (n:Node {id: randomUuid()})
```

The transaction logs again contain 10 additional log files that are waiting for the checkpoint to prune them.

To better understand how Neo4j handles unexpected shutdowns and how it recovers afterward, we'll now simulate a crash by forcefully terminating the process. This allows us to observe how transaction logs are used during recovery.

First, let's find the Neo4j Process Identifier (PID):

```
//007-pid-find.txt
ps aux | grep neo4j
```

You'll see output like this:

```
neo4j     12345  1.0  ... /path/to/java -cp ... org.neo4j.server....
```

Here, 12345 is the PID.

Kill the process, replacing 12345 with the correct PID:

```
//008-kill-neo4j.txt
sudo kill -9 12345
```

At this point, the Neo4j server has crashed, and while all committed transactions are safely stored in the transaction log, their corresponding changes may not yet be reflected in the store files.

Restart Neo4j:

```
//009-restart-neo4j.txt
./bin/neo4j start
```

Upon startup, Neo4j will automatically initiate the recovery process. It will detect that the store is not in sync with the latest committed transactions and will replay the transaction logs to bring the store up to date.

Once recovery is complete, Neo4j will trigger a checkpoint, allowing older transaction logs to be pruned safely. No manual intervention is required during recovery, but you can follow the process in real time by monitoring the *debug.log* file in Neo4j's logs directory:

```
2025-04-04 08:47:27.475+0000 INFO  [c.n.c.d.d.TopologyState] Database {bebc7d3a}
            /staging on {07a5a718}/ME! now has state STARTING
2025-04-04 08:47:27.483+0000 INFO  [c.n.c.d.d.TopologyState] Database {bebc7d3a}
/staging on {07a5a718}/ME! is discoverable in mode SINGLE and publishing
RaftMemberId{07a5a718}
2025-04-04 08:47:27.572+0000 INFO  [c.n.k.i.p.PageCacheWarmer] [staging/bebc7d3a]
Page cache warmup started. ❶
2025-04-04 08:47:27.572+0000 INFO  [o.n.k.d.Database] [staging/bebc7d3a]
Transaction logs recovery is required with the last check point (which points to
LogPosition{logVersion=20, byteOffset=1200196}, oldest log entry to recover
LogPosition{logVersion=20, byteOffset=1200196}). First observed post checkpoint
append index: 27.
```

```
2025-04-04 08:47:27.630+0000 INFO  [c.n.k.i.p.PageCacheWarmer] [staging/bebc7d3a]
Page cache warmup completed. 6666 pages loaded. Duration: 58ms. 114.93 pages/ms.
2025-04-04 08:47:27.637+0000 INFO  [o.n.k.d.Database] [staging/bebc7d3a] Recovery
required from position LogPosition{logVersion=20, byteOffset=1200196} ❷
2025-04-04 08:47:27.696+0000 INFO  [o.n.k.r.Recovery] [staging/bebc7d3a]
TransactionLogsRecovery
2025-04-04 08:47:27.733+0000 INFO  [o.n.k.r.Recovery] [staging/bebc7d3a]
10% completed
2025-04-04 08:47:27.795+0000 INFO  [o.n.k.r.Recovery] [staging/bebc7d3a]
20% completed
2025-04-04 08:47:27.866+0000 INFO  [o.n.k.r.Recovery] [staging/bebc7d3a]
30% completed
2025-04-04 08:47:27.912+0000 INFO  [o.n.k.r.Recovery] [staging/bebc7d3a]
40% completed
2025-04-04 08:47:27.985+0000 INFO  [o.n.k.r.Recovery] [staging/bebc7d3a]
50% completed
2025-04-04 08:47:28.507+0000 INFO  [o.n.k.r.Recovery] [staging/bebc7d3a]
60% completed
2025-04-04 08:47:28.718+0000 INFO  [o.n.k.r.Recovery] [staging/bebc7d3a]
70% completed
2025-04-04 08:47:28.943+0000 INFO  [o.n.k.r.Recovery] [staging/bebc7d3a]
80% completed
2025-04-04 08:47:29.094+0000 INFO  [o.n.k.r.Recovery] [staging/bebc7d3a]
90% completed
2025-04-04 08:47:29.243+0000 INFO  [o.n.k.r.Recovery] [staging/bebc7d3a]
100% completed
2025-04-04 08:47:29.255+0000 INFO  [o.n.k.d.Database] [staging/bebc7d3a]
Recovery in 'full' mode completed. Observed transactions range [first:27,
last:36]: 10 transactions applied, 0 not completed transactions rolled back,
skipped applying 0 previously rolled back transactions. Time spent: 1s 673ms.
2025-04-04 08:47:29.264+0000 INFO  [o.n.k.i.t.l.c.CheckPointerImpl]
[staging/bebc7d3a] Checkpoint triggered by "Recovery completed." @ txId: 36,
append index: 36 checkpoint started...
2025-04-04 08:47:29.647+0000 INFO  [o.n.k.i.t.l.c.CheckPointerImpl]
[staging/bebc7d3a] Checkpoint triggered by "Recovery completed." @ txId: 36,
append index: 36 checkpoint completed in 381ms. Checkpoint flushed 3186 pages
(0% of total available pages), in 2226 IOs. Checkpoint performed with IO limit:
600, paused in total 2 times( 133 millis).
2025-04-04 08:47:29.650+0000 INFO  [o.n.k.i.t.l.p.LogPruningImpl]
[staging/bebc7d3a] Pruned log versions 18 through 27. The strategy used was
'3 files'.
```

❶ Neo4j detects Recovery is necessary

❷ Recovery process started

In this section, we've explored how Neo4j handles write operations and ensures durability through its transaction lifecycle. You now understand the role of the page cache for in-memory changes, the importance of the transaction log (or WAL) for durability, and how checkpoints periodically flush changes to the store files. Together, these components form the foundation for crash recovery and safe persistence.

For ElectricHarmony, this architecture is critical. Their platform relies on consistent and reliable data updates, especially during peak periods when many users interact with the graph simultaneously. Knowing that Neo4j can recover from crashes without data loss gives their team the confidence to move fast without compromising on reliability.

You've also seen why transaction log rotation is essential to preventing unbounded growth and how checkpointing determines when old logs can safely be pruned. A well-tuned rotation and checkpointing strategy balances durability, disk usage, and recovery time.

Backups

Next, we'll explore how to protect data through backups.

A proper backup strategy is more than just copying files. It must ensure consistency, minimize downtime, and align with how Neo4j manages its internal state. Because of Neo4j's write-ahead architecture and memory-based page cache, thoughtlessly copying store files can result in incomplete or corrupt backups if you don't use the recommended tools.

Types of Backups

Neo4j provides built-in backup mechanisms tailored to its architecture, ensuring that backups are both consistent and restorable. In this section, you'll learn the different types of backups, how to perform them, and how to integrate them into a production-ready data protection strategy.

Full backup

Full backups perform a complete backup based on the database store files. This is done with the following command:

```
./bin/neo4j-admin database backup --to-path=<path/to/backups/directory>
--type=FULL <database-name>
```

First, prepare a directory to store your backups:

```
//010-create-backup-dir.txt
mkdir -p /tmp/backups/staging
```

Run the following command to perform a full backup on the staging database:

```
//011-neo4j-backup.txt
./bin/neo4j-admin database backup --to-path=/tmp/backups/staging
--type=FULL staging
```

This produces the following output:

```
[c.n.b.b.BackupOutputMonitor] Starting backup of database 'staging' from servers:
  [127.0.0.1:6362]
[c.n.b.b.BackupOutputMonitor] Start backup of database 'staging'.
[c.n.b.b.BackupOutputMonitor] Using remote server 127.0.0.1:6362
  for backup of database 'staging'.
[c.n.b.b.BackupOutputMonitor] Start full backup of database 'staging'.
[c.n.b.b.BackupOutputMonitor] Start receiving store files for database
  'staging'. Backups | 267
[c.n.b.b.BackupOutputMonitor] Finished receiving store files for database
  'staging', took 106ms.
[c.n.b.b.BackupOutputMonitor] Start receiving database 'staging' transactions
  from [36, 37].
[c.n.b.b.BackupOutputMonitor] Finished receiving transactions for database
  'staging' at 36, took 95ms.
[c.n.b.b.BackupOutputMonitor] Finished full backup of database 'staging'.
  Downloaded from tx -1 to tx 36.
[c.n.b.b.BackupOutputMonitor] Start recovering database 'staging'.
[c.n.b.b.BackupOutputMonitor] Finished recovering database 'staging',
  took 829ms.
[c.n.b.b.BackupOutputMonitor] Start creating artifact 'incomplete_backup0.tmp'
  for database 'staging'.
[c.n.b.b.BackupOutputMonitor] Finished artifact creation
  'staging-2025-04-04T10-42-57.backup' for database 'staging', took 296ms.
[c.n.b.b.BackupOutputMonitor] Backup of database 'staging' completed,
  took 1s 714ms.
```

When you analyze the *debug.log* file during a full backup, you'll notice that Neo4j begins by triggering a checkpoint. This flushes all recent transactions to the store files, allowing the backup to capture a consistent and up-to-date snapshot. As part of this process, transaction logs may also be pruned, since the checkpoint marks them as no longer needed for recovery:

```
2025-04-04 10:42:56.597+0000 INFO  [o.n.k.i.t.l.c.CheckPointerImpl]
[staging/bebc7d3a] Checkpoint triggered by "Store copy" @ txId: 36, append index:
36 checkpoint started...
2025-04-04 10:42:56.757+0000 INFO  [o.n.k.i.t.l.c.CheckPointerImpl]
[staging/bebc7d3a] Checkpoint triggered by "Store copy" @ txId: 36, append index:
36 checkpoint completed in 159ms. Checkpoint flushed 29 pages (0% of total
available pages), in 29 IOs. Checkpoint performed with IO limit: 600, paused in
total 0 times( 0 millis).
2025-04-04 10:42:56.757+0000 INFO  [o.n.k.i.t.l.p.LogPruningImpl]
[staging/bebc7d3a] No log version pruned. The strategy used was '3 files'.
```

This process produces a compressed archive containing the database backup. Check that your backup has been created:

```
ls -lha /tmp/backups/staging
```

The output is:

```
1 cwillemsen  wheel    15M  4 Apr 12:42 staging-2025-04-04T10-42-57.backup
```

Incremental backup

Incremental backups rely on transaction logs to identify changes since the last backup. Instead of copying the entire database, they transfer only the modified parts of the store files that correspond to transactions committed since the last known backup point. This makes them faster and more space-efficient than full backups, though they still require access to a complete backup chain starting from the last full backup.

The command for incremental backup is similar to the previous one, with just the backup type parameter changing:

```
./bin/neo4j-admin database backup --to-path=<path/to/backups/directory>
--type=DIFF <database-name>
```

To test this, let's add new data to the graph:

```
// do this 10 times
UNWIND range(1,20000) AS i
CREATE (n:Node {id: randomUuid()})
```

Now run an incremental backup:

```
//012-incremental-backup.txt
./bin/neo4j-admin database backup --to-path=/tmp/backups/staging
--type=DIFF staging
```

Here's what a successful differential backup looks like in the logs: output shows the start of a differential backup, the transaction range that was copied (from tx 37 to tx 47), the creation of the backup artifact, and the successful completion, all in under half a second:

```
2025-04-04 10:53:04.736+0000 INFO  [c.n.b.b.BackupOutputMonitor]
Starting backup of database 'staging' from servers: [127.0.0.1:6362]
2025-04-04 10:53:05.363+0000 INFO  [c.n.b.b.BackupOutputMonitor]
Start backup of database 'staging'.
2025-04-04 10:53:05.364+0000 INFO  [c.n.b.b.BackupOutputMonitor]
Using remote server 127.0.0.1:6362 for backup of database 'staging'.
2025-04-04 10:53:05.387+0000 INFO  [c.n.b.b.BackupOutputMonitor]
Start differential backup of database 'staging'.
2025-04-04 10:53:05.547+0000 INFO  [c.n.b.b.BackupOutputMonitor]
Start receiving database 'staging' transactions from [37].
2025-04-04 10:53:05.791+0000 INFO  [c.n.b.b.BackupOutputMonitor]
Finished receiving transactions for database 'staging' at 47, took 243ms.
2025-04-04 10:53:05.797+0000 INFO  [c.n.b.b.BackupOutputMonitor]
Finished differential backup of database 'staging'. Downloaded from tx 37
to tx 47.
2025-04-04 10:53:05.801+0000 INFO  [c.n.b.b.BackupOutputMonitor]
Start creating artifact 'incomplete_backup0.tmp' for database 'staging'.
2025-04-04 10:53:05.845+0000 INFO  [c.n.b.b.BackupOutputMonitor]
Finished artifact creation 'staging-2025-04-04T10-53-05.backup' for database
'staging', took 44ms.
2025-04-04 10:53:05.848+0000 INFO  [c.n.b.b.BackupOutputMonitor]
Backup of database 'staging' completed, took 483ms.
```

The produced incremental backup files will be stored along with the original full backup:

```
ls -lha /tmp/backups/staging/
```

The output is:

```
1 cwillemsen  wheel    15M  4 Apr 12:42 staging-2025-04-04T10-42-57.backup
1 cwillemsen  wheel   6.1M  4 Apr 12:53 staging-2025-04-04T10-53-05.backup
```

Incremental backups are especially recommended when your database has frequent write activity and you need a short *recovery point objective* (RPO) without the overhead of performing full backups too often. (RPOs are the maximum acceptable amount of data loss measured in time.) Incremental backups help you strike a balance between backup speed, storage efficiency, and recovery flexibility.

Restoring Backups

Creating backups is only one part of the story. Being able to reliably *restore* them is what ultimately protects your data.

Whether you're recovering hardware-level corruption or accidental deletion or you're setting up a staging environment from production data, Neo4j provides straightforward tools to restore both full and incremental backups. While the database is ACID-compliant, external factors such as disk failures or abrupt shutdowns can still result in file-level corruption.

In the following example, you'll restore a database using the backup files you created in the previous section. Neo4j can reconstruct a complete store from a combination of a full backup and one or more incremental backups.

You'll restore the backup chain into a new database named `staging2`. Use the following command:

```
//013-restore-backup.txt
./bin/neo4j-admin database restore \
--from-path=/tmp/backups/staging/staging-2025-04-04T10-53-05.backup staging2
```

The `--from-path` option must point to the latest file in the backup chain. In this case, it refers to the single incremental backup created earlier. Neo4j will automatically resolve and include the full backup and all preceding incremental files. It's important to run the `restore` command using the same Linux user as the one running the Neo4j server—otherwise, the restored database might not start due to file ownership issues.

What happens during the restore process?

Backup chain validation
: Neo4j verifies that all backups in the chain are valid and consistent. Each incremental backup must follow the previous one in transaction order and all must originate from the same full backup.

Full backup restoration
: The original full backup is unpacked and copied to initialize the new `staging2` database store.

Incremental recovery
: Each incremental backup is processed and applied in order. This step replays the transactions contained in the differential backups, bringing the store up to date.

This third step is especially important: the longer the backup chain (that is, the more incremental files there are), the longer the restore will take. Each incremental file adds recovery time, so balance granularity and frequency accordingly.

Once the restore is complete and the store files are in place, the final step is to create the database in the current Neo4j server instance:

```
CREATE DATABASE staging2 WAIT
```

With the restored store in place and the database created, your Neo4j instance is once again ready to serve queries, closing the loop between backup and recovery with confidence.

Cloud Backups

If you're running Neo4j on a virtual machine or cloud instance, storing backups locally on the same host introduces a major risk: if the VM is lost or corrupted, so are your backups.

To avoid this single point of failure, it's essential to store backups in a separate, durable location—ideally in object storage, such as Amazon S3, Azure Blob Storage, or Google Cloud Storage.

Neo4j offers built-in support for cloud backups and restore in the `neo4j-admin backup` command. This allows you to push full or incremental backups directly to cloud storage, without needing intermediate staging on local disk:

```
bin/neo4j-admin database backup --to-path=s3://myBucket/myDirectory/ mydatabase
```

For more information on cloud backups and how to set up your cloud object storage credentials, refer to the Neo4j documentation (*https://oreil.ly/lesMw*).

Remote Backups and VM Separation

In a busy production environment, running resource-intensive operations like full backups directly on the primary Neo4j server can introduce latency and affect performance. To avoid disrupting query throughput or interfering with other processes, it's often preferable to perform backups from a separate virtual machine.

Full backups are particularly well-suited to remote execution. Since they involve copying the entire store and triggering a checkpoint, running them from a different VM reduces I/O load on the main database host while still producing a consistent snapshot. This also allows full backups to run on their own schedule, independent of database activity peaks.

Incremental backups, by contrast, are lightweight and time-sensitive. They rely on access to recent transaction logs and are typically performed more frequently—every few minutes in some setups. Running these locally on the primary VM ensures fast execution and guarantees that the required logs are still available when the backup starts. Once you've created them, you can transfer these incremental backup files to remote storage for archiving or disaster recovery.

A common pattern is to:

- Run incremental backups locally at short intervals (such as every 5 to 15 minutes).
- Run full backups from a remote VM once per day or during low-traffic periods.
- Archive all backups to remote or object storage for long-term retention.

This strategy balances backup consistency, system performance, and fault tolerance so that backups protect data effectively without interfering with regular database workloads.

Designing a Backup Strategy

With a clear understanding of Neo4j's internal write lifecycle and recovery mechanisms, it's time to design a backup strategy suitable for production environments. The goal is simple: ensure that data can be restored reliably, with minimal data loss and downtime.

A good backup strategy must balance three key factors:

Durability
: Backups must be consistent and restorable.

Performance
: Backup and restore processes should not impact database throughput.

Recovery guarantees

Define how much data loss is acceptable and how quickly the system must be back online:

> The *recovery point objective* (RPO) defines how much data you're willing to lose in case of failure. It reflects the *maximum acceptable gap* between the latest data and the last successful backup.
>
> The *recovery time objective* (RTO) defines how quickly you need to restore the system and make it available again.

Table 9-1 provides recommended targets for production environments.

Table 9-1. Recommended RPO and RTO targets

Environment	RPO target	RTO target
Business-critical	5 minutes	<15 minutes
Standard production	15 minutes	<1 hour
Noncritical/testing	1 hour	Best effort

Why these numbers? In a production system with frequent writes (like ElectricHarmony), losing more than a few minutes of data can impact users and business operations. A 5- to 15-minute RPO ensures that even in the worst-case scenario, only a small window of transactions is lost. A low RTO ensures high availability, especially in customer-facing systems where downtime directly affects service levels.

The components of a good backup strategy are:

- Full backups (daily)
  - Schedule one full backup every 24 hours, preferably during off-peak hours.
  - Store it in a safe, reliable, redundant location outside of the database service and ideally in a different availability zone (such as object storage or an offsite backup repository).
  - This provides a baseline for restores and resets your backup chain.
- Incremental backups *(every 5–15 minutes)*
  - Depending on RPO requirements, perform incremental backups every 5 to 15 minutes.
  - These backups are lightweight and efficient since they only store transaction deltas.
- Transaction log retention
  - Retain logs for at least 2x the interval between full backups to allow point-in-time recovery.

    - For example: If you do full backups daily, keep at least 48 hours of logs.
- Frequent checkpointing
    - Use time or volume-based checkpoint settings that ensure transaction logs are not kept indefinitely but also do not rotate prematurely before backups occur.
- Validation and monitoring
    - Regularly test restores in a staging environment.
    - Monitor backup logs and Neo4j's *debug.log* for failures, skipped checkpoints, or unexpected retention behavior.
- Maintaining a restore playbook
    - Maintain clear procedures to restore from both full and incremental backups.
    - Automate where possible, and document how to validate restored data and bring systems back online.

Here is an example of Neo4j configuration for a 15-minute RPO:

```
db.checkpoint.interval.time=5m
db.tx_log.rotation.size=250MB
db.tx_log.rotation.retention_policy=7 days
```

The first line sets checkpoints to run every 5 minutes, ensuring that recent transactions are regularly flushed from memory to disk, reducing recovery time after a crash. The second sets the log size threshold for rotation to 250MB, and the third configures Neo4j to keep transaction logs for 7 days. This allows point-in-time recovery within the retention window, even if a backup is slightly older.

Additionally, schedule a full backup every 24 hours. In between, run incremental backups every 15 minutes to minimize potential data loss.

Summary

A solid backup strategy provides the foundation for resilience, recovery, and operational confidence in your Neo4j deployment. As your data volume and usage evolve, revisit these parameters regularly to align with new workloads, storage constraints, and business expectations.

In this chapter, you've explored the critical mechanisms that ensure Neo4j remains reliable and recoverable in production. Starting from the fundamentals of the write path, you learned how Neo4j handles in-memory and on-disk persistence through transaction logs and checkpoints. You've seen how log rotation and checkpointing work together to manage disk space, recovery speed, and data durability.

You also got hands-on with full and incremental backups and understood the importance of designing a strategy tailored to your system's recovery point objective (RPO) and recovery time objective (RTO). Finally, you walked through a complete restore workflow and saw how backups come together to ensure operational continuity even in the face of failure.

For ElectricHarmony, these practices are more than theoretical—they're critical to maintaining trust with users. Whether it's ensuring that music metadata stays consistent or recovering quickly from infrastructure hiccups, the backup and recovery setup they've adopted allows their team to move fast with confidence, knowing the data layer is solid and recoverable.

CHAPTER 10

Clustering and Sharding

As ElectricHarmony's graph grew in size and value, so did the expectations around reliability. Outages that were once tolerable became unacceptable. A failed write during a peak event could mean lost revenue, or worse, a corrupted view of their users' listening habits. The team knew it was time to move beyond a single-node setup.

This chapter introduces clustering in Neo4j, the foundation for building highly available graph deployments. You'll explore how Neo4j's architecture supports fault tolerance, how leader elections and replication work, and what trade-offs come with scaling for resilience.

From setting up a basic cluster to understanding how reads and writes behave across members, you'll learn how ElectricHarmony transitioned from a single point of failure to a robust cluster capable of handling both growth and unpredictability.

High availability isn't just a feature—it's a necessity. Let's dive in.

Clustering for High Availability

When performance and uptime are critical, running Neo4j as a standalone instance no longer cuts it.

Neo4j's clustering model is designed to keep your database available even in the face of hardware failures, maintenance windows, or surging traffic. Clustering doesn't just improve resilience; it also enables the system to scale read capacity across multiple machines.

Figure 10-1 starts with a very basic cluster to introduce you to some of the clustering concepts.

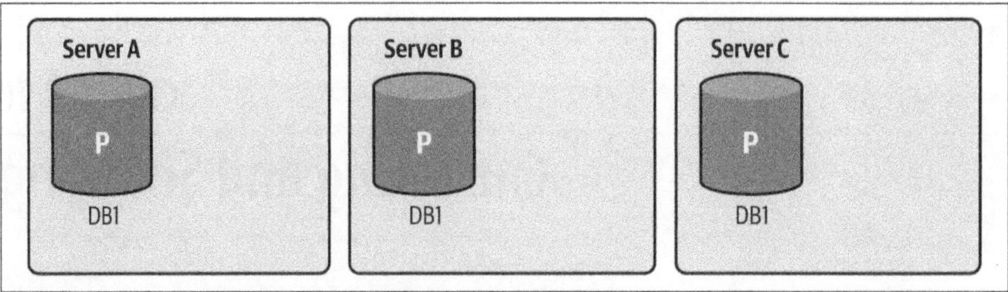

Figure 10-1. A basic Neo4j cluster with three primaries

Neo4j servers can operate in two modes: primary and secondary. A *primary* server (often simply called a *primary*) can handle both read and write operations for the databases it hosts. A *secondary* server (or just a *secondary*) only handles read operations.

Databases can be replicated across the cluster; each replica, also called an *instance*, can also be either primary or secondary. To achieve high availability, the system deploys multiple primary instances of the same database. When a database has multiple primaries, one of them is automatically selected as the leader (also referred to as the *writer*). The *leader* coordinates all write operations, while the other primaries act as followers, and the secondaries as readers.

Raft Protocol

To achieve high availability, Neo4j uses the Raft protocol (*https://oreil.ly/Fs9t6*), a consensus algorithm that elects a leader to manage log replication and maintain consistency across a cluster, to ensure that all transactions are safely replicated. Raft requires a majority of the primaries in a database, calculated as (N/2+1), to acknowledge a transaction before it is considered committed and is acknowledged to the client application.

In practice, only the leader accepts client write requests; it replicates those changes to the followers, ensuring durability and consistency across the cluster. Figure 10-2 illustrates this mechanism.

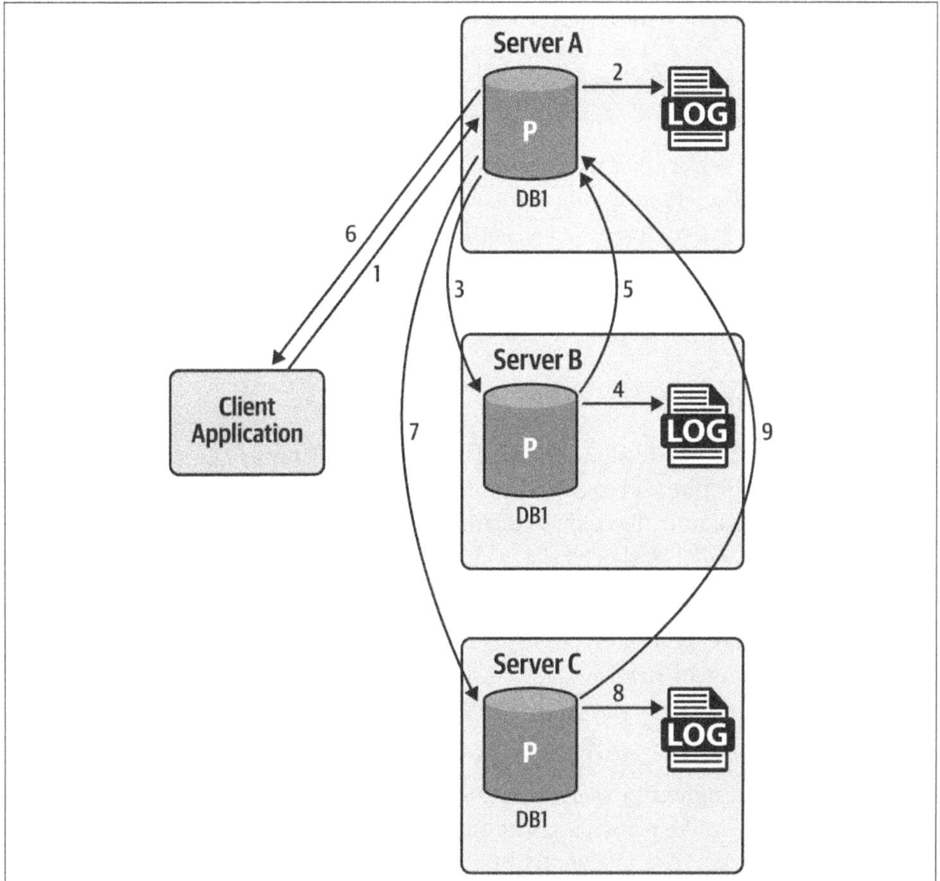

Figure 10-2. Commit sequencing

Here's the step-by-step sequencing:

1. The client application submits a transaction with a commit.
2. The leader tentatively writes the transaction to its local Raft log.
3. The leader then forwards the transaction to the follower primaries via the Raft protocol.
4. Each follower tentatively writes the transaction to its own Raft log.
5. The followers then acknowledge the transaction back to the leader.
6. Once a majority of primaries (N/2+1) have acknowledged the transaction, the leader marks the transaction as committed and instructs the followers to do the same.

In a three-member cluster (N=3), a majority is defined as N/2+1, which equals 2; this means the leader can acknowledge the transaction to the client once any two members (including itself) have confirmed it, even if the third (like server C) hasn't yet.

This synchronous replication mechanism has a direct impact on write latency: writes are acknowledged as soon as the fastest majority has responded. However, as the number of primaries increases, so does the number of acknowledgments required, potentially increasing write latency. This trade-off comes with a benefit: higher numbers of primaries improve availability and fault tolerance, as the system can tolerate more failures while still reaching quorum.

Fault Tolerance

The fault tolerance for a database is calculated with the formula $M = 2F + 1$, where M is the number of primaries required to tolerate F faults. For example, to tolerate one failure, the database must have three primaries. To tolerate two failures, it must have five primaries.

If the number of failed primaries exceeds what the cluster can tolerate, it halts write operations to ensure data safety. In this state, the database becomes read-only until a majority can be reestablished.

Secondaries

Secondaries are designed to scale read workloads by distributing query load across multiple replicas. Unlike primaries, secondaries do not participate in the Raft consensus protocol. Instead, they frequently pull updates from upstream primaries through a process known as log shipping, where changes to the database are recorded in logs and then sent to replicas so they can replay them and stay up to date.

A database can have many secondaries, and the loss of one does not affect availability or data safety. However, it does reduce the system's overall read capacity by removing one source of query throughput.

Deploying a Cluster

This book's GitHub companion repository offers a Docker Compose that is ready for you to deploy a cluster locally. Check out the chapter10/docker folder (*https://oreil.ly/e-5Ef*) and run the following command:

```
docker compose up -d
```

This will deploy a three-server cluster. The default mode for servers is `PRIMARY`. To change this, use the `initial.server.mode_constraint` setting.

Since two servers cannot be bound on the same port, the three servers are available on ports 17474, 27474, and 37474, respectively.

Open the server 1 browser on *http://localhost:17474* and select `neo4j://` as the scheme for the connection, as shown in Figure 10-3.

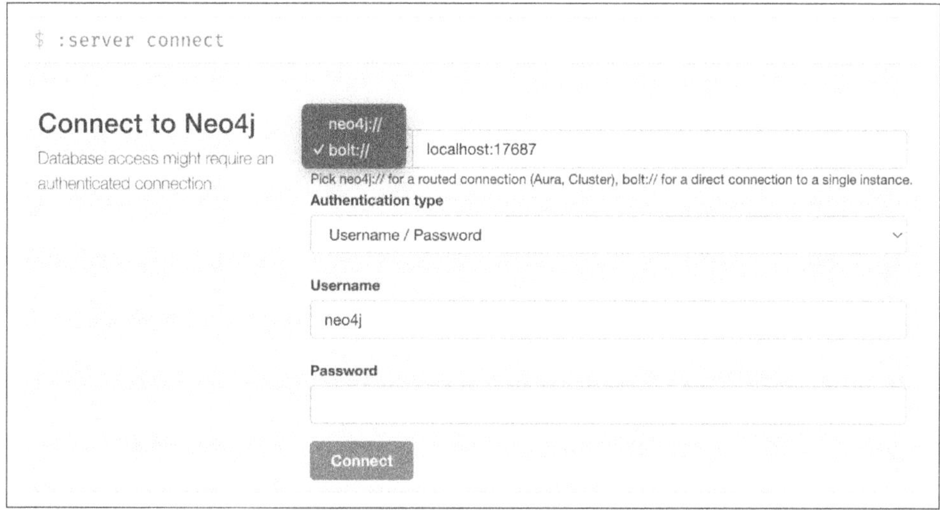

Figure 10-3. Connecting server 1

The `neo4j://` scheme ensures that even if you're not connected to the server hosting a database in "write/leader" mode, you will be able to perform write operations. You can find more information on the connection URIs in the driver manual of the Neo4j documentation (*https://oreil.ly/efEYi*).

Once you've logged in, using `password` as the password, run the following command:

```
SHOW SERVERS
```

This should give you output that looks like Figure 10-4.

```
neo4j$ show servers

|name                                  |address          |state    |health     |hosting              |
|"065a5d64-6180-4c8a-ab8b-faa2263317a3"|"primary2:7687"|"Enabled"|"Available"|["neo4j", "system"]|
|"3a435151-8491-4226-98fc-a8fcaa5057a8"|"primary1:7687"|"Enabled"|"Available"|["system"]         |
|"5823a2fc-e04c-40c7-80ab-96a9fdfe0c55"|"primary3:7687"|"Enabled"|"Available"|["system"]         |
```

Figure 10-4. Output of the `show servers` command

The system database is always present on all the servers. You might notice in Figure 10-4 that the default database, `neo4j`, has only one replica.

The default number of primaries when databases are created is dictated by the setting `initial.dbms.default_primaries_count`, which has a default value of 1. You can change the setting or specify the topology of a database at creation time. The following command creates a database with three primaries and no secondaries:

```
//001-create-db-3-primaries.cypher
CREATE DATABASE prod TOPOLOGY 3 PRIMARIES 0 SECONDARIES WAIT
```

You cannot create a database with a topology (number of primaries + number of secondaries) higher than the number of available servers.

Then run the following command:

```
//002-show-db-small.cypher
SHOW DATABASES

YIELD name, address, currentStatus, role, writer
```

This gives the output shown in Figure 10-5, showing that the production database has been replicated with three primaries, and the leader of the database is hosted by server 3 (primary-3).

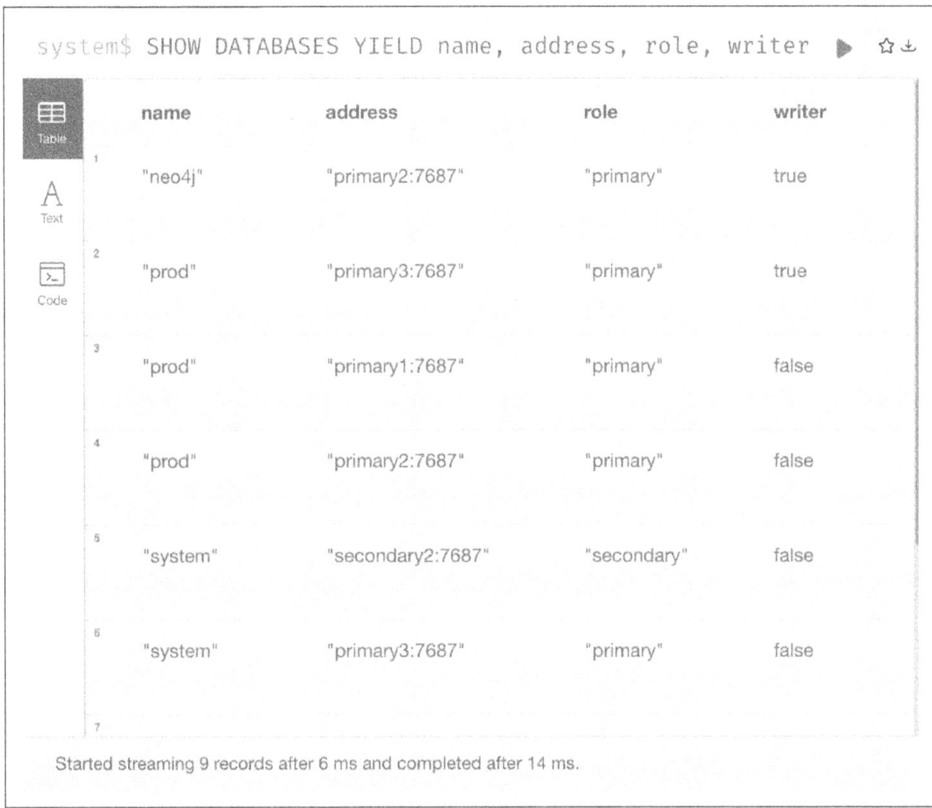

system$ SHOW DATABASES YIELD name, address, role, writer
Table
Text
Code
name address role writer
1 "neo4j" "primary2:7687" "primary" true
2 "prod" "primary3:7687" "primary" true
3 "prod" "primary1:7687" "primary" false
4 "prod" "primary2:7687" "primary" false
5 "system" "secondary2:7687" "secondary" false
6 "system" "primary3:7687" "primary" false
7
Started streaming 9 records after 6 ms and completed after 14 ms.

Figure 10-5. `SHOW DATABASES` command result, highlighting on which server a database writer is allocated

Now let's create some nodes in the database:

```
//003-create-nodes.cypher
:USE prod
UNWIND range(1,10) AS i
CREATE (n:Node)
```

Cluster Degradation

We told you that a three-node cluster can tolerate one failure. Let's put this into practice by killing server 3, which is hosting the production database in write mode. We expect that a new leader will be selected and that write operations will still be accepted:

```
docker kill neo4j-primary-3
```

Since we can't know ahead of time on which server the leader will be allocated, please amend these commands to reflect the correct server as you follow along with these steps.

Run the `SHOW DATABASES` command again and you'll see that the new leader for the prod database is now allocated to the server primary1 (see Figure 10-6).

```
system$ SHOW DATABASES YIELD name, address, currentStatus, role, writer
```

	name	address	currentStatus	role	writer
1	"neo4j"	"primary2:7687"	"online"	"primary"	true
2	"prod"	*null*	"unknown"	"primary"	false
3	"prod"	"primary1:7687"	"online"	"primary"	true
4	"prod"	"primary2:7687"	"online"	"primary"	false
5	"system"	"primary2:7687"	"online"	"primary"	false
6	"system"	*null*	"unknown"	*null*	false
7					

Started streaming 9 records after 250 ms and completed after 255 ms.

Figure 10-6. The state of the databases after killing one of the primary servers

You can find the relevant Raft lifecycle logs in server primary1's *debug.log* files:

```
.. [c.n.c.c.c.RaftMachine] [prod/72700f2a] Pre-election started with:
  PreVote.Request from RaftMemberId{e978e938} {term=1,
  candidate=RaftMemberId{e978e938}, lastAppended=4, lastLogTerm=1}
  and members: [RaftMem
.. [c.n.c.c.c.RaftMachine] [prod/72700f2a] Election started with reason:
  PRE_ELECTION_WON, Vote.Request from RaftMemberId{e978e938}
  {term=2, candidate=RaftMemberId{e978e938}, lastAppended=4, lastLogTerm=1} and
.. [c.n.c.c.c.RaftMachine] [prod/72700f2a] Moving to CANDIDATE state after
  successful pre-election stage
.. [c.n.c.c.c.RaftMachine] [prod/72700f2a] Moving to LEADER state at term 2
  (I am RaftMemberId{e978e938}), voted for by
// Logs truncated for readability
```

If you attempt to create more nodes on the database now, you should succeed.

The current cluster state can't tolerate any more failures. Indeed, if you kill server 2, the database will enter read-only mode, and no more writes will be accepted:

```
docker kill neo4j-primary-2
```

Figure 10-7 shows that no more writers exist for the prod database, and any attempt to write will lead to the exception illustrated in Figure 10-8.

system$ SHOW DATABASES YIELD name, address, currentStatus, role, writer

	name	address	currentStatus	role	writer
1	"neo4j"	null	"unknown"	"primary"	false
2	"prod"	null	"unknown"	"primary"	false
3	"prod"	null	"unknown"	"primary"	false
4	"prod"	"primary1:7687"	"online"	"primary"	false
5	"system"	null	"unknown"	null	false
6	"system"	"primary1:7687"	"online"	"primary"	false
7					

Started streaming 9 records after 5 ms and completed after 10 ms.

Figure 10-7. Result of `SHOW DATABASES` with no more writers available

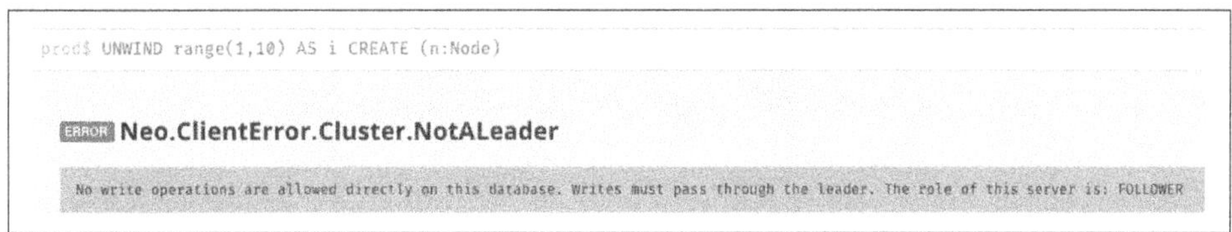
prod$ UNWIND range(1,10) AS i CREATE (n:Node)
ERROR Neo.ClientError.Cluster.NotALeader
No write operations are allowed directly on this database. Writes must pass through the leader. The role of this server is: FOLLOWER

Figure 10-8. This exception message appears if you attempt to write to a database that is in read-only mode.

Making one of the killed primaries available again will bring the database back to a writable state:

```
docker compose up -d primary-2
```

Multidatabase Clusters

In a cluster with multiple databases, each database can have its own leader on a different server. This means that leadership is distributed across the cluster, so the impact of a server going down varies, depending on which databases it was leading.

Figure 10-9 illustrates how leadership for each primary (P) database—DB1, DB2, and DB3—is distributed across three servers. Each database has one leader at any given time, and in this example, the leaders are spread out: DB1 on Server B, DB2 on Server A, and DB3 on Server C. This distribution helps balance the workload and improves fault tolerance by avoiding concentration of leadership on a single server. However, it's important to note that this distribution is not guaranteed. Leaders are elected dynamically using the Raft consensus algorithm, which means the actual placement can vary depending on the state of the cluster and recent elections.

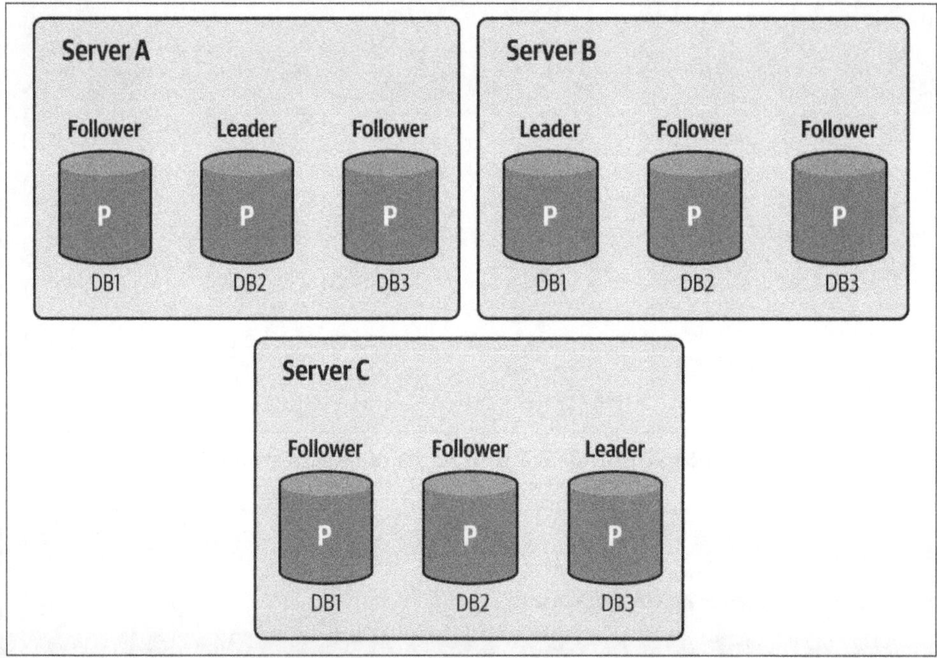

Figure 10-9. Multiple databases in a cluster setup

How Network Latency Affects Clustering

In clustered environments, low network latency is critical to ensuring fast, reliable synchronization between nodes. This is especially important for clusters that rely on synchronous replication, where the speed of coordination between nodes directly affects write performance and overall system responsiveness.

We recommend making sure that network latency between your cluster nodes supports fast and reliable synchronization, ideally with no more than 5ms round-trip time and never exceeding 10ms. Higher latencies can increase replication lag, delay consensus, and degrade availability in the face of failures.

You've now seen how a cluster of primary servers handles leader election and failover. Next, we look at how secondary servers (also known as read replicas) work and how to add them to your cluster.

Scaling Reads with Secondaries

To handle higher read workloads without overloading the primaries, Neo4j allows you to add secondary servers to your cluster. These servers are read-only and cannot host databases in primary mode. As we've noted, secondary servers do not participate in the Raft protocol, vote on transactions, or take part in leader elections. Instead, they stay in sync by pulling Raft logs from primaries at regular intervals, controlled by the `db.cluster.catchup.pull_interval` setting. This keeps them up to date without adding pressure on write operations.

In addition to scaling read queries across the cluster, secondary servers are also ideal for running analytical workloads, such as Graph Data Science. You can dedicate a secondary with higher memory and CPU specs to handle heavy analytics without impacting your transactional workload.

Figure 10-10 shows the previous three-node cluster extended with an additional secondary-only server.

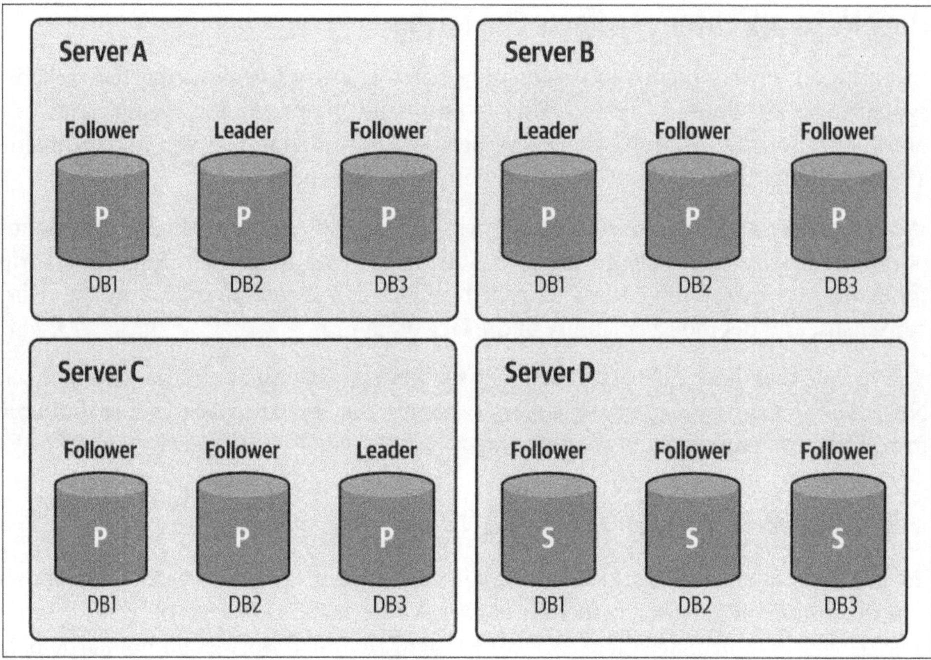

Figure 10-10. Cluster with secondaries

The cluster setup compose file in the companion repository has a commented section that adds two secondary servers. Uncomment those lines and run the following command to start the servers:

```
docker compose up -d
```

You will also see in the compose file that we explicitly specify the setting `initial.server.mode_constraint` as SECONDARY.

Run the following command in the Neo4j browser:

```
//004-show-servers.cypher
SHOW SERVERS
YIELD serverId, address, state, hosting
```

The result is shown in Figure 10-11.

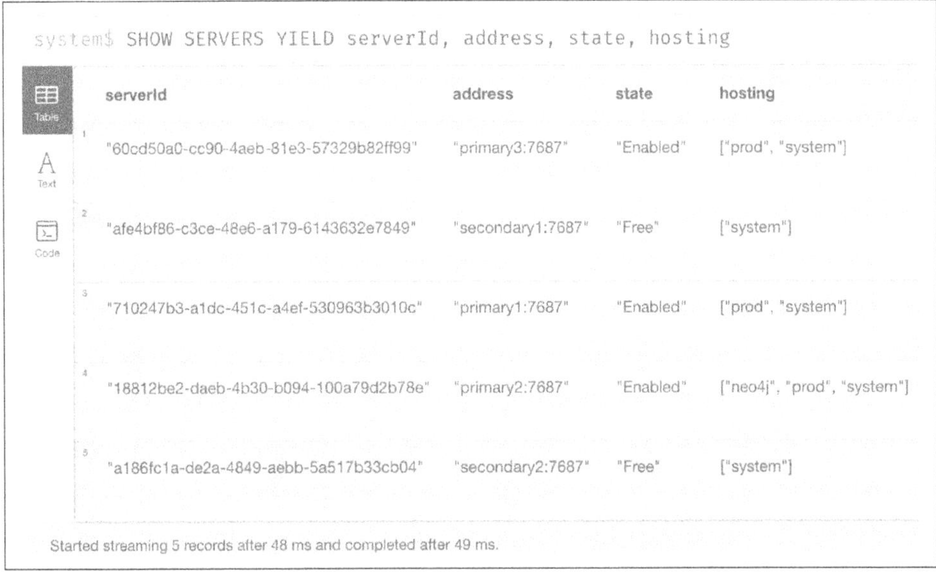

system$ SHOW SERVERS YIELD serverId, address, state, hosting

	serverId	address	state	hosting
1	"60cd50a0-cc90-4aeb-81e3-57329b82ff99"	"primary3:7687"	"Enabled"	["prod", "system"]
2	"afe4bf86-c3ce-48e6-a179-6143632e7849"	"secondary1:7687"	"Free"	["system"]
3	"710247b3-a1dc-451c-a4ef-530963b3010c"	"primary1:7687"	"Enabled"	["prod", "system"]
4	"18812be2-daeb-4b30-b094-100a79d2b78e"	"primary2:7687"	"Enabled"	["neo4j", "prod", "system"]
5	"a186fc1a-de2a-4849-aebb-5a517b33cb04"	"secondary2:7687"	"Free"	["system"]

Started streaming 5 records after 48 ms and completed after 49 ms.

Figure 10-11. Result of the `SHOW SERVERS` command with secondary servers

Secondary servers initially appear in a `Free` state, meaning they've been discovered by the cluster but are not yet active members. To add them to the cluster, you need to explicitly enable them.

Take the value from the `serverId` column for each secondary and run the following command:

```
ENABLE SERVER "<serverId>";
ENABLE SERVER "<serverId>";
```

Running `SHOW SERVERS` again will now show the secondary servers' state as `ENABLED`. For more details on various server states, refer to the cluster management section of the Neo4j documentation (*https://oreil.ly/F_VU1*).

Next, create a database with three primaries and two secondaries, using the following command:

```
//005-create-db-secondaries.cypher
CREATE DATABASE prod2 TOPOLOGY 3 PRIMARIES 2 SECONDARIES
```

Figure 10-12 shows that the prod2 database now runs on five instances in total: three primaries to ensure data integrity and two secondaries dedicated to scaling read throughput.

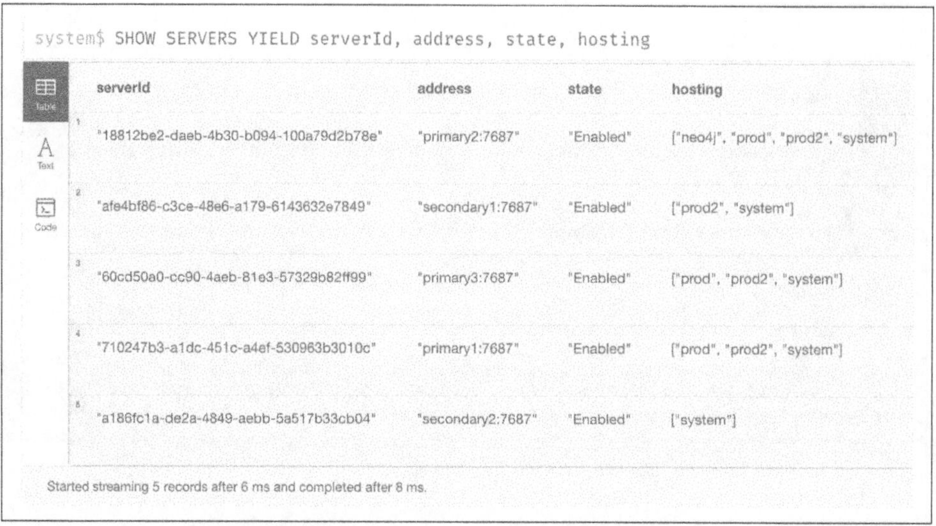
system$ SHOW SERVERS YIELD serverId, address, state, hosting

	serverId	address	state	hosting
1	"18812be2-daeb-4b30-b094-100a79d2b78e"	"primary2:7687"	"Enabled"	["neo4j", "prod", "prod2", "system"]
2	"afe4bf86-c3ce-48e6-a179-6143632e7849"	"secondary1:7687"	"Enabled"	["prod2", "system"]
3	"60cd50a0-cc90-4aeb-81e3-57329b82ff99"	"primary3:7687"	"Enabled"	["prod", "prod2", "system"]
4	"710247b3-a1dc-451c-a4ef-530963b3010c"	"primary1:7687"	"Enabled"	["prod", "prod2", "system"]
5	"a186fc1a-de2a-4849-aebb-5a517b33cb04"	"secondary2:7687"	"Enabled"	["system"]

Started streaming 5 records after 6 ms and completed after 8 ms.

Figure 10-12. Database with three primaries and two secondaries

Using Secondary Servers for Backups

While secondary servers aren't typically added to a cluster specifically for backups, their presence offers a valuable opportunity. Because they are read-only nodes that don't participate in Raft consensus or write operations, you can safely use them to run backups without affecting the transactional workload. This means that you can offload backup tasks to a secondary server, avoiding extra load on the primaries, which are busy handling writes and coordinating cluster state.

This setup allows you to take full advantage of your existing infrastructure, using secondary servers not only for read scaling and analytics, but also for operational tasks like backups. It's a simple yet effective way to improve reliability and reduce risk without adding complexity.

Beyond local backup use, secondary servers are also commonly deployed in offsite environments as part of disaster recovery (DR) strategies. In such setups, they act as continuously updated backup nodes located in a different datacenter or cloud region—providing an additional layer of protection in the event of a regional failure.

This setup allows you to maximize your existing infrastructure by using secondary servers not just for read scaling and analytics, but also for operational resilience, backups, and disaster recovery—all without adding complexity.

Causal Consistency

In a distributed Neo4j cluster, *causal consistency* guarantees that a client sees the effects of, at least, its previous writes, even when requests are routed to different servers. This is critical in systems where operations span multiple transactions or interact with different application components that use independent connections to the database.

Neo4j implements causal consistency through *bookmarks*: lightweight tokens that are returned to the client after a successful write transaction. Each token encodes a point in the causal history of the database (such as the last transaction the client has observed). When the client makes a subsequent request, it attaches the bookmark to ensure that the server it connects to has caught up to that point.

This mechanism ensures read-your-own-writes—meaning that a user can immediately read the data they just wrote, even when there is replication lag between primaries and secondaries.

Let's look at an example scenario for read after write across servers. Figure 10-13 illustrates causal consistency.

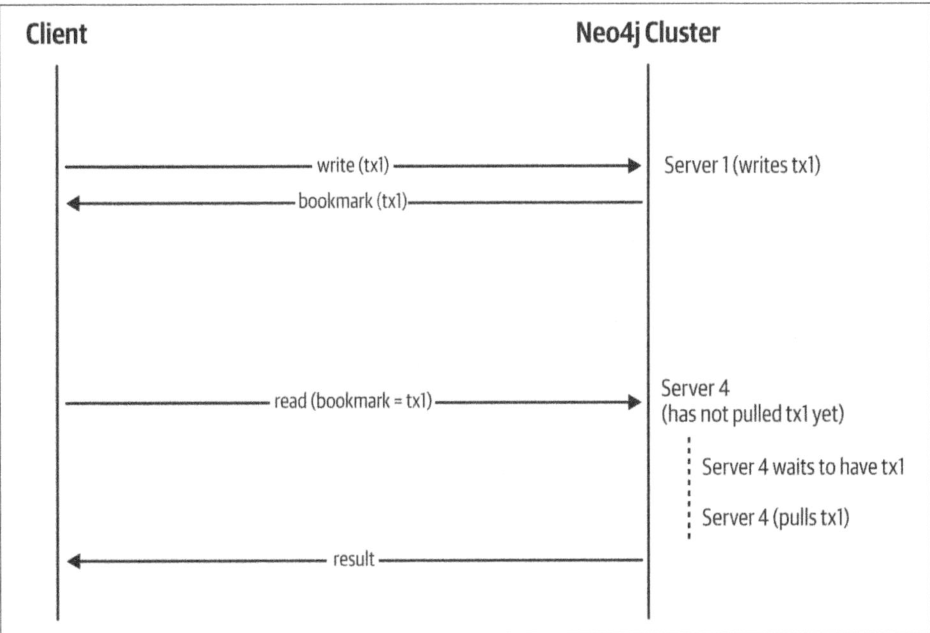

Figure 10-13. A causal-clustering transaction flow

In Figure 10-13, a client successfully performs a write on Server 1 and returns a bookmark. The client wants to read the data immediately, but the driver instead routes the read to Server 4, a secondary. If Server 4 hasn't yet replicated the write from Server 1, the read might not reflect the recent change. To prevent this, the client includes the bookmark with the read transaction. This is how Neo4j's driver ensures that the chosen server is caught up to the state represented by the bookmark, preserving causal consistency.

This system lets clients maintain a coherent view of the data across transactions, without requiring all operations to hit the primary. It's particularly effective in distributed environments, where routing and replication are abstracted away by the Neo4j driver.

The Mythical 1+1 Cluster

In their quests to cut costs, many organizations are tempted by a deceptively simple setup: one primary, one secondary. It looks like a cluster, sounds like a cluster, and even promises some level of fault tolerance. But in practice, this "1+1 cluster" is a fragile construct, more illusion than infrastructure. Here's why:

It's not really a cluster
: High availability requires consensus. With only two nodes, there's no quorum. If the primary fails, the secondary doesn't promote itself—it simply goes into read-only mode. Your application is suddenly unable to write, and you're left scrambling.

Data loss is a real risk
: The secondary is a follower, not a peer. It pulls updates from the primary and can lag behind it. If the primary fails before the secondary catches up, any unreplicated data is gone—no redo logs, no second chances.

Murphy's Law applies
: The danger isn't that this setup will always fail, it's that you *assume* it won't. And when you need high availability most, the unexpected happens. That one edge case, that one network glitch, that one kernel panic...if you assume nothing will fail, something inevitably will.

Recovery is painful
: Restarting services is one thing. Recovering a half-synced, unbalanced cluster without introducing split-brain or more data loss? That's another level of complexity. And every minute spent recovering is downtime you thought you were protected against.

If you're building for resilience, invest in a proper cluster, at least three members for online fault tolerance, proper monitoring, and tested failover procedures. The 1+1 cluster might seem like a shortcut, but more often than not, it's a trap.

Sharding and Federation

Chapter 8 introduced you to composite databases for offloading a portion of the data (the facts forming a fused resolved entity) to a separate graph when that data doesn't provide any more useful information to the main graph or would introduce too much noise. As you may recall, a *composite database* is a virtual construct that must be created explicitly and configured with references to its constituent databases.

Composite databases in Neo4j allow two things: sharding and federation.

Sharding is the practice of distributing data that shares the same model, labels, relationship types, and properties across multiple databases. Each shard holds a subset of the data, enabling better scalability and performance by spreading storage and query load. Sharding is useful when your dataset grows too large for a single database or when you want to isolate data for operational or geographical reasons.

Federation allows you to access and query across multiple graphs that may have different structures or serve different purposes. For example, one graph might contain user profiles, and another might store activity logs. With federation, you can combine insights from both in a single Cypher query without merging the data physically.

In both cases, the composite database acts as a logical entry point, giving you a unified view over multiple underlying databases, whether they are sharded replicas of the same model or diverse graphs used for federated analysis.

Let's circle back to the Chapter 8 use case and store the entity resolution facts in another database named `erfacts`:

```
//006-create-cs-1.cypher
CREATE DATABASE erfacts WAIT ;
:use erfacts ; // before next section
MERGE (a:Artist {id: "fused-3qm84nBOXUEQ2vnTfUTTFC"})
WITH a
UNWIND
[
{name: "Guns And Roses", id: "3qm84nBOXUEQ2vnTfUTTFC"},
{name: "G'N'R", id: "t5k9j2h7f1w6m3n8p4q0r2s6x"},
{name: "Guns n roses", id: "b7f3a2c9e5d1x8k6m4n0p2q9r"},
{name: "Guns n' roses", id: "z6r4k9n2h7p3m1j5f8x0w2d4q"}
] AS fact
MERGE (n:Artist {id: fact.id})
SET n.name = fact.name
SET n:Fact
MERGE (a)-[:FACT]->(n);
```

The main graph's original data can be created with the following query:

```
//007-create-cs-2.cypher
CREATE DATABASE songs WAIT ;
:use songs ; //before next section
```

```
MERGE (a:Artist {id: "fused-3qm84nBOXUEQ2vnTfUTTFC"})
WITH a
UNWIND [
"Patience", "Paradise City", "November Rain"
] AS track
MERGE (t:Track {id: randomUuid()})
SET t.name = track
MERGE (t)-[:ARTIST]->(a);
```

At this stage, you have two distinct databases, each holding a different portion of the data:

```
//008-create-composite.cypher
CREATE COMPOSITE DATABASE composed WAIT;
CREATE ALIAS composed.songs FOR DATABASE songs;
CREATE ALIAS composed.erfacts FOR DATABASE erfacts;
```

Figure 10-14 depicts the setup in one picture.

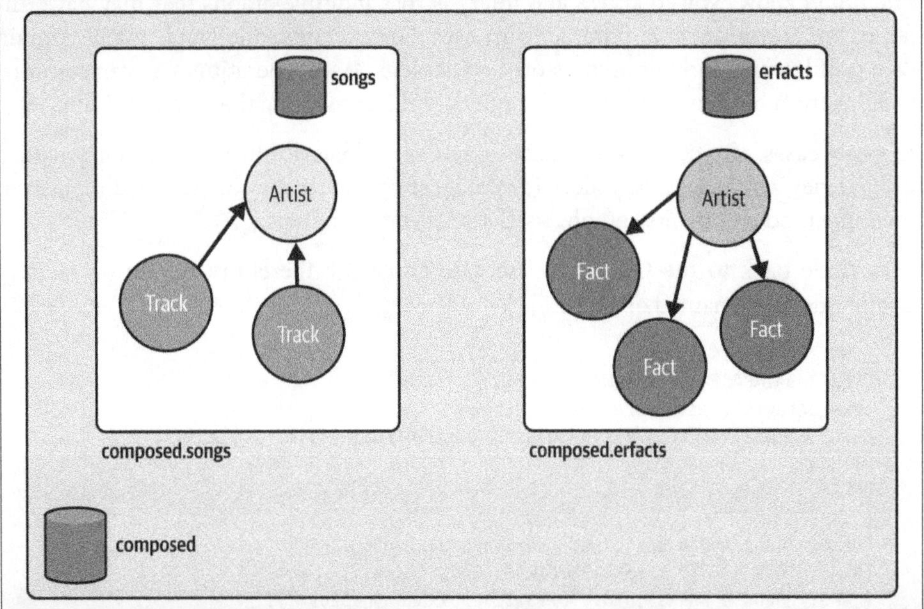

Figure 10-14. Composite databases setup

You can now either connect directly to one of the constituent databases or connect to the composite database in the same way you would connect to any individual database:

```
:USE composed
```

Running a query directly on the composite database won't fail, but it will return no results since the composite itself holds no data. To target a specific constituent, you need to use the special USE clause to route the query accordingly:

```
//009-composite-query-1.cypher
USE composed.songs
MATCH (n) RETURN count(n)
```

Although it's an easy mistake to make, don't confuse the USE clause with the :use command to connect to a database.

The query above returns only the count of nodes in the songs database. To query multiple constituents at once and get separate results for each, you can use the following query, which returns the node count from both constituents:

```
//010-composite-query-2.cypher
USE composed.songs
MATCH (n) RETURN count(n)
UNION
USE composed.erfacts
MATCH (n) RETURN count(n)
```

You can list all graphs, forming a composite:

```
UNWIND graph.names() AS name
RETURN name
```

Then use the exact same functions to execute a query on all constituents at once:

```
//011-composite-query-3.cypher
UNWIND graph.names() AS g
CALL(g) {
    USE graph.byName(g)
    MATCH (n) RETURN count(n) AS c
}
RETURN sum(c) AS totalNodes
```

Returning to the use case from Chapter 8, we can now traverse the songs graph and retrieve tracks along with their artist, without interference from the individual facts that originally formed the resolved `Artist` node. The result is the cleaner, focused graph shown in Figure 10-15:

```
//012-composite-query-4.cypher
USE composed.songs
MATCH (t:Track {name: "Patience"})
MATCH p=(t)-->(a:Artist)<--(t2)
RETURN p
```

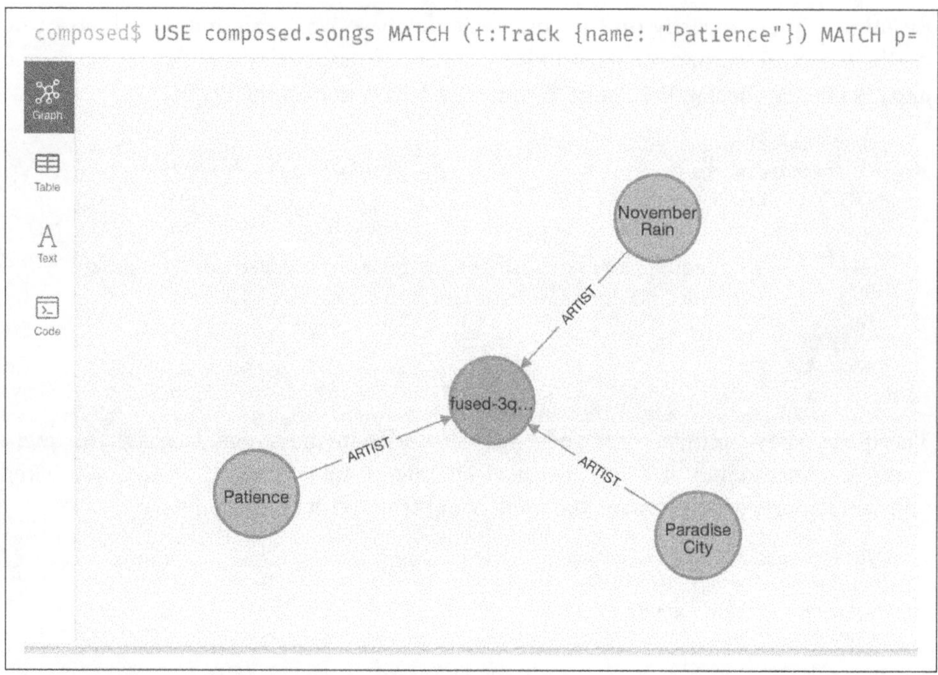

Figure 10-15. Composite query result from one graph

When needed, you can take advantage of the composite database structure to enrich your results with additional information from another constituent:

```
//013-composite-query-5.cypher
CALL {
    USE composed.songs
    MATCH (t:Track {name: "Patience"})
    MATCH p=(t)-->(a:Artist)<--(t2)
    RETURN a, p
}
WITH a.id AS artistId, p
CALL(artistId) {
    USE composed.erfacts
    MATCH (a2:Artist {id: artistId})
    MATCH fp=(a2)--(f:Fact)
    RETURN fp
}
RETURN p, fp
```

This yields a more comprehensive view, as illustrated in Figure 10-16.

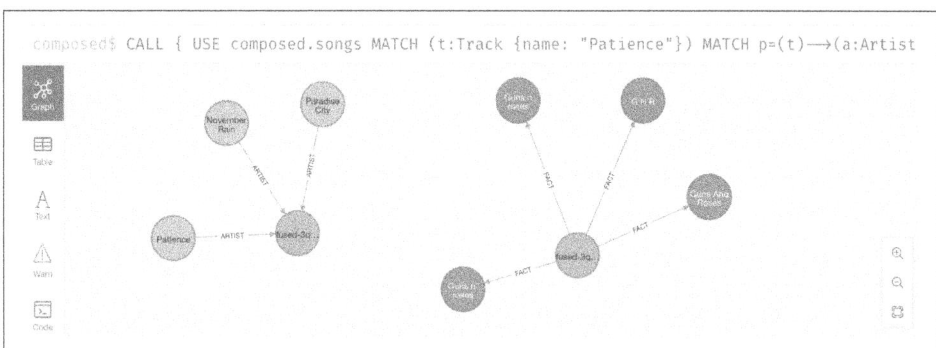

Figure 10-16. Composite database query result from two graphs

Nodes retrieved from two different databases will have distinct Neo4j internal IDs and therefore cannot be merged into a single node in the Neo4j browser. However, when building your own graph visualization, you can use business identifiers, such as a shared ID property, to represent them as a single logical entity.

Composite databases let you query multiple graphs, either sharded or federated, through a single logical entry point. They don't store data themselves but route queries to their defined constituents, enabling flexible, modular graph architectures.

Summary

As ElectricHarmony's reliance on Neo4j grew, so did its need for a resilient and scalable architecture. This chapter marked a key transition from a single-node setup to a robust cluster designed for fault tolerance, performance, and flexibility.

You've seen how Neo4j's clustering model ensures high availability through the Raft consensus protocol. Leader election, synchronous replication, and automatic failover protect against data loss and keep services running even in the face of hardware failures. Designing with the right number of primaries is essential to maintain quorum and ensure continued write capabilities.

Secondary servers extend the architecture's capabilities by scaling read throughput and supporting analytics and backups without impacting transactional performance. You deployed these components with Docker Compose, created databases with defined topologies, and simulated node failures to observe Neo4j's resilience in practice.

To ensure correctness in a distributed system, Neo4j uses causal consistency, with bookmarks allowing clients to safely read their own writes, even across different servers.

We also explored the limitations of simplistic deployments like the so-called 1+1 cluster, which may resemble a fault-tolerant setup but lacks quorum and promotes a false sense of reliability.

Finally, you were introduced to composite databases, Neo4j's solution for sharding and federation. Composite databases let you route queries across multiple graphs, whether partitioned for scale or purpose-built for different domains, through a single logical interface. This modular approach enables more scalable, maintainable graph solutions without compromising on expressiveness.

Clustering in Neo4j isn't just about uptime—it's about preparing your graph for the real world: failures, growth, and evolving data needs. It's the cornerstone of any serious deployment, enabling you to build systems that are dependable, elastic, and intelligent by design.

CHAPTER 11

Observability

ElectricHarmony has always prided itself on being a tech-forward, data-driven company. With a thriving business built around personalized music recommendations, its backbone is now Neo4j, a graph database that powers complex, real-time connections between users, songs, and trends. The company has been growing fast, and its Neo4j clusters are growing with it. However, with great scale comes great challenges.

As the system expands, the DevOps team starts to encounter occasional slowdowns and performance hiccups. What was once a flawless recommendation engine now sometimes falters—an unoptimized query here, a resource spike there—and these intermittent issues are becoming more frequent. ElectricHarmony's leadership is clear: the music can never stop.

It's time for the DevOps team to level up their game. They need to implement a robust observability strategy, something that allows them not only to react to incidents but proactively *prevent* them. The team understands that to keep the infrastructure modern and the services resilient, they have to evolve from traditional monitoring into full-scale observability. And Neo4j's logs and metrics hold the key.

This chapter details the next steps in ElectricHarmony's journey: how the DevOps team harnesses logs and metrics to understand what is really happening under the hood, pinpoint bottlenecks, and ensure the system can handle increasing user demand. They recognize that building modern, reliable infrastructure means more than just monitoring for crashes; it requires continuous insight into the health and performance of every component.

In this chapter, we'll show you how ElectricHarmony leverages Neo4j's logging and metrics capabilities to establish a robust observability framework. We explore the various types of logs generated by Neo4j, how to configure and manage them, and the key metrics that provide insights into system performance and health to ensure the reliability and efficiency of the graph-database infrastructure.

Harnessing the Power of Logs

Logs are the silent storytellers of any system, revealing the intricate events that occur behind the scenes. For ElectricHarmony, Neo4j's robust logging capabilities transform a continuous stream of raw data into meaningful insights that drive decision making and enhance system performance.

Consider a scenario where the Neo4j server unexpectedly exhausts its memory resources. Without detailed logs, diagnosing the root cause would be like searching for a needle in a haystack. However, with comprehensive logging in place, the team can swiftly identify the last query executed before the crash. This pinpoint accuracy allows them to address inefficient queries, optimize memory usage, and prevent similar incidents from disrupting the seamless experience ElectricHarmony is known for.

Security is another critical area where logs shine. Imagine a user attempting to access sensitive information, such as unauthorized personnel details. Through meticulous log analysis, the DevOps team can detect these unauthorized access attempts, thanks to the repudiation principles we discussed in Chapter 6.

Optimizing performance is equally crucial for maintaining a responsive and efficient system. Logs provide invaluable insights into query performance, revealing patterns that could indicate underlying issues. For instance, if certain queries consistently take longer than 10 seconds to execute, this may signal missing indexes or suboptimal query designs.

In essence, logs transform raw data into actionable intelligence, empowering ElectricHarmony's DevOps team to make informed decisions. Whether it's preventing system outages, enforcing security protocols, or optimizing performance, logs provide the clarity and depth they need to maintain a robust and efficient Neo4j infrastructure.

Types of Logs in Neo4j

Neo4j's sophisticated logging system provides four essential types of logs, each serving a distinct purpose:

Neo4j
: This log provides general information about the Neo4j server's operations. It is typically the first log you encounter and offers a broad overview of the system's status and activities.

Debug
: When investigating issues, the debug log becomes invaluable. It captures detailed information that helps in diagnosing and resolving problems within the Neo4j environment.

Query
: This log records all queries executed against the Neo4j database. It allows the team to monitor query performance, identify inefficient queries, and optimize database interactions.

Security
: Security events, such as user privilege escalations and unauthorized access attempts, are documented in the security log. This ensures that any security breaches or suspicious activities are promptly detected and addressed.

The location and configuration of these log files can vary depending on the deployment environment. For detailed information on their locations, refer to the Neo4j documentation (*https://oreil.ly/Kfpjf*).

Configuring Neo4j Logs

To utilize Neo4j's logging capabilities effectively, it is essential to understand the default logging configuration. Neo4j typically uses two primary configuration files:

- *user-logs.xml* for the Neo4j log
- *server-logs.xml* for the other logs

The locations of these files will depend on your specific Neo4j deployment and operating system. For instance, when using Docker, you can view the *server-logs.xml* configuration by executing the following command:

```
docker exec -it neo4j-tdg cat /var/lib/neo4j/conf/server-logs.xml
```

Refer to the Neo4j documentation (*https://oreil.ly/FMF0m*) to find the file locations for your environment.

These configuration files are structured into two main sections: appenders and loggers.

Appenders

Appenders define the destinations and formats for log output. They determine:

Output destinations
: Whether logs are written to files, the console, or a centralized logging system

File management
: How frequently log files are rolled over and how many historical files are retained

Log formats
: The format in which logs are recorded, such as plain text, JSON, or CSV

Event publication
: Which log events are published and how they are disseminated

Loggers

Loggers control the specifics of what gets logged and how it is managed. They specify:

Log event capture
: Which types of log events are captured and directed to specific appenders

Log levels
: The severity levels of log events to be recorded, such as `DEBUG`, `INFO`, `WARN`, or `ERROR`

Log forwarding
: Whether log events should be forwarded to other loggers for additional processing or storage

By combining loggers and appenders, the team can tailor their logging strategy to meet ElectricHarmony's specific needs. For example, they might configure logs from an internal ETL tool to be excluded from general logs; ensure that all security-related events at the `DEBUG` level and above are captured in the security log files; and set these files to a maximum size of 50MB each, while retaining the last 70 files to maintain sufficient history for investigating security incidents.

Inspecting Logs

Let's start with the Neo4j log.

Neo4j log

As outlined earlier, its configuration resides in the *user-logs.xml* file. Inspect it with the following command:

```
docker exec -it neo4j-tdg cat /var/lib/neo4j/conf/user-logs.xml
```

The result is displayed in Figure 11-1.

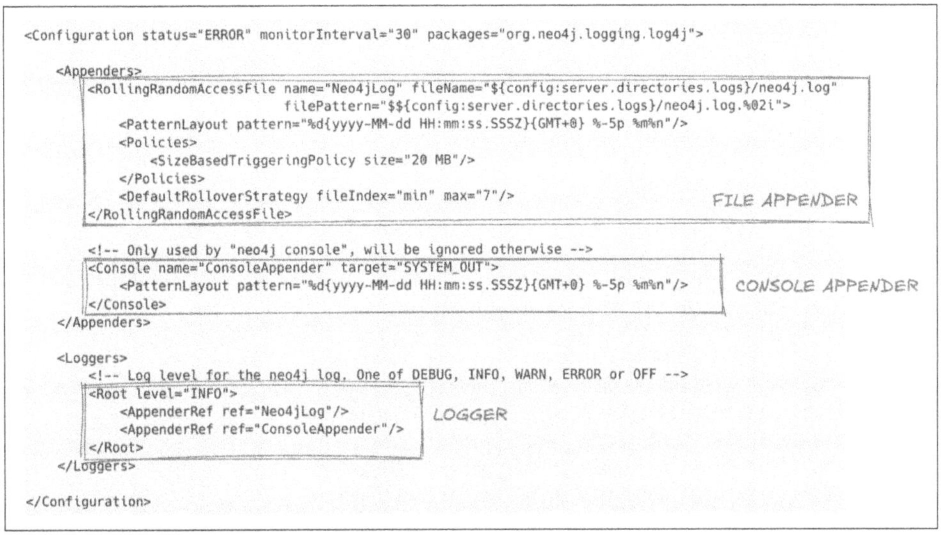

```
<Configuration status="ERROR" monitorInterval="30" packages="org.neo4j.logging.log4j">

    <Appenders>
        <RollingRandomAccessFile name="Neo4jLog" fileName="${config:server.directories.logs}/neo4j.log"
                                 filePattern="$${config:server.directories.logs}/neo4j.log.%02i">
            <PatternLayout pattern="%d{yyyy-MM-dd HH:mm:ss.SSSZ}{GMT+0} %-5p %m%n"/>
            <Policies>
                <SizeBasedTriggeringPolicy size="20 MB"/>
            </Policies>
            <DefaultRolloverStrategy fileIndex="min" max="7"/>
        </RollingRandomAccessFile>                                         FILE APPENDER

        <!-- Only used by "neo4j console", will be ignored otherwise -->
        <Console name="ConsoleAppender" target="SYSTEM_OUT">
            <PatternLayout pattern="%d{yyyy-MM-dd HH:mm:ss.SSSZ}{GMT+0} %-5p %m%n"/>   CONSOLE APPENDER
        </Console>
    </Appenders>

    <Loggers>
        <!-- Log level for the neo4j log. One of DEBUG, INFO, WARN, ERROR or OFF -->
        <Root level="INFO">
            <AppenderRef ref="Neo4jLog"/>                  LOGGER
            <AppenderRef ref="ConsoleAppender"/>
        </Root>
    </Loggers>

</Configuration>
```

Figure 11-1. The user-logs.xml configuration for the Neo4j log

The `Loggers` section specifies the use of two appenders: the `Neo4jLogAppender` and the `ConsoleAppender`.

The `ConsoleAppender` directs logs to the system console. In the context of this book, where Neo4j is deployed using Docker, the console corresponds to the Neo4j container's standard output logs. You can view these logs by executing the following command:

```
docker logs neo4j-tdg
```

The output is:

```
2024-10-11 12:11:09.693+0000 INFO  Starting...
2024-10-11 12:11:11.081+0000 INFO  ======== Neo4j 5.26.0 ========
(truncated)
2024-10-11 12:11:13.122+0000 INFO  Bolt enabled on 0.0.0.0:7687.
2024-10-11 12:11:13.125+0000 INFO  Bolt (Routing) enabled on 0.0.0.0:7688.
2024-10-11 12:11:13.496+0000 INFO  id: D5951A16D8861CA9DA4358097C4214323AFA4E41DD
2024-10-11 12:11:13.496+0000 INFO  name: system
2024-10-11 12:11:13.496+0000 INFO  creationDate: 2024-10-11T09:51:10.043Z
2024-10-11 12:11:13.496+0000 INFO  Started.
```

In addition to the console output, Neo4j writes logs to a dedicated *neo4j.log* file on disk. According to the Neo4j file locations documentation (*https://oreil.ly/l-0Yk*), this file is located at */var/lib/neo4j/logs/neo4j.log*. To view its contents, use the following Docker command:

```
docker exec -it neo4j-tdg cat /var/lib/neo4j/logs/neo4j.log
```

The Neo4j log primarily records essential events, such as the Neo4j server starting and stopping, errors encountered during startup (for example, if a port cannot be bound), and other general informational messages.

Security log

You will now inspect the security log file, located at */var/lib/neo4j/logs/security.log* using the following command:

```
docker exec -it neo4j-tdg tail -n 10 /var/lib/neo4j/logs/security.log
```

This will output the last 10 lines from its content, showing that the Neo4j user logged in at the times shown in the beginning of each line:

```
2024-10-11 12:11:17.994+0000 INFO  [neo4j]: logged in
2024-10-11 12:11:18.012+0000 INFO  [neo4j]: logged in
2024-10-11 12:50:10.977+0000 INFO  [neo4j]: logged in
2024-10-11 12:50:11.003+0000 INFO  [neo4j]: logged in
2024-10-11 12:50:11.017+0000 INFO  [neo4j]: logged in
2024-10-11 12:50:11.038+0000 INFO  [neo4j]: logged in
2024-10-11 13:48:53.444+0000 INFO  [neo4j]: logged in
2024-10-11 13:48:53.460+0000 INFO  [neo4j]: logged in
2024-10-11 13:48:53.474+0000 INFO  [neo4j]: logged in
2024-10-11 13:48:53.497+0000 INFO  [neo4j]: logged in
```

As you learned in Chapter 6, the security logs will log every event that affects the security of the system, run the following command in your Neo4j browser:

```
CREATE ROLE observer;
GRANT ACCESS ON DATABASE neo4j TO observer;
```

Now check the security logs again:

```
2024-10-11 14:25:55.241+0000 INFO  [neo4j]: CREATE ROLE observer
2024-10-11 14:26:48.197+0000 INFO  [neo4j]: GRANT ACCESS ON DATABASE neo4j
TO observer
```

Debug log

The debug log, located at */var/lib/neo4j/logs/debug.log*, can be quite verbose. Instead of displaying all the contents of this file, you will start following it from the last line. *Following* the log means that your command remains open and new log output is shown as it arrives. Run the following command and keep it running:

```
docker exec -it neo4j-tdg tail -n 0 -f /var/lib/neo4j/logs/debug.log
```

To produce logs, go to the Neo4j browser and create a new database:

```
CREATE DATABASE observability WAIT;
```

The full output of the log is too long to be meaningful on a book page, but here are the last lines, which show that the database has transitioned to a `STARTED` state:

```
2024-10-11 14:54:03.608+0000 INFO  [c.n.d.r.DbmsReconciler]
Database 'observability' transition is complete from
INITIAL{db=observability/baf33ee4} to STARTED{db=observability/baf33ee4}
(request by SystemGraph:Transaction:107 (requestCount:2))
2024-10-11 14:54:03.608+0000 INFO  [c.n.d.r.o.TopologyGraphOperators]
Reconciliation completed of Transaction:107
2024-10-11 14:54:03.811+0000 INFO  [c.n.c.d.d.TopologyState]
Leader for {baf33ee4}/observability is now
LeaderInfo{RaftMemberId{01e9a757} with term 0} on server {01e9a757}/ME!
2024-10-11 14:54:03.811+0000 INFO  [c.n.c.d.d.TopologyState]
Database {baf33ee4}/observability on {01e9a757}/ME! now has state STARTED
2024-10-11 14:54:03.811+0000 INFO [c.n.c.d.d.TopologyState]
Database {baf33ee4}/observability on {01e9a757}/ME!
is discoverable in mode SINGLE and publishing RaftMemberId{01e9a757}
```

A lot of valuable information can be found in the *debug.log* files, such as database startup issues, clustering events, and index population status.

Press `CTRL+C` to close the log output.

Query log

The query log is located at */var/lib/neo4j/logs/query.log*. The following command outputs the last three lines of the log:

```
docker exec -it neo4j-tdg tail -n 3 logs/query.log

2024-10-11 15:04:28.138+0000 INFO  id:1229 - transaction id:4614 - 3 ms:
(planning: 2, waiting: 0) - -1 B - 0 page hits, 0 page faults - bolt-session
bolt    neo4j-browser/v5.24.0        client/192.168.65.1:54645
server/172.19.0.2:7687>    system - neo4j - CALL dbms.showCurrentUser() - {}
- runtime=system - {app: 'neo4j-browser_v5.24.0', type: 'system'}
```

A query log entry can span multiple lines, so getting the last line of the query can return a partial entry.

Table 11-1 details the contents of the query log.

Table 11-1. Inventory of the query log

`2024-10-11 15:04:28.138+0000`	The timestamp of the log entry
`INFO`	The log category
`id:1229`	The query ID

`transaction id:4614`	The transaction ID
`3 ms: (planning: 2, waiting: 0)`	The total execution time of the transaction, time spent planning (for the execution plan to be created), and time spent waiting (for example, for other transactions to complete and a lock to be released)
`1B`	The amount of heap memory used during the lifetime of the query
`0 page hits, 0 page faults`	Amount of hits that were and were not returned from the page cache
`bolt-session`	The session type
`bolt`	The protocol used between the application and the database for the query
`neo4j-browser/v5.24.0`	The driver version
`client/192.168.65.1:54645`	The query client outbound IP:port used
`server/172.19.0.2:7687`	The server listening IP:port used
`system`	The database on which this query was executed
`neo4j`	Username of the query executioner
`CALL dbms.showCurrentUser() - {}`	The query and parameters
`runtime=system`	The runtime used to run the query
`{app: 'neo4j-browser_v5.24.0', type: 'system'}`	Transaction metadata

The query log contains a lot of information that can be useful for analysis and traceability. You can filter on each element of an entry in the logging configuration to determine which log events you want to appear in the query log, or to be used as filters in your centralized logging systems. For example, you might want to identify who has run a query on the system database in the last 5 minutes.

That leads to the question: who ran this query? In the case above, it was you, as the user `neo4j`. But you did not connect to the system database yourself, nor did you run the `CALL dbms.showCurrentUser()` query. In fact, the Neo4j browser runs system queries like these in the background; this one displays your username and roles in the side panel. Other queries that run in the background gather lists of property keys, labels, and relationship types for the database you are currently using in order to show statistics or provide autocompletion when you type your query.

In the next section, you will learn how to customize the logging system to fit your specific needs, ensuring that only relevant logs are retained.

GC log

The garbage collection (GC) log in Neo4j records detailed information about garbage-collection events in the Java virtual machine (JVM). It's useful for understanding memory-usage patterns, diagnosing performance issues, and identifying bottlenecks caused by excessive GC activity. By analyzing *gc.log*, you can detect symptoms like long GC pauses that can impact the database's throughput and latency. This helps the DevOps team make informed decisions about JVM tuning and memory management, for smoother operation and better performance.

You've learned about Neo4j logs, their purposes, configurations, and storage methods. This includes file-based logs with rolling strategies, console output logs, and the query log for analysis. Additionally, Neo4j browser's background queries enhance statistics and the developer experience.

Taming the Query Log

This section explores the ins and outs of the query log, including tailoring its configuration to suit your requirements. Before proceeding, it is important to understand that in addition to the logging configuration defined in *server-logs.xml*, other settings influence the behavior of the query log. These settings are located in the general Neo4j configuration file, *neo4j.conf*, and include:

`db.logs.query.enabled`
: Possible values are `OFF`, `INFO`, or `VERBOSE`. `OFF` disables query logging, `INFO` logs at the end of the queries that have either succeeded or failed, and `VERBOSE` logs at the beginning and end of the queries (more info on that later). The default value is `VERBOSE`.

`db.logs.query.parameter_logging_enabled`
: Whether or not query parameters should be logged, this can contain sensitive information. The default value is `true`.

`db.logs.query.threshold`
: If the query takes longer than the threshold time, the query will be logged when completed. A threshold of 0s will log all queries. The default value is 0s.

To configure other fine-grained settings, see the Neo4j logging documentation (*https://oreil.ly/CZF37*).

VERBOSE logging

The `VERBOSE` level of the `db.logs.query.enabled` setting logs queries at the beginning and end of their execution. If you take query `id:1229` from Table 11-1 and find all logs related to that ID, you will actually find two log entries. The first entry logs when the query starts, and the second records its completion:

```
2024-10-11 15:04:28.134+0000 INFO  Query started: id:1229 - transaction id:4614
- 0 ms: (planning: 0, waiting: 0) - 0 B - 0 page hits, 0 page faults -
bolt-session    bolt    neo4j-browser/v5.24.0        client/192.168.65.1:54645
server/172.19.0.2:7687>    system - neo4j - CALL dbms.showCurrentUser() - {}
- runtime=null - {app: 'neo4j-browser_v5.24.0', type: 'system'}

2024-10-11 15:04:28.138+0000 INFO  id:1229 - transaction id:4614 - 3 ms:
```

```
(planning: 2, waiting: 0) - -1 B - 0 page hits, 0 page faults - bolt-session
bolt     neo4j-browser/v5.24.0         client/192.168.65.1:54645
server/172.19.0.2:7687>    system - neo4j - CALL dbms.showCurrentUser() - {}
- runtime=system - {app: 'neo4j-browser_v5.24.0', type: 'system'}
```

At first glance, maintaining such detailed logs might seem excessive, potentially cluttering your log files with redundant information. However, there is a significant advantage to keeping `VERBOSE` logging enabled.

Imagine that a poorly optimized query consumes more heap memory than the server can handle, triggering an `OutOfMemory` exception and causing the server to crash. In this situation, the query never reaches completion, leaving you without any logs to trace the cause of the memory exhaustion. Capturing a log event at the start of each query ensures that even incomplete or failed queries are documented, allowing you to identify the problematic query and understand the underlying reasons for the server disruption.

Filtering out log events

You might not need to monitor the queries the Neo4j browser executes automatically; these can be filtered out. Each query log entry includes metadata that identifies the application running the query, such as `neo4j-browser_v5.24.0`. Additionally, as mentioned earlier in this chapter, the appenders section of the logging configuration can incorporate filters to determine which log events are captured. You can use this information to configure a filter on the appender that excludes log events originating from the Neo4j browser.

Exercise caution when filtering queries: users may execute queries directly within the Neo4j browser. To configure your filter, examine what occurs when you run a query yourself. Open the Neo4j browser and execute the following query:

```
MATCH (n:Playlist) RETURN count(n);
```

Now, locate the query logs that include the string `MATCH (n:Playlist)`. You will find eight log entries that match your search criteria:

```
docker exec -it neo4j-tdg cat /var/lib/neo4j/logs/query.log | grep \
 'MATCH (n:Playlist)'
```

The output is:

```
2024-10-11 10:08:23.676+0000 INFO  Query started: id:384 - transaction id:163
- 5 ms: (planning: 5, waiting: 0) - 0 B - 0 page hits, 0 page faults
- bolt-session  bolt    neo4j-browser/v5.24.0           client/192.168.65.1:22929
server/172.19.0.2:7687> neo4j - neo4j - EXPLAIN MATCH (n:Playlist)
2024-10-11 10:08:23.686+0000 INFO  id:384 - transaction id:163 - 15 ms:
(planning: 14, waiting: 0) - 0 B - 0 page hits, 0 page faults - bolt-session
bolt     neo4j-browser/v5.24.0           client/192.168.65.1:22929
server/172.19.0.2:7687> neo4j - neo4j - EXPLAIN MATCH (n:Playlist)
2024-10-11 10:08:23.692+0000 INFO  Query started: id:385 - transaction id:164
```

```
- 3 ms: (planning: 3, waiting: 0) - 0 B - 0 page hits, 0 page faults
- bolt-session  bolt    neo4j-browser/v5.24.0          client/192.168.65.1:36741
server/172.19.0.2:7687> neo4j - neo4j - MATCH (n:Playlist)
2024-10-11 10:08:23.693+0000 INFO  id:385 - transaction id:164 - 5 ms:
(planning: 4, waiting: 0) - 312 B - 0 page hits, 0 page faults - bolt-session
bolt    neo4j-browser/v5.24.0          client/192.168.65.1:36741
server/172.19.0.2:7687> neo4j - neo4j - MATCH (n:Playlist)
2024-10-11 17:21:29.557+0000 INFO  Query started: id:2612 - transaction id:889
- 5 ms: (planning: 5, waiting: 0) - 0 B - 0 page hits, 0 page faults
- bolt-session  bolt    neo4j-browser/v5.24.0          client/192.168.65.1:21950
server/172.19.0.2:7687> neo4j - neo4j - EXPLAIN MATCH (n:Playlist)
RETURN count(n) - {} - runtime=null - {app: 'neo4j-browser_v5.24.0',
type: 'user-action'}
2024-10-11 17:21:29.568+0000 INFO  id:2612 - transaction id:889 - 16 ms:
(planning: 15, waiting: 0) - 0 B - 2 page hits, 0 page faults - bolt-session
bolt    neo4j-browser/v5.24.0          client/192.168.65.1:21950
server/172.19.0.2:7687> neo4j - neo4j - EXPLAIN MATCH (n:Playlist)
RETURN count(n) - {} - runtime=pipelined - {app: 'neo4j-browser_v5.24.0',
type: 'user-action'}
2024-10-11 17:21:31.386+0000 INFO  Query started: id:2613 - transaction id:890
- 5 ms: (planning: 5, waiting: 0) - 0 B - 0 page hits, 0 page faults
- bolt-session  bolt    neo4j-browser/v5.24.0          client/192.168.65.1:21950
server/172.19.0.2:7687> neo4j - neo4j - MATCH (n:Playlist) RETURN count(n);
- {} - runtime=null - {app: 'neo4j-browser_v5.24.0', type: 'user-direct'}
2024-10-11 17:21:31.388+0000 INFO  id:2613 - transaction id:890 - 7 ms:
(planning: 6, waiting: 0) - 312 B - 1 page hits, 0 page faults - bolt-session
bolt    neo4j-browser/v5.24.0          client/192.168.65.1:21950
server/172.19.0.2:7687> neo4j - neo4j - MATCH (n:Playlist) RETURN count(n);
- {} - runtime=pipelined - {app: 'neo4j-browser_v5.24.0', type: 'user-direct'}
```

The Neo4j browser proactively executes an `EXPLAIN` on your query as you type, offering immediate feedback on potential syntax errors or unoptimized patterns. Fortunately, the metadata included in the Neo4j browser's query logs allows you to distinguish between queries initiated by the browser and those executed by the user. The `type` field within the metadata can have four distinct values, enabling precise filtering and analysis:

`system`
: A query automatically run by the app, such as the `dbms.showCurrentUser()` procedure shown in the previous section

`user-direct`
: A query directly submitted by the user, as you can see in the last lines of the logs you just got

`user-action`
: A query resulting from an action the user performed, like the automated `EXPLAIN` queries the browser is executing based on what you type in the browser

`user-derived`
: A query that has been *transpiled*, or rewritten by Neo4j from the user's original input into a form that the database engine can execute efficiently

You now have all the necessary information to create a filter that excludes all queries originating from the Neo4j browser while retaining user-direct queries.

Neo4j uses Log4j2 as its logging infrastructure. The following snippet shows a regular expression (regex)-based filter that will exclude log entries that match the regex provided. The regex complies with our requirement to keep user-direct queries, even if they come from the Neo4j browser:

```
<RegexFilter regex="(?si)^(?=.*neo4j-browser/v)(?!.*user-direct).*"
onMatch="DENY" onMismatch="ACCEPT"/>
```

Add this filter inside the Filters section of the `QueryLog` appender:

```
<RollingRandomAccessFile
    name="QueryLog"
    fileName="${config:server.directories.logs}/query.log"
    filePattern="$${config:server.directories.logs}/query.log.%02i">
  <PatternLayout pattern="%d{yyyy-MM-dd HH:mm:ss.SSSZ}{GMT+0} %-5p %m%n"/>
  <Policies>
    <SizeBasedTriggeringPolicy size="20 MB"/>
  </Policies>
  <DefaultRolloverStrategy fileIndex="min" max="7"/>
  <Filters>
    <RegexFilter regex="(?si)^(?=.*neo4j-browser/v)(?!.*user-direct).*"
                 onMatch="DENY"
                 onMismatch="ACCEPT"/>
  </Filters>
</RollingRandomAccessFile>
```

The companion Docker repository is configured to use the custom *server-logs.xml* file. To enable it, uncomment the following line in the Volumes section of the *docker-compose.yml* file, then restart Neo4j with the `docker compose up -d` command:

```
# - "./conf/server-logs.xml:/var/lib/neo4j/conf/server-logs.xml"
```

You can now test by running the `MATCH (n:Playlist) RETURN count(n)` query in the Neo4j browser a few times. Observe that the query log no longer includes queries run automatically by the Neo4j browser:

```
2024-10-11 17:43:04.030+0000 INFO  Query started: id:32 - transaction id:10 -
  5 ms: (planning: 5, waiting: 0) - 0 B - 0 page hits, 0 page faults -
  bolt-session    bolt    neo4j-browser/v5.24.0   client/192.168.65.1:35599
  server/172.1
2024-10-11 17:43:04.033+0000 INFO  id:32 - transaction id:10 - 7 ms:
  (planning: 6, waiting: 0) - 312 B - 1 page hits, 0 page faults -
  bolt-session    bolt    neo4j-browser/v5.24.0   client/192.168.65.1:35599
  server/172.19.0.2:7687>
2024-10-11 17:47:00.390+0000 INFO  Query started: id:156 - transaction id:57 -
```

```
  0 ms: (planning: 0, waiting: 0) - 0 B - 0 page hits, 0 page faults -
  bolt-session    bolt    neo4j-browser/v5.24.0   client/192.168.65.1:35599
  server/172.
2024-10-11 17:47:00.392+0000 INFO  id:156 - transaction id:57 - 2 ms:
  (planning: 1, waiting: 0) - 312 B - 1 page hits, 0 page faults -
  bolt-session    bolt    neo4j-browser/v5.24.0   client/192.168.65.1:35599
  server/172.19.0.2:7687>
```

The first line of the *server-logs.xml* file includes the setting `monitor Interval="30"`, indicating that Neo4j will reload the configuration every 30 seconds and apply changes as needed. This means you don't need to restart the Neo4j server to log configuration updates.

Enriching the metadata

In Chapter 6, you learned how to enhance Neo4j's transaction metadata with additional details. For example, when your application uses a Neo4j service account, it is a best practice to include the logged-in user in the metadata. Additionally, specifying your application's name allows you to trace queries back to their sources, which is especially useful in a microservices architecture.

We recommend you use the same metadata types as Neo4j, such as `system`, `user-direct`, `user-action`, and `user-derived`. For instance, if a user performs a search in your application, it is classified as a user-direct query. Conversely, if your application gathers information about indexes, it is considered a system query.

You can add metadata to transactions using the Neo4j drivers. The following example adds `electric_harmony` as the application name and `user-direct` as the type to the metadata, using the Python driver.

Python:

```
from neo4j import GraphDatabase
from neo4j import unit_of_work

URI = 'bolt://localhost:7687'
AUTH = ('neo4j', 'password')


@unit_of_work(
  timeout=5,
  metadata={"app": "electric_harmony", "type": "system"}
)
def count_playlists(tx):
    result = tx.run("MATCH (n:Playlist) RETURN count(n) AS count")
    record = result.single()
    return record["count"]

with GraphDatabase.driver(URI, auth=AUTH) as driver:
```

```
with driver.session(database="neo4j") as session:
    playlists_count = session.execute_read(count_playlists)
    print(playlists_count)
```

Inspect the query logs. You can see that the metadata correctly contains `electric_harmony` as app and `system` as type:

```
2024-10-11 19:18:14.618+0000 INFO  Query started: id:2 - transaction id:2 -
  0 ms: (planning: 0, waiting: 0) - 0 B - 0 page hits, 0 page faults -
  bolt-session    bolt    neo4j-python/5.25.0 Python/3.12.6-final-0 (darwin)
  client/192.168
2024-10-11 19:18:14.621+0000 INFO  id:2 - transaction id:2 -
  3 ms: (planning: 2, waiting: 0) - 312 B - 1 page hits, 0 page faults -
  bolt-session    bolt    neo4j-python/5.25.0 Python/3.12.6-final-0 (darwin)
  client/192.168.65.1:41691
```

Having this metadata in place allows you to inspect logs for a particular application only, or decide not to capture some logs—for example, queries executed by your internal application, `electric_harmony`.

Identifying long-running queries

Now that you're familiar with inspecting logs, simulating a long-running query, you can run the following command in the Neo4j browser, which will pause for 10 seconds:

```
CALL apoc.util.sleep(10000)
```

The query logs include the time it took for the query to complete:

```
2024-10-11 19:33:09.639+0000 INFO  id:147 - transaction id:55 -
  10012 ms: (planning: 5, waiting: 0) - 312 B - 0 page hits, 0 page faults -
  bolt-session    bolt    neo4j-browser/v5.24.0 client/192.168.65.1:53547
  server/172.19.0.2:7687>    neo4j - neo4j - CALL apoc.util.sleep(10000) -
  {} - runtime=pipelined - {app: 'neo4j-browser_v5.24.0', type: 'user-direct'}
```

You can now inspect the logs and return only the ones that took more than 5,000ms:

```
docker exec -it neo4j-tdg cat /var/lib/neo4j/logs/query.log | grep -E
  ' ([5-9][0-9]{3}|[1-9][0-9]{4,}) ms:'
```

This returns:

```
2024-10-11 10:18:14.370+0000 ERROR id:721 - transaction id:328 -
  77137 ms: (planning: 10, waiting: 0) - 664320 B - 82811 page hits,
  0 page faults - bolt-session  bolt  neo4j-browser/v5.24.0
  client/192.168.65.1:22929    server/172.19.0
2024-10-11 19:33:09.639+0000 INFO  id:147 - transaction id:55 -
  10012 ms: (planning: 5, waiting: 0) - 312 B - 0 page hits,
  0 page faults - bolt-session    bolt    neo4j-browser/v5.24.0
  client/192.168.65.1:53547    server/172.19.0.2:76 T
```

The command above is not something you'll run often. The last section of this chapter will demonstrate how centralized logging systems can make inspecting logs easier.

Monitoring queries that take longer than a specified threshold to complete is critically valuable: it can give you insights into which queries you could optimize or help you identify if you could create a valuable new index to help with such queries.

There are countless ways to implement Log4j2 filters for query logs, and our accompanying GitHub repository offers several examples to guide you.

Now that you know how to use, inspect, configure, and attach metadata to your logs, you are prepared to dive into another key aspect of observability: metrics.

Unveiling the Power of Metrics

Metrics are an essential pillar of observability, providing quantifiable insights into the health and performance of your Neo4j database. While logs tell the story of what has happened and are good for retrospective analysis, *metrics* offer a real-time snapshot of system behavior, helping you identify trends, detect anomalies, and make informed decisions to maintain system stability.

In this section, we focus on the most crucial metrics, including server load, Neo4j load, and Neo4j workload. Understanding these metrics allows you to pinpoint performance bottlenecks, optimize resource usage, and keep your database operating smoothly under varying workloads.

Enabling Metrics

By default, Neo4j's metrics system is enabled, but its default configuration outputs metrics as CSV files. This may be useful for some infrastructures, but it's not ideal for modern centralized logging systems. In this section, you will configure the metrics to be provided in Prometheus format.

Prometheus is an open-source monitoring and alerting toolkit designed for collecting and querying metrics from various services and applications. It uses a time-series database to store metrics data, making it an ideal solution for monitoring system performance and providing real-time insights into the health of your infrastructure.

To enable the Prometheus metrics and disable the CSV ones, provide the following configuration:

```
server.metrics.prometheus.enabled=true
server.metrics.csv.enabled=false
```

The Docker Compose deployment used throughout this book already contains the adapted configuration for metrics.

Prometheus metrics must be exposed over the HTTP(S) protocol to be scraped by the Prometheus server. You can view the metrics Neo4j exposes by opening the following URL in your browser: *http://localhost:2004*. Figure 11-2 shows part of its output. There are over 500 metrics available; you can find information about all of them in the Neo4j documentation (*https://oreil.ly/cZCi9*).

```
# HELP neo4j_database_system_db_query_execution_latency_millis Generated from Dropwizard metric import (metric=neo4j.database.s
# TYPE neo4j_database_system_db_query_execution_latency_millis summary
neo4j_database_system_db_query_execution_latency_millis{quantile="0.5",} 0.0
neo4j_database_system_db_query_execution_latency_millis{quantile="0.75",} 0.0
neo4j_database_system_db_query_execution_latency_millis{quantile="0.95",} 0.0
neo4j_database_system_db_query_execution_latency_millis{quantile="0.98",} 0.0
neo4j_database_system_db_query_execution_latency_millis{quantile="0.99",} 0.0
neo4j_database_system_db_query_execution_latency_millis{quantile="0.999",} 0.0
neo4j_database_system_db_query_execution_latency_millis_count 0.0
# HELP neo4j_database_system_pool_transaction_system_total_used Generated from Dropwizard metric import (metric=neo4j.database.
# TYPE neo4j_database_system_pool_transaction_system_total_used gauge
neo4j_database_system_pool_transaction_system_total_used 0.0
# HELP neo4j_database_system_pool_transaction_system_used_heap Generated from Dropwizard metric import (metric=neo4j.database.s
# TYPE neo4j_database_system_pool_transaction_system_used_heap gauge
neo4j_database_system_pool_transaction_system_used_heap 0.0
# HELP neo4j_database_system_cypher_cache_executable_query_stale_entries_total Generated from Dropwizard metric import (metric=
# TYPE neo4j_database_system_cypher_cache_executable_query_stale_entries_total counter
neo4j_database_system_cypher_cache_executable_query_stale_entries_total 0.0
# HELP neo4j_database_system_cypher_cache_executable_query_entries Generated from Dropwizard metric import (metric=neo4j.databa
# TYPE neo4j_database_system_cypher_cache_executable_query_entries gauge
neo4j_database_system_cypher_cache_executable_query_entries 0.0
# HELP neo4j_database_system_transaction_rollbacks_write_total Generated from Dropwizard metric import (metric=neo4j.database.s
# TYPE neo4j_database_system_transaction_rollbacks_write_total counter
neo4j_database_system_transaction_rollbacks_write_total 0.0
# HELP neo4j_database_system_transaction_committed_read_total Generated from Dropwizard metric import (metric=neo4j.database.sy
# TYPE neo4j_database_system_transaction_committed_read_total counter
neo4j_database_system_transaction_committed_read_total 40.0
# HELP neo4j_database_system_db_query_execution_failure_total Generated from Dropwizard metric import (metric=neo4j.database.sy
# TYPE neo4j_database_system_db_query_execution_failure_total counter
neo4j_database_system_db_query_execution_failure_total 0.0
```

Figure 11-2. Prometheus metrics results in part

Covering each metric in detail would require an entire book of its own, so we will focus on the essential metrics and how they assist ElectricHarmony's team in their Neo4j observability journey.

The figures in this chapter are intended as high-level illustrations to support the conceptual explanations. They are not optimized for print and may lack fine detail. For clearer versions, please refer to the companion GitHub repository (*https://oreil.ly/2wcKZ*).

Server Load Metrics

Server load metrics offer insights into your hardware resources and the strain on the server running Neo4j.

Key server load metrics include CPU usage, memory usage, and free disk space. If CPU usage is nearing 100%, this suggests the need to add more CPUs to improve server performance. High RAM usage indicates a risk of running out of memory, while low disk space can lead to out-of-disk events, which could potentially cause a server crash and risk corrupting Neo4j's data stores.

Neo4j does not provide those metrics itself. You can use utilities such as the `collectd` daemon to collect them. The last section of this chapter includes an example of collecting such metrics with your Docker containers.

Neo4j Load Metrics

Neo4j load metrics provide information about the strain that Neo4j is being put under and can help with capacity planning. The most notable load metrics Neo4j provides are:

Heap usage
: If Neo4j consistently uses 100% of its heap, consider increasing the initial and `max_heap_size` values to allocate more memory to the heap.

Page cache hit and usage ratio
: The *page cache hit* metric indicates the percentage of requests served by the page cache. When requests miss the page cache, data must be loaded from disk, which is significantly slower. Ideally, the hit ratio should be around 98%. The *usage ratio* shows the percentage of page cache memory used. If this approaches 100%, or if you observe query degradation despite a high hit ratio, consider increasing the memory allocated to the page cache.

JVM garbage collection
: This metric represents the proportion of time the JVM spends reclaiming heap memory rather than performing other tasks. It can spike when the database is running low on memory, potentially halting processing and causing query execution errors. If this occurs, consider increasing the memory allocated to your database.

The following examples show how to read some of the Neo4j load metrics:

- Amount of heap used (value in bytes):

  ```
  curl http://localhost:2004 | grep 'neo4j_dbms_vm_heap_used'
  ```

  The output is:

```
# HELP neo4j_dbms_vm_heap_used Generated from Dropwizard metric import
# TYPE neo4j_dbms_vm_heap_used gauge
neo4j_dbms_vm_heap_used 1.87379792E8
```

Approximately 178MB of heap memory is used.

- Accumulated garbage collection time (value in milliseconds):

```
curl http://localhost:2004 | grep 'vm_gc_time'
```

The output is:

```
# HELP neo4j_dbms_vm_gc_time_g1_young_generation_total Generated from Dropwizard
# TYPE neo4j_dbms_vm_gc_time_g1_young_generation_total counter
neo4j_dbms_vm_gc_time_g1_young_generation_total 109.0
# HELP neo4j_dbms_vm_gc_time_g1_old_generation_total Generated from Dropwizard
# TYPE neo4j_dbms_vm_gc_time_g1_old_generation_total counter
neo4j_dbms_vm_gc_time_g1_old_generation_total 0.0
```

- Page cache metrics:

```
curl http://localhost:2004 | grep 'page_cache'
```

The output is:

```
# HELP neo4j_dbms_page_cache_usage_ratio Generated from Dropwizard
# TYPE neo4j_dbms_page_cache_usage_ratio gauge
neo4j_dbms_page_cache_usage_ratio 0.07495404411764706
# HELP neo4j_dbms_page_cache_hit_ratio Generated from Dropwizard
# TYPE neo4j_dbms_page_cache_hit_ratio gauge
neo4j_dbms_page_cache_hit_ratio 1.0
# HELP neo4j_dbms_page_cache_page_faults_total Generated from Dropwizard
# TYPE neo4j_dbms_page_cache_page_faults_total counter
neo4j_dbms_page_cache_page_faults_total 4970.0
100 57547  100 57547    0     0  8827k      0 --:--:-- --:--:-- --:--:--
# HELP neo4j_dbms_page_cache_hits_total Generated from Dropwizard
# TYPE neo4j_dbms_page_cache_hits_total counter
neo4j_dbms_page_cache_hits_total 287626.0
```

All queries (1.0 = 100%) hit the page cache.

Neo4j Workload Metrics

Neo4j workload metrics provide insight into the workflow of a Neo4j instance. Key metrics include Bolt metrics, object count metrics, and throughput metrics.

Bolt metrics

Bolt metrics show the number of connections currently executing Cypher queries and returning results. For example, if you open two browser tabs and simulate long-running queries with `CALL apoc.util.sleep(30000)`, you can inspect the number of active connections using the following command:

```
curl http://localhost:2004 | grep 'connections_running'
```

The output is:

```
# HELP neo4j_dbms_bolt_connections_running Generated from Dropwizard
# TYPE neo4j_dbms_bolt_connections_running gauge
neo4j_dbms_bolt_connections_running 2.0
```

Object count metrics

Object count metrics provide node and relationship counts, prefixed with the database name. One of each metric is available per database:

```
curl -s http://localhost:2004 | grep 'count.node'
```

The output is:

```
# HELP neo4j_database_system_neo4j_count_node Generated from Dropwizard
# TYPE neo4j_database_system_neo4j_count_node gauge
neo4j_database_system_neo4j_count_node 60.0
# HELP neo4j_database_neo4j_neo4j_count_node Generated from Dropwizard
# TYPE neo4j_database_neo4j_neo4j_count_node gauge
neo4j_database_neo4j_neo4j_count_node 127669.0
# HELP neo4j_database_observability_neo4j_count_node Generated from Dropwizard
# TYPE neo4j_database_observability_neo4j_count_node gauge
neo4j_database_observability_neo4j_count_node 0.0
```

The neo4j database has 127,669 nodes.

A significant drop in the number of nodes or relationships in ElectricHarmony's Neo4j database could indicate an unintended action by an external process, such as the ETL. For instance, it would be highly unusual for 1,000 playlists to disappear from the graph within a short time frame. Monitoring this metric would enable your team to discover a possible issue early.

Throughput metrics

Throughput metrics provide a histogram of 95th- and 99th-percentile transaction latencies. The 95th and 99th percentiles are used to understand the performance of your system under most conditions, excluding the rare extreme outliers. For example, the 95th-percentile latency tells you that 95% of all transaction latencies are below this value, while the 99th percentile means that 99% are below that threshold. This helps you identify how well your system is performing for almost all users and whether there are any concerning spikes that impact a significant portion of the workload:

```
curl -s  http://localhost:2004 | grep 'execution_latency_millis' | grep neo4j_db
```

The output is:

```
# HELP neo4j_database_neo4j_db_query_execution_latency_millis Generated
# TYPE neo4j_database_neo4j_db_query_execution_latency_millis summary
neo4j_database_neo4j_db_query_execution_latency_millis{quantile="0.5",} 3.0
neo4j_database_neo4j_db_query_execution_latency_millis{quantile="0.75",} 5.5
```

```
neo4j_database_neo4j_db_query_execution_latency_millis{quantile="0.95",} 17.79999
neo4j_database_neo4j_db_query_execution_latency_millis{quantile="0.98",} 68.83999
neo4j_database_neo4j_db_query_execution_latency_millis{quantile="0.99",} 1144.060
neo4j_database_neo4j_db_query_execution_latency_millis{quantile="0.999",} 1166.0
neo4j_database_neo4j_db_query_execution_latency_millis_count 101.0
```

In the next section, we will combine logs and metrics to demonstrate a practical example, using Grafana and Loki for effective monitoring and analysis.

Bringing It All Together: Logs and Metrics with Grafana, Loki, and Prometheus

Grafana, Loki, and Prometheus are powerful tools. Together, they create a complete observability stack. Grafana provides rich visualizations and dashboards for monitoring system performance, Loki serves as a log-aggregation system that integrates seamlessly with Grafana, and Prometheus is responsible for collecting and storing metrics data in a time-series format.

In this practical example, Prometheus will collect Neo4j metrics, Grafana will visualize these metrics in customizable dashboards, and Loki will aggregate and analyze the Neo4j logs. We will also create a dashboard for monitoring essential metrics and inspecting logs. By combining these tools, we will create an integrated observability solution that offers a complete view of Neo4j's performance, from system metrics to detailed log events, empowering you to monitor, troubleshoot, and optimize your Neo4j deployment.

Setting Up the Observability Stack

Providing instructions on how to install and configure every one of these components would be way beyond the scope of this book. However, the companion GitHub repository comes with everything you need to get up and running.

First, you can start the whole stack along with Neo4j by running the following command:

```
docker compose -f docker-compose.yml -f docker-compose-observability.yml up -d
```

The following services will start:

Grafana
: Interactive visualization interface

Prometheus
: Metrics collector

Loki
: Logs aggregator service

Node exporter
: For collecting the operating system metrics

Promtail
: Logs collector

To begin, go to Grafana at localhost:3000 and log in with the username `neo4j-tdg` and password `password`. You should land on the welcome page, as shown in Figure 11-3. Note that these screenshots were taken in light mode for better rendering in the book, but your experience will be in dark mode by default.

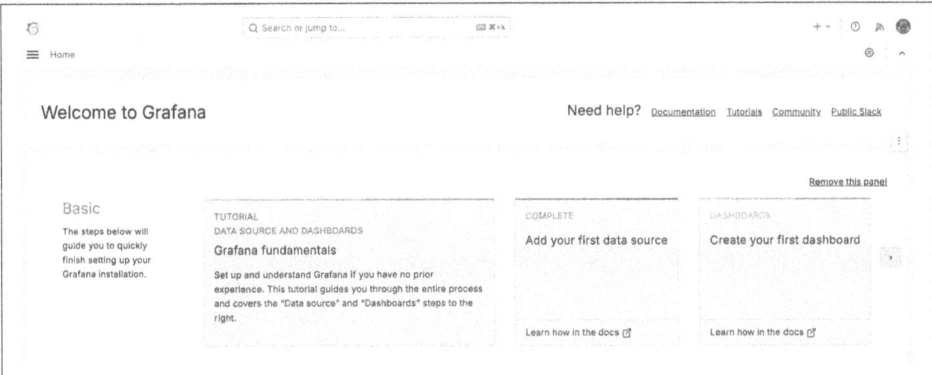

Figure 11-3. Grafana landing page

Prometheus and Loki for Grafana are preconfigured.

Visualizing Metrics

Go to the side panel and click on Metrics, then select Datasource: Prometheus, as shown in Figure 11-4.

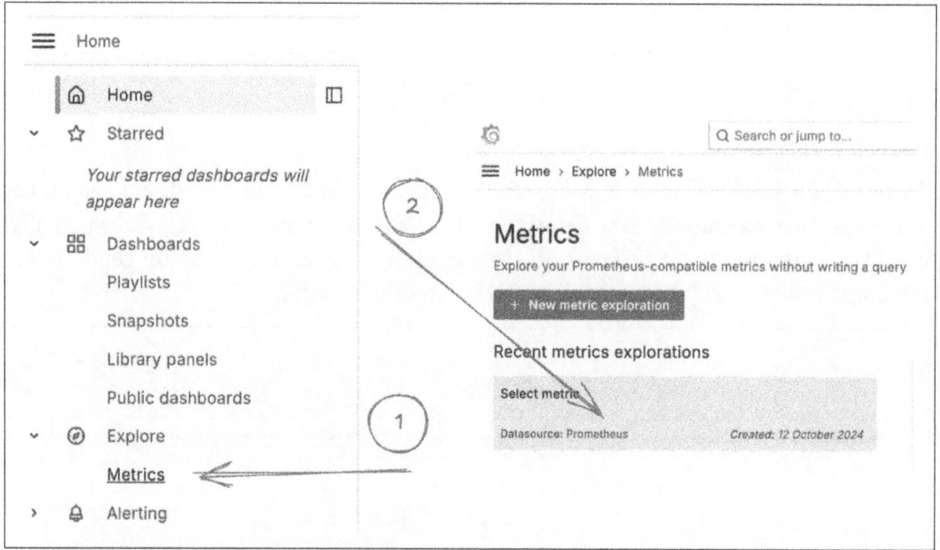

Figure 11-4. Grafana select metrics explorer

You will then land on a dashboard that shows all available metrics. While the order may vary, Figure 11-5 shows what your dashboard should look like.

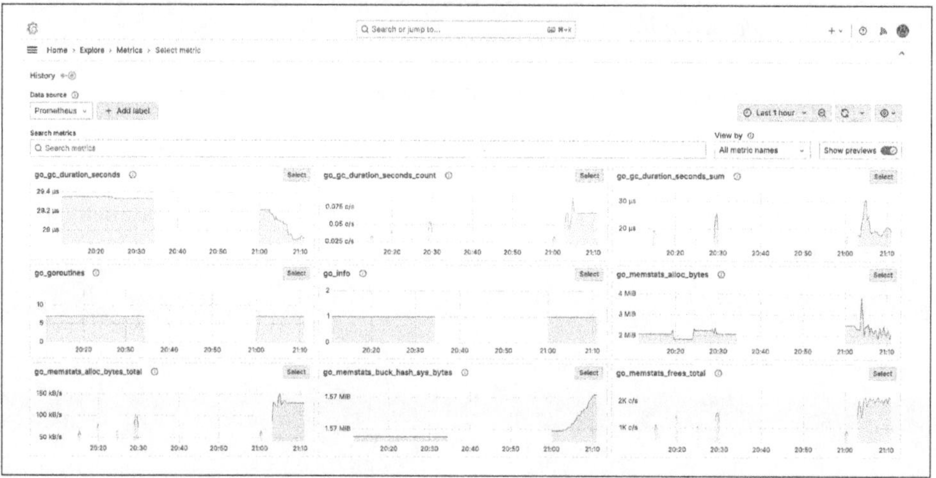

Figure 11-5. Grafana metrics dashboard

You will now see live metrics showing the increase or decrease of node counts in the database. You can search for a specific metric, such as `neo4j_database_neo4j_neo4j_count_node`, as shown in Figure 11-6.

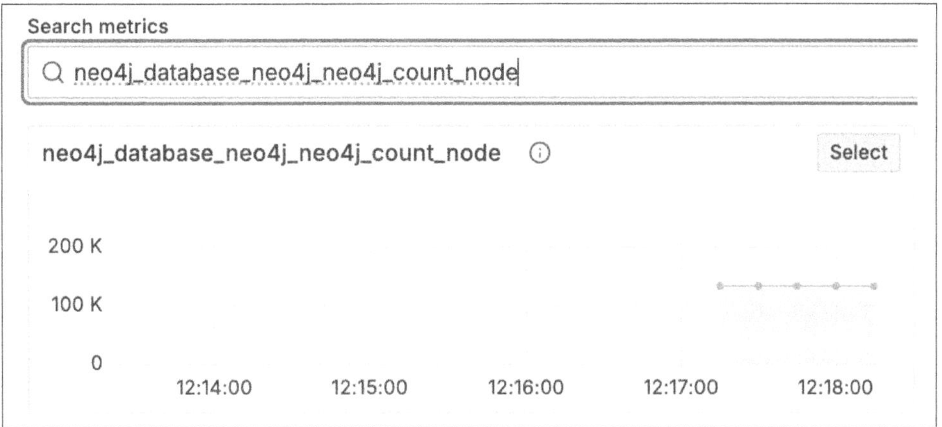

Figure 11-6. Grafana metrics for node count

Go to Neo4j and create or delete nodes with the following queries:

```
UNWIND range(1,5000) AS i CREATE (n:TestNode);
// wait a minute or two
MATCH (n:TestNode) WITH n LIMIT 1000 DELETE n;
```

Click on the refresh button to view the increase or decrease in the dashboard chart, as shown in Figure 11-7.

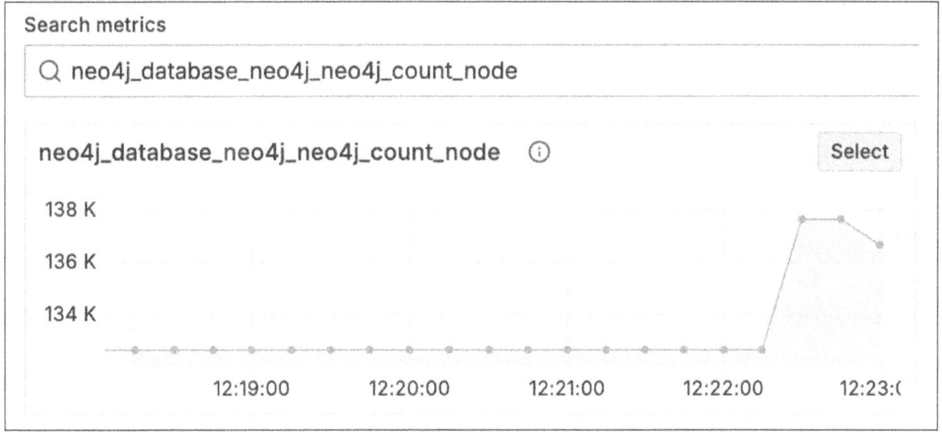

Figure 11-7. Grafana metrics observing node count increase and decrease

You can visualize the change in node count over the last defined time window using the delta function: `delta(neo4j_database_neo4j_neo4j_count_node{}[5m])`

You can also configure an alert for a decrease in node count. For example, you could send an email if more than 5,000 nodes are deleted within five minutes. Refer to the Grafana (*https://oreil.ly/1IPE4*) documentation for alert rules.

Querying Logs

Next, we'll show you how to query and filter logs based on your needs. The importance of well-defined metadata will become more apparent here.

In the side panel, click on Explore, and then select the Loki data source, as shown in Figure 11-8.

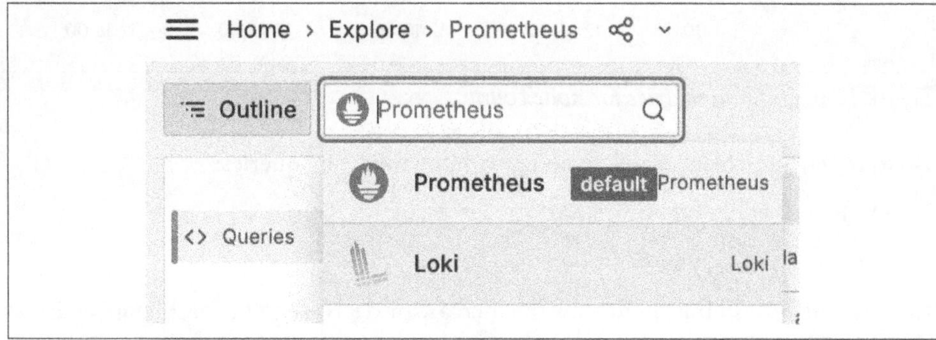

Figure 11-8. Grafana switch to Loki logs explorer

This brings you to the Logs explorer. To query logs, you will need to use the Loki query language. This is beyond the scope of this book, so please follow the provided query examples.

Step 1: Get all the logs

To retrieve all logs, run the following query:

```
{job="neo4j", filename="/logs/query.log"} | json
```

Note the end of the query, `| json`. The companion repository configures Neo4j logs to be written in JSON format, which is structured and works well with centralized logging systems like Loki. Figure 11-9 shows the latest Neo4j query logs.

Figure 11-9. Logs exploration with Grafana

Every field, such as database, query time, etc., becomes what is called a *label* in Loki and can be used to easily filter logs. For example, to search all logs for the neo4j database but exclude others, you can use the following query:

```
{job="neo4j", filename="/logs/query.log"} | json | database="neo4j"
```

Step 2: Filter by application

The following Python script will execute a query with parameters and add metadata, as discussed earlier in this chapter.

Python:

```
from neo4j import GraphDatabase
from neo4j import unit_of_work

URI = 'bolt://localhost:7687'
AUTH = ('neo4j', 'password')


@unit_of_work(
  timeout=5,
  metadata={"app": "electric_harmony", "type": "user-direct"}
)
def search_playlist(tx):
    result = tx.run(
        """
        MATCH (n:Track)
        WHERE toLower(n.name) CONTAINS $name
        RETURN n.name AS name
        LIMIT 1""",
```

```
        {'name': 'thunder'}
        )
    record = result.single()
    return record["name"]

with GraphDatabase.driver(URI, auth=AUTH) as driver:
    with driver.session(database="neo4j") as session:
        playlist_match = session.execute_read(search_playlist)
        print(playlist_match)
```

You can now adapt your Loki query to search only for logs whose metadata has `electric_harmony` as the app:

```
{job="neo4j", filename="/logs/query.log"} | json | database="neo4j" |
annotationData_app="electric_harmony"
```

The results are shown in Figure 11-10.

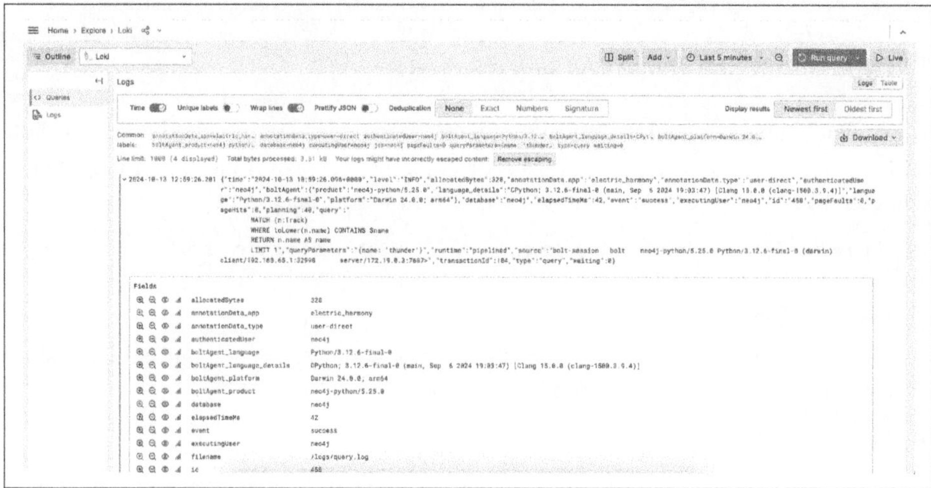

Figure 11-10. Logs filtering by application with Grafana

Step 3: Filter by query time

This quickly becomes routine: you have an available log label to filter on, such as query time, and you apply a filter accordingly. To find logs for queries that took more than 3 seconds, use the following query:

```
{job="neo4j", filename="/logs/query.log"} | json | database="neo4j" |
elapsedTimeMs >= 3000
```

Figure 11-11 shows the result.

Figure 11-11. Logs filtering by query time

Step 4: Combine them all

For the final query, we will combine multiple filters. We will search for entries where the database is `neo4j`, the source is the `electric_harmony` application, and parameters match the string `thunder`:

```
{job="neo4j", filename="/logs/query.log"} | json | database="neo4j" |
queryParameters =~ ".*thunder.*"
```

See the results in Figure 11-12.

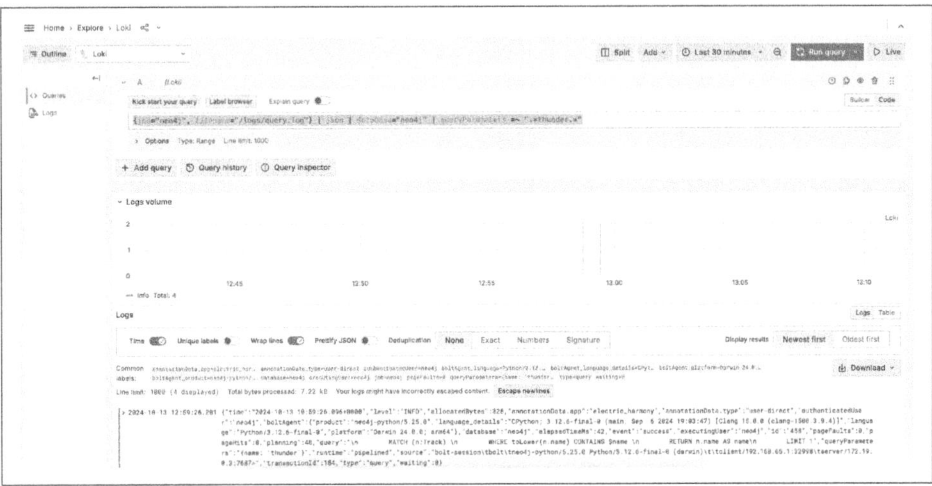

Figure 11-12. Logs filtering by query parameters

Other Tools

Neo4j Ops Manager (*https://oreil.ly/3uCZm*) is a UI-based tool to monitor metrics and logs and administer the database.

If you use Neo4j Aura, also check out the Query analyzer (*https://oreil.ly/Fk7Ju*). It's an easy way to review queries and shows a timeline of metrics about the number of queries, their latency, and failures, in addition to providing summary and detailed views of queries for a specific time period.

Summary

In this chapter, you covered the essentials of observability and its role in maintaining a robust Neo4j deployment. You learned about the different types of logs that Neo4j provides, with a focus on the query logs, which offer particularly insightful opportunities for analysis. You also explored the various types of metrics available, highlighting the most essential ones for understanding system performance and health.

You then learned how logs and metrics can be integrated into an observability stack using Grafana, Prometheus, and Loki. These tools work together to help you monitor, troubleshoot, and optimize your Neo4j environment effectively. With this knowledge, you are now equipped to leverage observability practices to ensure your database remains healthy and performs at its best.

CHAPTER 12

Practical Graph Data Science

ElectricHarmony is at the forefront of innovation. Now the data science team, always eager to explore new technologies, is faced with a challenge: how can they provide more personalized and engaging experiences for their users? Despite their advanced analytics and machine learning capabilities, they realize they're missing a crucial element—understanding the complex relationships within their data.

Enter the Graph Data Science (GDS) library in Neo4j. Unlike traditional data science methods, GDS offers a powerful way to model and analyze the intricate connections between entities, allowing for deeper insights and more effective solutions. Recognizing the potential of graphs, the team at ElectricHarmony decides to dive into this exciting field. In this chapter, we'll follow their journey as they leverage the power of graphs to revolutionize their service. We'll introduce the general concepts of GDS and demonstrate how to use it to uncover hidden patterns and insights.

One of the team's primary objectives is to enhance user engagement by understanding natural groupings in user behavior through community detection. Rather than starting from predefined genres or labels, they use algorithms to uncover clusters of users with similar listening habits. This insight enables features like collaborative playlists and targeted recommendations that reflect real user preferences, rather than editorial assumptions. By aligning musical content more closely with user behavior, the team creates a more relevant and enjoyable experience for listeners.

In this chapter, we will develop an effective process for creating GDS pipelines using Neo4j. We'll focus on how to iteratively build and refine these pipelines to analyze complex networks within ElectricHarmony's music streaming platform. By learning how to implement community detection algorithms and evaluate their results, you'll gain the skills needed to uncover meaningful patterns in your data. This iterative approach will enable you to continuously improve your models, leading to more accurate content recommendations and enhanced user engagement strategies.

It's time to elevate your data science game and make your data work harder for you. Welcome to the exciting world of graph-powered insights!

Introduction to the Graph Data Science Library

The Neo4j GDS library offers high-performance, parallel implementations of essential graph algorithms, accessible through Cypher procedures. Beyond algorithms, GDS also features ML pipelines designed to train predictive supervised models, enabling solutions for graph-centric challenges like predicting missing relationships.

Algorithms

Graph algorithms compute metrics for graphs, nodes, or relationships, providing insights into key entities (such as centralities and rankings) and underlying structures (like communities through community detection, graph partitioning, and clustering).

These algorithms often employ iterative approaches, usually traversing the graph using techniques like random walks, breadth-first searches, depth-first searches, pattern matching, graph embeddings, and pathfinding. Due to the exponential increase in possible paths as the graph distance grows, many graph algorithms have high computational complexity.

Fortunately, you can use optimized algorithms that leverage specific graph structures, memorize explored sections, and parallelize operations. Whenever feasible, these optimizations are incorporated into GDS. The Neo4j GDS library includes a comprehensive collection of these algorithms, detailed in the Neo4j documentation (*https://oreil.ly/Kw8Eb*).

The Graph Catalog

To maximize algorithm efficiency, GDS uses a specialized graph format that is compact and amenable to parallelism. This requires loading a subset of the graph data from the Neo4j database into an in-memory graph catalog. You can control the amount of data you load by using *graph projections*, which allow you to filter by node labels, relationship types, and other criteria.

You will often adopt the same flow when using GDS (pictured in Figure 12-1). First you'll read a relevant portion of the data stored in the database and load it into memory in the graph catalog as a named graph. From there, you will run your algorithms of choice on the named graph, which will return the algorithm results. Optionally, you can write those results back to the database.

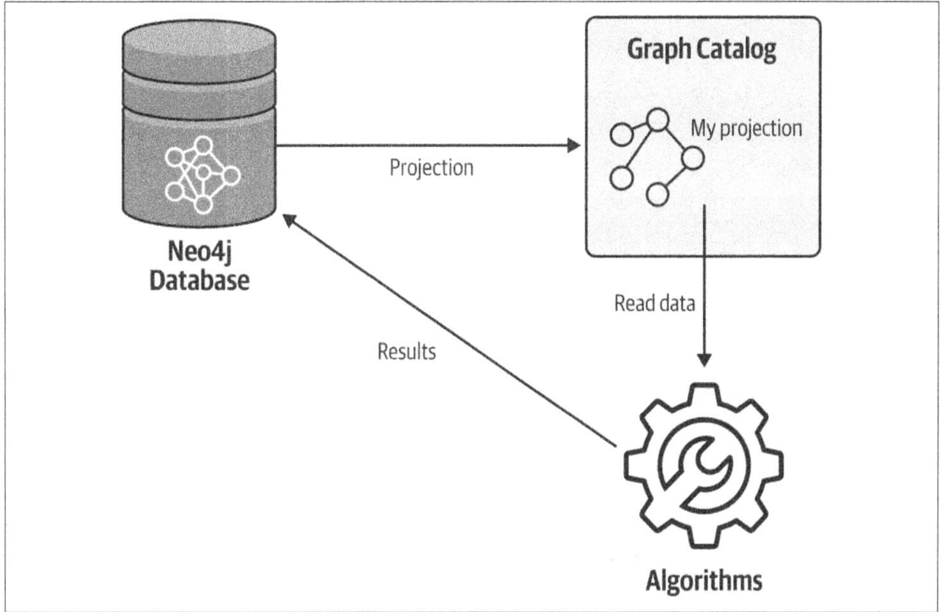

Figure 12-1. A basic GDS workflow

AI-Driven Playlist Communities

In ElectricHarmony's music streaming platform, playlists are connected to individual tracks, forming a rich and intricate graph of user preferences and musical relationships. You can uncover hidden patterns and groupings within your data by leveraging *community detection algorithms.*

Community detection is a fundamental technique in graph data science used to identify clusters or groups within a network. In the realm of ElectricHarmony's music streaming platform, the term *community* refers to groups of tracks and playlists that are more closely connected to *each other* than to the rest of the graph. These clusters often emerge from shared characteristics such as genre, mood, or user listening habits. For instance, they might represent genre-specific fan bases, demographic groups, or even generational cohorts. By detecting these communities, you can uncover hidden patterns in user preferences, enabling more personalized content recommendations and effective user engagement strategies.

Using community detection algorithms offers significant business benefits. First, these algorithms enhance your recommendation engine by suggesting playlists and tracks that are part of the same community, providing users with more personalized and relevant content. This leads to increased user satisfaction and retention, as listeners discover new music that aligns closely with their tastes. Additionally, by understanding the communities within your music graph, you can design targeted marketing campaigns, promoting playlists and tracks to specific user segments who are more likely to engage with them.

Moreover, these insights have practical applications in content curation and playlist creation. For example, your editorial team can use community detection results to curate thematic playlists that resonate with distinct user groups. This not only improves user experience but also increases the time users spend on your platform, boosting overall engagement metrics. By aligning your content strategy with the natural clusters identified by community detection, you can optimize your offerings to meet the diverse preferences of your user base, ultimately driving growth and revenue.

In simple terms, community detection helps you see the natural clusters in your data, as shown in Figure 12-2.

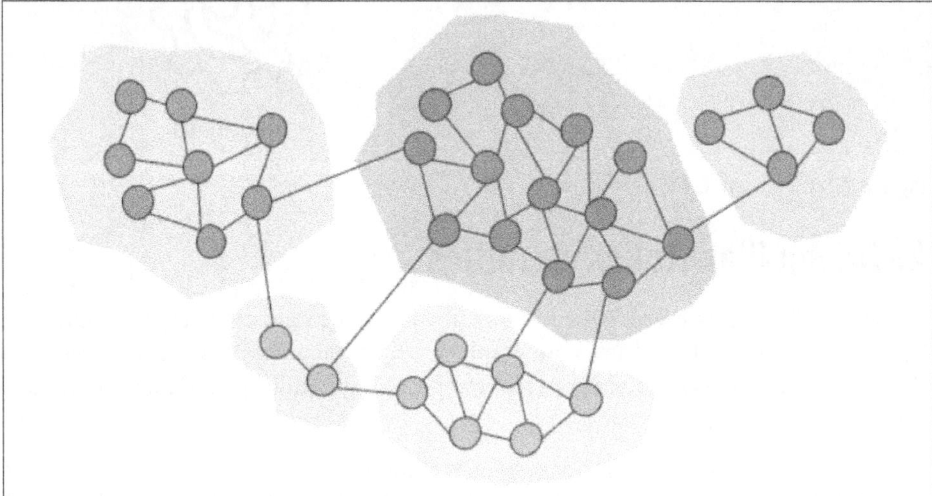

Figure 12-2. Natural clusters in graph data

Building a Co-Occurrence Graph

A *co-occurrence graph* between playlists represents the relationships between playlists based on the tracks they share. In this graph, each node represents a playlist, and an edge is drawn between two nodes if the corresponding playlists share 20 to 30% of the same tracks, a threshold that is typically chosen hypothetically at first and adjusted based on the results of iterative experimentation. The weight of the edge reflects the number of shared tracks, providing a measure of similarity between the playlists.

You will use a co-occurrence graph like the one in Figure 12-3 as input for community detection algorithms. By feeding the graph into these algorithms, you can identify clusters of playlists that share a significant number of tracks. This allows you to uncover natural groupings within your playlists, based on their shared content.

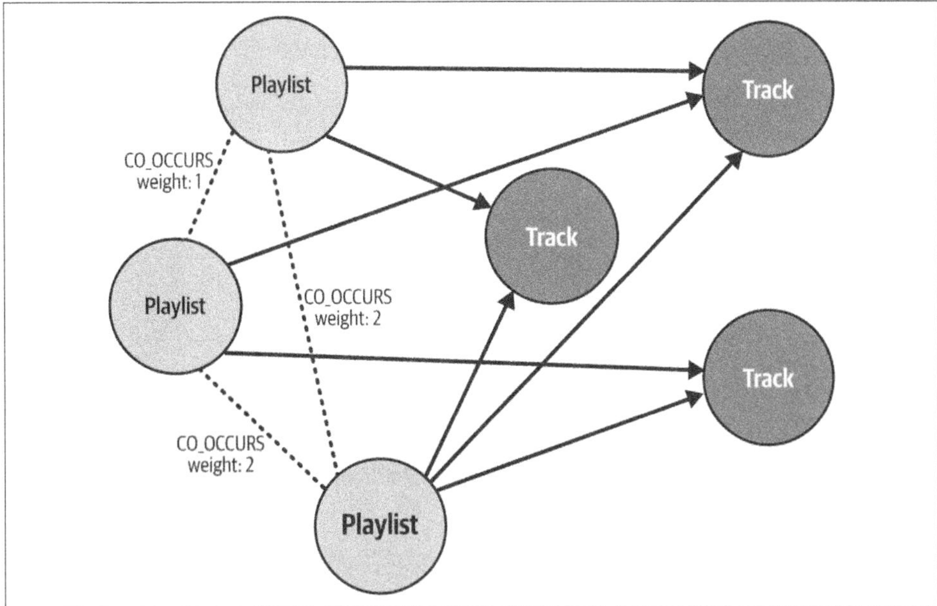

Figure 12-3. Co-occurrence graph of playlists and tracks

Start small

Consider the data in your graph: there are over a million playlists, with each playlist averaging 120 tracks. Some playlists contain as many as 10,000 tracks. If you attempt to create co-occurrence graphs on this entire dataset right away, you'll likely spend most of your time fine-tuning your queries. This can divert you from your initial goal: validating the process of implementing GDS pipelines and evaluating the benefits of the results.

You will use a simple heuristic for choosing a subset of the graph: for example, playlists that have between 20 and 25 tracks. This will give you about 80,000 tracks to work with. You can verify the total number of tracks using the following query:

```
MATCH (n:Playlist)
WHERE 20 <=  n.total_tracks <= 25
RETURN count(n)
```

Next, you'll need to mark your dataset.

Mark the experimental dataset. A straightforward way of marking the dataset to use for this experiment is to add an additional label to the Playlist nodes you want to use. Here we'll give them the label `ExperimentOne`:

```
MATCH (n:Playlist)
WHERE 20 <=  n.total_tracks <= 25
SET n:ExperimentOne
```

Now you can start experimenting by matching nodes with the `ExperimentOne` label. Let's build a query. We'll start from one playlist and retrieve other playlists with tracks in common:

```
MATCH (playlist1:ExperimentOne)
WITH playlist1 LIMIT 1
MATCH
(playlist1)-[:HAS_TRACK]->(track:Track)
<-[:HAS_TRACK]-(playlist2:ExperimentOne)
WHERE playlist1 <> playlist2
RETURN playlist1.id, playlist2.id, count(*) AS sharedTracks
ORDER BY sharedTracks DESC
LIMIT 5
```

The output is:

playlist1.id	playlist2.id	sharedTracks
"000DxSXqcMYmvxHYnYn2y5"	"5Tb5EhrZ2C7x990xplMwNr"	2
"000DxSXqcMYmvxHYnYn2y5"	"4wjZdvSC424JLpo0Wyq82O"	1
"000DxSXqcMYmvxHYnYn2y5"	"5DZR8Vcq1KHB709iAHVp0l"	1
"000DxSXqcMYmvxHYnYn2y5"	"5GMEw4ELCI3YaKc28bem7w"	1
"000DxSXqcMYmvxHYnYn2y5"	"3Mwx0m2jBdbzsJzWPTRPyV"	1

The query took about 15ms. and shows that there is a set of playlists that share two tracks in common. Let's expand the query to start from 10 tracks:

```
MATCH (playlist1:ExperimentOne)
WITH playlist1 LIMIT 10
MATCH
(playlist1)-[:HAS_TRACK]->(track:Track)
<-[:HAS_TRACK]-(playlist2:ExperimentOne)
WHERE playlist1 <> playlist2
RETURN playlist1.id, playlist2.id, count(*) AS sharedTracks
ORDER BY sharedTracks DESC
LIMIT 5
```

The output is:

playlist1.id	playlist2.id	sharedTracks
"00jpD4FlcJ8sLzBCdb5TH4"	"5UYwvrKUSTzhlNgq0hJfa4"	9
"00jxTGdpMMCaTJinbrKokM"	"1PgpJxKBAPkpTFMS3ecCYy"	8
"00jpD4FlcJ8sLzBCdb5TH4"	"1Twj76swzMiuPruyLs6yKR"	8
"00jxTGdpMMCaTJinbrKokM"	"1jSnEkKiUPIot6kRylGuff"	8
"00jpD4FlcJ8sLzBCdb5TH4"	"4of7gIEbMfwUengMZTDSZ6"	7

If you were to build the co-occurrences graph immediately using these results with about 80,000 playlists, it would generate approximately 10 million *co-occurrence relationships*. A *co-occurrence relationship* represents a connection between two entities based on their shared attributes or interactions. Within ElectricHarmony's music streaming platform, co-occurrence relationships can be established between playlists that share common tracks. When two playlists include the same songs, it indicates a similarity in musical themes, genres, or user preferences. By modeling these shared tracks as co-occurrence relationships between playlists, you create a network where playlists are nodes connected through their common content.

The purpose of this experiment is to build communities of similar playlists. Can we really consider two playlists to be similar if they have only one track in common?

Skip low co-occurrences. For this experiment, you will only create co-occurrence relationships for playlists that have at least two tracks in common. Is two tracks enough to establish a meaningful connection? You don't know yet—that's exactly what your experiment aims to discover. By starting with this threshold, you can analyze the results and adjust the approach based on the insights you gain. The following query adds that filter:

```
MATCH (playlist1:ExperimentOne)
WITH playlist1 LIMIT 10
MATCH
(playlist1)-[:HAS_TRACK]->(track:Track)
<-[:HAS_TRACK]-(playlist2:ExperimentOne)
WHERE playlist1 <> playlist2
WITH playlist1, playlist2, count(*) AS sharedTracks
WHERE sharedTracks > 1
RETURN playlist1.id, playlist2.id, sharedTracks
ORDER BY sharedTracks DESC
LIMIT 5
```

Create the co-occurrence relationships

As you saw in Chapter 2, you will likely exceed the amount of heap memory if you attempt to create these co-occurrence relationships in one transaction. Use the `CALL IN TRANSACTIONS` feature, which you know well by now, to commit after every 10,000 playlists:

```
:auto
MATCH (n:Playlist:ExperimentOne)
CALL (n) {
    MATCH (n)-[:HAS_TRACK]->(t)<-[:HAS_TRACK]-(other:ExperimentOne)
    WHERE n <> other
    WITH n, other, count(*) AS tracksInCommon
    WHERE tracksInCommon > 1
    MERGE (n)-[r:CO_OCCURS]-(other)
    SET r.weight = tracksInCommon
} IN TRANSACTIONS OF 10_000 ROWS
```

The preceding query is using MERGE without specifying the direction of the relationship to avoid unnecessary bidirectional relationships. Refer to Chapter 3 for an in-depth explanation of the MERGE clause.

The resulting graph (see Figure 12-4) shows small networks of co-occurrence forming.

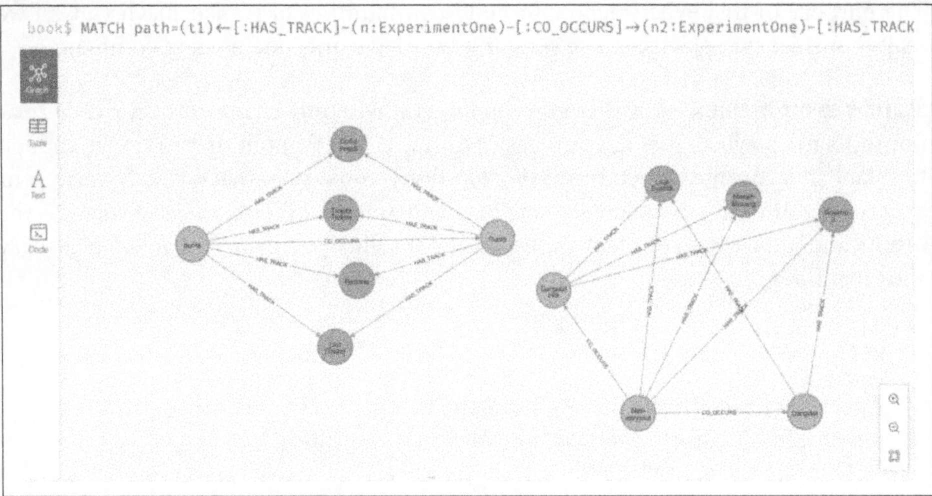

Figure 12-4. Small networks of co-occurrence begin to form.

Running this query will create a little over 3 million co-occurrence relationships. Each of these relationships includes a `weight` property, which represents the number of tracks shared between two playlists. By examining the minimum, maximum, and average weights of these co-occurrence relationships, you can understand how strongly playlists are connected based on shared content. You can retrieve these statistics with the following query:

```
MATCH (n:Playlist)-[r:CO_OCCURS]->(o)
RETURN min(r.weight), max(r.weight), avg(r.weight)
```

The output is:

min(r.weight)	max(r.weight)	min(r.weight)
2	25	3.327753173563246

You have successfully prepared your data to run data science algorithms. The relationships you just created also implicitly offer recommendations that are 1 hop away. In other words, if a user is listening to a playlist, to find similar playlists, you can use a query traversing the co-occurrence relationships and returning the playlists on the other side can be used.

Using GDS

In this section, we'll dive into how to use the GDS library to analyze our graph data effectively, from installation to storing the algorithm results.

Installing the GDS plugin

GDS is already preinstalled in the companion repository used in this book. For other deployment options, refer to the GDS installation documentation (*https://oreil.ly/1jYar*).

Projecting the subgraph

The very first step in using GDS is to create an in-memory projection of the portion of the graph to which you want to apply algorithms. You do not want to project *all* playlists—only the one you've marked with `ExperimentOne` for the experiment.

In GDS, you can perform projections in two different ways: as native projections or as Cypher projections. Native projections are ideal for performance and simplicity when your data can be used as is, while Cypher projections provide the flexibility to tailor the in-memory graph to specific analytical needs, at the cost of some performance.

In this scenario, all you need are the `ExperimentOne` label and the `CO_OCCURS` relationship type along with the weight property, so you will use the native projection.

Estimating memory usage

The GDS library operates completely on the heap, which means you'll need to adjust the `server.memory.*` configuration settings to accommodate the transactional (or operational) and analytical use cases of Neo4j altogether.

GDS is both computationally and memory-intensive, while Neo4j itself is IO- and memory-intensive. Running GDS and Neo4j transactional workloads on the same machine can lead to performance issues in production. A best practice is to dedicate one or more secondary nodes in your Neo4j cluster as GDS servers. This ensures that heavy graph analytics workloads don't interfere with transactional operations.

Figure 12-5 shows how GDS uses memory within the JVM heap, alongside Neo4j's transactional data.

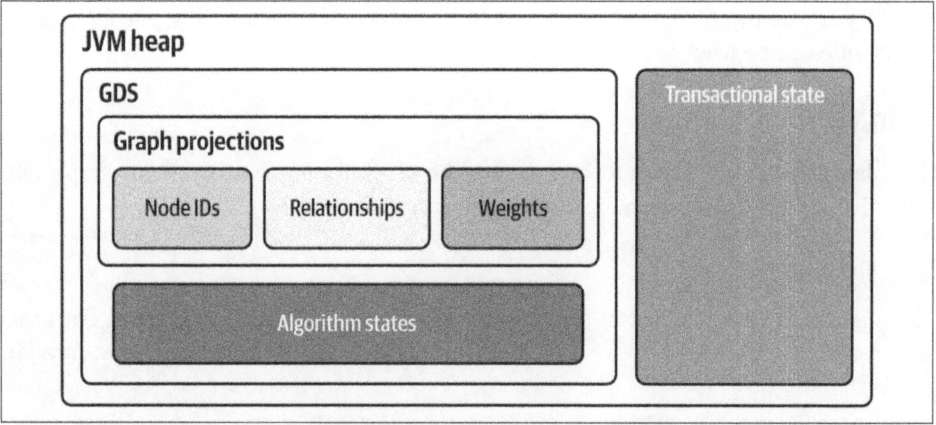

Figure 12-5. JVM heap usage with both GDS and Neo4j transactional data

Before running your GDS projections, it's important to estimate the memory they will require to ensure efficient execution.

The following query will return an estimate of how much memory the graph projection will use:

```
CALL gds.graph.project.estimate(
  'ExperimentOne',
  {CO_OCCURS: {orientation: 'UNDIRECTED', properties: 'weight'}}
)
YIELD requiredMemory, mapView,
heapPercentageMin, heapPercentageMax
```

This returns the estimates shown in Figure 12-6.

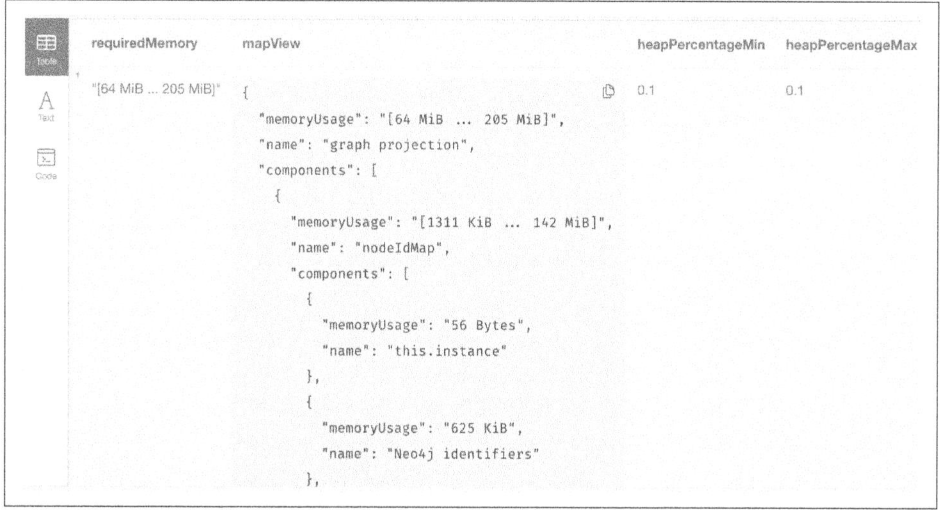

Figure 12-6. Memory usage estimates for a graph projection

The most important estimates to look at are the `requiredMemory`, `heapPercentageMin`, and `heapPercentageMax` columns. The results in the figure shows that projecting the graph would require using 0.1 percent of the configured max heap size.

Project the graph

The following query is very similar to the previous one, except that you'll remove the suffix `.estimate` from the function name and provide a name for your graph: `playlistCoOccurrences` (you can have more than one graph in memory at once to run different experiments):

```
CALL gds.graph.project(
  'playlistCoOccurrences',
  'ExperimentOne',
  {CO_OCCURS: {orientation: 'UNDIRECTED', properties: 'weight'}}
)
YIELD
  graphName AS graph,
  relationshipProjection AS relProjection,
  nodeCount AS nodes,
  relationshipCount AS rels
```

The query result points to something interesting: the number of relationships in memory is around 6 million, *twice* the existing number. Indeed, the GDS projections will create a relationship in each direction when you provide `orientation: 'UNDIRECTED'`:

graph	nodes	rels
"playlistCoOccurrences"	80119	6310572

In the context of graph data modeling, as seen in Chapter 5, creating redundant bidirectional relationships is often considered an antipattern because it can lead to unnecessary data duplication when it doesn't provide any additional semantic meaning. However, in the realm of graph analytics with GDS, representing relationships in both directions is not only acceptable but sometimes required.

Why is this the case? Many graph algorithms, especially those related to community detection, centrality measures, or pathfinding, operate under the assumption that relationships are undirected or that connections can be traversed in both directions. By projecting relationships in both directions, GDS ensures that these algorithms have the complete connectivity information they need to perform accurate calculations. This bidirectional projection allows the algorithms to consider all possible paths and influences between nodes, leading to more comprehensive and insightful analysis.

Therefore, while redundant relationships might be avoided in your stored data model to maintain efficiency, they are purposely introduced in the in-memory graph projections for GDS to facilitate analytical computations. This distinction clarifies why the number of relationships often doubles during the projection process, because GDS creates a reversed copy of each directed relationship to support bidirectional traversal. This is necessary not only for performance, but also because many graph algorithms interpret directed relationships differently, depending on their semantics. It highlights the different requirements between data modeling and graph analytics.

Executing the community detection algorithm

The GDS library includes many different community detection algorithms that are listed in the documentation (*https://oreil.ly/7PzuN*). There are many reasons you might select one algorithm over another, but the details of that decision fall outside the scope of this book. Just know that we've chosen the Louvain (*https://oreil.ly/cHzZu*) algorithm for this chapter because it is suitable for undirected relationships (`CO_OCCURS`) with *weighted properties* (the weight property representing the number of tracks shared by a pair of playlists).

The Louvain algorithm works by partitioning the graph into nonoverlapping communities, assigning each node to exactly one community where it fits best based on the network's modularity. This means that each playlist or track will belong to *only one* community, determined by where it has the strongest connections in terms of shared tracks. If two nodes have the same community ID, they're part of the same community.

You might wonder how this accounts for overlap; after all, in the real world, a playlist could fit into multiple genres or listener groups. For example, a playlist featuring death-metal covers of Taylor Swift songs might seem like it belongs to both metalheads and Swifties. However, the Louvain algorithm simplifies this complexity by placing each node into the community where it has the most significant connections. This approach helps to maximize the modularity of the network, making the communities as internally dense and externally sparse as possible.

While this means that nodes won't belong to multiple communities in this analysis, it provides a clear and straightforward grouping that is useful for many applications. If overlapping communities are important for your specific use case, other algorithms like Speaker-Listener Label Propagation (*https://oreil.ly/IcBSb*) or clique percolation (*https://oreil.ly/RB1ej*) might be more suitable. However, for our purposes in this chapter, using the Louvain algorithm allows us to effectively identify distinct communities within our graph.

Memory estimation

As with the graph projection, you should ensure that you have enough heap memory to run the algorithm. You can gather statistics with the following query:

```
CALL gds.louvain.write.estimate('playlistCoOccurrences',
  { writeProperty: 'community' })
YIELD nodeCount, relationshipCount, bytesMin, bytesMax, requiredMemory
```

The output is:

nodeCount	relationshipCount	bytesMin	bytesMax	requiredMemory
80119	6310572	5142921	"[5022 KiB ...	136 MiB]"

These results show that you will need 136MB of heap memory to run the algorithm.

Execution mode. You might have noticed, in the preceding query, that the `.write` component in the procedure is called `gds.louvain.write.estimate()`. This represents the algorithm's *execution mode*. In simple terms, an execution mode tells Neo4j how you want to run the algorithm and what you want to do with its results.

Neo4j has four execution modes:

`stream`
: Stream mode will stream the results of the algorithm as a Neo4j result, but will not modify the data or the in-memory graph.

`write`
: Write mode will write the community ID on each playlist node. The `writeProperty` parameter in the query tells the algorithm on which property it should write the value—in this case, community.

`stats`
: Stats mode returns a single summary; it does not write to the database or the in-memory graph.

`mutate`
: Mutate mode writes the result in the in-memory graph only. Use it when you want to apply another algorithm to the results of the first one in the in-memory graph.

To get familiar with the graph algorithm results, you will start with `stream` execution mode before modifying your original data.

The next query will execute the Louvain algorithm, in `stream` mode, on the `playlistCoOccurrences` graph:

```
CALL gds.louvain.stream('playlistCoOccurrences')
YIELD nodeId, communityId, intermediateCommunityIds
RETURN gds.util.asNode(nodeId).id AS playlist, communityId
ORDER BY communityId ASC
LIMIT 10
```

The result shows the IDs of playlists and their corresponding community IDs:

playlist	communityId
"3wZHPgTphrtR4XUqQXmMR4"	2
"3wFI09ZK3VzJ6vKwLxZlAi"	12
"3XCCbumeSAlzUHnwEreJho"	18
"3wFsmmXCzOSzxjJLG0flRc"	33
"3nJ0iHNtU6QQYjWK4mWvqf"	46
"3xCxt9FYGoSTmWwS2kUjxp"	52
"3ujbJhyZxTcvOytPbUqX5X"	64
"3RKqIXHWh7PDGGcVPJQb2x"	72
"3UzrzGzxm97FPp24WEIoLb"	78
"3NJI6ErnJSHWo0Yi8C7DcR"	87

Storing results. Two of the four execution modes allow you to store your results. `write` mode stores the community ID on a property on the `Playlist` nodes; in `stream` mode, you can take the results and continue the Cypher query to store them as you like.

In Chapter 5, you learned that how you design your graph heavily relies on how you want to access your data later on and how you treat business entities internally. Storing the community ID as a property on the playlist node prevents you from treating communities as first-class citizens. By representing communities as first-class citizens—that is, modeling them as separate nodes in your graph—you make it much easier to navigate between communities. This approach allows you to traverse directly to a related `Community` node and efficiently find connected playlists. Recommending similar playlists based on a given one, or the tracks they contain, becomes more straightforward, as you can simply navigate through the `Community` nodes and their relationships.

Additionally, treating communities as nodes enables you to apply other graph algorithms directly on them, such as PageRank (*https://oreil.ly/TomAM*) or betweenness centrality algorithms (*https://oreil.ly/zp14y*), to identify influential playlists or communities within the graph. These algorithms can help uncover key nodes that play significant roles in connecting different parts of the network or that have high influence within their community. By analyzing communities with these algorithms, you gain deeper insights into the structure and dynamics of your data, which can enhance recommendation systems and user engagement strategies.

In contrast, if you only store the community ID as a property on the `Playlist` node, performing such analyses becomes more challenging. Without `Community` nodes, navigating between communities is more tedious, and you miss out on the powerful benefits of graph traversals and algorithms that can simplify recommendation processes and highlight important nodes in your network.

Look at the diagrams on the left and right of Figure 12-7. Which one is more "graphy"?

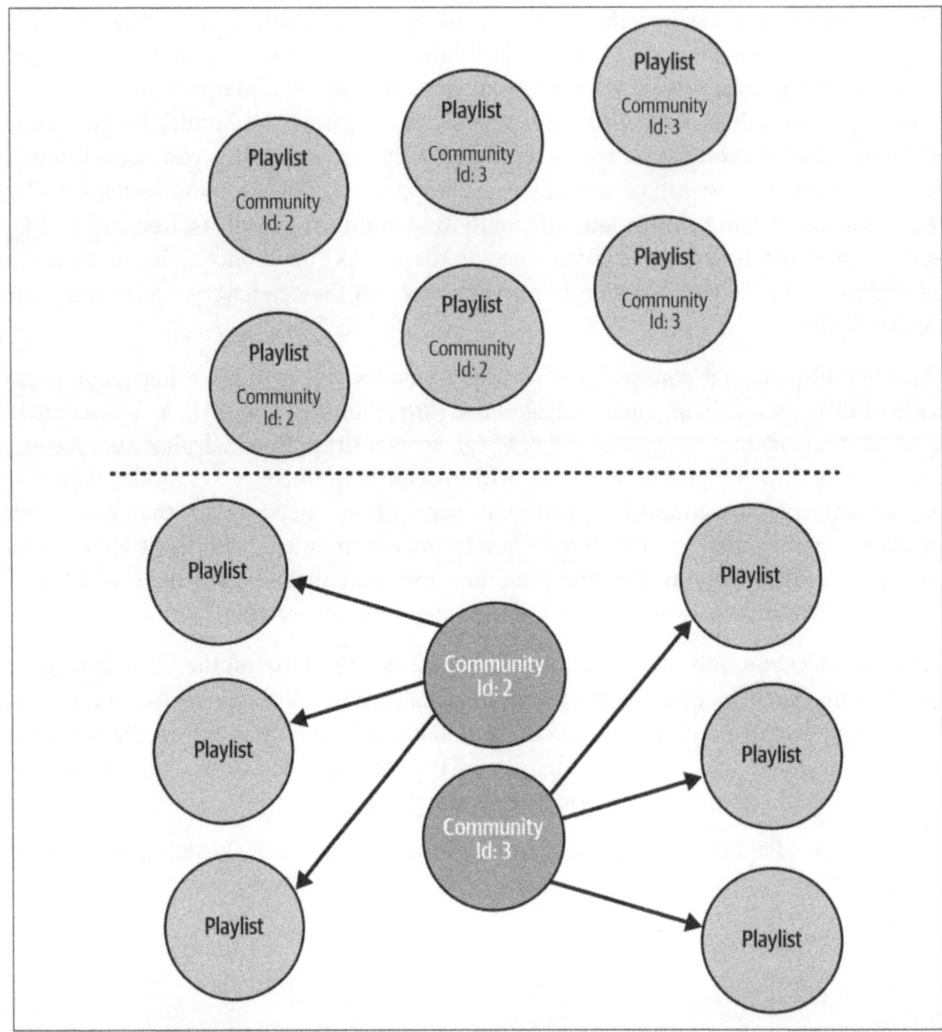

Figure 12-7. Two ways of storing the community ID

To store the results—as shown on the right side of Figure 12-7—you'll first need to create a unique constraint on the nodes labeled `Community`, ensuring that each node's `id` property (the community ID) is unique:

```
CREATE CONSTRAINT communityIdUnique
FOR (n:Community)
REQUIRE n.id IS UNIQUE
```

Then adapt the algorithm query to create those communities from the stream and connect the playlists:

```
CALL gds.louvain.stream('playlistCoOccurrences')
YIELD nodeId, communityId, intermediateCommunityIds
WITH gds.util.asNode(nodeId) AS playlist, communityId
MERGE (c:Community {id: communityId})
MERGE (c)-[:HAS_PLAYLIST]->(playlist)
```

Now that you've stored the community results, let's move on to analyze them.

Analytical queries

It's very important to understand how communities are distributed. This can reveal insights about the data, such as isolated or weakly connected nodes.

First, check how many communities were created when you ran the algorithm:

```
MATCH (c:Community)
RETURN count(c) AS count
```

The output is:

count
6885

How many of them contain only one playlist?

```
MATCH (c:Community)
WHERE COUNT { (c)-[:HAS_PLAYLIST]->() } = 1
RETURN count(c) AS count
```

The output is:

count
6407

Approximately 93% of the communities you just created contain only one playlist. Why are we getting these results?

It could be that most of the data subset you used is not representative enough for the experiment. The Louvain algorithm tends to favor communities that are sufficiently connected. A playlist is *sufficiently connected* when it shares enough tracks with other playlists to form strong relationships, contributing positively to the modularity within a community. You might also have skipped creating the CO_OCCURS relationship when two playlists have only one track in common. This can lead to isolated nodes in the in-memory graph. This behavior is not always a problem, though. Indeed, it is better not to provide recommendations at all than to provide bad recommendations.

Rinse and repeat

You will often need to use iterative approaches, try new heuristics and different projections, or tune the algorithm parameters and evaluate the results on your data.

The previous section demonstrated that the graph model, combined with Cypher and the GDS library, offer developers and data scientists a rapid, easy-to-use framework for executing graph data science tasks. You can "rinse and repeat" faster than ever before.

Given the insights from your initial experiment, it's evident that tweaking certain parameters may yield better results. Let's try another experiment that iterates on the first one.

Creating a second experiment

The second experiment will evaluate if increasing the number of tracks in common between playlists to at least four will reduce the number of single-playlist communities. For the purposes of this experiment, you will not change the playlists used. You will, however, create a distinct relationship type for the co-occurrence graph, named `CO_OCCURS_TWO`.

Create the new `CO_OCCURS_TWO` relationships between playlists with at least four tracks in common:

```
:auto
MATCH (n:Playlist:ExperimentOne)
CALL {
    WITH n
    MATCH (n)-[:HAS_TRACK]->(t)<-[:HAS_TRACK]-(other:ExperimentOne)
    WHERE n <> other
    WITH n, other, count(*) AS tracksInCommon
    WHERE tracksInCommon >= 4
    MERGE (n)-[r:CO_OCCURS_TWO]-(other)
    SET r.weight = tracksInCommon
} IN TRANSACTIONS OF 500 ROWS
```

The next steps are similar to the first experiment, except that you will project the graph with the newly created co-occurrence relationships into an in-memory graph with a new name: `playlistCoOccurrencesTwo`. Here it is:

```
CALL gds.graph.project(
   'playlistCoOccurrencesTwo',
   'ExperimentOne',
   {CO_OCCURS_TWO: {orientation: 'UNDIRECTED', properties: 'weight'}}
)
YIELD
  graphName AS graph,
  relationshipProjection AS relProjection,
  nodeCount AS nodes,
  relationshipCount AS rels
```

Finally, run the Louvain algorithm on the newly created projected graph and store the new communities. You will need to use a dedicated label (`CommunityTwo`) to distinguish them from the communities you created in the first experiment. Let's apply that:

```
CALL gds.louvain.stream('playlistCoOccurrencesTwo')
YIELD nodeId, communityId, intermediateCommunityIds
WITH gds.util.asNode(nodeId) AS playlist, communityId
MERGE (c:CommunityTwo {id: communityId})
MERGE (c)-[:HAS_PLAYLIST]->(playlist)
```

Comparing the count of communities with only one playlist to the total number of communities reveals that approximately 72% of them contain only a single playlist. While this is a slight improvement from the previous results, you might still find the outcome less than ideal.

In our next and final experiment, you will utilize Cypher projections. The issue with the native projection is that it inherently includes all playlists labeled with `ExperimentOne` into the in-memory graph, regardless of whether they have a `CO_OCCURS` relationship or not. This inclusion of isolated nodes could be the root cause of the high percentage of communities consisting of a single playlist.

The following query will project the `CO_OCCURS_TWO` relationships along with their nodes into a new in memory graph named `playlistCoOccurrencesThree` using the Cypher projection:

```
MATCH (source:ExperimentOne)-[r:CO_OCCURS_TWO]->(target:ExperimentOne)
WITH gds.graph.project(
  'playlistCoOccurrencesThree',
  source,
  target,
  { relationshipProperties: r { .weight } }
) AS g
RETURN
  g.graphName AS graph, g.nodeCount AS nodes, g.relationshipCount AS rels
```

If you pay attention to the result of the query, you will spot that the in-memory graph contains fewer nodes than the previous experiments using the native projection:

graph	nodes	rels
"playlistCoOccurrencesThree"	51179	905535

Next, we will run the Louvain community detection algorithm again and stream the results back as `CommunityThree` nodes:

```
CALL gds.louvain.stream('playlistCoOccurrencesThree')
YIELD nodeId, communityId, intermediateCommunityIds
WITH gds.util.asNode(nodeId) AS playlist, communityId
MERGE (c:CommunityThree {id: communityId})
```

```
MERGE (c)-[:HAS_PLAYLIST]->(playlist)
You now can verify if it made improvements to the quality of the communities:
MATCH (c:CommunityThree)
WHERE COUNT { (c)-[:HAS_PLAYLIST]->() } = 1
RETURN count(c) AS count;
// 2246

MATCH (c:CommunityThree)
RETURN count(c) AS count
// 4158
```

By leveraging Cypher projections, you effectively reduced the number of singleton communities to 50%, demonstrating a significant improvement over previous experiments. This highlights the importance of choosing the appropriate projection method, as it can greatly enhance the quality of your community detection results.

Real-World Applications of Community Detection

Now that you've stored the community structure in your graph, the next step is making those results useful. In this section, we'll explore practical applications of community detection within ElectricHarmony's music platform. These use cases can be implemented immediately using Cypher and GDS, without the need for additional infrastructure.

Playlist recommendations

Once a playlist has been assigned to a community, recommending similar playlists becomes trivial. Instead of calculating similarity in real time based on overlapping tracks, artists, or metadata, which can be computationally expensive, you can simply retrieve other playlists that belong to the same community. This significantly boosts performance and ensures that the recommendations reflect deeper, graph-based patterns of user behavior or curation logic. As a result, users receive more cohesive and personalized suggestions, often uncovering playlists that share a common thematic or stylistic thread.

The following query is an example of recommending similar playlists in the same community from a given playlist ID:

```
MATCH (p:Playlist {id: "01wvUa0flceLMo1IYWD3vB"})
MATCH (p)<-[:HAS_PLAYLIST]-(c:CommunityThree)-[:HAS_PLAYLIST]->(other:Playlist)
WHERE other<> p
RETURN p.name AS playlistFrom,
other.name AS recommendation
ORDER BY rand()
LIMIT 5
```

The output is:

playlistFrom	recommendation
"Electro Swing"	"Electro-Swing"
"Electro Swing"	"Chandelier Swinging (Electro Swing)"
"Electro Swing"	"electro swing"
"Electro Swing"	"Electro Swing"
"Electro Swing"	"Electro Swing"

User segmentation

Community information can also be leveraged to enrich user profiles and power intelligent segmentation. By analyzing the playlists a user follows and identifying the most frequent community among those playlists, you can assign each user to a behavior-driven segment. Unlike static demographic segmentation, these segments are dynamic and grounded in actual user activity. As communities shift, through the evolution of shared interests or playlist curation, user segments naturally adapt, ensuring that the system stays relevant over time.

The following Cypher query demonstrates how to assign each user to their dominant community:

```
MATCH (u:User)-[:FOLLOWS]->(p:Playlist)<-[:HAS_PLAYLIST]-(c:Community)
WITH u, c.id AS communityId, count(*) AS score
ORDER BY score DESC
WITH u, collect(communityId)[0] AS topCommunity
SET u.segment = topCommunity
```

This approach enables a variety of personalization strategies:

- Onboarding optimization: Automatically suggest relevant playlists or themes when a new user signs up or logs in for the first time.
- Dynamic content feeds: Populate homepages with playlists curated from the user's community, increasing engagement and time spent in-app.
- A/B testing and UX personalization: Adapt UI elements, like color schemes, promotional banners, or feature prioritization, based on the user's segment.
- Marketing and messaging: Craft notifications, emails, or in-app prompts that speak directly to the interests of users within a given community.

By aligning personalization efforts with communities, you're not just optimizing for individual behavior; you're amplifying the shared, emergent preferences of groups. This makes recommendations more meaningful and contributes to a sense of belonging, which in turn fosters loyalty and long-term user retention.

Influencer discovery

Not all playlists are created equal; some act as hubs, bridging multiple listeners and genres, and influencing the direction of a community's taste. Within each community, these high-impact playlists can be surfaced using centrality algorithms like PageRank, which score nodes based on how well-connected and important they are within the broader playlist network. These are often expertly curated lists that consolidate emerging trends, introduce fresh content, or reflect the collective preferences of a large listener base.

The following Cypher query identifies these key playlists using GDS:

```
CALL gds.pageRank.stream('playlistCoOccurrencesThree')
YIELD nodeId, score
WITH gds.util.asNode(nodeId) AS playlist, score
MATCH (c:CommunityThree)-[:HAS_PLAYLIST]->(playlist)
RETURN c.id AS communityId, playlist.name AS playlist, score
ORDER BY score DESC
LIMIT 5
```

The output is:

communityID	playlist	score
49080	"Emo rap"	33.90834539160779
15634	"Dangdut"	33.52388370579392
46317	"rock en espanol"	30.69971592058743
48627	"Nu Metal"	28.499416881364887
28685	"girl group songs"	27.875836332597363

Highlighting these influential playlists has tangible product benefits:

- It boosts engagement. These playlists often act as entry points into a genre or niche tastes. Featuring them increases the chance of resonating with new or curious users.
- It supports discovery. Influence often correlates with novelty or quality. Elevating these playlists helps users uncover what's trending or worth listening to within a community.
- It allows for editorial curation: editorial teams can review top-ranked playlists for manual curation or promotion, using algorithmic insight to guide their choices.
- It builds trust. Promoting well-connected, trusted playlists helps establish a perception of quality and reliability, especially for new users exploring the platform.

Over time, you can track changes in PageRank to observe shifts in influence, spot emerging tastemakers, or even identify declining trends before they fade completely. Influence isn't static, and neither is your graph.

Behavioral clusters

Even in the absence of explicit genre or mood tags, the structure of playlist communities often reveals rich behavioral patterns. These clusters naturally emerge from shared curation habits and listening preferences. A community might reflect themes like "morning motivation," "rainy day instrumentals," or "deep focus," without ever being labeled as such. By sampling a few representative tracks from each community, you can begin to intuit the underlying mood, use case, or sonic identity of that cluster.

This Cypher query provides a quick lens into what each community "sounds like" with a sneak peek at the results in Figure 12-8:

```
CYPHER runtime=parallel
MATCH (c:CommunityThree)-[:HAS_PLAYLIST]->(p:Playlist)-[:HAS_TRACK]->(t:Track)
WHERE t.name IS NOT NULL AND t.name <> ""
WITH c.id AS communityId, collect(DISTINCT t.name)[0..3] AS sampleTracks,
count(DISTINCT p) AS size
RETURN communityId, sampleTracks, size
ORDER BY size DESC
LIMIT 10
```

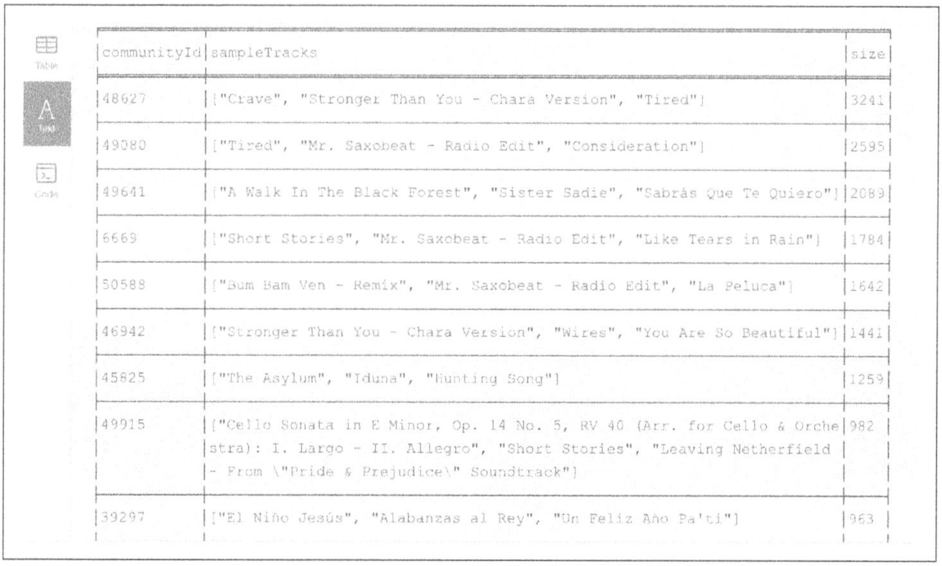

communityId	sampleTracks	size
48627	["Crave", "Stronger Than You - Chara Version", "Tired"]	3241
49080	["Tired", "Mr. Saxobeat - Radio Edit", "Consideration"]	2595
49641	["A Walk In The Black Forest", "Sister Sadie", "Sabrás Que Te Quiero"]	2089
6669	["Short Stories", "Mr. Saxobeat - Radio Edit", "Like Tears in Rain"]	1784
50588	["Bum Bam Ven - Remix", "Mr. Saxobeat - Radio Edit", "La Peluca"]	1642
46942	["Stronger Than You - Chara Version", "Wires", "You Are So Beautiful"]	1441
45825	["The Asylum", "Iduna", "Hunting Song"]	1259
49915	["Cello Sonata in E Minor, Op. 14 No. 5, RV 40 (Arr. for Cello & Orchestra): I. Largo - II. Allegro", "Short Stories", "Leaving Netherfield - From \"Pride & Prejudice\" Soundtrack"]	982
39297	["El Niño Jesús", "Alabanzas al Rey", "Un Feliz Año Pa'ti"]	963

Figure 12-8. Behavioral cluster results

It retrieves a few distinct track titles from each community, along with the community's size, offering a data-driven snapshot of what listeners in that group gravitate toward.

Applications include:

Editorial guidance
: Sampled track titles can act as inspiration for naming and promoting new themed playlists, especially when genre metadata is sparse or noisy.

Human-in-the-loop labeling
: Teams can audit communities and apply light-touch labels (such as "ambient focus" or "party starters") to boost content discoverability without requiring deep manual curation.

Automated categorization
: If paired with audio analysis or NLP on track metadata, these communities can be automatically classified into mood or activity segments.

Emergent-trend detection
: Behavioral clusters allow you to surface newly forming trends, whether it's a regional sound, a seasonal mood, or an evolving subgenre.

This approach gives you a high-signal alternative to traditional metadata enrichment pipelines. Instead of relying solely on genre labels, you're listening to the community itself, letting real-world usage patterns shape how content is understood, categorized, and surfaced.

Content licensing strategy

Understanding which tracks appear most frequently across top communities gives your content team a strategic edge. These are the high-leverage songs—the tracks that travel well, gain traction across different listener segments, and frequently resurface in user-generated or editorial playlists. Such tracks are prime candidates for licensing deals, artist spotlights, promotional partnerships, or catalog prioritization.

This Cypher query identifies those high-impact tracks:

```
MATCH (c:Community)-[:HAS_PLAYLIST]->(p:Playlist)-[:HAS_TRACK]->(t:Track)
WITH t, count(DISTINCT p) AS playlistCount
RETURN t.id, t.title, playlistCount
ORDER BY playlistCount DESC
LIMIT 50
```

It surfaces the 50 most reused tracks across all communities, highlighting songs that function as connective tissue in the graph, regardless of genre or artist popularity.

This allows for opportunities such as:

Licensing negotiations
: Focus efforts on acquiring or renewing rights for tracks that consistently drive engagement across clusters.

Catalog expansion
: Use insights to identify sonic patterns and discover similar, potentially undervalued songs worth adding to the platform.

Artist promotion
: Prioritize artists with multiple high-recurrence tracks for features, interviews, or curated takeovers.

Editorial planning
: Use highly embedded tracks as anchors for new playlists, knowing they already perform well in a variety of contexts.

This level of strategic foresight is difficult to achieve with flat relational data. But once you've modeled playlists and communities as a graph, patterns like these emerge naturally, enabling smarter, more data-driven decisions across content and business operations.

Summary

In this chapter, you explored Neo4j's Graph Data Science (GDS) library to perform advanced graph analytics, using the Louvain algorithm to uncover patterns within ElectricHarmony's music streaming data. GDS offers an accessible interface via Cypher procedures, bridging the gap between machine learning and engineering. This simplifies complex analytical tasks that traditionally required deep data science expertise, allowing you to run sophisticated algorithms with familiar Cypher queries.

You learned how easily you can iterate through experiments using GDS, enabling rapid adjustments and refinements. Since data science involves exploration and your initial results may not be perfect, having a flexible tool like GDS is crucial for effective experimentation.

Additionally, you discovered the differences between native and Cypher projections in GDS and when to use each. Understanding these options helps optimize performance and tailor your in-memory graphs to specific analytical needs.

Beyond the fundamentals, this chapter guided you through practical experiments and strategic decisions that impact both model quality and business value. From building co-occurrence graphs at scale to comparing projection methods and exploring real-world applications like user segmentation, playlist recommendations, and influencer discovery, you've seen how graph data science unlocks actionable insights. With iterative experimentation and the ability to model relationships and communities directly in the graph, you can go far beyond traditional analytics, powering features that feel deeply personalized, dynamic, and relevant to your users.

By mastering these concepts, you're now better equipped to harness graph data science in Neo4j, making more informed decisions and developing innovative solutions.

CHAPTER 13

The Future of Graphs with Generative AI

The AI landscape continues to evolve rapidly. No doubt, by the time you have this book in your hands, the field will have advanced significantly. In this final chapter, you'll find out why graphs make such a difference and how Neo4j has embraced GenAI, one of the most promising frontiers of innovation.

When ChatGPT made its dramatic entrance in 2022, it captured the world's imagination. It was primarily used to answer questions but quickly evolved to text summarization and image generation. It was soon clear that GenAI models excel at content creation and pattern recognition—but they struggle with factual accuracy, resulting quite often in unreliable results. When LLMs generate content, they're predicting what should come next based on the statistical patterns they learned during training. But without being trained on more recent or relevant information, they tend to hallucinate, producing confident "facts" that cannot always be trusted. For any nontrivial business domain, this phenomenon is alarming.

Retrieval-augmented generation (RAG) architectures improve the reliability of GenAI systems by ensuring that LLM responses are based on facts and come from various sources of knowledge. Knowledge graphs represent real-world entities and the complex relationships that exist between them. LLMs can produce less biased and more accurate responses by relying on a knowledge graph as the source of facts.

The rise of GenAI has brought knowledge graphs back into the spotlight and has also created a symbiotic relationship of sorts. Knowledge graphs ground LLMs in factual information, and LLMs assist in drastically reducing the time and effort it takes to create knowledge graphs from unstructured text.

In this final chapter, you'll gain a clear picture of what knowledge graphs really are and where they're used, why they're the cornerstone of GraphRAG, and where LLMs can play a role in speeding up the creation of a knowledge graph from unstructured data. We don't cover specific tools and frameworks in this chapter, since they'll almost certainly have been superseded by new ones by the time this book goes to print. The Neo4j for GenAI (*https://oreil.ly/0-Jy5*) page is the one to track to learn of the latest advancements in this area. True to the core domain you're used to by now, you'll take ElectricHarmony into the year 3000 with GenAI, but you'll also expand your horizons and explore how so many other domains can benefit from knowledge graphs.

Knowledge Graphs

Knowledge graphs capture knowledge of real-world entities and their relationships and are typically stored in graph databases like Neo4j. Knowledge graphs incorporate some form of *organizing principle*: a framework that specifies how nodes and relationships are organized. It can be as simple as a schema, or it can include taxonomies and ontologies and be complex enough to power an inference engine.

A *taxonomy* is primarily a classification system. It groups entities into categories based on certain properties or characteristics and organizes these categories hierarchically. A taxonomy typically implies an `IS-A` or `SUBCLASS-OF` relationship.

One of the earliest taxonomies you might be familiar with is in biology, which is actually where the term originated. Living organisms are classified into the hierarchy of domain, kingdom, phylum, class, order, family, genus, and species. Having this taxonomy allows you to infer characteristics of living organisms. For example, the silky anteater on the cover of this book, or the *Cyclopes didactylus*, belongs to the family Cyclopedidae, which is a family of anteaters. This family belongs to the order Pilosa (*https://oreil.ly/ZcoIG*), which is a group of xenarthran placental mammals, already alluding to how the silky anteater is a specific type of mammal.

Can you guess a taxonomy for ElectricHarmony? Given its classifications and categories, an obvious one is genres. Music genres are diverse and sprawling, but a simplistic partial taxonomy could look like the one in Figure 13-1.

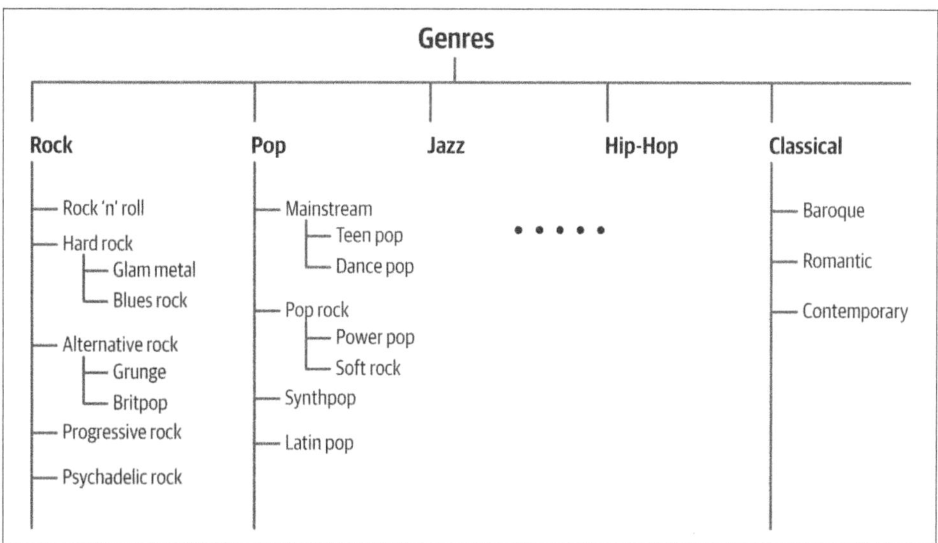

Figure 13-1. A partial taxonomy of music genres

An *ontology* is an organizing principle and formal specification of concepts and how they relate, typically representing a semantic network. Maintaining an ontology can get complex and often involves a number of frameworks, tools, and languages, such as the Web Ontology Language (OWL). Ontologies are richer than hierarchical taxonomies and capture the context and rules of behavior or constraints.

Look at the musicontology.com specification for `MusicArtist`. It gives music artists properties such as discography, biography, fanpage, and activity. The `MusicArtist` class also specifies two subclasses: `MusicGroup` and `SoloMusicArtist`. A representation of a track in the Resource Description Framework (RDF), a standard for describing data interchange that is popular with ontologies, might be:

```
<#track-1>
  a mo:Track ;
  dc:title "Turnover" ;
  foaf:maker
  <http://musicbrainz.org/artist/233fc3f3-6de2-465c-985e-e721dbabbace#_> .
<http://musicbrainz.org/artist/233fc3f3-6de2-465c-985e-e721dbabbace>
  a mo:MusicGroup ;
  foaf:name "Fugazi" .
```

This particular example (*https://oreil.ly/bg0HM*) shows a track titled "Turnover," created by a `MusicGroup` named `Fugazi`.

Both taxonomies and ontologies can be organizing principles for knowledge graphs. You can view them as an abstract mapping over a graph, such as in Figure 13-2.

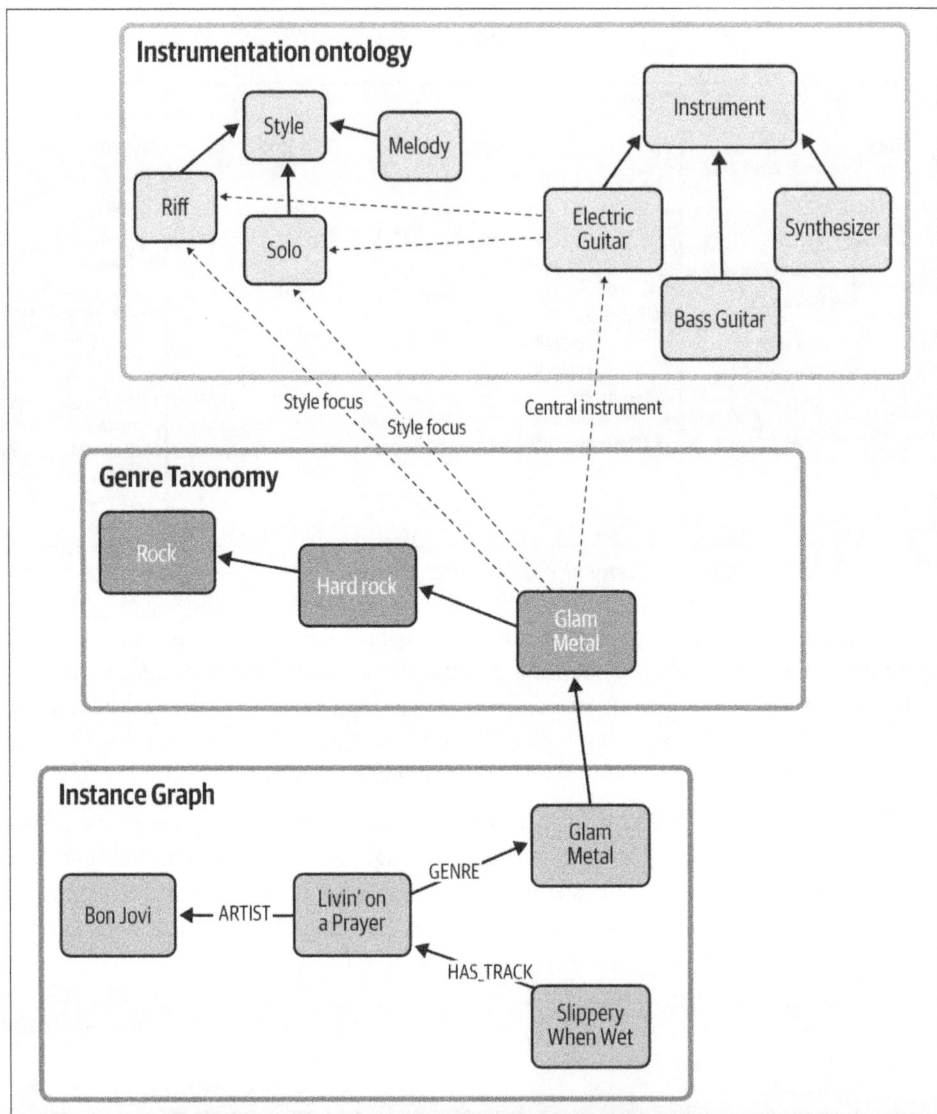

Figure 13-2. Mapping an instance graph to taxonomies and ontologies

In Neo4j, aim to include just enough semantics in your labeled property graph to preserve the practicality, whiteboard-friendliness, and intuitiveness of a knowledge graph. A music knowledge graph will expand ElectricHarmony's value proposition by inferring listeners' musical tastes to improve its recommendations. ElectricHarmony might even introduce a natural language search feature that lets users give instructions, such as "Create a playlist that is composed of rock songs that feature powerful guitar solos and heavy distortion."

Applications of Knowledge Graphs

Let's step out of the music world for a moment to explore how knowledge graphs power use cases in other domains. Understanding the role of LLMs highlights why knowledge graphs are the perfect companions to GenAI applications.

Customer 360

A *customer 360 knowledge graph* is a good example of *master data management*, a practice that brings data about a customer together from various organizational silos, such as services, vendors, marketing, support, and sales.

These graphs use *entity resolution*, an important technique used to identify the same customer across different departments or suborganizations—a classic problem in large enterprises with poor customer service. The knowledge graph here serves as a single source of truth. Businesses can use their own ontologies—for instance, about lifetime value, churn, or high-value potential customers—to enrich the knowledge graph and support its behavior prediction.

An LLM use case in this domain is to chat about your customers: "Show me customers who have purchased over $5,000 in the last quarter who are likely to churn. What complaints did they file, and what promotions can bring them back?"

You can continuously enrich the knowledge graph itself by using an LLM to process unstructured text from customer reviews, feedback, or complaints and extract entities and relationships to add back to the graph.

The benefits of the combined graph and LLM approach include:

- Painting an accurate picture of the customer, without people having to slowly piece together information from across departments.
- Providing contextual information grounded in facts when GraphRAG is used.
- Surfacing rich insights that power personalized customer service.

Cybersecurity

Events, network topologies, access rights, and devices fit naturally into knowledge graphs due to the complex relationships between them. In January 2025, MITRE released a cybersecurity ontology (*https://oreil.ly/p2FOc*) to establish a common language for techniques to counter cyberattacks. This knowledge graph can be used to monitor for known attack patterns, privilege escalation risks, and similar. When paired with an LLM that can extract entities (like domains and IP addresses) from emails, the knowledge graph can be queried for malicious associations. GenAI applications in this domain can produce incident reports by creating summaries of the attack path and recommending mitigation steps, using the knowledge graph as context. Any inferences or link prediction can always be supported by facts from the knowledge graph, resulting in higher trust and quicker response times, rather than relying on a human to manually query the graph and piece together a plan.

Life Sciences

In life sciences and healthcare, knowledge graphs play a vital role in bringing together data about patients, genomic data, clinical trials, medical literature, and various well-established medical ontologies. They enable powerful inferences across related entities such as drugs, genes, and diseases, as well as complex queries such as "Which drugs target the pathways implicated by disease A?"

Here, too, LLMs play a dual role. They enrich the graph by extracting entities and relationships from medical literature and clinical studies, in addition to prescriptions and notes. The second role is to answer natural-language questions, making this vast trove of information accessible to clinicians. Furthermore, an LLM may also infer connections, such as a certain drug inhibiting a protein. Again, with GraphRAG, hallucinations are reduced, and answers are traceable to facts in the graph.

Retail

One of the earliest use cases of graphs was in ecommerce, specifically recommendations. Product catalogs, supply chains, marketing campaigns, and user behavior can all be modeled in knowledge graphs. Pairing them with LLMs to create personalized shopping assistants is a new use case. LLMs can also be used to interpret events produced by the knowledge graph, such as inventory levels dropping or a surge prediction due to a marketing campaign and can summarize action items in natural language.

Criminal Investigations

Law enforcement is the perfect domain for a knowledge graph. Criminal investigations rely on uncovering relationships between entities such as people, objects such as weapons or vehicles, locations, and events (commonly referred to as the POLE graph). The volume of unstructured data is high in this domain—think of witness reports, surveillance footage, images, voice recordings and more. Manually collating all this information and trying to connect the dots under the constraint of time is extremely challenging. A knowledge graph brings it all together and enables investigators to find paths quickly and explore related entities. This pattern should now be evident to you: an LLM assists in enriching the knowledge graph by analyzing unstructured data and enables investigative teams to work more efficiently by conversing with it to ask questions such as "Do these suspects have common associates?" and "Is there anything similar about all the locations at which these events have occurred?"

The following sections explore the symbiotic relationship between knowledge graphs and GenAI. Now that you've seen how this pair can be applied effectively in diverse domains, you'll better relate to the concepts of GraphRAG and knowledge graph building.

GraphRAG

RAG is a technique that enhances GenAI applications by retrieving key information and context to answer a user's query from external data sources, including private or proprietary ones, and ranking this information based on relevance to the query. This ranked, sorted information is combined with the user's question and additional instructions to augment the prompt supplied to the LLM. The LLM now generates answers based on these supplied facts, instead of relying solely on a pretrained model. High quality in RAG's retrieval and augmentation components can help reduce hallucinations in its generated answers.

GraphRAG relies on a knowledge graph as its external data source, which it uses to improve the retrieval phase. The superpower of graphs is connecting the dots and inferring hidden relationships. Knowledge graphs provide much-needed relevance and context, resulting in more accuracy, explainability, and traceability. Figure 13-3 shows what a GraphRAG architecture encompasses at a very high level.

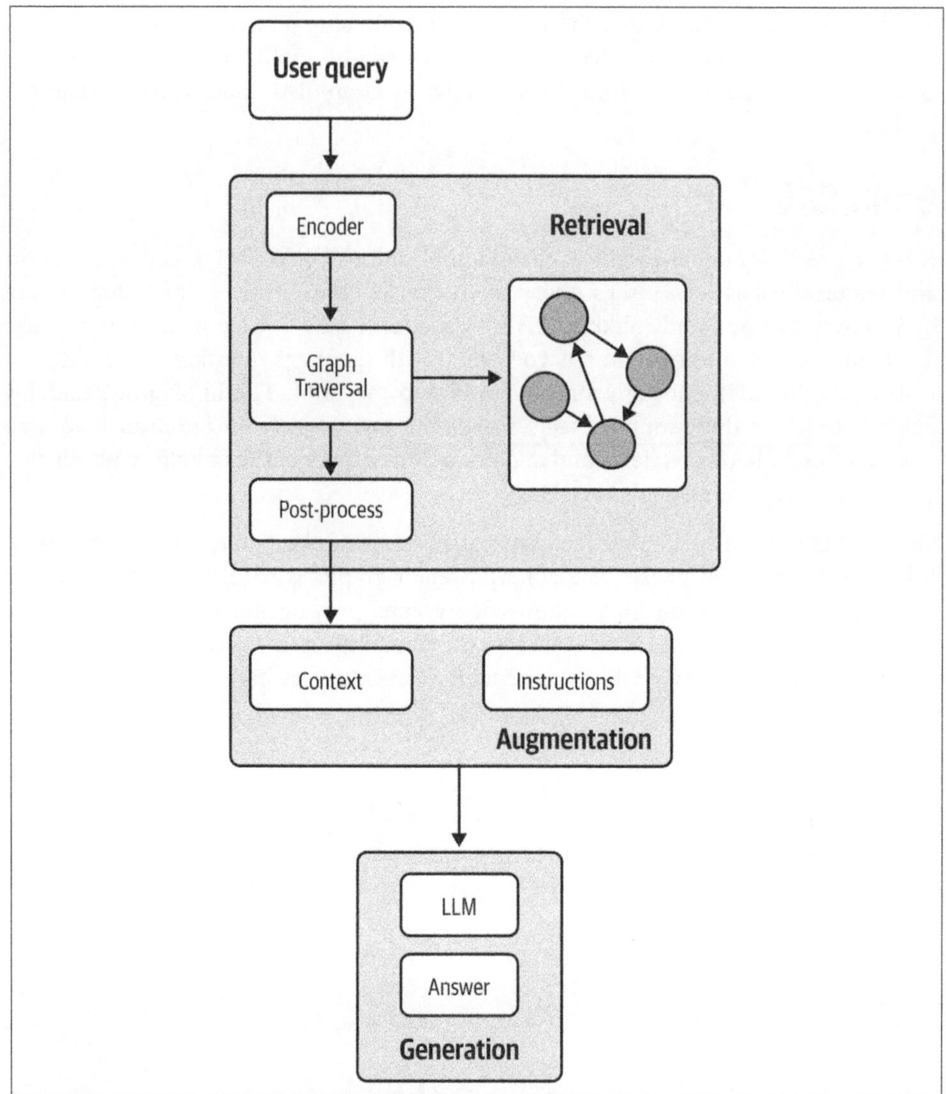

Figure 13-3. A high-level GraphRAG flow

The retrieval phase can be as simple or complex as needed. In its most basic form, the user's query is encoded or translated to find the starting point in the graph. The Cypher query can be generic, like the node neighborhood or the subgraph connecting all starting points. It can also involve predefined queries written by subject-matter experts, who identify which subgraph is relevant for answering certain questions, then use query routing and content extraction techniques to retrieve the appropriate information. GraphRAG then traverses the graph via a Cypher query to retrieve related entities, structures the results, and sends them with instructions to the LLM.

In more advanced cases, graph data-science algorithms are used to further rank results or infer relationships that provide important context to the LLM. These techniques are constantly evolving, and we recommend browsing through GraphRAG's catalog of currently available patterns (*https://graphrag.com*).

What About Vector Search?

Information retrieval based on vector search over text embeddings is a popular RAG technique. A *text embedding* is a numerical representation of text (a word, sentence, document, or the like) that captures its meaning, context, and relationships to other pieces of text in a way that computers can understand and compare. An embedding maps text into a *vector* (an array of numbers), often in hundreds or thousands of dimensions, and this vector representation captures the entity's semantics or qualities statistically. In a piece of text, for example, the source text is typically chunked into smaller fragments, embedded, and stored. Vector search over text embeddings then matches semantically similar text. In the retrieval phase, vector search can be used to match user queries to semantically similar pieces of information, which are then provided as context to the LLM.

However, relying on vector search alone can be problematic, especially in large, highly specific domains with complex relationships. There are a few reasons for this. First, vector search is confined to the text fragments in the chunks it has retrieved. These may be incomplete if some relevant information in another chunk was missed. Second, multihop traversals and inferring relationships, which give invaluable context to the LLM to synthesize new insights or summarize semantic concepts, are weaknesses for vector searches. Finally, vector searches are a closed box: their results are hard to explain or trace.

Fortunately, you don't have to choose one or the other. Vector searches are great for finding a starting point in the graph based on the user's query—in other words, finding relevant chunks of text that are semantically close to the query. They do this by computing the Euclidean distance or angle (cosine) between the search text and stored vector in a high dimensional space. They *aren't* as well suited to queries that require reasoning over relationships and connecting documents, chunks, domain entities, and so on. That's where graph traversals come in, providing meaningful, explainable context to the LLM.

In summary, complementing GenAI with techniques such as vector search can enable a rich context window, supplied with highly relevant content that results in more accurate and explainable answers.

Agentic AI Architectures

Agentic architectures are popular because they equip LLMs with tools that not only retrieve information (similar to RAG) but also *take action* on behalf of the user. A simplified process flow, from the user query back to the answer, is shown in Figure 13-4.

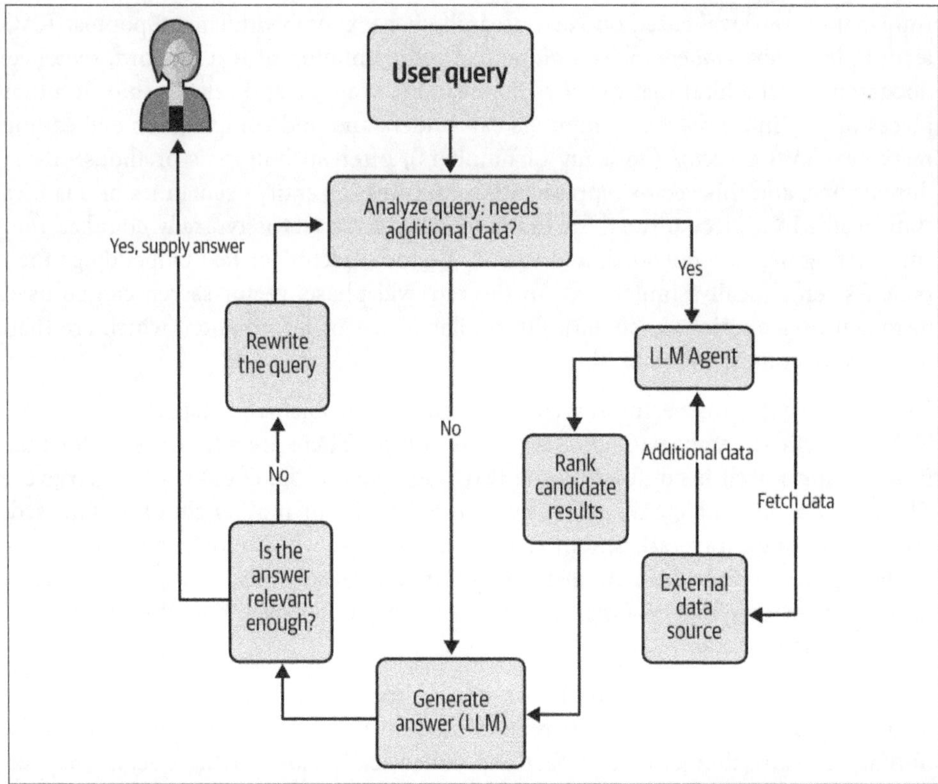

Figure 13-4. AI agent process flow

The LLM formulates a plan to compose the set of tools it needs to reliably answer the user's query. During execution, the LLM can use these tools in various ways: it can invoke them in a sequence, run them in a loop, or use the output from one tool to augment its input to another. It constantly evaluates whether the data it has collected is sufficient to answer the user's query and, if the data is insufficient, it persists with its tools to get close enough to a good answer.

Agents aren't only information retrievers. They can also be employed as guardrails to apply security checks or ensure data privacy, or to improve the relevance of results by ranking and sorting candidate answers and intermediate information inputs.

In November 2024, Anthropic developed the *Model Context Protocol* (MCP)—a protocol for AI applications that standardizes a universal way for external tools and APIs to connect and provide context to an agent's model. The MCP architecture includes a main program called the MCP Host, which can be set up with several MCP servers that offer tools, resources, and prompts. At the time of writing this book, Neo4j has three MCP servers:

- `mcp-neo4j-cypher` to interact with the Neo4j database via Cypher
- `mcp-neo4j-memory` for storing facts as graph memory
- `mcp-neo4j-cloud-aura-api` to manage Neo4j Aura instances

Figure 13-5 illustrates a case where an agent requests a task during an interaction that can be handled by an MCP server capability. In this scenario, the LLM selects the appropriate tool, extracts the necessary parameters, and invokes the tool via an MCP client connected to the MCP server.

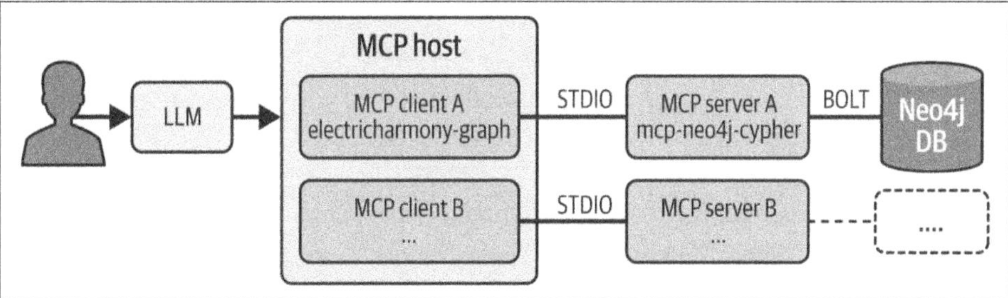

Figure 13-5. The LLM selects the appropriate tool and invokes it via the MCP client connected to an MCP server.

Google's MCP Toolbox for Databases, a collaboration between Google and LangChain, addresses common database challenges such as connections, security, and tool updates. An integration with Neo4j (*https://oreil.ly/ALa8-*) is available as part of this toolbox, bringing knowledge graph capability to AI agents. The impact of the MCP Toolbox on AI agents has been tremendous. It now takes much less effort to federate agents across data sources in a more standard manner. It's still early days, but it looks like MCP—and AI agents in general—are here to stay.

Knowledge Graph Creation

The importance of GraphRAG underscores the need for a comprehensive knowledge graph to connect siloes of business information. When data is fragmented across a large organization, constructing a rich context for RAG is difficult. Knowledge graphs are easier to create or enrich with unstructured data when using an LLM. The Neo4j LLM knowledge graph builder (*https://oreil.ly/Fkro5*) transforms documents, PDFs, video transcripts, and the like into a lexical graph of documents and chunks, which are stored, with their embeddings, in your Neo4j database, in addition to an entity graph that stores nodes and their relationships to the document chunks. Most of the heavy lifting is done by LLMs, enabling you to create or enhance your knowledge graph rapidly. The ecosystem is rich and involves players such as LangChain (*https://oreil.ly/jmvwy*), LlamaIndex (*https://oreil.ly/nEjyo*), and the GraphRAG Python package (*https://oreil.ly/rWS6W*).

The general idea is to ingest data from unstructured sources, use an LLM to extract entities and relationships from it, perform entity resolution, and merge these entities and relationships into the business graph to enrich it. Figure 13-6 also shows how GenAI applications use this knowledge graph.

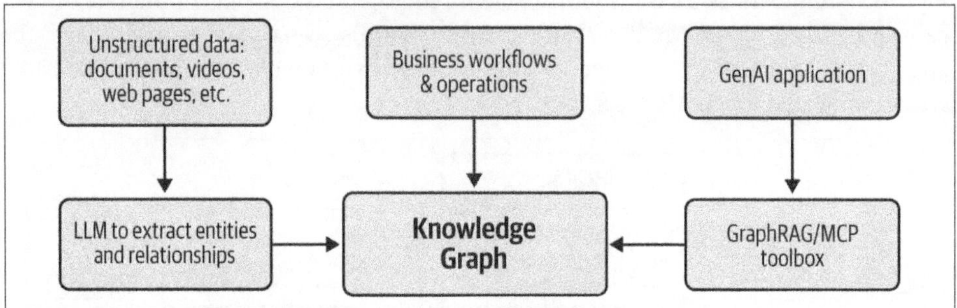

Figure 13-6. The knowledge graph builder builds and/or enriches a knowledge graph, which GenAI applications can then use.

The beauty of building your knowledge graph quickly is that these graphs' qualities enable faster development of Gen AI applications. First, a flexible schema encourages iterative development. Start with a high-impact area of the business first—you don't need to wait to gather every siloed data source to pull into the graph. Second, you can go wide easily by modeling the most important data connections across various systems first. The knowledge graph now spans the most important use cases across your entire business. Later, you can expand and enrich it with more business context as your Gen AI application evolves.

A Practical Example: Playlist Recommendations from Natural Language

Let's wrap up the chapter and the book by bringing everything together into a practical example using ElectricHarmony. This example showcases how graph data science, vector similarity, and natural language interfaces can work in harmony to offer personalized music recommendations powered by GenAI.

The code for this example is available in the GitHub companion repository (*https://oreil.ly/kQhL3*). Follow the instructions in the `README.md` for a step-by-step guide on how to run it yourself.

Imagine a user saying: "Recommend a playlist of jazz music with a chic style." Let's see how ElectricHarmony makes this happen.

Step 1: Communities from GDS

In Chapter 12, you used the Louvain algorithm from Neo4j Graph Data Science (GDS) to detect communities of playlists. Each community groups together playlists that are closely connected by the number of tracks they share in common, represented by a `CO_OCCURS` relationship.

For a given community, you can use the following Cypher query to retrieve a sample of tracks along with their artist names (as shown in Figure 13-7):

```
//001-community-samples.cypher
MATCH (c:Community)-[:HAS_PLAYLIST]->(p)
WHERE c.id = 44386
MATCH (p)-[:HAS_TRACK]->(t)-[:ARTIST]->(a)
RETURN t.name AS track, a.name AS artist
ORDER BY rand()
LIMIT 10
```

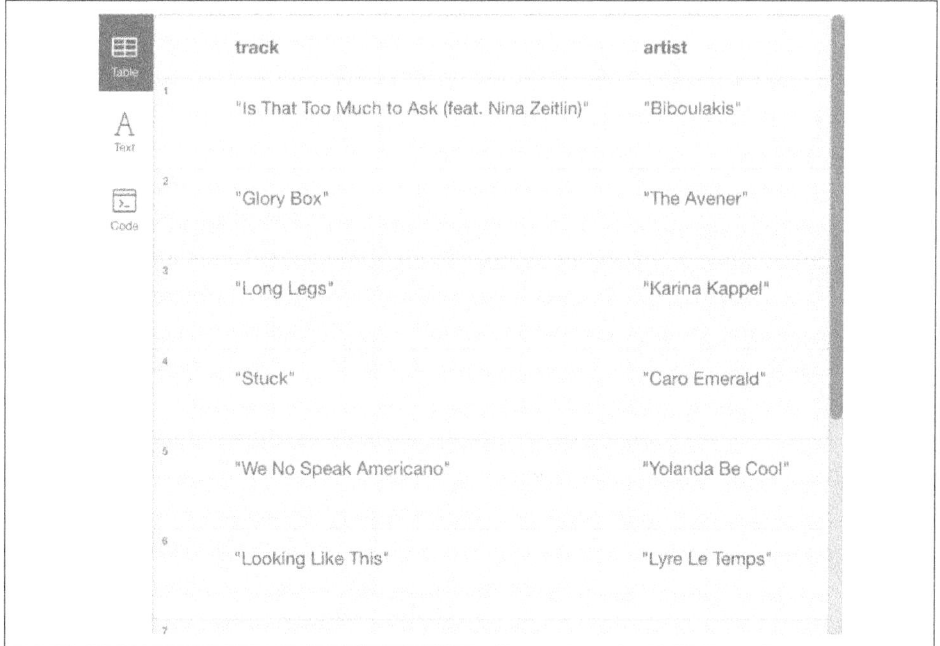

Table
Text
Code
track
artist
"Is That Too Much to Ask (feat. Nina Zeitlin)"
"Biboulakis"
"Glory Box"
"The Avener"
"Long Legs"
"Karina Kappel"
"Stuck"
"Caro Emerald"
"We No Speak Americano"
"Yolanda Be Cool"
"Looking Like This"
"Lyre Le Temps"

Figure 13-7. Sample tracks for a given community

Step 2: Generate Summaries and Questions with an LLM

The approach here is to retrieve a sample of tracks from the community playlists along with their artist names. Since LLMs have been trained on publicly available information, their knowledge is useful for generating realistic text summaries.

The LLM will generate two important pieces of information:

- A summary of the musical identity of the community
- A list of natural-language queries a user might ask when referring to this community (without knowing it exists)

A prompt is crafted to instruct the LLM on what to generate and how to format the response:

```
You will be given a sample of 100 songs belonging to similar playlists. For each
song, you have the track name and artist name.
Your task is to generate a comprehensive summary for the community of playlists.
Additionally, generate 5 hypothetical search phrases a listener could type in
order to find such playlists, for example if the summary contains "Influential
rock a billy", then a question could be "I'm looking for rockabilly themed
playlists."
**You must return the data in the following JSON format**:
{{
  "questions": ["question1", "question2", ...],
  "summary": "text"
}}
Tracks: {text}
```

The {text} placeholder in the prompt will be replaced with the sample tracks retrieved in Step 1.

If you're using Claude or ChatGPT, you can try it right away: simply paste the prompt above, along with the results of the Cypher query, and you'll be amazed by the response. It might look similar to what's shown in Figure 13-8.

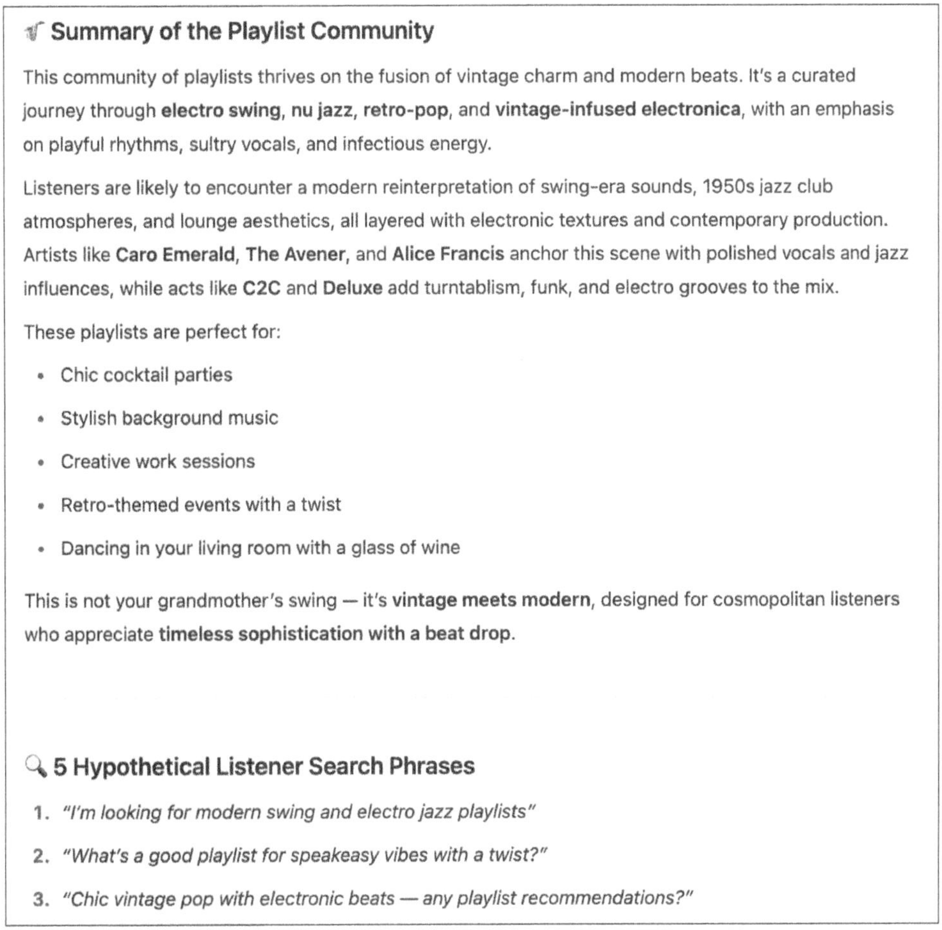

Summary of the Playlist Community

This community of playlists thrives on the fusion of vintage charm and modern beats. It's a curated journey through **electro swing, nu jazz, retro-pop**, and **vintage-infused electronica**, with an emphasis on playful rhythms, sultry vocals, and infectious energy.

Listeners are likely to encounter a modern reinterpretation of swing-era sounds, 1950s jazz club atmospheres, and lounge aesthetics, all layered with electronic textures and contemporary production. Artists like **Caro Emerald, The Avener**, and **Alice Francis** anchor this scene with polished vocals and jazz influences, while acts like **C2C** and **Deluxe** add turntablism, funk, and electro grooves to the mix.

These playlists are perfect for:

- Chic cocktail parties
- Stylish background music
- Creative work sessions
- Retro-themed events with a twist
- Dancing in your living room with a glass of wine

This is not your grandmother's swing — it's **vintage meets modern**, designed for cosmopolitan listeners who appreciate **timeless sophistication with a beat drop**.

5 Hypothetical Listener Search Phrases

1. *"I'm looking for modern swing and electro jazz playlists"*
2. *"What's a good playlist for speakeasy vibes with a twist?"*
3. *"Chic vintage pop with electronic beats — any playlist recommendations?"*

Figure 13-8. ChatGPT result of the summary

Step 3: Vectorize and Store in Neo4j

It's unlikely that a user would phrase their question *exactly* as it appears in the summary, which makes traditional search techniques less effective. A common strategy is to convert both the summaries and the questions into mathematical representations—vector embeddings—that capture their meaning and can be compared using similarity functions. As you learned earlier in this chapter, vector embeddings allow us to find semantically similar items efficiently.

We store both the original summary and question texts in Neo4j, along with their corresponding embeddings, using the model shown in Figure 13-9. At this point, the graph is no longer just a network of direct relationships—it's also enriched with semantic understanding through vectors.

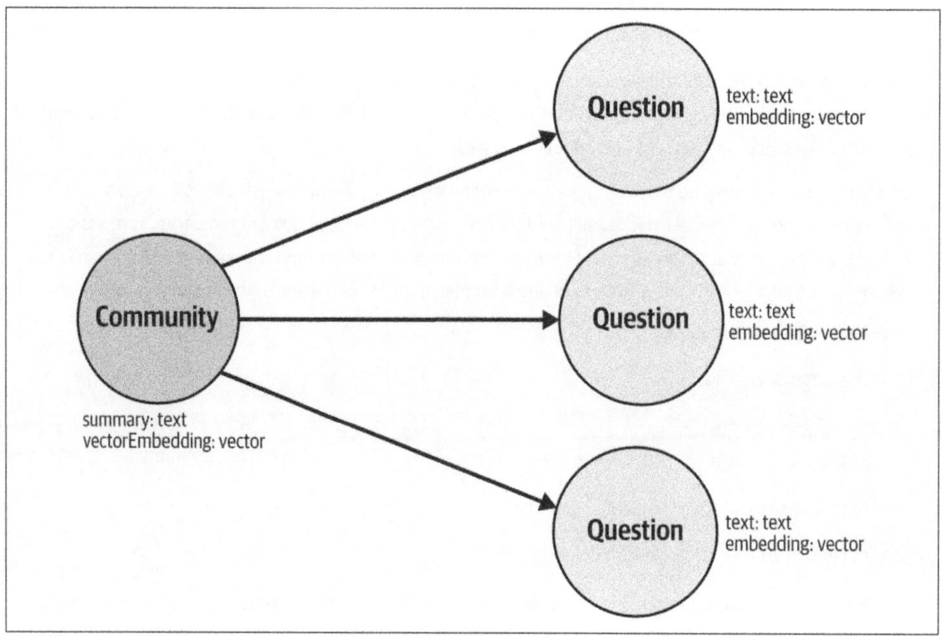

Figure 13-9. Graph model of summary and questions.

Step 4: The User Asks a Question

Now it's showtime. The user asked: "Recommend a playlist of jazz music with a chic style."

Here's what happens behind the scenes, pictured in Figure 13-10:

- The user query is embedded into a vector.
- A vector similarity search finds the most semantically relevant questions or community summaries.
- These hits point to the best-matching communities or questions.

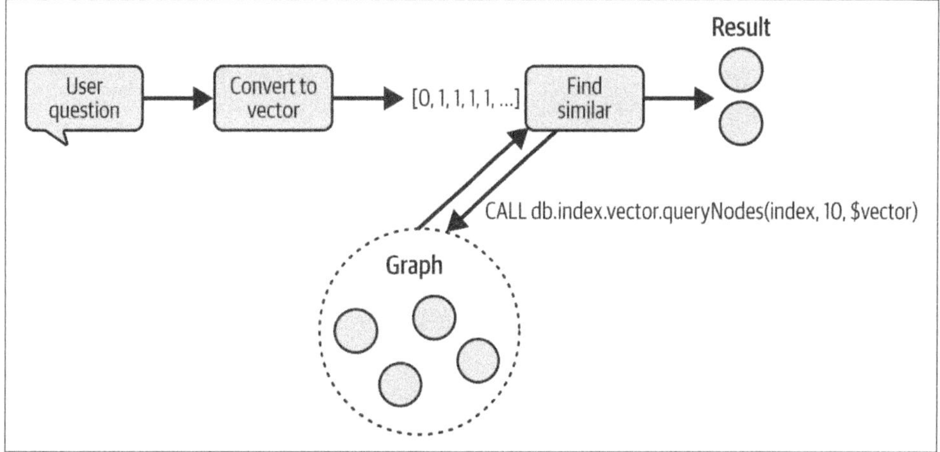

Figure 13-10. First phase of the retrieval

Step 5: Generate an answer

Once the most similar questions or communities have been identified based on the user's query, the graph is traversed again to retrieve a sample of tracks. This information is then passed to the LLM, which uses it to generate a comprehensive answer—often including reasoning as to why a playlist from that community is a good match.

The following prompt is used to guide the LLM, and Figure 13-11 shows an example response generated manually using ChatGPT:

```
You will receive a summary of a community of playlists, some playlists and some
sample tracks of them.
For each playlist, create a "here is a recommended playlist" answer to the user
and explain why based on the songs.
Question : {user_question}
Data : {data}
```

Recommended Playlist: "Jazz & Big Band"

If you're looking for jazz with a *chic style*, I highly recommend the **"Jazz & Big Band"** playlist. This collection embodies timeless elegance and polished sophistication—perfect for refined moments, cocktail evenings, or simply when you're in the mood for a smooth, classy ambiance.

Why this playlist fits your request:

- **Frank Sinatra** sets the tone with "Come Fly With Me" and "Witchcraft," both of which are iconic examples of suave vocal jazz with lush arrangements.
- **Michael Bublé** brings modern polish to the classic big band sound, with tracks like "Come Dance With Me" and "Haven't Met You Yet," maintaining a luxurious feel.
- **Lady Gaga**'s jazz covers, such as "I Can't Give You Anything But Love," channel vintage glamour with contemporary edge.
- **Count Basie** and his rendition of "Fly Me to the Moon" add orchestral jazz richness.
- **Tony Bennett** and **Billy Joel** contribute urbane New York-style flair with "New York State of Mind."

Together, these artists craft a jazz experience that is chic, urbane, and timeless.

Figure 13-11. ChatGPT-generated playlist recommendation

In addition to generating an immediate response, the user's query can also be stored in the graph along with its vector embedding. This opens up several powerful possibilities. For example, during traversal, you can enrich the results by comparing the current query not only to stored community summaries but also to previously asked questions, either generated by the LLM or submitted by other users.

This enables a feature like "Users who asked similar questions also searched for...", where the system suggests semantically related queries based on vector similarity. These suggestions can be displayed as clickable prompts, allowing users to explore related musical themes or moods with a single tap, enhancing the discovery experience while keeping the interface intuitive and engaging.

Storing user queries also has long-term benefits: it allows you to analyze popular intent patterns over time, improve recommendations, and even fine-tune your vector models to better match your user base.

Step 6: Wrapping Up

This example demonstrates the power of combining structured graph data, vector embeddings, and generative AI. What's especially exciting is that the LLM contributes both knowledge (via its pretrained model) and contextual understanding (via the

RAG flow), while the graph ensures that the recommendations are grounded in real-world data.

ElectricHarmony can generate summaries and natural questions from the graph, and it can use those same elements to power retrieval. It's a beautiful feedback loop where your own domain knowledge (tracks, playlists, genres) meets the world's shared knowledge (musical trends, language, and patterns).

Together, graphs and GenAI don't just recommend content, they understand it.

Summary

Knowledge graphs serve as a factual foundation for generative AI systems. They support RAG to address hallucinations fueled by limited context window size, lack of access to private data, and LLMs' knowledge cutoff (based on their last training data). We expect knowledge graphs to be the backbone of future GenAI applications.

GraphRAG improves upon RAG by adding rich contextual information; integrating Neo4j into the MCP Toolbox for Databases makes GraphRAG much more accessible to agents, and LLMs are making it easier to create knowledge graphs from unstructured data. The convergence of Neo4j graph databases and GenAI represents a significant leap forward in the ability to extract value from connected data. As these technologies continue to develop at blistering speed, we will see sophisticated solutions that leverage both graph data and the flexible reasoning of generative AI. The future of data is not just about information itself but about understanding and leveraging the complex webs of relationships that give information meaning.

Index

Symbols

1+1 clusters, 292

A

abstract syntax tree (AST), 138
access controls
  implementing role-based access control, 187-193
  information disclosure considerations, 196
  label-based, 252-256
  property-based, 252-256
ACID properties, transactions, 51
admin import feature, 73-75
agentic AI architectures, 362-363
AI agents, 362-363
algorithms
  clique percolation, 339
  community detection, 329
    storing results, 340-343
  execution modes, 339-340
  GDS library, 328
  Louvain, 338-346
  Speaker-Listener Label Propagation, 339
analytical queries, Louvain algorithm results, 343
analytical workloads, secondary servers, 287
analyzers, 212-214
  tokenization, 220-221
anchors, 138-139
  global graph queries, 139
  queries based on labels, 139-140
  query performance
    selectivity, 151-153
    using predicates, 156-161
apoc library, 132
appenders (log file section), 302
ASCII art, visual query languages, 12
AST (abstract syntax tree), 138
atomicity property, transactions, 51, 54
audit logs, 194
authentication
  Neo4j login, 15
  provider support, 182
  security best practices, 184
  spoofing, 182-183
authorization, RBAC, 187-193
auto-committing transactions, 56
availability, clusters, 277-278
  fault tolerance, 280
  Raft protocol, 278-280
  secondary servers, 280

B

backups, 267
  cloud, 271
  full, 267-268
  incremental, 269-270
  remote, 272
  restoring, 270-271
  secondary servers, 290
  securing, 185
  security considerations, 194
  strategy, 272-274
  transaction log rotation strategy
    example, 261-267
    schedule considerations, 260
backward compatibility, refactoring data, 120
behavioral clusters, user communities, 349-350

bidirectional relationships, 98-104
graph analytics with GDS, 338
block-storage engine, 11
bolt metrics, queries, 316
bookmarks, 291
browser credential timeouts, 183
browsers, securing Neo4j databases, 183
bucketed relationships, 97-98
build inputs, 173
built-in roles, 189
business domain models, comparison, 5

C

cache
authentication
TTL setting, 183
turning off, 182-183
unencrypted user credentials, turning off, 183
CALL IN TRANSACTIONS, 54-57
concurrent transactions, 230
CALL subqueries, 227-229
cardinality, relationships, 83
Cartesian products, 148-150
case sensitivity, searches, 204
categorical variables, 85
causal consistency, clusters, 291-292
CDC (Change Data Capture), 75
checkpoints
database housekeeping, 258-259
performing manually, 263
recommended frequency, 274
Claude.ai, resolving duplicate entities, 239-241
clean datasets, 75
client applications, importing data from, 57
clique percolation algorithm, 339
cloud backups, 271
clustered deployments, security, 185
clusters
1+1 clusters, 292
causal consistency, 291-292
deployment, 280-283
fault tolerance, 283-285
multidatabase, 286
network latency, 287
performance
fault tolerance, 280
high availability, 277-278
Raft protocol, 278-280
secondary servers, 280
read queries, distribution, 287-289
co-occurrence graphs, 332
co-occurrence relationships, 333-335
marking datasets, 331-333
selecting subsets of data, 331
skipping low co-occurrences, 333
communication channels, default ports, 184-185
community detection algorithms, 329
behavioral clusters, 349-350
co-occurrence graphs, creating, 330-335
content licensing strategy, 350-351
dynamic user segmentation, 347
generating recommendations, 346
influencer discovery, 348
Louvain, 338-346
storing results, 340-343
composite databases, 248
sharding and federation, 293-297
composite indexes, 160
compound privileges, 193
concurrent transactions, 230
transaction locking, 65-66
nodes and relationships, 67-69
configuration files, logs, 301-302
connection URIs, 281
consistency checks, 185-186
consistency property, transactions, 51
constraints
indexes, 159
types, 194
CONTAINS search operator, 207
count store, 139
crash recovery, 259, 265-266
CREATE privilege, 192
credential timeouts, setting, 183
cross joins, 148
CSV files
importing, admin import feature, 73-75
loading, 62
previewing, 16-18
customer 360 knowledge graphs, 357
cybercrime networks, graph use case, 8-9
cybersecurity, knowledge graphs, 357-358
Cypher projections, 335
Cypher query language, 12-13
importing data, parameters, 57
injection attacks, 186-187

MERGE clause, avoiding duplicate data, 24-28
parameters, 59
pathfinding query example, 22-23
procedures, 67
processing pipeline, 137-138
runtime, 138, 176-178
writing queries, 23-32
Cypher Shell, 143

D

data at rest, security, 185
data ingestion, 15-16
batch processing
batch sizing, 61-62
UNWIND clause, 58-64
CALL IN TRANSACTIONS operation, 54-57
client applications, query parameters, 57
LOAD CSV command, 193
offline, 73-75
reingesting, 120
speed, improving, 32-38
tools, 75
data integrity, transactions, 50-52
data persistence, transaction lifecycle, 257-258
data previews, 16-18
data representation, relational databases, 5
data siloes (see siloed data)
data storage
block-storage engine, 11
index-free adjacency, 11
database store directory, inspecting, 262
databases
access, securing, 183
composite databases, sharding and federation, 293-297
constraints, transactions, 50
creating, 16, 261
files location, 261
housekeeping process, 258-259
instances, 278
leaders, 278
fault tolerance, 283-285
multidatabase clusters, 286
Raft protocol, 278-280
new, creating, 55
relationships, cardinality, 83
scale considerations, 49
topology, 282
transactions, 50-52
CALL IN TRANSACTIONS operation, 54-57
heap feature overview, 52, 54
parallel writes, 64-73
DateTime type, 114
debug logs, 301
inspecting, 304-305
debug.log file, 264
full backups, 268
declarative query languages, 12
DELETE privilege, 193
denial-of-service (DoS) attacks (see DoS (denial-of-service) attacks)
deployment, clusters, 280-283
fault tolerance, 283-285
direction, relationships, 98
disaster recovery, secondary servers, 290
DoS (denial-of-service) attacks, mitigation and prevention techniques, 197-198
drivers, interfacing with applications, 57-58
durability property, transactions, 51
dynamic user segmentation, 347

E

Eager operator, 167
EagerAggregation operator, 168
eagerness, queries, 165-168
elevation of privilege attacks, mitigation and prevention techniques, 198-200
encrypting
data, 185
properties, information disclosure considerations, 196
ENDS WITH search operator, 207
entities
fused, composite databases, 248
fusing, 242-248
merged properties, 245
modeling as nodes, 84-85
property graph models, 10
resolved
entity groups, 241-242
modeling, 238-241
quantified path patterns, 248-252
entity resolution, 357
error messages, security considerations, 187
execution modes, algorithms, 339-340

EXPLAIN command, query plans, 141-143
explicit eagerness, 168
extensions, security considerations, 199

F

fact nodes, query participation, 248
fault tolerance, 280
  1+1 clusters, 292
  clusters, 283-285
federation, queries, 293-297
file permissions, 185
  security considerations, 200
filters
  creating queries, 310
  eliminating redundant, 153-156
full backups, 267-268
  recommended schedule, 273
  remote, 272
full text indexes, searches, 211-216
full-disk encryption, 185
fused entities, composite databases, 248
fuzzy searches, 219-220

G

garbage collection logs, inspecting, 306-307
GDS (Graph Data Science) library, 327
  community detection algorithms, 329
  graph algorithms, 328
  graph catalogs, 328
  graphs, projecting, 337-338
  installing plugin, 335
  Louvain algorithm, 338-346
  memory usage, estimating, 335-337
  subgraphs, projecting, 335
  workflow, 329
GenAI, 353
  knowledge graphs, 2
global graph queries, 139
GQL (Graph Query Language), 12
Grafana, 318
  logs explorer, 322
  select metrics explorer, 320
graph algorithms, GDS, 328
Graph Analytics, 15
graph catalogs, GDS, 328
Graph Data Science (GDS) library (see GDS (Graph Data Science) library)
graph databases
  relational databases
    comparison, 4
  testing, 28-32
graph local queries, 140
graph modeling
  commonalities, traversing across, 84-85
  decorating properties, 83-84
  labels, performance considerations, 85-87
  node fanout, 87-90
  overview, 77
  principles, 82
  properties and nodes, 83
  relationships
    bidirectional, 98-104
    bucketed, 97-98
    granularity, 92-95
    n-way, 109-111
    performance considerations, 238
    types compared to properties, 96-97
  sequences, 114-119
  supernodes, 90-92
  versioning, time-based, 112-114
graph models
  business domain models, comparison, 5
  designing, 18-19
graph projections
  GDS library, 328
  memory, 339
Graph Query Language (GQL), 12
graph stores, nonnative compared to native, 11
GraphAcademy, Neo4j training, 13
GraphRAG, 2
  knowledge graphs, 359-361
    creating, 363
graphs
  data representation advantages, 2
  knowledge, 354-356
  projecting, 337-338
  use cases, 6

H

heap
  CALL IN TRANSACTIONS operation, 54-57
  memory allocation configuration, 54
    parallel writes, 64-65
  query rows, 146
  transactions, 52-54
heap usage metric, 315
hints, query planner, 172-175

housekeeping process, databases, 258-259
hyperedge nodes, 109-111

I

identifiers
  in searches, 222
  searchability, 203
immutable privileges, 198
impedance mismatch, 5
implicit eagerness, 166
implicit relationships, 40
importing data (see data ingestion)
incremental backups, 269-270
  recommended schedule, 273
  remote, 272
index-free adjacency, data storage, 11
indexes
  analysis phase, 212
  composite, 160
  data ingestion, improving speed, 33
  full-text searches, 211-216
  hints, 173
  performance considerations, 161
  point, 159
  property constraints, 194
  query performance, 140-141, 157-161
  range, 158
  sorting results, 170-172
  string-based, 210
  text, 159
  text searches, 203-204
  TEXT searches, 208-211
  token lookup, 158
  token-based, 211
    tokenization, 220-221
  usage history, 223
influencer discovery, 348
information disclosure, 196
  access control, 196
  properties, encryption, 196
  query logs, 196
instances, databases, 278
IP addresses, in searches, 222
isolation property, transactions, 51

J

join tables, relational databases, 6
JVM garbage collection metric, 315

K

Kafka Connect, data ingestion, 75
know your customer (KYC), 6
knowledge graphs, 2, 354-356
  creating, 363
  customer 360, 357
  cybersecurity, 357-358
  GraphRAG, 359-361
  law enforcement, 358
  life sciences, 358
  retail industry, 358
KYC (know your customer), 6

L

label scan hints, 175
label-based access control, 252-256
labeled property graphs, 10
labels
  constraints, adding, 33
  dynamic, 247
  performance considerations, 85-87
large language models (LLMs) (see LLM)
law enforcement
  graph use case, 7-8
  knowledge graphs, 358
LDAP provider, configuration, 182-183
leaders, databases, 278
  fault tolerance, 283-285
  multidatabase clusters, 286
  Raft protocol, 278-280
least privileges, 199
life sciences knowledge graphs, 358
linked lists, 116-119
  apoc library, 132
lists
  recalculating item position, 115-116
  sequences, 114
    finding last item, 115
live refactoring, 120
LLM knowledge graph builder, 363
LLMs (large language models)
  cautions, 353
  customer 360 knowledge graphs, 357
LOAD CSV command
  concurrent transactions, 230
  ingesting data, 193
load testing, queries, 179
locking, parallel writes, 65-66
  nodes and relationships, 67-69

loggers (log file section), 302
logs
  authentication attempts, 184
  configuration files, 301-302
  debug.log file, 264
  differential backups, 269
  filtering log events, 308-311
  inspecting, 302-307
  Loki
    filtering by application, 323
    filtering by query time, 324
    multiple filters, 325
  nonrepudiation considerations, 195
  queries, 179
  query, information disclosure considerations, 196
  replication, Raft protocol, 278-280
  retrieving, Loki, 322-323
  sections, 302
  security
    audits, 194
    contents, 184
  transactions, rotation strategy, 260-267
  types, 195, 300-301
  usefulness of, 300
  VERBOSE logging, 307-308
  write-ahead logging, 258
Loki, 318
  logs
    filtering by application, 323
    filtering by query time, 324
    multiple filters, 325
    retrieving, 322-323
Louvain algorithm, 338-346
  analytical queries, 343

M

master data management, 357
MATCH privilege, 190
MCP (Model Context Protocol), 363
MCP Toolbox for Databases, 363
memory
  configuration, parallel writes, 64-65
  graph projections, 339
  heap, configuration, 54
  logs, 300
  page cache, queries, 146
  query rows, 146
  usage, estimating, 335-337
MERGE clause, avoiding duplication, 24-28
metrics
  Grafana metrics explorer, 320
  monitoring, 313
    configuring Prometheus format, 313-314
    Neo4j load metrics, 315-316
    Neo4j workload metrics, 316-318
    server load, 315
Model Context Protocol (MCP), 363
model design, 18-19
monitoring, 318
  (see also observability stack)
  backups, 274
  metrics, 313
    configuring Prometheus format, 313-314
    Neo4j load metrics, 315-316
    Neo4j workload metrics, 316-318
    server load, 315
  Neo4j Ops Manager, 326
multidatabase clusters, 286
multitoken searches, 216-219

N

n-way relationships, 109-111
native auth provider, 182
native graph databases, 10-12
native projections, 335
Neo4j
  access, securing, 183
  authentication, 15
  Cypher query language, 12, 13
  data storage, index-free adjacency, 11
  databases, creating new, 55
  drivers, 57-58
  Graph Analytics, 15
  launching, 15
  load metrics, 315-316
  logs, 300-301
  overview, 9-10
  password, initial login, 182
  proof of concept example
    creating nodes and relationships, 21-22
    creating SIMILAR relationships, 38-39
    dataset ingestion, 15-16
    finding similarities, 35-37
    generating recommendations, 40-42
    implicit relationships, 40
    improving data ingestion speed, 32-38
    installing Neo4j, 15

model design, 18-19
overview, 13-14
previewing data, 16-18
testing and refactoring, 28-32
testing recommendations, 42-47
walking the graph, 20
writing queries, 23-32
Query analyzer, 326
training, GraphAcademy, 13
workload metrics, 316-318
Neo4j Aura, 185
Neo4j log, inspecting, 302-304
Neo4j Ops Manager, database administration, 326
neo4j-admin copy, 186
neo4j-jdbc, data ingestion, 75
nested objects, nodes, 83
network latency, clustering, 287
nodes
adding concurrently, 70-73
communities, treating as, 341
creating, 21-22
concurrently, 69-70
from properties, 123-126
from relationships, 126-135
degrees, 230-233
querying, 163-165
fusing, 243-245
graph modeling, 83
decorating properties, 83-84
hyperedge, 109-111
nested objects, 83
node fanout, 87-90
object count metrics, 317
organizing principles, 354
property graph models, 10
random, creating, 262
relationships, n-way, 109-111
simultaneous updates, locking mechanisms, 67-69
supernodes, 90
traversal efficiency considerations, 234-238
traversal problems , 88
nonrepudiation, logs, 195
nonword terms in searches, 222

O

object count metrics, nodes and relationships, 317
observability stack, 318
(see also monitoring)
metrics, selecting and displaying, 320-322
services, 318-319
ontologies, 355-356
operators, searches, 207

P

page cache
queries, 146
transactions, 259
page cache hit metric, 315
parallel batch execution, concurrent transactions, 230
parallel runtime, 176-178
parallel writes
memory configuration, 64-65
transaction locking, 65-66
nodes and relationships, 67-69
parameters, queries, 178-179, 186
partitioned operators, 176
passwords
forcing change, 182
initial, setting, 182
patches, 200
path patterns, matching repeated, 248-252
pathfinding
native graph databases, 12
query example, 22-23
pattern anchors, 138-139
global graph queries, 139
queries based on labels, 139-140
pattern comprehension, subqueries, 228
performance
clusters
fault tolerance, 280
high availability, 277-278
Raft protocol, 278-280
secondary servers, 280
data ingestion, improving speed, 33
indexes, 161
logs, 300
memory, estimating usage, 335-337
properties, access considerations, 162-163
queries
eagerness, 165-168
eliminating redundant filters, 153-156
increasing anchor selectivity, 151-153

increasing anchor selectivity with predicates, 156-161
indexing, 140-141, 157-161
large datasets, 225-227
monitoring and measuring, 179-180
parameterizing, 178-179
row cardinality, 147-148
subqueries on large datasets, 227-229
traversal efficiency considerations, 234-238
query planner, improving with hints, 172-175
refactoring data
creating nodes from properties, 123-126
creating nodes from relationships, 126-135
overview, 120-121
relationship types, 121-123
relationships, granularity, 92-95
search queries, 206
speed, improving with SIMILAR relationships, 38-39
symmetric relationships, 98-104
transaction logs, 260
phrase indexes, 216-219
pipelined runtime, 176, 177
point indexes, 159
ports, default communication channels, 184
post-union processing, 229
postings list, full-text indexes, 214
primary servers, 278
default number of, 282
privileges
auditing, 199
granting, 190
probe tables, 173
procedure calls, full-text indexes, 215
procedures, queries, 67
PROFILE command, query plans, 144
DB hits, 146
rows, 144-146
projections, native compared to Cypher, 335
Prometheus, 318
configuring Neo4j metrics, 313-314
proof of concept example, song recommendation system
creating nodes and relationships, 21-22
creating SIMILAR relationships, 38-39
dataset ingestion, 15-16
finding similarities, 35-37
generating recommendations, 40-42
implicit relationships, 40
improving data ingestion speed, 32-38
installing Neo4j, 15
model design, 18-19
overview, 13-14
previewing data, 16-18
testing and refactoring, 28-32
testing recommendations, 42-47
walking the graph, 20
writing queries, 23-32
properties
accessing, performance considerations, 162-163
constraints, types, 194
creating nodes from, 123-126
encryption, information disclosure considerations, 196
graph modeling, 83
decorating properties, 83-84
merged, fused entities, 245
new, granting permission to create, 192
property graph models, 9
relationships, 96-97
weighted, 338
property graph models, 9
property keys, dynamic, 247
property-based access controls, 252-256

Q

QPPs (quantified path patterns)
queries, 225
(see also subqueries)
across disconnected patterns, 148-150
analytical, Louvain algorithm results, 343
based on labels, 139-140
bolt metrics, 316
Cartesian products, 148-150
cross joins, 148
Cypher injection attacks, 186-187
distributing across clustered servers, 287-289
duplicate data, avoiding, 24-28
dynamic labels, 247
eagerness, performance considerations, 165-168
fact nodes, 248
federation, 293-297

filtering, 308
filters, creating, 310
graph local, 140
large datasets
performance issues, 225-227
subqueries, 227-229
load testing, 179
long-running, finding, 312-313
monitoring and measuring, 179-180
node degrees, 163-165
page cache, 146
parameters, 59
importing data from client applications, 57
path patterns, matching repeated, 248-252
performance
increasing anchor selectivity, 151
increasing anchor selectivity with predicates, 156-161
indexing, 140-141
relationship granularity, 92-95
performance considerations
eliminating redundant filters, 153-156
indexing, 157-161
parameterizing, 178-179
row cardinality, 147-148
procedures, 67
processing pipeline, 137-138
relationships, traversal efficiency considerations, 234-238
searches, performance optimization, 206
sorting results, 168-172
stop-the-world pauses, 226-227
syntax errors, 309
unions, 229
post-union processing, 229
writing, 23-32
Query analyzer, 326
query languages, Cypher, 12-13
query logging, 179
query logs, 301
configuring, 307
filtering log events, 308-311
VERBOSE logging, 307-308
information disclosure considerations, 196
inspecting, 305-306
metadata values, 309
query optimizer (see query planner)
query planner, 138
anchors, 138-139
global graph queries, 139
queries based on labels, 139-140
indexing, 140-141
performance, improving with hints, 172-175
TEXT indexes, 210
viewing plans
DB hits, 146
overview, 141-144
rows, 144-146

R

Raft protocol, 278-280
RAG (retrieval-augmented generation) architectures, 359
reliability of, 353
vector searches, 361
range indexes, 158
RBAC (role-based access control), 187-193
RDF (Resource Description Framework), 355
READ privilege, 190
read privileges, 190
read queries, distributing across clustered servers, 287-289
real-time recommendations, graph use case, 7
recommendation systems
example build, 364-371
proof of concept example, 14
recommendations
community detection algorithms, 329
generating, 40-42
generating for communities, 346
real-time, graph use case, 7
testing, 42-47
recovery point objective (RPO), 270, 273
recovery time objective (RTO), 273
refactoring
apoc library, 132
nodes
creating from properties, 123-126
creating from relationships, 126-135
overview, 120-121
relationship types, changing, 121-123
relational databases
compared to graph databases, 4
data accessibility, 6
data representation, 5
join tables, 6
relationship types

dynamic, 247
refactoring, 121-123
relationships
adding concurrently, 70-73
bidirectional, 98-104
graph analytics with GDS, 338
bucketed, 97-98
cardinality, 83
co-occurrence, 332
counting, 121
creating, 21-22
concurrently, 69-70
creating nodes from, 126-135
granularity, 92-95
node degrees, 230-233
object count metrics, 317
organizing principles, 354
property graph models, 10
qualifying, types compared to properties, 96-97
simultaneous updates, locking mechanisms, 67-69
relationships, characteristics, 98
remote access, security, 185
remote backups, 272
REMOVE LABEL privilege, 193
replication, Raft protocol, 278-280
resolved entities
entity groups, 241-242
modeling, 238-241
quantified path patterns, 248-252
Resource Description Framework (RDF), 355
restore playbook, 274
retail industry knowledge graphs, 358
retrieval-augmented generation (RAG) architectures (see RAG (retrieval-augmented generation) architectures)
role-based access control (RBAC), 187-193
roles
access, granting to, 254-256
auditing, 199
authentication, 187
creating, 189, 253-254
row cardinality, query performance considerations, 147-148
rows, query results, 144-146
RPO (recovery point objective), 270, 273
RTO (recovery time objective)
backup strategies, 273
runtimes, Cypher query language, 138, 176-178

S

searches
agentic AI, 362-363
case sensitivity, 204
operators, 207
query performance optimization, 206
special characters, 221
stopwords, 222
techniques
full text indexes, 211-216
fuzzy, 219-220
multitoken, 216-219
partial searches, 207-208
TEXT indexes, 208-211
transforming data, 204-206
wildcards, 219
text indexes, 203-204
text, determining eligibility, 202-203
vector, 361
with graph patterns, 223
secondary servers, 278, 280
analytical workloads, 287
backups, 290
disaster recovery, 290
distributing read queries, 287-289
enabling, 289
security
audit logs, 194
authentication best practices, 184
authorization, RBAC, 187-193
backups, 185, 194
built-in roles, 189
clustered deployments, 185
communication channels default ports, 184-185
consistency checks, 185-186
Cypher injection attacks, 186-187
data at rest, 185
data encryption, 185
DoS attacks, mitigation and prevention techniques, 197-198
elevation of privilege attacks, mitigation and prevention techniques, 198-200
error messages, 187
extensions, 199
file permissions, 185, 200
full-disk encryption, 185

immutable privileges, 198
information disclosure, 196
access control, 196
property encryption, 196
query logs, 196
least privileges, 199
logs, 300
contents, 184
nonrepudiation considerations, 195
neo4j-admin copy command, 186
patches, upgrading, 200
property constraints, 194
remote access, 185
service accounts, 188
spoofing, 182
authentication, 182-183
STRIDE, 181
security logs, 301
inspecting, 304
sequences, lists, 114
finding last item, 115
recalculating item position, 115-116
server load metrics, 315
servers, changing default mode, 280
service accounts
nonrepudiation considerations, 195
security, 188
SET LABEL privilege, 193
SET PROPERTY privilege, 193
sharding data, 293-297
SHOW DATABASES command, 282
SHOW INDEXES, 159
SHOW SERVERS command, 281
shutdowns, recovering from unexpected, 265-266
siloed data, 2
compared to graphs, 2
overcoming disadvantages, 4
SIMILAR relationships, improving performance, 38-39
slotted runtime, 176
sorting query results, 168-172
Speaker-Listener Label Propagation algorithm, 339
special characters, searches, 221
spoofing, 182
authentication, 182-183
protecting against, 184
STARTS WITH search operator, 207
statistics, 139
collected by Neo4j, 151
stop-the-world pauses, 226-227
stopwords in searches, 222
stream execution mode, algorithms, 340
string-based indexes, 210
subgraphs, projecting, 335
subqueries, 225
large datasets, resolving performance issues, 227-229
pattern comprehension, 228
supernodes, 90-92
symmetric relationships, performance considerations, 98-104
synchronous replication, Raft protocol, 280
syntax errors, queries, 309
system database, 282

T

taxonomies, 354-356
temporal instant types, 114
term dictionaries, full-text indexes, 214
text embedding, 361
text indexes, 159
TEXT indexes, searches, 208-211
text searches
determining eligibility, 202-203
full text indexes, 211-216
fuzzy, 219-220
indexes, 203-204
multitoken, 216-219
partial searches, 207-208
TEXT indexes, 208-211
transforming data, 204-206
wildcard, 219
threat assessment models, STRIDE, 181
throughput metrics, transaction latencies, 317
time decay, time-based versioning, 112
time-based versioning, 112-114
Timestamp type, 114
token lookup indexes, 158
token-based indexes, 211
tokenization, 220-221
transaction latency, throughput metrics, 317
transaction lifecycle, 257-258
transaction logs, 51
checking contents, 261
cleanup, 259
incremental backups, 269

location, 261
retention intervals, 273
rotation strategy, 260
example, 261-267
schedule considerations, 260
write-ahead logging, 258
transactions, 50-52, 258
ACID properties, 51
auto-committing, 56
committing rows incrementally, 55
committing, write-ahead logging, 258
concurrent, 230
default row value, 55
enhancing metadata, 311-312
executing in batches, 230
flow diagram, 52
heap feature, 52-54
CALL IN TRANSACTIONS operation, 54-57
page cache, 259
parallel writes, 64-73
splitting, 54
TRAVERSE privilege, 190
trigram indexes, 208
type mismatches, avoiding, 34-35
types
relationships, 96-97
temporal instant, 114

U

UBO (ultimate beneficial ownership), graph use case, 6
unexpected shutdowns, recovering from, 265-266
unions, 229
post-union processing, 229
UNWIND clause, batch data processing, 58-64
usage ratio metric, 315
user accounts, creating, 188
User nodes, granting access, 191
users
auditing, 199
behavioral clusters, 349-350
dynamic segmentation, 347
influencer discovery, 348

V

validation, backups, 274
vector searches, 361
VERBOSE logging, 307-308
versioning, time-based, 112-114
virtual machines (VMs) (see VMs (virtual machines))
visual query languages, ASCII art, 12
VMs (virtual machines)
backups, 271
remote backups, 272
Vormetric Data Security Manager, 185

W

walking the graph, 20
weighted properties, 338
whitespace in searches, 222
wildcard searches, 219
workflows, GDS library, 329
write execution mode, algorithms, 340
write latency, synchronous replication, 280
write privileges, 192
write-ahead logging, 258

About the Authors

Luanne Misquitta is one of the world's most experienced Neo4j consultants. She discovered graph databases and Neo4j in 2009 while she was researching techniques to model and traverse connected data. Since that defining moment in her career, she has been a graph advocate, Neo4j instructor, key community contributor, blogger, and frequent speaker at GraphConnect.

Luanne was previously VP of engineering at GraphAware, where she spent a decade consulting with clients around the world on graph modeling and Cypher. She was an open source committer and a core contributor to the Neo4j OGM and Spring Data Neo4j 4 frameworks. Luanne led the development of GraphAware's Hume, an enterprise mission-critical graph analytics solution.

Christophe Willemsen is the chief technology officer at GraphAware, leading strategic R&D, security, and technical thought leadership initiatives. As the driving force behind the early development of GraphAware's flagship product, Hume—a connected data analytics platform—he embedded his expertise to address the complex needs of organizations working with highly connected data. Today, Hume supports mission-critical investigations and intelligence analysis across law enforcement and intelligence sectors. Since joining GraphAware in 2014, Christophe has continued to innovate in the graph technology space, guiding product evolution and advising clients through advanced consulting and strategic initiatives.

Colophon

The animal on the cover of *Neo4j: The Definitive Guide* is a silky anteater (*Cyclopes didactylus*). Also known as the pygmy anteater, it is the smallest species of anteater. Its natural range stretches from southern Mexico to Bolivia and Brazil, and it spends nearly all of its time in trees, with hind feet that are specially adapted for climbing. They are named for their soft, dense fur, which is grayish-yellow and has a silvery sheen.

The silky anteater is nocturnal and feeds primarily on ants and termites found in trees, though it may also eat other insects. Adults reach up to 14 to 18 inches long, with prehensile tails making up about half of that length.

The silky anteater is considered a species of least concern. Many of the animals on O'Reilly covers are endangered; all of them are important to the world.

The cover illustration is by José Marzan Jr., based on an antique line engraving from Lydekker's *Royal Natural History*. The series design is by Edie Freedman, Ellie Volckhausen, and Karen Montgomery. The cover fonts are Gilroy Semibold and Guardian Sans. The text font is Adobe Minion Pro; the heading font is Adobe Myriad Condensed; and the code font is Dalton Maag's Ubuntu Mono.

www.ingramcontent.com/pod-product-compliance
Lightning Source LLC
Jackson TN
JSHW052351150825
89470JS00008B/473

* 9 7 8 1 0 9 8 1 6 5 6 5 9 *